HA-MEEM PUBLICATIONS
🌐 www.hameemstore.com
📷 @hameemstore
✉ orders@hameemstore.com
📞 +1 (416) 879-2545

All rights reserved by HA-MEEM PUBLICATIONS, aside from fair use, meaning a few pages or less for non-profit educational purposes, review, or scholarly citation. No part of this publication maybe reproduced, stored in a retrieval system or transmitted in any form or means, electronic, online, mechanical, photocopying, recording or otherwise, without the prior permission of the copyright owner.

شَرْحُ الْعَقِيْدَةِ النَّسَفِيَّةِ

Sharh Al-Aqeedah An-Nasafiyyah

A Commentary on the Creed of
Imaam an-Nasafi رحمة الله عليه

Author
Imaam Sa'd-ud-Deen at-Taftaazaani رحمة الله عليه

Translator
Maulana Muhammad Huzaifah Ibn Adam aal-Ebrahim

Edited, Checked and Approved by
Mufti Afzal Hoosen Elias رحمة الله عليه

Index:

Translator's Preface	P.5
Biography of Imaam an-Nasafi	P.8
Biography of Imaam at-Taftaazaani	P.11
Author's Preface	P.14
Types of Shar`i Ahkaam	P.16
Emergence of the Mu`tazilah	P.18
The Debate between Imaam al-Ash`ari and al-Jubbaa'i	P.19
The Basis of `Ilm-ul-Kalaam	P.22
The Causes of Knowledge	P.28
The First Cause: The Senses	P.32
The Second Cause: The Truthful Report	P.35
The Third Cause: The Intellect	P.45
A Discussion on Sifaat Al-Ma`aani	P.84
The Attribute of the Kalaam of Allaah	P.98
The Qur'aan is the Kalaam of Allaah	P.103
Al-Iraadah (The Intending)	P.120
Seeing Allaah Ta`aalaa	P.121
A Discussion on Sam`iyyaat	P.128
A Discussion on the Creation of the Actions of People	P.130
The Actions of People	P.138
Good and Bad	P.143
Burdening with the Impossible	P.150
Al-Ajal (The Appointed Term)	P.154
Ar-Rizq (Sustenance)	P.156
Deviation and Guidance Comes from Allaah Ta`aalaa	P.158
What is Best and What is Better	P.160
The Punishment in the Grave	P.162
The Questioning in the Grave	P.162
The Resurrection	P.166
The Meezaan (Scale of Deeds)	P.168
The Kitaab (Book of Deeds)	P.169
The Questioning of the Slaves by Allaah Ta`aalaa	P.170
Al-Hawdh	P.171
As-Siraat (The Bridge)	P.172
Jannah and Jahannam	P.173
The Major Sins	P.177
Intercession and Eternity in Jahannam	P.189
A Discussion on Imaan	P.195
Imaan Increasing and Decreasing	P.202
The Risaalat	P.214
The Sending of the Rusul	P.215

The Miracles of the Ambiyaa	P.217
The Descension of Nabi `Eesa عليه السلام	P.221
A Discussion on the Number of Ambiyaa	P.222
The Sinlessness of the Ambiyaa	P.224
The Malaa'ikah	P.226
The Virtue of Some Parts of the Qur'aan over Other Parts	P.228
The Mi`raaj (Ascension)	P.229
The Karaamaat (Miracles) of the Awliyaa	P.231
The Order of Khilaafah	P.239
The Duration of Khilaafah	P.242
The Khaleefahs Must Be From the Quraish	P.247
The Sinlessness of the Khaleefah	P.249
The Conditions of Wilaayat	P.251
The Wali (Saint)	P.262

Translator's Preface

بِسْمِ اللهِ الرَّحْمَنِ الرَّحِيْمِ

الحمد لله رب العالمين والصلاة والسلام على سيدنا ونبينا وحبيبنا محمد وعلى آله وأصحابه أجمعين وعلى كل من تبعهم بإحسان إلى يوم الدين

أما بعد:

The virtue of any knowledge lies in the virtue of what it is connected to. `Ilm-ul-`Aqaa'id (The Knowledge of Beliefs) is connected to Allaah Ta`aalaa, to Ma`rifat of Him, His Sifaat, His Rusul, the matters pertaining to the Aakhirah such as Jannah, Jahannam, the scale of deeds, the weighing of deeds, the books of deeds, the bridge over Jahannam, and others; the Ghaybi (Unseen) matters such as the Malaa'ikah, the Jinn, etc. For this reason, `Ilm-ul-`Aqaa'id is considered to be the noblest of all `Uloom, and in fact, the pinnacle of `Uloom.

The reason behind this is that, all of the other `Uloom of Islaam are dependent on `Aqeedah, for, if a person does not have the correct `Aqeedah, if his beliefs are Kufr, corrupt, baatil, then of what use is his knowledge of Fiqh, or Hadeeth, or Taareekh, or Usool, or any other? All of those `Uloom will only benefit him if his `Aqeedah is in order.

The study of `Aqeedah, then is of utmost importance. One aspect of `Aqeedah pertains to the subject-matters discussed in this Kitaab, such as the Sifaat of Allaah Ta`aalaa, how we are to understand the Mutashaabihaat Aayaat and Ahaadeeth, etc. However, another aspect of `Aqeedah is the Tawheed itself and the matters that are connected to it such as al-Walaa wal-Baraa' (Allegiance and Disavowal), something that in the present day and age is regarded as a foreign concept, something alien to Islaam, possibly an invention of the Khawaarij. People are unaware of the fact that Walaa wal-Baraa is rooted in Islaam; in fact, rooted in the very Kalimah that we recite every day. The very Kalimah itself, "Laa Ilaaha Illallaah, Muhammadur Rasoolullaah صلى الله عليه وسلم" very loudly, clearly and emphatically announces this concept of Walaa wal-Baraa.

In the study of `Aqeedah, teachers should endeavour to engrain within the minds and hearts of the students the complete understanding of "Laa Ilaaha

Illallaah". The majority of those who profess to be Muslims do not understand the meaning of "*Laa Ilaaha Illallaah*". By this we are not referring to simply the English translation, because even the Kuffaar know that.

"*Laa Ilaaha Illallaah, Muhammadur Rasoolullaah* صلى الله عليه وسلم" is the foundation of `Aqeedah*, and it is much more than merely words that are to be rendered lip-service. If only they knew what "*Laa Ilaaha Illallaah*" entails...

The subject-matter of this *kitaab*, however, is the aspect of `Aqeedah* that deals with *Imaan* in Allaah Ta`aalaa, in His Ambiyaa, in His Malaa'ikah, in His Kutub, in Jannah and Jahannam, in the Day of Qiyaamah, in the Signs of the Hour, etc.

Part of Imaam at-Taftaazaani's intention when he wrote this *sharh* was to thoroughly refute the Ahl-e-Baatil, such as the Mu`tazilah, the Karraamiyyah, the Khawaarij, the Philosophers, etc. However, a person might object at this juncture saying that those groups died out long ago so of what use is the study of this *kitaab*?

The answer to that objection is that what he intended to achieve in this *sharh* was not merely to refute those groups and there arguments of those groups, but to open up the minds of the readers, those who study this *kitaab*, so that whatever *baatil* groups emerge in later generations and whatever *baatil* arguments they may bring for their corrupt views, their *baatil* may be easily and adequately refuted, إن شاء الله.

His intention, then, was not merely to teach the readers the subject matter mentioned in this book, but to teach them how to think.

In the present age, there are numerous *baatil* groups promoting their own *baatil* beliefs that are in conflict with the age-old beliefs of Ahlus Sunnah wal-Jamaa`ah. This *kitaab* is meant to ground the readers in the correct `Aqaa'id (beliefs) of Ahlus Sunnah wal-Jamaa`ah.

Sharh al-`Aqeedah an-Nasafiyyah* is a Maatureedi *kitaab*, but the differences between the Ash`aris and the Maatureedis are very few, and really are just semantical. There are no major differences between Ash`aris and Maatureedis in terms of `Aqeedah - the differences are all minor. In this *kitaab*, when it comes to an issue wherein the Ash`aris have a belief different to the Maatureedis, Imaam at-Taftaazaani mentions it, so this *kitaab* serves to impart both Maatureedi `Aqeedah* and Ash`ari `Aqeedah*.

We make *Du`aa* that Allaah Ta`aalaa makes this *kitaab* a means of benefit to us and to all those who read it, and that He lets us live and die upon the correct *`Aqeedah* and *Manhaj*, آمين يا رب العالمين.

Biography of Imaam an-Nasafi رحمة الله عليه

His name was `Umar ibn Muhammad ibn Ahmad ibn Ismaa`eel ibn Muhammad ibn `Ali ibn Luqmaan.

He was regarded as one of the greatest `Ulamaa of the Ahnaaf who ever lived.

He was known as "an-Nasafi" because he came from the town of Nasaf, one of the lands of Maa Waraa'an Nahr. It lies south-east of Bukhara.

He was given the title of "Najm-ud-Deen", meaning "The Star of the Deen". He was also one of those who were referred to as Shaykh-ul-Islaam.

Imaam an-Nasafi was born in the year 461 A.H., which corresponds to 1069 C.E.

Imaam an-Nasafi traveled far and wide during his lifetime in search of *Ilm*, and thus had the good fortune of acquiring *Ilm* from a very large number of `Ulamaa. He himself compiled a book wherein he listed all of the `Ulamaa from whom he acquired *Ilm*, and their number reached 550. The historians only give the names of a few of those `Ulamaa, however. They are:

1. Abu-l Qaasim ibn Bayaan
2. Ismaa`eel ibn Muhammad an-Noohi an-Nasafi
3. Hasan ibn `Abdil Malik al-Qaadhi
4. Madhi ibn Muhammad al-`Alawi
5. `Abdullaah ibn `Ali ibn `Eesa an-Nasafi
6. Abu-l Yusr Muhammad ibn Muhammad ibn al-Husain al-Bazdawi an-Nasafi
7. Abu Muhammad al-Hasan ibn Ahmad as-Samarqandi
8. `Ali ibn al-Hasan al-Maatureedi
9. Abu `Ali al-Hasan ibn `Abdil Malik an-Nasafi

He had many, many students, but we know the names of only a few. Among them are:

1. Muhammad ibn Ibraaheem at-Toorubushti
2. Abu-l Layth Ahmad ibn `Umar ibn Muhammad an-Nasafi
3. `Umar ibn Muhammad ibn `Umar al-`Uqayli
4. Abu Sa`d `Abdul Kareem as-Sam`aani

The most famous of his students, however, is without a doubt Imaam Burhaan-ud-Deen al-Margheenaani, "*Saahib-e-Hidaayah*".

Imaam an-Nasafi wrote extensively in his life, having been an `Aalim with encyclopaedic knowledge in every one of the `*Uloom* of Deen. His authored works exceed 100 publications, and from among them are:

1. *Ajnaas al-Fiqh*
2. *Tatweel al-Asfaar li-Tahseel al-Akhbaar*
3. *Mustatraf `alal Huroof Mustatar*
4. *At-Tayseer fit-Tafseer*
5. *Al-Jumal al-Ma'thoorah*
6. *Al-Hasaa'il fil-Masaa'il*
7. *Al-Khasaa'is fil-Furoo`*
8. *Da`awaat al-Mustaghfireen*
9. *Talabat al-Talabah fil-Lughah `alaa Alfaazhi Kutubi As-haab al-Hanafiyyah*
10. *Fataawaa Najm ad-Deen Abi-l Hasan `Ataa ibn Hamzah as-Saghdi*
11. *Al-Fataawaa An-Nasafiyyah*
12. *Majma` al-`Uloom*
13. *Mashaari` ash-Shaari` fee Furoo` al-Hanafiyyah*
14. *Al-Mu`taqad*
15. *Manzhoomah an-Nasafi fil-Khilaaf*
16. *Al-`Aqeedah An-Nasafiyyah*
17. *Al-Akmal wal-Atwal fit-Tafseer*
18. *Risaalah fil-Khata' fee Qiraa'atil Qur'aan*
19. *Kitaab al-Yawaaqeet fil-Mawaaqeet*
20. *Al-Manzhoomah fil-Fiqh*
21. *Kitaab al-Masaarih fil-Fiqh*
22. *Qayd al-Awaabid limaa feehi min Ta'leef ash-Shawaarid*
23. *Risaalah fee Bayaani Madh-habil Mutasawwifah*
24. *Al-Munabbihaat*
25. *Kitaab al-Qand fee Ma`rifati `Ulamaa-e-Samarqand*
26. *Taareekh Bukhara*
27. *Al-Ash`aar bil-Mukhtaar minal Ash`aar*

And many more.

Imaam adh-Dhahabi said regarding him: "The `Allaamah, the Muhaddith."

Imaam Qaasim ibn Qutloobughaa said: "He was a Faqeeh, an `Aarif in the Madh-hab (i.e. Hanafi Madh-hab) as well as in literature."

Imaam as-Sam`aani said: "He was an Imaam, a virtuous Faqeeh, an `Aarif (one who is extremely well-versed) in the Madh-hab as well as literature. He authored many works in *Fiqh* and *Hadeeth*. He took *al-Jaami` as-Sagheer* and turned it into poetic form. He wrote approximately 100 books."

Imaam ibn an-Najjaar said: "He was a virtuous Faqeeh, a Mufassir, a Muhaddith, an Adeeb, a Mufti."

Imaam al-Qurashi described him saying: "The Imaam, the Zaahid, Najm-ud-Deen Abu Hafs."

Imaam an-Nasafi passed away in Samarqand on the 12th of Jumaadal Oolaa, the year 537 A.H., which corresponds to the 2nd of December, the year 1142 C.E.

It is mentioned that he used to teach both human beings and Jinn, and for this reason he was known as "Mufti ath-Thaqalayn" (The Mufti of Both Man and Jinn).

After Imaam an-Nasafi passed away, someone saw him in a dream and asked him how the questioning went with Munkar and Nakeer. He said, "Allaah Ta`aalaa returned my *Rooh* to my body, and Munkar and Nakeer questioned me. I asked them, "Should I answer in prose or in poetry?" They said, "In poetry." I said:

ربي الله لا إله سواه ونبي محمد مصطفاه

وديني الإسلام وفعلي ذميم أسأل الله عفوه وعطاه

"My Rabb is Allaah - there is no Ilaah besides Him. My Nabi is Muhammad صلى الله عليه وسلم, *his Chosen One.*

My Deen is Islaam and my actions are blameworthy - I ask Allaah for His Pardon and His Gift (i.e. Jannah)."

Biography of Imaam at-Taftaazaani رحمة الله عليه

His name is Mas`ood ibn `Umar ibn `Abdillaah at-Taftaazaani. This is the name agreed upon by all of the historians except one: Imaam ibn Hajar al-`Asqalaani, in Durar al-Kaaminah, mentions him as "Mahmood" instead of Mas`ood.

There are differences of opinion regarding his date of birth: some said he was born in the year 722 A.H., whereas some said he was born as early as 712, which was Imaam ibn Hajar's opinion.

His date of death is agreed upon as being in the year 792 A.H. If he was born in 722, he would have been 70 at the time of death. If he was born in 712, however, he would have been 80 years of age at the time of death.

Imaam at-Taftaazaani was born in - as his name suggests - Taftaazaan, which is in Khurasaan, in Iran.

He studied in various Madaaris in the cities of Herat, Ghijduvan, Feryumed, Gulistan, Khwarizm, Samarqand and Sarakhs. He lived in many different places during his lifetime but spent a significant portion of it in Sarakhs.

Imaam ibn Hajar al-`Asqalaani had very high praise for him, commenting about him that, "no one could ever replace him."

Imaam at-Taftaazaani was a Maatureedi, and in fact was one of the most famous Maatureedi `Ulamaa of all time.

He was also a Hanafi, according to most historians. He was regarded by some as being the "Fakhr-ud-Deen Raazi" of the Hanafi Madh-hab.

However, there were some who claimed that he was a Shaafi`ee, but that opinion is incorrect. Mullah `Ali al-Qaari lists him as a great `Aalim of the Hanafi Madh-hab in his *Tabaqaat*.

Imaam at-Taftaazaani passed away in Samarqand but was buried in Sarakhs, the place where he lived the longest.

Imaam at-Taftaazaani was a master in every field of *`Ilm*, whether it be in Arabic, or *`Aqeedah*, or *`Ilm-ul-Kalaam*, or *Fiqh*, or *Usool-ul-Fiqh*, or any other.

He authored many books in his life, among which are the following:

1. *Irshaad al-Haadi fin-Nahw*
2. *At-Talweeh fee Kashf Haqaa'iq at-Tanqeeh*
3. *Al-Isbaah fee Sharh Deebaajah al-Misbaah fin-Nahw*
4. *Tarkeeb al-Jaleel fin-Nahw*
5. *Tahdheeb al-Mantiq wal-Kalaam*
6. *Al-Jadhar al-Asamm fee Sharh Maqaasid at-Taalibeen*
7. *Haashiyah `alal Kash-shaaf liz-Zamakhshari*
8. *Daf` an-Nusoos wan-Nukoos*
9. *Risaalah al-Ikraah*
10. *Sharh Tasreef az-Zanjaani*
11. *Sharh Talkhees al-Miftaah lis-Sakaakee fil-Ma`aani wal-Bayaan*
12. *Sharh Hadeeth al-Arba`een*
13. *Sharh ash-Shamsiyyah fil-Mantiq*
14. *Sharh al-`Aqeedah an-Nasafiyyah*
15. *Sharh Faraa'idh as-Siraajiyyah lis-Sajaawandi al-Hanafi*
16. *Sharh al-Kash-shaaf*
17. *Sharh Muntahas-Su'l wal-Amal libnil Haajib*
18. *Fataawaa al-Hanafiyyah*
19. *Qawaaneen as-Sarf*
20. *Kashf al-Asraar wa `Uddah al-Abraar fee Tafseer al-Qur'aan (Farsi)*
21. *Sharh Talkhees al-Jaami`*
22. *Al-Mukhtasar min Sharh Talkhees al-Miftaah fil-Ma`aani*
23. *Al-Mutawwal fil-Ma`aani wal-Bayaan*
24. *Miftaah al-Fiqh*
25. *Maqaasid at-Taalibeen fee `Ilm Usool ad-Deen*
26. *An-Ni`m as-Sawaabigh fee Sharh al-Kalim an-Nawaabigh liz-Zamakhshari*
27. *Sharh al-Maqaasid*

And others. The book, "*Sharh al-Maqaasid*", is regarded by some as being the greatest Kitaab ever written on `*Ilm-ul-Kalaam*, but also notoriously the most difficult. Many *haashiyas* have been written on it.

Imaam at-Taftaazaani enjoyed the great favour from Allaah Ta`aalaa that his *kitaabs* are studied as part of the syllabus for those becoming `Ulamaa. His *kitaab*, *Sharh al-`Aqeedah an-Nasafiyyah*, has been taught in Deoband since their inception. Another *kitaab* of his, "*Mukhtasar al-Ma`aani*", is taught in Madaaris as the highest level *kitaab* in the field of *Balaaghah* and is also considered to be one of the most difficult *kitaabs* in the *Dars-e-Nizaami* syllabus.

Imaam at-Taftaazaani studied under a number of different `Ulamaa, including:

1. `Adhud-ud-Deen `Abdur Rahmaan ibn Ahmad ibn `Abdil Ghaffaar al-Eeji (d. 756 A.H.), the then Qaadhi al-Qudhaat in the east, and the Shaykh of the Shaafi`is in the lands of Maa Waraa'an Nahr. Imaam at-Taftaazaani studied for a long time under him, and qualified under him in the fields of *Ilm-ul-Kalaam, Usool, Mantiq* and *Balaaghah.*
2. Qutb-ud-Deen Mahmood ibn Muhammad Nizaam-ud-Deen ar-Raazi at-Tahtaani (d. 766 A.H.)
3. Bahaa'-ud-Deen as-Samarqandi al-Hanafi
4. Dhiyaa'-ud-Deen `Abdullaah ibn Sa`d ibn Muhammad `Uthmaan al-Qazweeni, well-known as al-Qarami and as "ibn Qaadhi al-Qaram" (d. 780 A.H.)

Many students studied under Imaam at-Taftaazaani, but the most well-known among them were:

1. Husaam-ud-Deen Hasan ibn `Ali al-Abeewardi al-Khateebi (761 - 816 A.H.)
2. Haidar ibn Ahmad ibn Ibraaheem ar-Roomi al-Hanafi, well-known as "Shaykh at-Taaj" (780 - 854 A.H.)
3. `Alaa-ud-Deen `Ali ibn Muhammad ar-Raazi ash-Shaafi`ee, Qaadhi al-Qudhaat in his time (767 - 829 A.H.)
4. Shams-ud-Deen Muhammad ibn Fadhlillaah ibn Majd-id-Deen al-Kareemi (773 - 861 A.H.)
5. `Alaa-ud-Deen Muhammad ibn Muhammad ibn Muhammad ibn Muhammad al-Bukhaari al-Hanafi (770 - 841 A.H.)
6. Jamaal-ud-Deen Yusuf ibn Rukn ad-Deen Maseeh al-Awbahi al-Khuraasaani as-Samarqandi

When Imaam Sa`d-ud-Deen Mas`ood Taftaazaani passed away, it was written above his *qabr*:

"O those who have come to visit: visit and send Salaam upon the rawdhah of the Imaam, the Muhaqqiq, the Ocean of Knowledge, the Mudaqqiq, the Sultaan of the `Ulamaa and Writers, the Heir of the Knowledge of the Ambiyaa and Rusul, the Balance between Logic and Naql, the Seal of the Mujtahideen, Abu Sa`eed Sa`d al-Haqq wad-Deen Mas`ood, the Qaadhi (Judge), the Imaam, the Exemplar of the people, ibn `Umar al-Mowlaa al-Mu`azh-zham, the best of all Judges in the world (in his era), the Proof of the Millat and the Deen, son of the Imaam, ar-Rabbaani, as-Samdaani, the Mufti of Both Groups, the Sultaan of the `Aarifeen, the Qutb of the Waasileen, Shams al-Haqq wad-Deen, al-Ghaazi at-Taftaazaani, may Allaah Ta`aalaa sanctify their Arwaah and enter them into Jannat-ul-Firdows."

بِسْمِ اللهِ الرَّحْمَنِ الرَّحِيْمِ

Author's Preface

الحمد لله المتوحد بجلال ذاته وكمال صفاته , المتقدس في نعوت الجبروت عن شوائب النقص وسماته , والصلاة على نبيه محمد المؤيد بساطع حججه وواضح بيانه , وعلى آله وأصحابه , هداة طريق الحق وحماته

وبعد فإن مبنى علم الشرائع والأحكام وأساس قواعد عقائد الإسلام هو علم التوحيد والصفات , الموسوم بالكلام , المنجي عن غياهب الشكوك وظلمات الأوهام , وإن المختصر المسمى بالعقائد للإمام الهمام , قدوة علماء الإسلام نجم الملة والدين عمر النسفي – أعلى الله درجته في دار السلام – يشتمل من هذا الفن على غرر الفرائد , ودرر الفوائد , في ضمن فصول هي للدين قواعد وأصول , وأثناء نصوص هي لليقين جواهر وفصوص , مع غاية من التنقيح والتهذيب , ونهاية من حسن التنظيم والترتيب , فحاولت أن أشرحه شرحاً يفصّل مجملاته ويبيّن معضلاته وينشر مطوياته ويظهر مكنوناته , مع توجيه للكلام في تنقيح , وتنبيه على المرام في توضيح , وتحقيق للمسائل غب تقرير , وتدقيق للدلائل إثر تحرير , وتفسير للمقاصد بعد تمهيد , وتكثير للفوائد مع تجريد , طاوياً كشح المقال عن الإطالة والإملال , متجافياً عن طرفي الإقتصاد : الإطناب والإخلال

والله الهادي إلى سبيل الرشاد , والمسؤول لنيل العصمة والسداد , وهو حسبي ونعم الوكيل

All praises are due to Allaah Ta`aalaa Alone, the One Who is Al-Mutawahhid (attributed with perfect Tawheed, i.e. Alone, without partners) with the loftiness of His Being and the perfection of His Attributes (*Sifaat*); the One Who is Al-Mutaqaddis (free from any imperfections) in His Qualities of Power and Majesty from being mixed with any kind of imperfection or blemishes. Salutations be upon His Nabi, Muhammad صلى الله عليه وسلم, who has been aided with His radiant proofs and clear explanations, and (salutations be also upon) his family and his companions, who were the guides and protectors of the Path of Truth.

Thereafter:

Indeed, the foundation of the `Ilm of the Sharee`ahs and *Ahkaam* (Rulings) and the foundations of the beliefs of Islaam is the Knowledge of Tawheed and *Sifaat* (the Attributes of Allaah Ta`aalaa), which has been named "*al-Kalaam*", and which saves one from the darkness of doubts and false notions.

The summary (*Mukhtasar*), entitled "*al-`Aqaa'id*" by the great Imaam, the leader of the `Ulamaa of Islaam, the Star of the Millat and the Deen, Imaam Najm-ud-Deen `Umar an-Nasafi - may Allaah raise high his rank in the Land of Peace - includes, in this subject (of `Aqeedah), many unique gems and beneficial pearls, scattered among (the) chapters (of the book) which is a foundation and basis for the Deen, and amidst texts which for *yaqeen* (conviction) is as priceless gems and stones, with the greatest of revisal and rectification, and the utmost of proper order and structure.

I (i.e. Imaam at-Taftaazaani) have tried to give such a *sharh* of this Kitaab which explains in detail its ambiguous matters; clarifies its intricate matters; spreads wide open its folded-up matters, and makes apparent and visible its hidden gems. At the same time, focusing on improving the speech, drawing attention to the objective when clarifying, establishing the *masaa'il* with their *daleel* (evidence), going deep into the evidence amidst writing (i.e. establishing the *daleel* of the *mas'alah* with other *daleel*), explaining the goals and objectives after preparation, increasing the benefits and beneficial points despite brevity, trying to drive away from the treatise unnecessary prolonging and weariness, staying away from the two extremities of making it (the treatise) too long or too brief, and instead adopting a balanced approach.

And Allaah is the One Who guides to the Path of Righteousness, and we ask Him to grant us protection and steadfastness, and He is sufficient for me, and He is the greatest Wakeel (Guardian over all affairs).

أنواع الأحكام الشرعية

Types of *Shar`I Ahkaam* (Rulings):

إعلم أن الأحكام الشرعية منها ما يتعلق بكيفية العمل, وتسمى فرعية وعملية, ومنها ما يتعلق بالإعتقاد, وتسمى أصلية واعتقادية, والعلم المتعلق بالأولى يسمى علم الشرائع والأحكام, لما أنها لا تستفاد إلا من جهة الشرع, ولا يسبق الفهم عند إطلاق الأحكام إلا إليها, وبالثانية علم التوحيد والصفات لما أن ذلك أشهر مباحثه وأشرف مقاصده

Know that from the *Ahkaam Shar`iyyah*, there are those that deal with the method of doing *a`maal* (deeds), and this is called "*far`iyyah*" (derived), or the branch matters, and "*`amaliyyah*" (practical), and others that deal with matters of belief (*i`tiqaad*), and those are termed "*usooliyyah*" (roots or fundamentals) and *i`tiqaadiyyah* (creedal). The knowledge that is connected to the first is known as *`Ilm-ush-Sharaa'i` wal-Ahkaam* (The Knowledge of the Sharee`ah and the Rulings), because they are not derived except from the Sharee`ah, and because when the term "*Ahkaam*" is used in a general, unrestricted manner, the understanding of people go only to that. The second is *`Ilm-ut-Tawheed was-Sifaat* (The Knowledge of Tawheed and the Attributes of Allaah Ta`aalaa), because that is the most prominent of its subject-matter and the noblest of its goals.

وقد كان الأوائل من الصحابة والتابعين – رضوان الله عليهم أجمعين – لصفاء عقائدهم ببركة صحبة النبي عليه السلام, وقرب العهد بزمانه, ولقلة الوقائع والإختلافات, وتمكنهم من المراجعة إلى الثقافات متسغنين عن تدوين العلمين وترتيبهما أبواباً وفصولاً, وتقرير مباحثهم فروعاً وأصولاً, إلى أن حدثت الفتن بين المسلمين وغلب البغي على أئمة الدين, وظهر إختلاف الآراء والميل إلى البدع والأهواء, وكثرت الفتاوى والواقعات, والرجوع إلى العلماء في المهمات, فاشتغلوا بالنظر والإستدلال والإجتهاد والإستنباط, وتمهيد القواعد والأصول, وترتيب الأبواب والفصول, وتكثير المسائل بأدلتها وإيراد الشبه بأجوبتها وتعيين الأوضاع والإصطلاحات, وتبيين المذاهب والإختلافات

The first ones among the Sahaabah and the Taabi`een - may Allaah Ta`aalaa be pleased with all of them - because of the purity of their `Aqeedah due to being in the *mubaarak* company of Nabi صلى الله عليه وسلم and (the Taabi`een) being near to his time, and due to the scarcity of occurrences and arguments, and because they were able to return to (in the event of disagreement) to the most reliable and trustworthy authorities (i.e. the Taabi`een were able to refer their questions to Sahaabah-e-Kiraam), they were not in need of writing down these two branches of knowledge (i.e. `Ilm-ush-Sharaa'i` wal-Ahkaam and `Ilm-ut-Tawheed was-Sifaat) and arranging them in chapters, and establishing their subject-matters into *furoo`* (derived, or branch) and *usool* (fundamental, or root), and it remained as such until *fitnah* broke out among the Muslims and rebellion overcame the leaders of the Deen, and differences of opinion arose, and people inclined to *bid`ah* (innovation) and desires, and the Fataawaa and events (from which matters arose) increased, and people turned to the `Ulamaa for the important matters, so they devoted their time to research, and *ijtihaad* and *istimbaat* (derivation of rulings), and laying down the foundations and the principals (*usool*), and arranging the chapters and sections, and increasing the evidences for the *masaa'il* and providing responses to objections and doubts, and defining the (general) usage (of the words) and the technical terminology, and clarifying the Madhaahib and the differences of opinion.

وسموا ما يفيد معرفة الأحكام العملية عن أدلتها بالفقه, ومعرفة أحوال الأدلة إجمالاً في إفادتها الأحكام بأصول الفقه, ومعرفة العقائد عن أدلتها بالكلام, لأن عنوان مباحثه كان قولهم الكلام في كذا وكذا, ولأن مسألة الكلام كان أشهر مباحثه وأكثرها نزاعاً وجدالاً, حتى أن بعض المتغلبة قتل كثيراً من أهل الحق لعدم قولهم بخلق القرآن ولأنه يورث قدرة على الكلام في تحقيق الشرعيات, وإلزام الخصوص, كالمنطق للفلسفة, ولأنه أول ما يجب من العلوم التي إنما تعلم وتتعلم بالكلام, فأطلق هذا الإسم لذلك ثم خص به, ولم يطلق على غيره تمييزاً, ولأنه إنما يتحقق بالمباحثة وإدارة الكلام من الجانبين, وغيره قد يتحقق بالتأمل ومطالعة الكتب, ولأنه أكثر العلوم خلافاً ونزاعاً, فيشتد إفتقاره إلى الكلام مع المخالفين والرد عليهم, ولأنه لقوة أدلته صار كأنه هو الكلام دون ما عداه من العلوم, كما يقال للأقوى من الكلامين هذا هو الكلام, ولأنه لابتنائه على الأدلة القطعية المؤيد أكثرها بالأدلة السمعية أشد العلوم تأثيراً في القلب وتغلغلاً فيه, فسمي بالكلام المشتق من الكلم وهو الجرح

They named that which gives knowledge and recognition of the *Ahkaam* and practical matters, with their evidences, as "*Fiqh*", and they named that which gives knowledge and recognition of the conditions of the evidences, in brief, in providing the *Ahkaam*, as "*Usool-ul-Fiqh*", and they named the knowledge of `*Aqaa'id*, with its evidences, as "Al-Kalaam" (or `Ilm-ul-Kalaam), because the subject of its investigations or subject-matters was their saying, "The *kalaam* (speech) regarding such-and-such," and because the matter of *Kalaam* (`*Ilm-ul-Kalaam*, literally, "The Knowledge of Speech") was the most famous of its investigations or subject-matters and the field in which there was the most disagreement and argumentation, so much so that some of the leaders who took power by force killed many of the Ahl-ul-Haqq (People of the Truth, or the Reality) because the Ahl-ul-Haqq refused to proclaim that the Qur'aan is created (a belief of the Mu`tazilah sect). Another reason as to why this field (i.e. specialisation in `Aqeedah*) was termed `*Ilm-ul-Kalaam* is because it results in a person becoming very strong in speaking in determining the matters of the Sharee`ah, in silencing his opponents, like *mantiq* (logic) of the philosophers, and also because it was the first field of `Ilm which was learnt and taught through *kalaam* (speaking) alone, and thus this term of "*Kalaam*" because exclusive to it and was not used for other than it, for the purpose of distinction.

Another reason behind it being named `*Ilm-ul-Kalaam* is because it is established through mutual research and discussion from two sides, whereas with the other fields of `Ilm, they can be acquired through pondering and researching the *kutub* (books). Another reason for it being named this is because from all of the `Uloom (sciences), it is the one in which there is the most argumentation and differences of opinion, and thus it became severely in need of "*kalaam*" (speaking) with the opponents and refuting them.

Another reason for it being named `*Ilm-ul-Kalaam* is because, due to its proofs being so strong, it became as though it alone was the "*Kalaam*" (speech), in exclusion from what was other than it, like how it is said regarding the stronger one from two speeches: "This is the speech (*kalaam*)."

Also, because it was based upon *qat`iyy* evidences (i.e. evidences that are absolute, decisive, and firmly established in their nature), most of which are aided by *adillah* (evidences) that are *sam`iyyah* (based on hearing), it became - from the `Uloom - the one that had the greatest effect in penetrating the hearts of people and permeating therein, and so it was named "*al-Kalaam*", derived from "*al-Kalm*", which means a wound.

ظهور مذهب المعتزلة

The Emergence of the *Madh-hab* of the Mu`tazilah:

وهذا هو كلام القدماء, ومعظم خلافياته من الفرق الإسلامية, خصوصاً المعتزلة, لأنهم أول فرقة أسسوا قواعد الخلاف, لما ورد به ظاهر السنة, وجرى عليه جماعة الصحابة – رضوان الله عليهم أجمعين – في باب العقائد, وذلك أن رئيسهم واصل بن عطاء إعتزل مجلس الحسن البصري رحمه الله, يقول: إن مرتكب الكبيرة ليس بمؤمن ولا كافر, ويثبت المنزلة بين المنزلتين, فقال

الحسن: قد اعتزل عنا, فسموا المعتزلة, وهم سموا أنفسهم أصحاب العدل والتوحيد لقولهم بوجوب ثواب المطيع وعقاب العاصي على الله تعالى, ونفي الصفات القديمة عنه

This was how "*Kalaam*" was understood and defined by the ancients (the `Ulamaa of the past). The majority of the differences of opinion and controversies caused by `Ilm-ul-Kalaam existed among the Mu`tazilah from among all of the sects of Islaam, and that is because they were the first *firqah* (sect) to have laid down the foundations of controversy and opposition to that which appears in the apparent and clear of the Sunnah and that the Sahaabah - رضوان الله عليهم أجمعين - were upon in the matter of beliefs. That is because their leader, whose name was Waasil ibn `Ataa, held the belief that the person who commits a major sin is neither a Muslim nor a Kaafir, but rather, he is in a middle stage (*al-manzilah baynal manzilatayn*), i.e. a stage between Imaan and Kufr. He used to attend the *majlis* of Imaam Hasan Basri رحمة الله عليه. After fabricating this belief, and Imaam Hasan Basri and the Muslims in the gathering not accepting this belief of his, he withdrew himself from them, so Imaam Hasan Basri said: "He has withdrawn himself from us (*i`tazala `annaa*)." Thus, they became known as the "Mu`tazilah", literally: "The Withdrawers," because by their beliefs they had "withdrawn" themselves from Ahlus Sunnah wal-Jamaa`ah.

They became known as the Mu`tazilah, but the name they used for themselves was, "*As-haab al-`Adl wat-Tawheed*" (The People of Justice and Tawheed), because of the fact that they believed it is *waajib* on Allaah Ta`aalaa to reward the obedient one and to punish the sinner, and they denied that the Attributes (*Sifaat*) of Allaah Ta`aalaa are *Qadeem* (Eternal, without a beginning).

مناظرة الأشعري للجبائي

The Debate of Imaam al-Ash`ari with al-Jubbaa'i:

ثم إنهم توغلوا في علم الكلام وتشبثوا بأذيال الفلاسفة في كثير من الأصول وشاع مذهبهم فيما بين الناس, إلى أن قال الشيخ أبو الحسن الأشعري لأستاذه أبي علي الجبائي: ما تقول في ثلاثة إخوة, مات أحدهم مطيعاً, والآخر عاصياً, والثالث صغيراً؟

فقال: الأول يثاب بالجنة, والثاني يعاقب بالنار, والثالث لا يثاب ولا يعاقب

قال الأشعري: فإن قال الثالث: يا رب, لِمَ أمتني صغيراً وما أبقيتني إلى أن أكبر فأومن بك وأطيعك فأدخل الجنة؟ ماذا يقول الرب تعالى؟

فقال: يقول الرب: إني كنت أعلم أنك لو كبرت لعصيت فدخلت النار, فكان الأصلح لك أن تموت صغيراً

فقال الأشعري: فإن قال الثاني: يا رب, لِمَ لم تمتني صغيراً لئلا أعصي فلا أدخل النار؟ فماذا يقول الرب؟

فبهت الجبائي وترك الأشعري مذهبه واشتغل هو ومن تبعه بإبطال رأي المعتزلة وإثبات ما ورد به السنة ومضى عليه الجماعة, فسموا أهل السنة والجماعة

ثم لما نقلت الفلسفة إلى العربية وخاض فيها الإسلاميون, وحاولوا الرد على الفلاسفة فيما خالفوا فيه الشريعة, فخلطوا بالكلام كثيراً من الفلسفة, ليتحققوا مقاصدها فيتمكنوا من إبطالها, وهلم جراً, إلى أن أدرجوا فيه معظم الطبيعيات والإلهيات, وخاضوا في الرياضيات حتى كاد لا يتميز عن الفلسفة, لولا اشتماله على السمعيات, وهذا هو كلام المتأخرين

وبالجملة هو أشرف العلوم لكونه أساس الأحكام الشرعية, ورئيس العلوم الدينية, وكون معلوماته العقائدية الإسلامية, وغايته الفوز بالسعادات الدينية والدنيوية, وبراهينه الحجج القطعية المؤيد أكثرها بالأدلة السمعية وما نقل عن بعض السلف من الطعن فيه والمنع عنه, فإنما هو للمتعصب في الدين والقاصر عن تحصيل اليقين, والقاصد إلى إفساد عقائد المسلمين, والخائض فيما لا يفتقر إليه من غوامض المتفلسفين, وإلا فكيف يتصور المنع عما هو أصل الواجبات وأساس المشروعات؟

Thereafter, they went deep into the field of `Ilm-ul-Kalaam and began clinging onto the tails of the philosophers in much of the usool (of kalaam), and their Madh-hab spread among the people (i.e. the Madh-hab of I`tizaal), until the time came when Imaam Abu'l Hasan al-Ash`ari رحمة الله عليه (who until this point had been from the Mu`tazilah) said to his ustaadh, Abu `Ali al-Jubbaa'i: "What do you say regarding three brothers, one of whom dies whilst he had been obedient unto Allaah Ta`aalaa, the other dies whilst he had been disobedient unto Allaah Ta`aalaa, and the third dies as an infant?"

Al-Jubbaa'i responded: "The first will be rewarded with Jannah. The second will be punished in Jahannam. The third will neither be rewarded nor punished."

Imaam al-Ash`ari asked him, "What if the third, who died as an infant, says to Allaah Ta`aalaa: "O Allaah, why did You cause me to die as an infant and not let me grow up so that I could have believed in You and thus entered Jannah?" What will Allaah Ta`aalaa say?"

Al-Jubbaa'i responded: "Allaah Ta`aalaa will say to him: "I knew that had you grown up, you would have been disobedient and thus would have entered the fire of Jahannam, so it was best for you to have died as an infant."

Imaam al-Ash`ari asked him, "What if the second one says: "O Allaah, why did You not let me also pass away as an infant, so that I would not have been disobedient and thus would not have entered the fire of Jahannam?" Al-Jubbaa'i had no answer.

After that, Imaam al-Ash`ari abandoned him and abandoned the *Madh-hab* of the Mu`tazilah, and he and those with him devoted their time and energy to refuting the views and arguments of the Mu`tazilah sect, and establishing that which has reached us from the Sunnah of Rasoolullaah صلى الله عليه وسلم as well as what the Sahaabah were upon, and thus they were named: "Ahl-us-Sunnah wal-Jamaa`ah" (The People of the Sunnah and the Group, i.e. the Sahaabah).

Thereafter, the works of the philosophers (which formerly were in Greek) were translated into Arabic, and the people of Islaam began engrossing themselves in these works, trying to refute the philosophers in those views of theirs which conflicted with the Sharee`ah, and thus they mixed Kalaam with a lot of philosophy, their goal being to understand the objectives of philosophy and thus be in a better position to refute it, etc. This carried on until *Kalaam* became mixed with physics and metaphysics and later on even mathematics, until it reached a stage where it was difficult to distinguish between philosophy and Kalaam, were it not for the fact that Kalaam still included the belief in *as-Sam`iyyaat* (those things that are to be believed in just from hearing, such as the matters of the Ghayb), and this was the *Kalaam* of the *Muta'akh-khireen* (later ones from the scholars of Kalaam).

In a nutshell, *Kalaam* was originally the noblest of the `Uloom due to it being the very foundation of the *Shar`i Ahkaam* and the leader of the Deeni sciences, and because its subject matter was that of Islaamic beliefs, and its end result was success with the happiness of the *Dunyaa* and the *Aakhirah*, and its evidences, most of which were strengthened with the *adillah* (proofs) of *as-Sam`iyyaat*.

As for what has been reported from certain of the Salaf criticising *Kalaam* and prohibiting it, then this refers to those who became *muta`assib* (extreme, going beyond bounds of the Sharee`ah and the Sunnah) in matters of Deen and who became lax in acquiring *yaqeen* (conviction), and the one who intended by his study of *`Ilm-ul-Kalaam* to ruin the beliefs of the Muslims, and those who engrossed themselves in unnecessary matters like the obscurities of the philosophers.

Otherwise, how can it be possible to prohibit that thing which is the very root of the *waajibaat* (compulsory matters) and the foundation of the legislated matters?

مبنى علم الكلام

The Foundation of `Ilm-ul-Kalaam:

ثم لما كان مبنى علم الكلام على الإستدلال بوجود المحدثات على وجود الصانع وتوحيده وصفاته وأفعاله, ثم منها إلى سائر السمعيات, ناسب تصدير الكتاب بالتنبيه على وجود ما يشاهد من الأعيان والأعراض, وتحقق العلم بهما ليتوصل بذلك إلى معرفة ما هو المقصود الأهم, فقال:

Because the foundation of *`Ilm-ul-Kalaam* was that of using as proof the argument that the existence of created beings proves the existence of a Creator, and then going further to deduce from it His *Sifaat*, His *Af`aal* (Actions), and then from there to deduce the rest of the *Sam`iyyaat* (those things believed in just from hearing them), it was fitting for the author to have begun the Kitaab by drawing the attention of the readers to the existence of those things which are witnessed, such as individuals and substances, and verifying the knowledge about them, to be able to reach - from there - to the recognition of that which is the most important objective, so he (the author) says:

(قال أهل الحق)

وهو الحكم المطابق للواقع, يطلق على الأقوال والعقائد والأديان والمذاهب, باعتبار اشتمالها على ذلك, ويقابله الباطل. وأما الصدق فقد شاع استعماله في الأقوال خاصة, ويقابله الكذب, وقد يفرق بينهما بأن المطابقة تعتبر في الحق من جانب الواقع, وفي الصدق من جانب الحكم, فمعنى صدق الحكم مطابقته للواقع, ومعنى حقيقته مطابقة الواقع إياه

[**Translator's Note:** The bolded text is the speech of the author of the matn, which is Imaam an-Nasafi رحمة الله عليه. This is then followed by the sharh (commentary) by the commentator, which is Imaam at-Taftaazaani رحمة الله عليه.]

"The people of *Haqq* said:"

Haqq is the judgement or ruling which corresponds to reality. The word *Haqq* is used for sayings, beliefs, religions and *Madhaahib*, taking into consideration the fact that it includes all of that. The opposite of *haqq* is *baatil* (falsehood).

As for *sidq* (truthfulness), then it is used exclusively for sayings or speech. Its opposite is *kidhb* (lying).

The difference between them is that when it comes to *haqq*, it must correspond to the reality or fact (*al-waaqi`*), and when it comes to *sidq*, it must correspond to the ruling or judgement (*al-hukm*), so the meaning of "the truthfulness of the ruling" is that it corresponds to the reality or fact (*al-waaqi`*), and the meaning "its *haqeeqat*" (i.e. state of being Haqq) is that the reality or fact corresponds to it.

(حقائق الأشياء ثابتة)

"The realities of things are affirmed."

حقيقة الشيء وماهيته ما به الشيء هو هو, كالحيوان الناطق للإنسان, بخلاف مثل الضاحك والكاتب مما يمكن تصور الإنسان بدونه, فإنه من العوارض, وقد يقال: إن ما به الشيء هو هو باعتبار تحققه حقيقة, وباعتبار تشخصه هوية, ومع قطع النظر عن ذلك ماهية

والشيء عندنا: الموجود, والثبوت, والتحقق, والوجود, والكون, ألفاظ مترادفة, معناها بديهي التصور

The *haqeeqat* of a thing (*shay'*) and its *maahiyat* (essence, or essential nature) are the factors that make a thing what it is. It is like the application of the term "talking animal" to human beings, unlike, for example, "the one who laughs," "the writer," which are things which it is possible to imagine a person without (possessing those qualities). In other words, it is possible to be *insaan* despite not being a laugher or a writer, because those qualities are simply contingents and do not make a person a person.

It has also been said that the factor which makes a thing what it is, is determined by taking into consideration its establishment as having a *haqeeqat* (reality), and taking into consideration its assuming of individuality, giving it a *huwiyyah* (identity or personality). Without looking at either of these, it is a *maahiyah*.

A shay' (thing), according to us, is that which exists (*al-mawjood*), and the terms *ath-thuboot* (the affirmed), *at-tahaqquq* (that thing which has been established to possess a *haqeeqat*), *al-wujood* (the existent), and *al-kawn* (coming into existence), are terms which are near-synonyms and their meanings are immediately understood by the intellect.

فإن قيل: فالحكم بثبوت حقائق الأشياء يكون لغواً بمنزلة قولنا: الأمور ثابتة، قلنا: المراد أن ما تعتقده حقائق الأشياء ونسميه بالأسماء, من الإنسان والفرس والسماء والأرض, أمور موجودة في نفس الأمر, كما يقال: واجب الوجود موجود, وهذا الكلام مفيد, ربما يحتاج إلى البيان, وليس مثل قولك: الثابت ثابت, ولا مثل قوله: أنا أبو النجم وشعري شعري, على ما لا يخفى

If an objection is raised that, saying that the realities of things are affirmed (true) is unnecessary, futile, like saying, "Things exist," then to this objection we would respond by saying: "That which we believe to be the realities of things and which we name by (their particular) names, such as human being, horse, heaven, earth, etc., are matters which exist in and of themselves, and it is similar to the saying: "That Being Who is *Waajib-ul-Wujood* (His Existence is compulsory) exists." This is a statement which provides beneficial information. In fact, it might even need to be explained. It is not like you saying, "That which is affirmed is affirmed." It is also not like a person saying, "I am Abu Najm, and my poetry is my poetry." The (obviousness) of that is not hidden.

وتحقيق ذلك أن الشيء قد يكون له إعتبارات مختلفة, يكون الحكم عليه بالشيء مفيداً بالنظر إلى بعض تلك الإعتبارات دون البعض, كالإنسان إذا أخذ من حيث أنه جسم ما, كان الحكم عليه بالحيوانية مفيداً, وإذا أخذ من حيث أنه حيوان ناطق, كان ذلك لغواً

The verification of this lies in the fact that a thing (*shay'*) may have different aspects to be taken into consideration, and applying upon it the classification of "a thing" (*shay'*) may be beneficial when looking at some of those aspects to be taken into consideration in exclusion of others. For example, a human being (*insaan*); when taken from the aspect of being a body (*jism*), applying upon him the label of animality gives beneficial information, but if taken from the aspect of him being a "talking animal" (*haywaanun naatiq*), then the application of that label would be futile.

(والعلم بها)

"And that the knowledge of them -"

أي بالحقائق من تصوراتها, والتصديق بها وبأحوالها

Meaning, the knowledge of the realities of things, from their perceptions, and their verification, and their states:

(متحقق)

" - Is verified (as having a *haqeeqat*)."

وقيل: المراد العلم بثبوتها للقطع بأنه لا علم بجميع الحقائق, والجواب أن المراد الجنس

It has also been said that the intended meaning of that statement is, knowledge of their affirmation only, not knowledge of all of their realities, and the response to this is that the intended meaning is that of *jins* (species).

رداً على القائلين بأنه لا ثبوت لشيء من الحقائق ولا علم بثبوت حقيقة ولا بعدم ثبوتها

خلافاً للسوفسطائيا

فإن منهم من ينكر حقائق الأشياء ويزعم أنها أوهام وخيالات باطلة, وهم العنادية

ومنهم من ينكر ثبوتها ويزعم أنها تابعة للإعتقادات, حتى إن إعتقدنا الشيء جوهراً فجوهراً, أو عرضاً فعرض, أو قديماً فقديم, أو حادثاً فحادث, وهم العندية

ومنهم من ينكر العلم بثبوت شيء ولا ثبوته ويزعم أنه شاك, وشاك في أنه شاك, وهلم جراً, وهم اللا أدرية

لنا – تحقيقاً – أن نجزم بالضرورة بثبوت بعض الأشياء بالعيان وبعضها بالبيان – وإلزاماً – أنه إن لم يتحقق نفي الأشياء فقد ثبتت, وإن تحقق, والنفي حقيقة من الحقائق لكونه نوعاً من الحكم, فقد ثبتت شيء من الحقائق فلم يصح نفيها على الإطلاق, ولا يخفى أنه إ نما يتم على العنادية. قالوا: الضروريات منها حسيات, والحس قد يغلط كثيراً, كالأحول يرى الواحد إثنين, والصفرائي يجد الحلو مراً, ومنها بديهات, وقد يقع فيها إختلافات, وتعرض شبه يفتقر في حلها إلى أنظار دقيقة, والنظريات فرع الضروريات, ففسادها فسادها, ولهذا كثر فيها إختلاف العقلاء

This is as a refutation of those who claim that there is no affirmation to anything from the realities, nor is there knowledge of the affirmation of a *haqeeqat* (reality) for anything nor is there knowledge of there not being an affirmation of a *haqeeqat* (reality) for something.
"Contary to the Sophists."

Because among them were those who rejected the realities of things, claiming that they are merely imaginary, existing only in the imagination, false, not really existing. This group was known as *al-`Inaadiyyah* (the obstinate ones).

The second group rejected the affirmation of the realities of things, claiming that (the realities) are hinged upon beliefs; thus, if we believe that a thing is a jewel, then it is a jewel. If we believe a thing is a contingent, it is a contingent. If we believe a thing to be pre-eternal, then it is pre-eternal (i.e. always having existed, not having a beginning), and if we believe that a thing came into existence, then it came into existence. This group was known as *al-`Indiyyah* (the Opinioners).

A third group rejected knowledge of the affirmation or non-affirmation (of the realities) of anything, claiming that they are doubters, and that they are in doubt about the fact that they are in doubt, and so on and so forth. This group was known as the *Laa Adriyyah* (The people who say, "I do not know.")

For us, we first - as a verification and establishing (of the *haqaa'iq* or realities of things) - state firmly, necessarily, the affirmation of some things through perception or some through explanation or demonstration. We then go on from there to state that if the negation of things has not been established, then their existence has been established. But if their negation (*nafi*) has been established, then negation is a reality from amongst the realities due to it being a type (*naw'*) of judgement or ruling, and thus something of the realities has been affirmed and so it is not valid to negate it in a general, unrestricted way. However, this applies only to the `Inaadiyyah (Obstinates).

(As for the other two groups, they) said: With regards to those things deemed *dharooriyyaat* (necessarily existing), some of them are *hissiyyaat* (established through the senses), and the senses can err, like a person who is squint seeing a single thing as being two, or a person who is bilious tasting something sweet as being bitter. Some (of these *dharooriyaat*) are *badeehaat* (clearly perceived by the intellect), but differences arise among (*badeehaat*), and there are doubts which, for the sake of clarification require the need of in-depth views. Then, among the *dharooriyyat* there are also the *nazhriyyaat* (opinions or assumptions arrived at through analogical deductions), but (they argue that) these are a sub-branch of *dharooriyyaat* (necessarily existent things), so if they (the root) are corrupt, then the *nazhriyyaat*, which is the sub-branch, will be corrupt as well.

For this reason, there are many arguments and differences of opinion concerning them among the thinkers.

قلنا: غلط الحس في البعض لأسباب جزئية, لا ينافي الجزم بالبعض بانتفاء أسباب الغلط, والإختلاف في البديهي لعدم الإلف أو لخفاء في التصور, لا ينافي البداهة, وكثرة الإختلافات لفساد الأنظار لا ينافي حقيقة بعض النظريات, والحق أنه لا طريق إلى المناظرة معهم خصوصاً اللا أدرية لأنهم لا يعترفون بمعلوم ليثبت به مجهول, بل الطريق تعذيبهم ليعترفوا أو يحترقوا

وسوفسطا إسم للحكمة المموهة, والعلم المزخرف, لأن سوفا معناه العلم والحكمة, واسطا: معناه المزخرف والغلط, ومنه اشتقت السفسطة كما اشتقت الفلسفة من فيلا سوفا, أي محب الحكمة

We say: the erring of one or more of the senses is due to particular causes, and this does not negate certainty of a thing in the case where the causes of erring are not there.

[An example of this is a person who is squint-eyed and thus sees singular objects as dual. The cause for erring, in this case, is because of a particular reason, and this particular reason is in a part (*juz'*) of this person, namely, his eyes, and the error does not lie in his as a whole. In the case where this particular cause of erring is not there, nor other similar causes of erring in the faculty of sight, then the person can safely say with conviction that he has seen a particular object, because there is no error in his faculty of vision.]

Differences of opinions and arguments arising in the matter of those things which are clearly and immediately perceptible by the intellect are simply due to an absence of acquaintance (with the subject-matter), or due to a cloudiness in (one's ability to) correctly picture or form a notion, and this does not negate the fact that the item itself is such that it is immediately perceived by the (correctly functioning) intellect.

The many arguments due to the corruption of views do not negate the *haqeeqat* of some of the views or opinions.

The truth is that there is no way to debate with them (the Sophists), especially the group among them knows as the *Laa Adriyyah* (the ones who say, "We do not know," akin to Agnostics), because they do not admit to anything known through which an unknown thing may be affirmed. Rather, the only way (to deal with them) is to punish them with fire; that they may either admit or be burnt to death.

Soofastaa is a word used to refer to wisdom that is disguised or masked, and to refer to adorned knowledge, because "*soofaa*" means knowledge and wisdom, and "*astaa*" means adorned, but it also means false. From it is derived the word "*safsatah*", just like "*falsafah*" is derived from "*feelaa soofaa*" (philosopher), which means "lover of wisdom".

أسباب العلم

The Causes of Knowledge:

(وأسباب العلم)

"And the causes of knowledge."

وهو صفة يتجلى بها المذكور لمن قامت هي به, أي يتضح ويظهر ما يذكر, ويمكن أن يعبر عنه موجوداً كان أو معدوماً, فيشمل إدراك الحواس وإدراك العقل من التصورات والتصديقات اليقينية وغير اليقينية, بخلاف قولهم صفة توجب تمييزاً لا يحتمل النقيض, فإنه وإن كان شاملاً لإدراك الحواس بناء على عدم التقييد بالمعاني والتصورات, بناء على أنها لا نقائض لها على ما زعموا, لكنه لا يشتمل غير اليقينيات من التصديقات, هذا ولكن ينبغي أن يحمل التجلي على الإنكشاف التام الذي لا يشمل الظن, لأن العلم عندهم مقابل للظن

Knowledge itself is a quality by which any mentioned (*madhkoor*) object becomes clear (*yatajallaa*) to the one who possesses it, i.e. it becomes apparent to him and he becomes able to express himself regarding it, be it something that is existent (*mawjood*) or even such a thing as is non-existent (*ma`doom*).

Knowledge encompasses the comprehension by the senses as well as the comprehension by the intellect (*`aql*), with regards to those things as are conceived (by the mind) and those things that are asserted, those things which are certain and those which are uncertain.

This is contrary to the statement of the Sophists who believed that knowledge is an attribute which necessitates a distinction which does not carry the possibility of contradiction, because that statement, even though it might encompass comprehension by the senses due to it not being restricted to meanings, and conceived things based on the fact that there are no contradictions for them according to what they have claimed; however, it does not encompass those things which are uncertainties from the asserted matters (*at-tasdeeqaat*). At the same thing, it is necessary that *tajalli* be interpreted as being a complete uncovering and revealing which does not include speculation, because to them, knowledge is the opposite of speculation.

(للخلق)

"For the creation."

أي للمخلوق من الملك والإنس والجن, بخلاف علم الخالق تعالى فإنه لذاته لا لسبب من الأسباب

Meaning, for all the created beings from the Malaa'ikah, human beings and Jinn, contrary to the Knowledge of The Creator (Allaah Ta`aalaa), because

His Knowledge belongs to His *Dhaat* (Being) and is not due to a cause from the causes.

(ثلاثة: الحواس السليمة, والخبر الصادق, والعقل)

"Are three: the healthy senses, the truthful report, and the intellect."

بحكم الإستقراء, ووجه الضبط أن السبب إن كان من خارج فالخبر الصادق, وإلا فإن كان آلة غير المدرك فالحواس, وإلا فالعقل

This is by way of enumeration. From the aspect of exactness, if the cause is something outside (the knower), then it will be from the (facet of) truthful reports. If not, i.e. if it is within the knower himself, then, if it is an instrument other than the instrument of comprehension, then it is the (five) senses, otherwise, it is the intellect.

فإن قيل: السبب المؤثر في العلوم كلها هو الله تعالى, لأنها بخلقه وإيجاده من غير تأثير للحاسة, والخبر الصادق والعقل, والسبب الظاهري كالنار للإحراق هو العقل لا غير, وإنما الحواس والأخبار آلات وطرق في الإدراك, والسبب المفضي في الجملة بأن يخلق الله فينا العلم معه بطريق جري العادة, ليشمل المدرك كالعقل والآلة كالحس والطريق كالخبر, لا ينحصر في الثلاثة, بل هاهنا أشياء أخر, مثل الوجدان والحدس والتجربة ونظر العقل بمعنى ترتيب المبادئ والمقدمات

If it is said: the True Cause for all types of knowledge is only Allaah Ta`aalaa Himself, because it is He Who created it and brought it into existence without any effect from the senses, or truthful reports, or intellect, and the apparent cause, as in the case of fire burning (a person), in the intellect (`aql), and the senses and reports are merely instruments and roads to comprehending.

Another objection might be raised that the ultimate cause (*as-sabab al-mufdhi*), altogether, in which Allaah Ta`aalaa creates within us knowledge according to the usual way in order to include that which comprehends and perceives, such as the `aql; the instrument, such as the senses; and the road, such as the (truthful) report - an objection might be raised that the methods of acquiring knowledge are not confined simply to these three; rather, there are other ways, such as *wijdaan* (sentiment; emotion; feeling), *hads* (guessing), *tajribah* (experience), and the speculating of the intellect (`aql), meaning, to arrange the principles and the premises.

قلنا: هذا على عادة المشايخ في الإقتصار على المقاصد والأعراض عن تدقيقات الفلاسفة, فإنهم لما وجدوا بعض الإدراكات حاصلة عقيب استعمال الحواس الظاهرة التي لا شك فيها سواء كانت من ذوي العقول أو غيرهم, جعلوا الحواس أحد الأسباب, ولما كان معظم المعلومات الدينية مستفاداً من الخبر الصادق جعلوه سبباً آخر, ولما لم يثبت عندهم الحواس الباطنة المسماة بالحس المشترك والوهم وغير ذلك, ولم يتعلق لهم غرض بتفاصيل الحدسيات والتجربيات والبديهيات والنظريات, وكان مرجع الكل إلى العقل, جعلوه سبباً ثالثاً يفضي إلى العلم بمجرد التفات, أو بانضمام حدس أو تجربة أو ترتيب مقدمات, فجعلوا السبب في العلم بأن لنا جوعاً وعطشاً وأن الكل أعظم من الجزء, وأن نور القمر مستفاد من نور الشمس, وأن السقمونيا مسهل, وأن العالم حادث, هو العقل, وإن كان في البعض باستعانة من الحس

We respond to this by saying: this is according to the habit of the Mashaayikh, that, they would suffice with the actual objectives and goals and not enter into the deep, intricate matters of the philosophers. These Mashaayikh, when they found that certain things were comprehended and known after making use of the external senses (i.e. sight, hearing, etc.) in which there is no doubt, be it from those with intellect or those without, they declared the *hawaas* (senses) to be one of the methods of acquiring knowledge.

Then, due to the fact that the vast majority of what we know regarding the Deen is learnt from truthful reports, they made truthful reports as another method of acquiring knowledge.

Because they had not affirmed internal senses, known as "common sense" (*al-hiss al-mushtarak*), nor *wahm* (estimation), etc., nor did they attach importance to the details of *hadsiyyaat* (guesswork), or *tajribiyyaat* (experiences), or *badeehiyyaat* (things immediately perceptible by the intellect), or *nazhriyyaat* (speculations) and all of those things return and refer back to the intellect, thus they made the intellect the third source of acquiring knowledge, because the intellect could acquire knowledge merely by turning (its attention) to something, or by making use of guesswork, or experience, or the arrangement of premises, and therefore they made it the cause of knowledge, of knowing that, for example, we are hungry or thirsty, or that a whole is greater than a part, or that the light of the moon is derived from the light of the sun, or that scammony can be used as a laxative, or that the world came into existence. All of this can be learnt by using the intellect, even though the intellect may take assistance from the senses.

السبب الأول: الحواس

The First Cause of Knowledge: The Senses

(فالحواس)

"The senses-"

جمع حاسة بمعنى القوة الحساسة

Plural of *haassah* (sense), meaning the sensory faculty.

(خمس)

" - Are five."

بمعنى أن العقل حاكم بالضرورة بوجودها, وأما الحواس الباطنية التي يثبتها الفلاسفة, فلا تتم دلالتها على الأصول الإسلامية

Meaning, the intellect affirms their existence by necessity. As for the internal senses which the philosophers affirm, then there is no proof for them in the *Usool* of Islaam.

(السمع)

"The first is the hearing."

وهو قوة مودعة في العصب المفروش في مقعر الصماخ, يدرك بها الأصوات بطريق وصول الهواء المتكيف بكيفية الصوت إلى الصماخ, بمعنى أن الله تعالى يخلق الإدراك في النفس عند ذلك

And hearing is the ability which has been placed in the nerves that are spread out within the cavity of the ear. Through it, the person perceives sounds, by means of the air - which has been changed by the sound - reaching the cavity of the ear. Meaning, Allaah Ta`aalaa then creates within the soul of the person the capability of comprehension, at that time.

(والبصر)

"The second is that of sight."

وهو قوة مودعة في العصبيتين المجوفتين اللتين تتلاقيان في الدماغ, ثم تفترقان فتتأديان إلى العينين يدرك بها الأضواء والألوان والأشكال والمقادير والحركات والحسن والقبح وغير ذلك مما يخلق الله تعالى إدراكها في النفس عند استعمال العبد تلك القوة

Meaning, it is an ability, or faculty, which has been placed in the two hollow nerves that connect with one another in the brain and then separate and go to the eyes. With it, the person perceives brightness, and colours, and shapes and forms, and quantities, and movements, and beauty and ugliness, etc. Allaah Ta`aalaa creates this ability of perception within the soul of His slave when the slave makes use of this faculty.

(والشم)

"The third is that of smell."

وهي قوة مودعة في الزائدتين الناتئتين من مقدم الدماغ الشبيهتين بحلمتي الثدي, يدرك بها الروائح بطريق وصول الهواء المتكيف بكيفية ذي الرائحة إلى الخيشوم

It is a faculty which has been placed in the two protruding lumps in the front of the brain which resemble nipples. With it, the person is able to perceive smells, by way of the air - which has been altered with the quality of the particular smell - reaching his nasopharynx.

(والذوق)

"The fourth is that of taste."

وهي قوة منبثة في العصب المفروش على جرم اللسان, يدرك بها الطعوم مخالطة الرطوبة اللعابية التي في الفم بالمطعوم, ووصولها إلى العصب

It is a faculty situated in the nerves spread out on the organ of the tongue. Through it, the person is able to perceive tastes, through the thing which is tasted mixing with the saliva of the mouth, and from there reaching the nerves.

(واللمس)

"The fifth is that of touch."

وهي قوة منبثة في جميع البدن يدرك بها الحرارة والبرودة والرطوبة واليبوسة ونحو ذلك, عند التماس والإتصال به

It is a faculty situated in the entire of the body. Through it, the person is able to perceive heat, and cold, and wetness and dryness, etc., when coming into contact with them.

(وبكل حاسة منها)

"And with every faculty from these faculties,"

أي من الحواس الخمس

Meaning, from the five senses or five faculties.

(يوقف)

"A person becomes aware."

أي يطلع

Meaning, he comes to know.

(على ما وضعت هي)

"That for which it was placed."

أي تلك الحاسة

Meaning, that particular sense or faculty.

(له)

"For it."

يعني أن الله تعالى قد خلق كلا من تلك الحواس لإدراك أشياء مخصوصة كالسمع للأصوات, والذوق للمطعوم, والشم للروائح, لا يدرك بها ما يدرك بالحاسة الأخرى, وأما أنه هل يجوز أن يمتنع ذلك؟ ففيه

خلاف, والحق الجواز, لما أن ذلك محض خلق الله من غير تأثير للحواس, فلا يمتنع أن يخلق الله عقيب صرف الباصرة إدراك الأصوات مثلاً

Meaning, Allaah Ta`aalaa created each one of those faculties for the perception of particular things, like how the faculty of hearing has been created for the perception of sounds, and the faculty of taste has been created for the perception of taste, and the faculty of smell has been created for the perception of smells, etc. What is perceived through one faculty cannot be perceived through the use of a different faculty.

However, as to the issue of whether or not that is possible (i.e. perceiving through one faculty that which is generally perceived through a different faculty), then there is a difference of opinion about it, but the correct opinion is that it is possible, because perceiving anything by the senses only comes about through Allaah Ta`aalaa creating that perception within the soul of the person, so there is nothing to prevent that Allaah Ta`aalaa creates a perception of sounds after a movement of the person's eye, for example (because all perception is created within the person by Allaah Ta`aalaa and that can be done even without any of the senses, so Allaah Ta`aalaa can cause a person to hear and be addressed by speech without the faculty of hearing, for example.)

فإن قيل: أليست الذائقة تدرك بها حلاوة الشيء وحرارته معاً؟ قلنا: لا , بل الحلاوة تدرك بالذوق والحرارة باللمس الموجود في الفم واللسان

If an objection is raised that, is it not the case that the faculty of sense perceives the sweetness of a thing as well as its heat at the same time?

We say: No. Rather, the sweetness is perceived with the faculty of taste and the heat is perceived with the faculty of touch which exists in the mouth and tongue as well (because the faculty of touch exists throughout the body).

السبب الثاني: الخبر الصادق

The Second Cause of Knowledge: Truthful Reports

(والخبر الصادق)

"The second cause of knowledge is truthful reports."

أي المطابق للواقع, فإن الخبر كلام يكون لنسبته خارج تطابقه تكل النسبة فيكون صادقاً, أو لا يطابقه فيكون كاذباً

فالصدق والكذب على هذا من أوصاف الخبر, وقد يقالان بمعنى الإخبار عن الشيء على ما هو به, ولا على ما هو به, أي الإعلام بنسبة تامة تطابق الواقع أو لا تطابقه, فيكونان من صفات المخبر, فمن هاهنا يقع في بعض الكتب الخبر الصادق بالوصف, وفي بعضها خبر الصادق بالإضافة

Meaning, that which confirms to reality, because *khabr* (news, or a report) is speech which, there is something external to which it conforms, and thus it is *saadiq* (truthful), or it does not conform to it, in which case if it *kaadhib* (false).

Sidq (truthfulness) and *kidhb* (false) are the qualities of the report. It is possible to use them to give information about a thing according to how it is, or on the other hand, according to how it is not, i.e. making something known with a complete link or connection which either agrees with reality or does not agree with it, and thus they are the qualities of the giver of information (*mukhbir*).

For this reason, in some books it is mentioned as "*al-khabr as-saadiq*" (the truthful report), i.e. in the form of a description (i.e. *mawsoof*, *sifah*), whereas in others it is mentioned as, "*khabr as-saadiq*" (a report of a truthful person), i.e. in the form of *idhaafah* (attaching, i.e. *mudhaaf*, *mudhaaf ilayhi*).

(على نوعين)

"It is of two types:"

النوع الأول

The First Type:

(أحدهما: الخبر المتواتر)

"One of them is the *mutawaatir* (continuous) report."

سمي بذلك لما أنه لا يقع دفعة بل على التعاقب والتوالي

It has been named as such because it does not occur just one time, but rather, with continuity and sequence.

(وهو الخبر الثابت على ألسنة قوم لا يتصور تواطؤهم)

"It is that report which is affirmed upon the tongues of such a people who, it is not possible to imagine that they would all agree (on a lie)."

أي لا يجوز العقل توافقهم

Meaning, the intellect does not view as being possible their agreement.

(على الكذب)

"On a lie."

ومصداقه وقوع العلم من غير شبهة

Its *misdaaq* (that which proves it as being true) is that knowledge occurs without any doubt.

(وهو)

"And it-"

بالضرورة

By necessity.

(موجب للعلم الضروري, كالعلم بالملوك الخالية في الأزمنة الماضية والبلدان النائية)

"Necessitates the knowledge which is necessary, like the knowledge of the kings of old and times past and countries far away."

يحتمل العطف على الملوك وعلى الأزمنة, والأول أقرب وإن كان أبعد

The statement of the author, "of countries far away" can be `atf* on *mulook* (kings) but it can also be `atf* on "times", but it is more likely that it is `atf* on *mulook* even though it is further away in the sentence.

فهاهنا أمران: أحدهما أن المتواتر موجب للعلم, وذلك بالضرورة, فإنا نجد من أنفسنا العلم بوجود مكة وبغداد, وأنه ليس إلا بالاخبار

So there are two matters here: the first is that mutawaatir necessitates knowledge, and that is with necessity, because we find in ourselves knowledge of the existence of Makkah and Baghdad, and that is acquired except through reports (*akhbaar*).

والثاني أن العلم الحاصل به ضروري, وذلك لأنه يحصل للمستدل وغيره حتى الصبيان الذين لا إهتداء لهم بطريق الإكتساب وترتيب المقدمات, وأما خبر النصارى بقتل عيسى عليه السلام واليهود بتأبيد دين موسى عليه السلام, فتواتره ممنوع

The second issue is that the knowledge acquired through it is necessary, and that is because it is acquired by a person capable of making deductions as well as even children who have no knowledge or guidance pertaining to the method of acquisition and the arrangement of premises.

As for the reports of the Christians (Nasaaraa) regarding the killing of Nabi `Eesa عليه السلام, and the reports of the Jews (Yahood) regarding the perpetuity of the Deen of Nabi Moosaa عليه السلام, then that kind of tawaatur is prohibited.

فإن قيل: خبر كل واحد لا يفيد إلا الظن, وضم الظن إلى الظن لا يوجب اليقين, وأيضاً جواز كذب كل واحد يوجب جواز كذب المجموع, لأنه نفس الآحاد

قلنا: ربما يكون مع الإجتماع ما لا يكون مع الإنفراد, كقوة الحبل المؤلف من الشعرات

If it is said: the report of each person does not bring about anything except *zhann* (speculation), and attaching speculation to speculation does not necessitate *yaqeen* (conviction). Additionally, the fact that it is possible for each individual person to lie necessitates the possibility of the entire group lying, because the group is made up of those very same people.

We respond to this by saying: many a time there is, with *ijtimaa`* (gathering) that which there is not with *infiraad* (individuality), just like the strength of a rope, which is made up of individual hairs.

فإن قيل: الضروريات لا يقع فيها التفاوت ولا الإختلاف, ونحن نجد العلم بكون الواحد نصف الإثنين أقوى من العلم بوجود إسكندر, والمتواتر قد أنكر إفادته العلم جماعة من العقلاء كالسمنية والبراهمة.

If it is said: in matters of *dharooriyyaat* (knowledge that is known by necessity), there is no differing stages or differences of opinion, and we have found that the knowledge that one is half of two is stronger than the knowledge of the existence of Alexandria.

A group of the thinkers had rejected the bringing about of knowledge through *mutawaatir* (reports), like the Sumaniyyah and the Brahmins.

قلنا: هذا ممنوع, بل قد تتفاوت أنواع الضروري بواسطة التفاوت في الإلف والعادة والممارسة, والأخطار بالبال وتصورات أطراف الأحكام, وقد يختلف فيه مكابرة وعناداً, كالسوفسطائية في جميع الضروريات

We say: this is prohibited. Rather, the types of *dharoori* (necessary knowledge) differ in ranks through their different stages in terms of usage, and custom, and practice, and passing through the minds of people, and the conceiving of the ends of the rulings. It is also possible for there to be differences of opinion (in *mutawaatir* reports) due to arrogance and obstinacy, like the Sophists in (their rejection of) all types of *dharooriyyaat* (knowledge known by necessity).

النوع الثاني

The Second Type:

(والنوع الثاني: خبر الرسول المؤيد)

"The second type is that of the report of a Rasool who is aided."

أي الثابت رسالته

"Meaning, the one whose *Risaalat* (being a Rasool) is affirmed."

(بالمعجزات)

"With mu`jizaat (miracles)."

والرسول إنسان بعثه الله تعالى إلى الخلق لتبليغ الأحكام, وقد يشترط فيه الكتاب بخلاف النبي صلى الله عليه وسلم فإنه أعم

والمعجزة أمر خارق للعادة قصد به إظهار صدق من ادعى أنه رسول الله تعالى

A Rasool is a human being whom Allaah Ta`aalaa sends to the creation to convey to them the *Ahkaam*. The bringing of a Kitaab (Divine Book) is a condition in the case of a Rasool, unlike in the case of a Nabi, because a Nabi is more `*aam* (general).

A *mu`jizah* is a matter which breaks the norm (of how the world works), and its purpose is to show the truthfulness (*sidq*) of the one who says that he is a Rasool of Allaah Ta`aalaa.

(وهو)

"And it-"

أي خبر الرسول

Meaning, the report of a Rasool.

(يوجب العلم الإستدلالي)

" - Necessitates deductive knowledge."

أي الحاصل بالإستدلال, أي بالنظر في الدليل, وهو الذي يمكن التوصل بصحيح النظر فيه إلى العلم بمطلوب خبري, وقيل قول مؤلف من قضايا يستلزم لذاته قولا آخر, فعلى الأول: الدليل على وجود الصانع هو العالم, وعلى الثاني: قولنا العالم حادث, وكل حادث له صانع, وأما قولهم الدليل هو الذي يلزم من العلم به العلم بشيء آخر, فبالثاني أوفق

Meaning, knowledge which is acquired through *istidlaal* (deduction), i.e. looking into the evidences, and it is such a thing that through looking at (the evidences) with a sound look (speculation), one is able to arrive at the sought-after, report-based knowledge.

It has been said that the statement of the author is from the cases that necessitates, by itself, another statement.

According to the first (definition), the proof for the existence of a Creator is the world. According to the second (definition), the proof is our saying that the world came into existence (*haadith*), and everything that came into existence requires a Creator.

As for their statement that *daleel* (evidence) is such a thing that, by knowing it, a person acquires other knowledge, then this is more suited for the second (definition).

أما كونه موجباً للعلم, فللقطع بأن من أظهر الله المعجزة على يده تصديقاً له في دعوى الرسالة, كان صادقاً فيما أتى به من الأحكام, وإذا كان صادقاً يقع العلم بمضمونها قطعاً

As for its being a necessitator of knowledge, then that is because of the certainty of the fact that, the one whom Allaah Ta`aalaa lets a *mu`jizah* occur by his hands, this is a confirmation (*tasdeeq*) for him in his claim of being a Rasool, and that he is truthful in those *Ahkaam* which he has brought, and if he is truthful, then the knowledge of whatever it contains is absolute (beyond doubt).

وأما أنه إستدلالي فلتوقفه على الإستدلال, واستحضار أنه خبر من ثبتت رسالته بالمعجزات, وكل خبر هذا شأنه فهو صادق, ومضمونه واقع

As for its being *istidlaali* (deductive), then that is because of its being hinged upon *istidlaal* (deduction), and it brings to mind the fact that it is the report of one whose *Risaalat* has been established through *mu`jizaat* (miracles), and every report which, this is its status, then it is truthful and its content-matter is factual.

(والعلم الثابت به)

"And the knowledge that is affirmed through it."

أي بخبر الرسول

Meaning, with the report of a Rasool.

(يضاهي)

"Imitates."

أي يشابه

Meaning, resembles.

(العلم الثابت بالضرورة)

"The knowledge that is affirmed by necessity."

كالمحسوسات والبديهات والمتواترات

Like those things perceived by the senses (*mahsoosaat*), and the things immediately perceived by the intellect (*badeehaat*), and the *mutawaatiraat* (continuous reports).

(في التيقن)

"In establishing certainty."

أي عدم احتمال النقيض

Meaning, the absence of a possibility of contradiction.

(والثبات)

"And affirmation."

أي عدم احتمال الزوال بتشكيك المشكك, فهو علم بمعنى الإعتقاد المطابق الجازم الثابت, وإلا لكان جهلاً أو ظناً أو تقليداً

Meaning, the absence of the possibility of removal through the casting of doubts by that which is ambiguous, so it is a knowledge in the meaning of *i'tiqaad* (firm belief) which is in conformity (with the reality) and which is absolute and affirmed. Otherwise, it would have been ignorance, or speculation, or blind-following.

فإن قيل: هذا إنما يكون في المتواتر فقط, فيرجع إلى القسم الأول

قلنا: الكلام فيما علم أنه خبر الرسول بأن سمع من فيه, أو تواتر عنه ذلك, أو بغير ذلك إن أمكن, وأما خبر الواحد فإنما لم يفد العلم لعروض الشبهة في كونه خبر الرسول

If it is said: this only applies in the case of *mutawaatir*, so it returns to the first type (of *khabr saadiq*).

We say: the discussion regarding that which is known to be a report of a Rasool, such as it being heard from his mouth, or there are *mutawaatir* reports from him regarding it, or through other than that, if possible. As for a *khabr-e-waahid*, then it does not bring about knowledge due to the doubt regarding it actually being the report of Rasoolullaah صلى الله عليه وسلم.

فإن قيل: فإذا كان متواتراً أو مسموعاً مِنْ في رسول الله عليه السلام, كان العلم الحاصل به ضرورياً, كما هو حكم سائر المتواترات والحسيات, لا إستدلالياً

قلنا: العلم الضروري في المتواتر عن رسول الله, هو العلم بكونه خبر الرسول عليه الصلاة والسلام, لأن هذا المعنى هو الذي تواترت الأخبار به, وفي المسموع من في رسول الله صلى الله عليه وسلم, هو إدراك الألفاظ وكونها كلام رسول الله

If it is said: if it is *mutawaatir* or heard directly from the mouth of Rasoolullaah صلى الله عليه وسلم, then the knowledge acquired from it is *dharoori* (necessary), just as is the case with the rest of the *mutawaatiraat*, and the *hissiyyaat* (those perceived by the senses), and it will not be *istidlaali* (deductive).

We respond to this by saying that the necessary knowledge with regards to the *mutawaatir* reports from Rasoolullaah صلى الله عليه وسلم, is the knowledge of it being a report of Rasoolullaah صلى الله عليه وسلم, because this meaning is the one that, there are *mutawaatir akhbaar* (reports) concerning. And in the case of that which is heard directly from the mouth of Rasoolullaah صلى الله عليه وسلم then (the necessary knowledge) in this case is that of comprehending the words and its being the speech of Rasoolullaah صلى الله عليه وسلم.

والإستدلالي: هو العلم بمضمونه وثبوت مدلوله, مثلاً قوله عليه الصلاة والسلام: البينة على المدعي واليمين على من أنكر

As for *istidlaali* (deductive knowledge), then it is, in this case, the knowledge of its subject-matter and the affirmation of what it proved. For example, the Hadeeth:

"The onus of proof is upon the claimant, and the defendant must take an oath."

علم بالتواتر أنه خبر الرسول صلى الله عليه وسلم وهو ضروري, ثم علم منه أنه يجب أن تكون البينة على المدعي وهو إستدلالي

It is known through *tawaatur* that it is a report of Rasoolullaah صلى الله عليه وسلم, and it is necessary (knowledge). Thereafter, it is known from it that it binding upon the claimant to produce evidence, and that (fact) is *istidlaali* (deductive knowledge).

فإن قيل: الخبر الصادق المفيد للعلم لا ينحصر في النوعين, بل قد يكون خبر الله تعالى, أو خبر الملك, أو خبر أهل الإجماع, أو الخبر المقرون بما يرفع احتمال الكذب, كالخبر بقدوم زيد عند تسارع قومه إلى داره

If it is said: a truthful report that brings about knowledge is not restricted to these two types; rather, it can be a report from Allaah Ta`aalaa, or one of the Malaa'ikah, or a report from the people of *ijmaa`* (consensus), or a report tied to that which precludes any possibility of falsehood, like the report that "Zaid has arrived," when people are rushing to his house.

قلنا: المراد بالخبر خبر يكون سبب العلم لعامة الخلق, بمجرد كونه خبراً, مع قطع النظر عن القرائن المفيدة لليقين بدلالة العقل, فخبر الله تعالى أو خبر الملك إنما يكون مفيداً للعلم بالنسبة إلى عامة الخلق, إذا وصل إليهم من جهة الرسول عليه السلام, فحكمه حكم خبر الرسول, وخبر أهل الإجماع في حكم التواتر

We say: the intended meaning of *khabr* (report) is a report which acts as a cause (*sabab*) for knowledge for all of the creation, simply by it being a report whilst not looking at any of the *qaraa'in* (supporting evidences and context) which bring out *yaqeen* (conviction) by the evidence of the intellect. Thus, the report of Allaah Ta`aalaa or one of the Malaa'ikah brings out knowledge with regard to all of the creation when it reaches them through the medium of a Rasool عليه السلام. So, its ruling is the ruling of the report of the Rasool and the report of the people of ijmaa` in the ruling of *tawaatur*.

وقد يجاب بأنه لا يفيد بمجرده, بل بالنظر في الأدلة على كون الإجماع حجة

This has been responded to by saying that it does not bring about information by itself, but rather, by looking into the evidences regarding *ijmaa`* (consensus) being an evidence.

قلنا: وكذلك خبر الرسول, ولهذا جعل إستدلالياً

We say: similar is the case of a report of a Rasool, and for this reason it was made *istidlaali* (deductive).

السبب الثالث: العقل

The Third Cause of Knowledge: The Intellect

(وأما العقل)

"As for the intellect-"

وهو قوة للنفس بها تستعد للعلوم والإدراكات, وهو المعنى بقولهم: غريزة, يتبعها العلم بالضروريات عند سلامة الآلات

وقيل: جوهر يدرك به الغائبات بالوسائط, والمحسوسات بالمشاهدة

And it is a faculty of the soul. With it, the person is prepared to acquire the various sciences and matters to be comprehended. It is the intended meaning by the saying: "The intellect is an innate property (*ghareezah*). When the instruments are sound, knowledge of the necessary matters shall follow."

It has also been said that the `*aql* (intellect) is a substance by which unseen matters via mediums, and the *mahsoosaat* (matters perceived through the senses) through witnessing (*mushaahadah*).

(فهو سبب للعلم أيضاً)

"So it is a cause for knowledge as well."

صرح بذلك لما فيه من خلاف الملاحدة والسمنية في جميع النظريات, وبعض الفلاسفة في الإلهيات, بناء على كثرة الإختلاف وتناقض الآراء

والجواب أن ذلك لفساد النظر, فلا ينافي كون النظر الصحيح من العقل مفيداً للعلم, على أن ما ذكرتم إستدلال بنظر العقل, ففيه إثبات ما نفيتم فيتناقض

He clearly stated that, due to the arguments which exist regarding it among the atheists and the Sumaniyyah in all of the speculative matters (*nazhriyyaat*), and some of the philosophers in metaphysical matters, based on excessive different and confliction points of view.

The response is, that is due to the corruption of (their) speculation, so it does not negate the fact that a sound speculation from the intellect is capable of bringing about knowledge, based on the fact that what you have mentioned is *istidlaal* (deduction) using the speculation of the intellect. Thus, in that is the very thing which you have negated, so they contradict one another.

فإن زعموا أنه معارضة للفاسد بالفاسد

قلنا: إما أن يفيد شيئاً فلا يكون فاسداً, أو لا يفيد فلا يكون معارضة

If they claim that this is opposing the corrupt (invalid) with what is corrupt (invalid), we say: either it brings about something and therefore is not corrupt (invalid), or it does not bring about anything, in which case it will not be an opposition.

فإن قيل: كون النظر مفيداً للعلم إن كان ضرورياً لم يقع فيه خلاف, كما في قولنا: الواحد نصف الإثنين, وإن كان نظرياً لزم إثبات النظر بالنظر, وإنه دور

If it is said: the fact that speculation brings about knowledge if it is *dharoori* (necessary), there is no argument regarding that, like in our statement: "One is half of two." If it is *nazhri* (speculative), then it necessitates the affirmation of speculation with speculation, and that is *dawr* (an infinite cycle).

قلنا: الضروري قد يقع فيه خلاف, إما لعناد أو لقصور في الإدراك, فإن العقل متفاوتة بحسب الفطرة باتفاق من العقلاء, واستدلال من الآثار, وشهادة من الأخبار, والنظري قد يثبت بنظر مخصوص لا يعبر عنه بالنظر, كما يقال: قولنا العالم متغير, وكل متغير حادث, يفيد العلم

بحدوث العالم بالضرورة, وليس ذلك لخصوصية هذا النظر بل لكونه صحيحاً مقروناً بشرائطه, فيكون كل نظري صحيح مقرون بشرائطه مفيداً للعلم, وفي تحقيق هذا المنع زيادة تفصيل لا يليق بهذا الكتاب

We say: there is argument regarding the *dharoori* (necessary knowledge) as well, either due to obstinacy or due to a deficiency of comprehension, because the intellect is of different stages proportionate to the *fitrah* (nature), according to *ittifaaq* (unanimous agreement) of the thinkers. This is arrived at through *istidlaal* from the *Aathaar* and testification from the reports.

Nazhri (speculative knowledge) can be affirmed with specific speculation (*nazhr makhsoos*) which is not termed *nazhr* (speculation), like how it is said: our statement: "The world changes, and everything that changes is *haadith* (came into existence)." This by necessity brings about knowledge of the fact that the world came into existence, and that is not because of a speciality of this speculation, but rather, because of it being *saheeh* (valid; sound), connected to its conditions. Thus, every sound, speculative knowledge that is attached to its *sharaa'it* (conditions) can bring about knowledge. In the verification of this prohibition there is the need for additional details which is not suitable for this Kitaab.

(وما ثبت منه)

"And what is established from it-"

أي من العلم الثابت بالعقل

Meaning, from the knowledge affirmed by the intellect (`aql).

(بالبديهة)

" - With immediate perception."

أي بأول التوجه من غير احتياج إلى الفكر

Meaning, the moment one's attention is turned to it, without the need for contemplation.

(فهو ضروري, كالعلم بأن كل شيء أعظم من جزئه)

"Then it is *dharoori* (necessary knowledge), like the knowledge that every whole (*kull*) is greater than its part (*juz'*)."

فإنه بعد تصور معنى الكل والجزء والأعظم لا يتوقف على شيء, ومن توقف فيه حيث زعم أن جزء الإنسان كاليد مثلاً قد يكون أعظم من الكل, فهو لم يتصور معنى الكل والجزء

Because, after a person has perceived the meaning of "*kull*" (all; whole) and *juz'* (part) and "*a`zham*" (greater than), he has no reservations. A person who hesitates regarding it, claiming that it is possible for a part (*juz'*) of a human being, like his hand, for example, is greater than the whole (*kull*), then he has not correctly understood the meaning of *kull* and *juz'*.

(وما ثبت بالإستدلال)

"And what is affirmed from istidlaal (deduction)-"

أي بالنظر في الدليل سواء كان إستدلالا من العلة على المعلوم, كما إذا رأى ناراً فعلم أن لها دخاناً, أو من المعلول على العلة كما إذا رأى دخاناً فعلم أن هناك ناراً, وقد يخص الأول باسم التعليل والثاني بالإستدلال

Meaning, by speculating regarding the evidence, regardless of whether it is through *istidlaal* (deduction) from the `*illat* upon the *ma`lool* (i.e. cause and effect), such as by a person seeing fire, so he knows that there must be smoke, or from the *ma`lool* (effect) upon the `*illat* (cause), like a person seeing smoke, so he knows that there must be a fire there. The first has been specified with the term, "*ta`leel*" (assigning an `*illat*, or cause) and the second has been called "*istidlaal*" (deduction).

(فهو اكتسابي)

" - Then it is iktisaabi (earned; acquired)."

أي حاصل بالكسب, وهو مباشرة الأسباب بالإختيار, كصرف العقل والنظر في المقدمات في الإستدلالات والإصغاء, وتقليب الحدقة, ونحو ذلك في الحسيات, فالإكتسابي أعم من الإستدلالي لأنه الذي يحصل بالنظر في الدليل, فكل إستدلالي إكتسابي ولا عكس, كالإبصار الحاصل بالقصد والإختيار

Meaning, acquired through *kasb* (earning), directly through the *asbaab* (causes) and with choice (*ikhtiyaar*), such as by application of the intellect, and speculating regarding the premises in *istidlaalaat* (deductions), and by listening, and turning the pupil (of the eye), etc., in the *hissiyaat* (matters perceived by the senses). So, *iktisaabi* is more general (*a`ammu*) than *istidlaali*, because *iktisaabi* is acquired through speculation and looking into the evidence. Thus, every *istidaali* is *iktisaabi*, but not every *iktisaabi* is *istidlaali*, as, for example, making use of one's sight, which results from intention and choice.

وأما الضروري فقد يقال في مقابلة الإكتسابي, ويفسر بما لا يكون تحصيله مقدوراً للمخلوق, وقد يقال في مقابلة الإستدلالي, ويفسر بما يحصل بدون فكر ونظر في دليل, فمن هاهنا جعل بعضهم العلم الحاصل بالحواس إكتساباً, أي: حاصلاً بمباشرة الأسباب بالإختيار, وبعضهم ضرورياً أي حاصلا بدون الإستدلال, فظهر أنه لا تناقض في كلام صاحب البداية حيث قال: إن العلم الحادث نوعان:

Dharoori has been said to be the opposite of *iktisaabi*, and it has been explained (made *mufassar*) with that which, its acquisition is not within the control of the creation. It has also been said to be the opposite of *istidlaali* (deductive), and thus been explained (made *mufassar*) as being that which is acquired without contemplation or speculation into the evidences. From this aspect, some of them classified the knowledge that is acquired through the senses as being *iktisaabi*, i.e. acquired directly from the *asbaab* (causes), with *ikhtiyaar* (choice), and some of them classified it as *dharoori* (necessary), i.e. acquired without *istidlaal* (deduction).

It is thus apparent that there is no contradiction in the speech of the author of *al-Bidaayah*, when he said: "*`Ilm* that is *haadith* (originated) is of two types:"

ضروري: وهو ما يحدثه الله في نفس العبد من غير كسبه واختياره, كالعلم بوجوده وتغير أحواله

Dharoori, which is what Allaah Ta`aalaa brings into existence in the soul of the slave without any earning (on the part of the slave), and without the choice or volition of the slave either, like the knowledge of his existence and the changing of his conditions.

واكتسابي: وهو ما يحدثه الله فيه بواسطة كسب العبد, وهو مباشرة أسبابه, وأسبابه ثلاثة: الحواس السليمة, والخبر الصادق, ونظر العقل

And *iktisaabi* (acquired), which is what Allaah Ta`aalaa brings into existence via the medium of the earning of the slave, directly through its *asbaab* (causes), and its causes are three: sound sensory faculties (i.e. sight, hearing, speech, smell, and touch); truthful reports and the speculation of the intellect (`aql).

ثم قال: والحاصل من نظر العقل نوعان: ضروري, يحصل بأول النظر من غير تفكر كالعلم بأن الكل أعظم من الجزء, واستدلالي يحتاج فيه إلى نوع تفكر, كالعلم بوجود النار عند رؤية الدخان

Thereafter, he stated: that which is derived from the speculation of the intellect is of two types: *dharoori* (necessary), which is attained by the first glance or speculation, without the need for contemplation, like the knowledge that a whole is greater than a part. The second type is *istidlaali* (deductive), in which a type of contemplation is required, like the knowledge of the existence of fire when seeing smoke.

(والإلهام)

"And *ilhaam*."

المفسر بإلقاء معنى في القلب بطريق الفيض

Ilhaam has been explained as the casting of a meaning (or a concept, or an idea, or a thought, or an explanation, or even a strong feeling) into the heart by means of *faydh* (spiritual lights or blessings).

(ليس من أسباب المعرفة بصحة الشيء عند أهل الحق)

"It is not from the causes of recognition (*asbaab al-ma`rifah*) capable of declaring a thing as being sound, according to the people of reality."

حتى يرد به الإعتراض على حصر الأسباب في الثلاثة المذكورة, وكان الأولى أن يقول: من أسباب العلم بالشيء, إلا أنه حاول التنبيه على أن مرادنا بالعلم والمعرفة واحد, لا كما اصطلح عليه البعض من تخصيص العلم بالمركبات أو الكليات, والمعرفة بالبسائط أو الجزئيات, إلا أن تخصيص الصحة بالذكر مما لا وجه له, ثم الظاهر أنه أراد أن الإلهام ليس سبباً يحصل به العلم لعامة الخلق, ويصلح للإلزام على الغير, وإلا فلا شك أنه قد يحصل به العلم, وقد ورد القول به في الخبر, نحو قوله عليه الصلاة والسلام: ألهمني ربي, وحكي عن كثير من السلف

This was stated as a counter to an objection raised by some against the *asbaab* (causes of knowledge) being restricted to three. It would have been better had he (the author) said: "From the causes of knowledge of a thing." However, he tried to draw attention to the fact that the meaning we intend by `ilm (knowledge) and ma`rifah (recognition) is one, not like some have done, in making a technical definition, which is that of restricting `ilm (knowledge) to compounds (*murakkabaat*), or universals (*kulliyyaat*), and recognition of basics (*basaa'it*) or particulars (*juz'iyyaat*). However, the specification of soundness with what has been mentioned has no purpose (i.e. otherwise there had would have been no purpose in saying, "the soundness of a thing" rather than saying, "a thing".)

Thereafter, the apparent is that he had intended that *ilhaam* is not a *sabab* (cause) through which knowledge is acquired for most of the creation and which is valid to make binding upon another; otherwise, it would have been something through which knowledge is acquired.

The statement regarding it has been has appeared in the reports, like in the Hadeeth:

"My Rabb gave me *ilhaam*."

It has also been narrated from many of the Salaf.

وأما خبر الواحد العدل, وتقليد المجتهد, فقد يفيدان الظن, والإعتقاد الجازم الذي لا يقبل الزوال, فكأنه أراد بالعلم ما لا يشملهما, وإلا فلا وجه لحصر الأسباب في الثلاثة

As for the solitary report (*khabr al-waahid*) and the *talqeed* of a Mujthaid, then both of these bring about *zhann* (speculation), and *i`tiqaad* (creed) is fixed, clear-cut and does not accept removal. Thus, it is as though he intended by "knowledge" that which does not encompass them; otherwise, there would have been no purpose to restrict the causes of knowledge to three.

(فالعلم)

"So, knowledge (`ilm) -"

أي ما سوى الله تعالى من الموجودات مما يعلم به الصانع, يقال: عالم الأجساد, وعالم الأعراض, وعالم النبات, وعالم الحيوان, إلى غير ذلك, فيخرج عنه صفات الله تعالى, لأنها ليست غير الذات, كما أنها ليست عينها

Meaning, whatever is besides Allaah Ta`aalaa, all of the things which exist, it is known that they have a creator. It is said: the world of bodies, the world of substanes, the world of plants, the world of the animals, etc. The *Sifaat* of Allaah Ta`aalaa are excluded (from being part of the created things, because they are not created, and they did not come into existence, Rather, they are pre-existing, without a beginning or an end.) because the *Sifaat* are not other than the *Dhaat* of Allaah Ta`aalaa, but at the same time, they are not the *Dhaat* itself either.

(بجميع أجزائه)

" - With all of its parts -"

من السماوات وما فيها والأرض وما عليها

From the heavens and what is in them and the earth and what is upon it.

(محدث)

"Came into existence."

أي مخرج من العدم إلى الوجود, بمعنى أنه كان معدوماً فوجد, خلافاً للفلاسفة حيث ذهبوا إلى قدم السماوات بموادها وصورها وأشكالها, وقدم العناصر بموادها وصورها, لكن بالنوع, بمعنى أنها لم تخل عن صورة قط, نعم أطلقوا القول بحدوث ما سوى الله تعالى, لكن بمعنى الإحتياج إلى الغير, لا بمعنى سبق العدم عليه

Meaning, brought out from the state of non-existence into the state of existence. Meaning, they had not existed, and then they were brought into existence. This is contrary to the view of the philosophers, because they held the view of "*qidam as-samaawaat*" (the eternity of the heavens), with its *mawaadd* (essences; natures), its forms and its shapes, and also the eternity (qidam) of the elements, with their *mawaadd* (essences) and their forms; however, only a type, i.e. they were never without a form. Yes, the term "*hudooth*" (coming into existence) has been applied to whatever is besides Allaah Ta`aalaa, but in the meaning of "needing something else," not in the meaning of being preceded by non-existence.

ثم أشار إلى دليل حدوث العالم بقوله:

Thereafter, he (the author) points out an evidence of the *hudooth* of the world, by saying:

(إذا هو)

"Because it -"

أي العالم

Meaning, the world.

(أعيان وأعراض)

"Consists of individuals and substances."

لأنه إن قام بذاته فعين, وإلا فعرض, وكل منهما حادث لما سنبين, ولم يتعرض له المصنف رحمه الله تعالى, لأن الكلام فيه طويل لا يليق بهذا المختصر, كيف وهو مقصور على المسائل دون الدلائل

Because, if something exists by itself, then it is an individual; otherwise, it is a substance. Both of them came into existence, as we will explain. The author رحمة الله عليه did not discuss it because a discussion regarding it would be very prolonged and would not be appropriate for this summary. How can it, when it is restricted to the *masaa'il* alone, and not the evidences.

(فالأعيان ما)

"So, the individuals are-"

أي ممكن يكون

Meaning, they are capable of.

(له قيام بذاته)

" - those which exist by themselves."

بقرينة جعله من أقسام العالم

With the evidence that they have been made from the categories of the world.

ومعنى قيامه بذاته عند المتكلمين: أن يتحيز بنفسه, غير تابع تحيزه لتحيز شيء آخر, بخلاف العرض, فإن تحيزه تابع لتحيز الجوهر الذي هو موضوعه, أي محله الذي يقوّمه, ومعنى وجود العرض في الموضوع: هو أن وجوده في نفسه هو وجوده في الموضوع, ولذها يمتنع الإنتقال عنه, بخلاف وجود الجسم في الحيز, لأن وجوده في نفسه أمر, ووجوده في الحيز أمر آخر, ولهذا ينتقل عنه, وعند الفلاسفة معنى قيام الشيء بذاته: إستغناؤه عن محل يقومه, ومعنى قيامه بشيء آخر: إختصاصه به, بحيث يصير الأول نعتاً والثاني منعوتاً, سواء كان متحيزاً كما في سواد الجسم أم لا, كما في صفات الله تعالى, والمجردات

The meaning of "*qiyaam bi-dhaatihi*" (existing by itself), according to the Mutakallimeen (specialists in '*Ilm-ul-Kalaam*), is that it is bound by itself, its *tahayyuz* (being bounded) not being subsequent to the *tahayyuz* of something else, unlike the substance, because the *tahayyuz* of substances (*a`raadh*) follows the *tahayyuz* of the *jawhar* (atom, or smallest particle) which is its subject, i.e. its place which keeps up the substances.

And, the meaning of the substances existing in the subject is that its existence in itself is its existence in the subject, and for this reason, it cannot move away from it, unlike the existence of a body inside a boundary, because its existence in itself is one matter and its existence in a boundary is another, and therefore it can move away from it.

According to the philosophers, the meaning of a thing existing by itself is that it is independant of a *mahall* (place) to upkeep it. The meaning of it existing by something else is that it is specified by it, in such a way that the first becomes the quality and the second becomes the thing which has been qualified, regardless of whether it is within a boundary, as in the case of the mass of the body, or without being within a boundary, as in the case with the *Sifaat* of Allaah Ta`aalaa and the absolutes.

(وهو)

"And it-"

أي ما له قيام بذاته من العالم

Meaning, that which exists by itself, from the created things.

(إما مركب)

"Is either a compound."

من جزأين فصاعداً عندنا

Made up of two or more parts, according to us.

(وهو الجسم)

"Which is the body (jism)."

وعند البعض لابد من ثلاثة أجزاء لتحقق تقاطع الأبعاد الثلاثة, أعني الطول, والعرض, والعمق, وعند البعض من ثمانية أجزاء ليتحقق تقاطع الأبعاد على زوايا قائمة, وليس هذا نزاعاً لفظياً راجعاً إلى الإصطلاح, حتى يدفع بأن لكل أحد أن يصطلح على ما شاء, بل هو نزاع في أن المعنى الذي وضع لفظ الجسم بإزائه هل يكفي فيه التركيب من جزأين أم لا؟

According to some, there has to be at least three parts (*ajzaa'*) for the three dimensions to be realised, which are: length, width and depth.

According to some, there has to be at least eight parts for the dimensions to be realised along with the angles. This is not simply a semantical difference going back to technicalities, so that it could have been said that each one is free to use whatever technical term he wishes to; rather, it is a difference of opinion regarding the issue of the meaning for which the word "*jism*" (body) has been used, is it sufficient to be compounded or made up of two parts or not?

إحتج الأولون بأنه يقال لأحد الجسمين إذا زيد عليه جزء واحد أنه أجسم من الآخر, فلولا أن مجرد التركيب كاف في الجسمية لما صار بمجرد زيادة الجزء أزيد في الجسمية, وفيه نظراً لأن أفعل من الجسامة بمعنى الضخامة وعظم المقدار, يقال جسم الشيء, أي أعظم, فهو جسيم وجسام بالضم, والكلام في الجسم الذي هو إسم لا صفة

The First Ones argued that it is siad to one of two bodies, if the one is one part more than the other, that it is "*ajsam*" (bulkier, or has more body) than the other. So, if simply being made up (of parts) was not sufficient in *jismiyyah* (being a body), then one body would not have been "bulkier" or "having more body" due to having an additional *juz'* (part).

There is some consideration to be given to this, because the word-form "*af'al*" from the word "*jasaamah*", means "*dhakhaamah*" (thickness; bulkiness: voluminous) and greatness of amount. It is said, "*jasumash-shay*", i.e. "a thing became big/bulky", so it is "*jaseem*", or "*jusaam*" (with a *dhammah*). This discussion pertains to jism as an *ism* rather than as a *sifah*.

(أو غير مركب كالجوهر)

"Or not a compound, like a jawhar (atom, or smallest particle)."

يعني العين الذي لا يقبل الإنقسام, لا فعلاً ولا وهماً ولا فرضاً

Meaning, the individual or matter which does not accept division, not actuality, nor in imagination, nor by surmise.

(وهو الجزء الذي لا يتجزأ)

"And it is the *juz'* (part) which cannot be divided any further."

ولم يقل وهو الجوهر, إحترازاً عن ورود المنع, فإن ما لا يتركب لا ينحصر عقلاً في الجوهر, بمعنى الجزء الذي لا يتجزأ, بل لا بد من إبطال الهيولي والصورة والعقول والنفوس المجردة ليتم ذلك, وعند الفلاسفة لا وجود للجوهر الفرد, أعني الجوهر الذي لا يتجزأ, وتركب الجسم إنما هو من الهيولي والصورة

He did not say, "it is the *jawhar*," in order to avoid coming across a restriction, because that which is not compounded (made up of parts) cannot be restricted, logically, in a *jawhar*, meaning, "the indivisible part" (*al-juz' alladhee laa yatajazza'*). Rather, it is necessary to abolish *hayooli* (primordial matter) and soorah (form), intellects and absolute souls (*an-nufoos al-mujarradah*), in order to achieve that.

According to the philosophers, an individual atom does not exist (*al-jawhar al-fard*), i.e. the *jawhar* which cannot be further divided.

They (the philosophers) also claim that the *jism* (body) is made up of *hayooli* (primordial matter) and *soorah* (form).

وأقوى أدلة إثبات الجزء الذي لا يتجزأ أنه لو وضع كرة حقيقية على سطح حقيقي لم تماسه إلى بجزء غير منقسم, إذ لو ماسته بجزأين لكان فيها خط بالفعل, فلم تكن كرة حقيقية على سطح حقيقي

The strongest of evidences for the affirmation of "the indivisible part" (*al-juz' alladhee laa yatajazza'*) is the fact that, were a real ball to be placed on a real stretch of land, it would make contact (i.e. the ball and the land) at one point which is undivisible (*ghayr munqasim*), because were they to connect at two parts (*juz'ayn*), there would have been a line, so it would not have been a real ball nor a real stretch of land.

وأشهرها عند المشايخ وجهان:

The most famous proof (for the existence of the indivisible part) according to the Mashaayikh is two facets:

الأول: أنه لو كان كل عين منقسماً لا إلى نهاية لم تكن الخردلة أصغر من الجبل, لأن كلاً منهما غير متناهي الأجزاء, والعظم والصغر إنما هو بكثرة الأجزاء وقلتها, وذلك إنما يتصور في المتناهي

The first is that, if every substance were capable of being infinitely divided (further and further, having no end), then a mustard seed would not have been smaller than a mountain, since each would have been - according to that logic - made up of infinite parts. Being bigger or smaller only takes place when there is more parts or less parts (*ajzaa'*), and that cannot take place except if there is an end to the amount of times it can be divided.

الثاني: أن اجتماع أجزاء الجسم ليس لذاته, وإلا لما قبل الإفتراق, فالله تعالى قادر على أن يخلق فيه الإفتراق حتى ينتهي إلى الجزء الذي لا يتجزأ, لأن الجزء الذي تنازعنا فيه إن أمكن افتراقه لزم قدرة الله تعالى عليه دفعاً للعجز, وإن لم يمكن ثبت المدعى, والكل ضعيف

The second is that, the coming together of the parts (*ajzaa'*) of the body is not by itself; otherwise, it (the body) would not have been able to separate (into parts). Allaah Ta`aalaa is All-Powerful over creating within it *iftiraaq* (separation), causing it to divide and divide until it reaches *al-juz' alladhee laa yatajazza'* (the indivisible part). The *juz'* (part) which we are arguing about (is this part): if it is possible to be separated further, then Allaah Ta`aalaa has the power to bring it about, because Allaah Ta`aalaa is free from any kind of weakness or being incapable. If this part is not capable of separating further, then the claim (of it being the indivisible part) has been established.

However, all (of these proofs) are weak.

أما الأول, فلأنه إنما يدل على ثبوت النقطة, وهو لا يستلزم ثبوت الجزء, لأن حلولها في المحل ليس حلول السريان حتى يلزم من عدم انقسامها عدم انقسام المحل

As for the first, then it is weak because it only points out to the affirmation of the spot, but that does not necessitate the affirmation of the *juz'* (part), because its inhabiting a place is not inhabiting *sarayaan* (circulation), and thus it does not necessitate from the absence of its divisibility the non-divisibility of the place (*mahall*).

وأما الثاني والثالث, فلأن الفلاسفة لا يقولون بأن الجسم متألف من أجزاء بالفعل, وأنها غير متناهية, بل يقولون: إنه قابل لانقسامات غير متناهية, وليس فيه اجتماع أجزاء أصلاً, وإنما العظم والصغر باعتبار المقدار القائم به, والإفتراق ممكن لا إلى نهاية, فلا يستلزم الجزء

As for the second and third (proofs), then they are weak because the philosophers do not say that the *jism* (body) is made up of parts (*ajzaa'*) in actuality and that these parts have no end; rather, they say that the parts are capable of endless division and that there is no *ijtimaa`* (gathering) of parts at all, and that largeness or smallness is only according to the value present (in the body). They also say that *iftiraaq* (separation) is possible endlessly, and thus there is no "indivisible part".

وأما أدلة النفي أيضاً فلا تخلو من ضعف, ولهذا مال الإمام الرازي رحمه الله في هذه المسألة إلى التوقف

As for the evidences of negation, then they too are not free from weakness, and for this reason, Imaam ar-Raazi رحمة الله عليه inclined towards *tawaqquf* (reserving judgement) in this issue.

فإن قيل: هل لهذا الخلاف ثمرة؟

If it is asked: is there any benefit in this argument?

قلنا: نعم, له ثمرة وهي أن في إثبات الجوهر الفرد نجاة عن كثير من ظلمات الفلاسفة, مثل إثبات الهيولي والصورة, المؤدي إلى قدم العالم, ونفي حشر الأجساد, وكثير من أصول الهندسة المبني عليها دوام حركة السماوات والأرض, وامتناع الخرق والإلتئام عليها

We say: Yes, it has a benefit, and that is: in the affirmation of a singular atom there is salvation from many of the darknesses of the philosophers, like their affirmation of hayooli and soorah (form) which lead to their belief in qidam al-`aalam (the world being pre-eternal), and the belief in there being no resurrection of the bodies, and many of the principles of geometry, upon which is based the constancy of the movement of the heavens and the earth, (and their belief) in their being no rending of them nor being joined together again.

(والعرض ما لا يقوم بذاته)

"`Ardh (substance) does not exist by itself."

بل بغيره, بأن يكون تابعاً له في التحيز أو مختصاً به إختصاص الناعت بالمنعوت على ما سبق, لا بمعنى أنه لا يمكن تعلقه بدون المحل على ما توهم فإن ذلك إنما هو في بعض الأعراض

Rather, with other than it, such as by it being a follower of it in tahayyuz (boundary) or specified with it like the specification of the qualifier with the qualified thing as has preceded, not in the meaning that it is not possible for it to connected to it without a mahall (place) as has been imagined (by some), because that is only the case in some a`raadh (substances).

(ويحدث في الأجسام والجواهر)

"It originates in the bodies and the substances."

قيل هو من تمام التعريف إحترازاً عن صفات الله تعالى, وقيل لا بل هو بيان حكم العرض, كالألوان وأصولها, قيل: السواد والبياض, وقيل: الحمرة, والخضرة, والصفرة أيضاً, والبواقي بالتركيب

It has been mentioned that this was added to complete the definition and to avoid including the *Sifaat* of Allaah Ta`aalaa. Others said that it was to clarify the ruling of substance, like colours and their bases (i.e. primary colours), which is said to be black and white. Others say that red, green and yellow are included among these, and that all other colours come about through mixing these (primary colours) together.

(والأكوان)

"And the states of coming into existence."

هي الإجتماع والإفتراق, والحركة والسكون

Which is *ijtimaa`* (coming together) and *iftiraaq* (separating), and movement and stillness.

(والطعوم)

"And tastes."

وأنواعها تسعة وهي: المرارة والحرافة والملوحة والعفوصة والحموضة والقبض والحلاوة والدسومة والتفاهة, ثم يحصل بحسب التركيب أنواع لا تحصى

There are nine types of tastes, and they are: bitterness, pungency, saltiness, astringency, sourness, puckeriness, sweetness, greasiness and insipidity. From the combination of these, innumerable kinds of tastes are made.

(والروائح)

"And smells."

وأنواعها كثيرة, وليست لها أسماء مخصوصة, والأظهر أن ما عدا الأكوان لا يعرض إلا للأجسام, فإذا تقرر أن العالم أعيان وأعراض, والأعيان أجسام وجواهر, فنقول الكل حادث

There are many types and they do not have specific names.

What is apparent is that besides the states coming into existence, the rest do not occur except when *ajsaam* (bodies). When it is thus confrmed that the world is made up of individuals and substances, and the individuals (*a`yaan*) are bodies and atoms (*jawaahir*), we say: all of it came into existence.

أما الأعراض فبضعها بالمشاهدة, كالحركة بعد السكون, والضوء بعد الظلمة, والسواد بعد البياض, وبعضها بالدليل, وهو طريان العدم كما في أضداد ذلك, فإن القدم ينافي العدم, لأن القديم إن كان واجباً لذاته فظاهر, وإلا لزم استناده إليه بطريق الإيجاب, إذ الصادر عن الشيء بالقصد والإختيار يكون حادثاً بالضرورة, والمستند إلى الموجب القديم قديم, ضرورة إمتناع تخلف المعلول عن العلة التامة.

As for the *a`raadh*, then some of them are known through observation, like movement after stillness, and light after darkness, and blackness after whiteness. Some of them are known through evidence, such as the occurence (*tarayaan*) of non-existence like in the opposites of those ones, because *qidam* (being pre-eternal) negates non-existence, because something that is *qadeem* (pre-eternal), if it is necessary by its own self then it is apparent; however, it would have to be ascribed (to eternity) by way of affirmation, because that which comes from a thing through intention and choice is necessarily originated, and something that is attributed to a pre-eternal cause (*moojib*) is pre-eternal as well because it is impossible for a *ma`lool* (effect) to lag behind the complete `*illat* (cause).

وأما الأعيان فلأنها لا تخلو عن الحوادث, وكل ما لا يخلو عن الحوادث فهو حادث

As for the *a`yaan*, (then they are originated as well) because they are not free from *hawaadith* (things which came into existence), and every such thing which is not free from *hawaadith* is itself *haadith* (originated).

أما المقدمة الاولى, فلأنها لا تخلو عن الحركة والكسون, وهما حادثان, أما عدم الخلو عنهما فلأن الجسم أو الجوهر لا يخلو عن السكون في حيز, فإن كان مسبوقاً بكون آخر في ذلك الحيز بعينه فهو ساكن, وإن لم يكن مسبوقاً بكون آخر في ذلك الحيز, بل في حيز آخر فمتحرك, وهذا معنى قولهم الحركة كونان في آنين في مكانين, والسكون كونان في آنين في مكان واحد

As for the first premise (that they are not free from originated things), then it is because they are not free from movement and stillness, and both movement and stillness are things which come into existence. As for them not being free from both of them (movement or stillness), then it is because the body or atom is not free from being still (motionless) without a boundary. If it is preceded by another *kawn* (something which came into existence) in that same boundary, then it is *saakin* (still; motionless), and if it is not preceded by a *kawn* within that boundary, but rather in a different boundary, then it is *mutaharrik* (moving), and this is the meaning of their statement that, "Movement is two *kawn's* at two times in two places, and stillness is two *kawn's* in two times in one place."

فإن قيل: يجوز أن لا يكون مسبوقاً بكون آخر أصلاً كما في آن الحدوث, فلا يكون متحركاً كما لا يكون ساكناً, قلنا:

If it is said: it is possible that it had not bee preceded by another kawn (some state which came into being) at all, as for example at the time of origination, for then it was neither moving nor still, then to this we reply:

هذا المنع لا يضرنا لما فيه من تسليم المدعي على أن الكلام في الأجسام التي تعددت فيها الأكوان وتجددت عليها الأعصار والأزمان, وأما حدوثهما فلأنهما من الأعراض, وهي غير باقية, ولأن ماهية الحركة لما فيها من انتقال من حال إلى حال تقتضي المسبوقية بالغير والأزلية تنافيها, ولأن كل حركة فهي على التقضي وعدم الإستقرار, وكل سكون فهو جائز الزوال, لأن كل جسم فهو قابل للحركة بالضرورة, وقد عرفت أن ما يجوز عدمه يمتنع قدمه

This prevention does not harm us due to the fact that it admits the claim that the speech has been made regarding *ajsaam* (bodies) in which there are a number of *kawn's* (states which came into existence) and over which passed many eras and times. As for their coming into existence, then it is because they are from the *a`raadh*, and those are not everlasting, and also because the very nature or quiddity of motion is such that in it there is a movement from one condition (*haal*) to another, which necessitates precedence by something else, and eternity negates this. It is also because every movement or motion comes to an end and is not permanent, and every stillness or motionlessness is capable of ending, because every *jism* (body) is capable of movement with necessity, and you know that whatever is capable of having not existed, it is impossible for that thing to be pre-eternal (having always existed, without a beginning).

وأما المقدمة الثانية, فلأن ما لا يخلو عن الحوادث لو ثبت في الأزل لزم ثبوت الحادث في الأزل, واللازم باطل والملزوم مثله, وهو محال

وهانا أبحاث:

As for the second premise (that whatever is not free from things which came into existence itself came into existence), then, it is because that which is not free from *hawaadith* (originated matters), were eternity to be affirmed for it, it would necessitate eternity for an originated matter. The necessitator and that which is necessitated are both *baatil* (false), and it is impossible.

Here are some researches (regarding the objections concerning substances):

الأول: أنه لا دليل على انحصار الأعيان في الجواهر والأجسام, وأنه يمتنع وجود ممكن يقوم بذاته, ولا يكون متحيزاً أصلاً, كالعقول والنفوس المجردة التي تقول بها الفلاسفة

The first objection is that there is no evidence to restrict *a`yaan* to simply atoms and bodies, and that such a belief restricts the possibiility of the existence of something which subsists by itself and which is free from boundaries completely, like the intellects, and the absolute souls which the philosophers speak about.

والجواب عنه: أن المدعى حدوث ما ثبت وجوده بالدليل من الممكنات, وهو الأعيان المتحيزة والأعراض, لأن أدلة وجود المجردات غير تامة على ما بين في المطولات

The response to this is as follows: the claim is the originated of that thing, the existence of which is affirmed with evidence from the possible things, and that is: the *a`yaan* and *a`raadh* which have boundaries, because the evidences for the existence of the absolute souls is not complete, as has been explained in detail in the lengthier books.

الثاني: أن ما ذكر لا يدل على حدوث جميع الأعراض, إذ منها ما لا يدرك بالمشاهدة حدوثه ولا حدوث أضداده, كالأعراض القائمة بالسماويات من الأشكال والإمتدادات والأضواء

The second objection is: that which has been mentioned does not prove the origination or coming into existence of all of the *a`raadh*, because among them are those which, their coming into existence is not perceived through observation, nor the coming into existence of their opposites, like the *a`raadh* which subsist in the heavens, such as shapes, extensions and lights.

والجاب: أن هذا غير مخل بالغرض, لأن حدوث الأعيان يستدعي حدوث الأعراض, ضرورة أنها لا تقوم إلا بها

The response to this is: this does not break the objective, because the coming into existence of the *a`yaan* necessarily demands that the *a`raadh* came into existence as well, since they cannot subsist except through them.

الثالث: أن الأزل ليس عبارة عن حالة مخصوصة حتى يزلم من وجود الجسم فيها وجود الحوادث فيها, بل هو عبارة عن عدم الأولية, أو عن استمرار الوجود في أزمنة مقدرة غير متناهية في جانب الماضي, ومعنى أزلية الحركات الحادثة: أنه ما من حركة إلا وقبلها حركة أخرى, لا إلى بداية, وهذا هو مذهب الفلاسفة, وهم يسلمون أنه لا شيء من جزئيات الحركة بقديم, وإنما الكلام في الحركة المطلقة

The third objection is that *azal* (eternity) does not refer to a specific state such that the existence of a body (*jism*) in it would necessitate the existence of *hawaadith* (originated matters) within it; rather, it refers to the absence of a beginning, or the continuation of existence in times which are considered never-ending in the past. The meaning of the *azaliyyah* (pre-eternity) of movement is that there is no movement except that before it there had been another movement, and so on and so forth, without a beginning. This is the view of the philosophers, and they admit that there is nothing from the particulars of motion that are eternal, but the discussion is regarding (what they term) "the unrestricted motion".

والجواب: أنه لا وجود للمطلق إلا في ضمن الجزئي, فلا يتصور قدم المطلق مع حدوث كل جزء من الجزئيات

The answer is that, *mutlaq* (unrestricted) does not exist except within the particular, so it is inconceivable for mutlaq to be eternal whilst all of the particulars (*juz'iyyaat*) were originated.

الرابع: أنه لو كان كل جسم في حيز لزم عدم تناهي الأجسام لأن الحيز هو السطح الباطن من الحاوي المماس للسطح الظاهر من المحوى

والجواب: أن الحيز عند المتكلمين هو الفراغ المتوهم الذي يشغله الجسم وينفذ فيه أبعاده, ولما ثبت أن العالم محدَث, ومعلوم أن المحدث لابد له من محدِث, ضرورة امتناع ترجيح أحد طرفي الممكن من غير مرجح, ثبت أن له محدِثاً

The fourth objection is that if every *jism* (body) is within a boundary, that would necessitate the non-limitation of bodies, because the boundary is the inner surface of a container which touches the outer surface of that which is contained.

The answer is that boundary, according to the Mutakallimeen (experts in `Ilm-ul-Kalaam) is the imaginary space (al-faraagh al-mutawahham) which is occupied by the body and in which its dimensions spread out.

Once it has been affirmed that the world is originated, then, it is known that every originated thing has a creator, one who brought it into existence, by necessity of the impossibility of preference being given to one of the two sides of possibility without someone to do *tarjeeh* (give preference), and from this it is affirmed that it has an originator.

(والمحدِث للعالم هو الله تعالى)

"The Originator of the world is Allaah Ta`aalaa."

أي الذات الواجب الوجوب, الذي يكون وجوده من ذاته ولا يحتاج إلى شيء أصلاً, إذ لو كان جائز الوجود لكان من جملة العالم, فلم يصلح محدثاً للعالم ومبتدئاً له, مع أن العالم إسم لجميع ما يصلح علماً على وجود مبدئ له, وقريب من هذا ما يقال إن مبدئ الممكنات بأسرها لابد أن يكون واجباً, إذ لو كان ممكناً لكان من جملة الممكنات, فلم يكن مبدئاً لها

Meaning, that Being Who is necessarily existent; He Whose existence is by His Being, and He has absolutely no need for anything at all. Had His existence been only "possible" then He would have been part of the world (`aalam) and would not have been suitable to be the Originator of the world and the One Who began it, along with the fact that `aalam (world) is a noun used to refer to all that which is capable of being a sign (`alam) of the existence of the One Who began it.

What is near to this is the statement that, the One Who began all of the possible things, it is necessary that His Existence be necessary (*waajib*), because had it simply been "possible" (*mumkin*), then He would have been part of the "possible things" and so would not have been the One Who began it.

وقد يتوهم أن هذا دليل على وجود الصانع من غير افتقار إلى إبطال التسلسل, وليس كذلك, بل هو إشارة إلى أحد أدلة بطلان التسلسل, وهو أنه لو ترتبت سلسلة الممكنات لا إلى نهاية لاحتاجت إلى علة, وهي لا يجوز أن تكون نفسها ولا بعضها, لاستحالة كون الشيء علة لنفسه ولعلله, بل خارجاً عنها, فتكون واجباً فتنقطع السلسلة

It is imagined that this is evidence for the existence of the Creator without the need for nullifying the endless chain (*at-tasalsul*), but it is not as such. Rather, it is pointing out to one of the evidences of the invalidity of tasalsul (the endless chain), and (this proof) is that if a chain of possibilities were to be arranged infinitely, it would require an `*illat* (cause), and the `*illat* cannot be the thing itself nor part of it due to the impossibility of a thing being the `*illat* for itself and its own causes (`*ilal*). Rather, it has to be outside of it, so it has to be *waajib* (necessary), so the chain is broken.

ومن مشهور الأدلة برهان التطبيق, وهو أن نفرض من المعلول الأخير إلى غير النهاية جملة, ومما قبله بواحد مثلاً إلى غير النهاية جملة أخرى, ثم تطبق الجملتين لأن تجعل الأول من الجملة الأولى بإزاء الأول من الجملة الثانية, والثاني بالثاني, وهلم جراً, فإن كان بإزاء كل واحد من الأولى واحد من الثانية, كان الناقص كالزائد, وهو محال, وإن لم يكن فقد وجد في الأولى ما لا يوجد بإزائه شيء من الثانية, فتنقطع الثانية وتتناهى, ويلزم منه تناهي الأولى, لأنها لا تزيد على الثانية إلا بقدر متناه, والزائد على المتناهي بقدر متناه يكون متناهياً بالضرورة

Of the well-known proofs is that of the evidence of *tatbeeq* (tallying), and that consists of us assuming from the last *ma`lool* (effect) an infite series (of effects), and another series, for example, just one short of this last effect to infinity. Then, we apply the two series by putting the first of the first series face-to-face (or corresponding with) the first of the second series, and the second with the second, etc.
Thus, if there is face-to-face with every one from the first series one from the second, then the deficient is like that which has extra, and that is impossible. If it is not as such, then there is found in the first what is not found - corresponding to it - anything from the second, so the second (series) breaks and ends, and that necessitates the ending of the first (series) because it is not more than the second except by a finite amount, and that which exceeds the finite by a finite amount is necessarily finite.

وهذا التطبيق إنما يكون فيما دخل تحت الوجود دون ما هو وهمي محض, فإنه ينقطع بانقطاع الوهم, فلا يرد النقض بمراتب العدد, بأن يطبق جملتان, إحداهما من الواحد لا إلى نهاية, والثانية من الإثنين لا إلى نهاية, ولا بمعلومات الله تعالى ومقدوراته, فإن الأولى أكثر من الثانية مع لا تناهيهما, وذلك لأن معنى لا تناهي الأعداد والمعلومات والمقدورات أنها لا تنتهي إلى حد واحد لا يتصور فوقه آخر, لا بمعنى أن ما لا نهاية له يدخل تحت الوجود, فإنه محال

This *tatbeeq* (tallying) can only be in that which enters under existence, not that which is simply imaginative, because that cuts off with the cutting off of imagination, so it does not repel the contradiction by the arragement of numbers,, such as by applying the two series, one of them from one to infinity and the secone from two to infinity, nor by things pertaining to the Knowledge of Allaah Ta`aalaa or things pertaining to the *Qudrat* (Power) of Allaah Ta`aalaa, because the first is more than the second despite the fact that both are infinite, and that is because the meaning of infinity of numbers, and (the infinity of) things pertaining to the Knowledge of Allaah Ta`aalaa and (the infinity of) things pertaining to the Power of Allaah Ta`aalaa, means that they do not end in one definite limit beyond which no other limit can be conceived. This does not mean that whatever is infinite enter under existence, because that is impossible.

(الواحد)

"The One."

يعني أن صانع العالم واحد, فلا يمكن أن يصدق مفهوم واجب الوجود إلا على ذات واحدة, والمشهور في ذلك بين المتكلمين برهان التمانع المشار إليه بقوله تعالى:

لَوْ كَانَ فِيهِمَا آلِهَةٌ إِلَّا اللهُ لَفَسَدَتَا

Meaning, the Creator of the world is One, so it is not possible for the understanding of "The Necessarily Existent" to apply to anyone except One Being, and the well-known evidence for that among the Mutakallimeen is the evidence of *tamaanu`* (mutual hindrance), which is pointed out by the Aayah:

{"*Had there been in them gods besides Allaah, they (the heavens and the earth) would have been corrupted...*"}

وتقرير أنه لو أمكن إلهان لأمكن بينهما تمانع, بأن يريد أحدهما حركة زيد والآخر سكونه, لأن كلاً منهما في نفسه أمر ممكن, وكذا تعلق الإرادات بكل منهما, إذا لا تضاد بين الإرادتين, بل بين المرادين. وحينئذ إما أن يحصل الأمران فيجتمع الضدان وإلا فيلزم عجز أحدهما وهو أمارة الحدوث والإمكان لما فيه من شائبة الإحتياج

The explanation of this is that had it been possible for there to have been two Ilaahs, then it would have been possible for there to be mutual hindrance (*tamaanu`*) between them, such as by one of them wanting Zaid to move and the other wanting Zaid to remain still, because of those things are possible in themselves, as is the connection of the will with each of those two (actions), because there is no mutual opposition between the two wills but rather, between the two things that are willed. Thus, either both matters are achieved, in which case two opposites unite (which is impossible), or both are not achieved, which would necessitate the powerlessness of one of them, and (powerlessness) is an indication of being originated and of possibility, because in it is the defect of being in need.

فالتعدد مستلزم لإمكان المتانع المستلزم للمحال فيكون محالاً , وهذا تفصيل ما يقال إن أحدهما إن لم يقدر على مخالفة الآخر لزم عجزه, وإن قدر لزم عجز الآخر , وبما ذكرنا يندفع ما يقال إنه يجوز أن يتفقا من غير تمانع أو أن تكون الممانعة والمخالفة غير ممكن لاستلزامها المحال , أو أن يمتنع اجتماع الإرادتين كإرادة الواحد حركة زيد وسكونه معاً

Plurality necessitates the possibility of *tamaanu`* (mutual hindrance), which necessitates the impossible, so it is impossible. This is an explanation of what has been said, that if one of them is unable to oppose the other, then that necessitates powerlessness, and if he is able to oppose the other, then that necessitates the powerlessness of the other one. From what we have said refutes the claim that it is possible for them to agree to not hinder one another, or that mutual hindrance and opposition is not possible, because both of that necessitate the impossible, or that it is not possible for the two wills to come together like one of them willing Zaid to move and the other willing him to stand still, at one and the same time.

واعلم أن قول الله تعالى:

لَوْ كَانَ فِيهِمَا آلِهَةٌ إِلَّا اللَّهُ لَفَسَدَتَا

حجة إقناعية والملازمة عادية على ما هو اللائق بالخطابيات, فإن العادة جارية بوجود التمانع والتغالب عند تعدد الحاكم على ما أشير إليه بقوله تعالى:

وَلَعَلَا بَعْضُهُمْ عَلَى بَعْضٍ

Know that the Aayah:

{"*Had there been in them (the heavens and the earth) gods other than Allaah, they (the heavens and earth) would have been corrupted...*"}

It is satisfactory as evidence. The necessary consequence is customary according to what conforms to rhetorical syllogisms (*khitaabiyyaat*), because it is usual that when there are multiple rulers, then *tamaanu`* (mutual hindering of one another) takes place as well as *taghaalub* (overpowering one another). This is pointed out in the Aayah:

{"*Some of them would have overcome others...*"}

وإلا فإن أريد به الفساد بالفعل أي خروجهما عن هذا النظام المشاهد, فمجرد العدد لا يستلزمه لجواز الإتفاق على هذا النظام المشاهدة, وإن أريد إمكان الفساد فلا دليل على انتفائه, بل النصوص شاهدة بطيّ السماوات ورفع هذا النظام, فيكون ممكناً لا محالة.

Otherwise, if actual corruption (*fasaad*) is meant, i.e. the universe leaving the present system and state of affairs which is observed, then the mere existence of plural (Ilaahs) does not necessitate that due to the possibility of them agreeing upon keeping in place the current system and order which is observed. If what is meant is the possibility of corruption (*fasaad*), then there is no evidence for its denial; rather, the *nusoos* (clear texts) bear testimony to the folding up of the heavens and the raising of the present order and system, so definitely it is possible.

لا يقال الملازمة قطعية, والمراد بفسادهما عدم تكوّنهما, بمعنى أنه لو فرض صانعان لأمكن بينهما تمانع في الأفعال, فلم يكن أحدهما صانعاً, فلم يوجد مصنوع لأنا نقول: إمكان التمانع لا يستلزم إلا عدم تعدد الصانع, وهو لا يستلزم انتفاء المصنوع, على أنه يرد منع الملازمة إن أريد عدم التكون بالفعل, ومنع انتفاء اللازم إن أريد بالإمكان.

It is not to be said that *mulaazamah* (the necessary consequence) is absolute, and the meaning of their (heavens and earth) becoming corrupted is the absence of their existing, meaning that if it were to be assumed that there are two creators, then it would have been possible for there to have been *tamaanu`* between them in matters of actions, so one of them would not have been the creator, and then no creation would have been created. Because we say: "The possibility of *tamaanu`* does not necessitate except the absence of plurality of creators, and that does not necessitate the negation of what was created, though it does come to mean the prevention of *mulaazamah* (the necessary consequence) if actual non-existence is meant, and the prevention of the negation of the necessitator if what is meant is possibility.

فإن قيل: مقتضى كلمة لو أن انتفاء الثاني في الزمان الماضي بسبب انتفاء الأول, فلا يفيد إلا الدلائل على أن انتفاء الفساد في الزمان الماضي بسبب انتفاء التعدد

If it is said: what is necessitated by the word "*low*" (used in the Aayah) is the negation of the second (statement) in the past tense on account of the negation of the first, so it does not bring about except evidence that the negation of corruption in the past tense is on account of the negation of plurality (of gods).

قلنا: نعم بحسب أصل اللغة, لكن قد تستعمل للإستدلال بانتفاء الجزاء على انتفاء الشرط, من غير دلالة على تعيين زمان, كما في قولنا: لو كان العالم قديماً لكان غير تمغير, والآية من هذا القبيل, وقد يشتبه على بعض الأذهان أحد الإستعمالين بالآخر فيقع الخبط

We say: Yes, according to the law of the language. However, it can also be used to indicate the negation of the *jazaa* (result) in the case of the negation of the *shart* (condition), without pointing out to a particular tense (i.e. past, present or future), like in our statement: "If the world was *qadeem* (eternal), then it would have been unchanging."

The Aayah is from this kind. One of the uses may resemble the other in the minds of some people, and thus confusion arises.

(القديم)

"The Eternal."

هذا تصريح بما علم إلتزاماً, إذ الواجب لا يكون إلا قديماً أي لا إبتداء لوجوده, إذ لو كان حادثاً مسبوقاً بالعدم لكان وجوده من غيره ضرورة, حتى وقع في كلام بعضهم أن الواجب والقديم مترادفان, لكنه ليس بمستقيم للقطع بتغاير المفهومين, وإنما الكلام في التساوي بحسب الصدق, فإن بعضهم على أن القديم أعم لصدقه على صفات الواجب, بخلاف الواجب فإنه لا يصدق عليها, ولا استحالة في تعدد الصفات القديمة, وإنما المتسحيل تعدد الذوات القديمة

This is a clear statement of what is known by necessity, because that which is necessarily existent can not be except *qadeem* (eternal), i.e. not having a beginning for its existence, because if it were to have been originated, preceded by non-existence, then its coming into existence from something else would have been necessary. This resulted in some of them saying that *waajib* (necessarily existent) and *qadeem* (eternal) are synonymous. However, due to the difference in the meanings, that is not accurate.

The discussion regarding their being equal (in meaning) is proportionate to *sidq* (truthfulness), because some of them held the view that *qadeem* is more `*aam* (general) due to its truthfulness concerning the attributes of the necessarily existent, contrary to the necessarily existent, because it is true of the attributes.

It is not impossible for there to be a plurality of eternal attributes, but it is impossible for there to be a plurality of eternal beings or essences (*dhawaat*, pl. of "*dhaat*").

وفي كلام بعض المتأخرين كالإمام حميد الدين الضرير رحمه الله ومن تبعه, تصريح بأن واجب الوجود لذاته هو الله تعالى وصفاته, وقد استدلوا على أن كل ما هو قديم فهو واجب لذاته, بأنه لو لم يكن واجباً لذاته لكان جائز العدم في نفسه فيحتاج في وجوده إلى مخصص فيكون محدثاً, إذ لا نعني بالمحدث إلا ما يتعلق وجوده بإيجاد شيء آخر

In the speech of the Muta'akh-khireen (latter ones) like Imaam Hameed-ud-Deen adh-Dhareer رحمة الله عليه and those who followed him, there is a clear mention that the One Who is Necessarily Existent by His *Dhaat* (Being; Essence) is Allaah Ta`aalaa and His *Sifaat* (Attributes). They deduced from the fact that everything which is *qadeem* is necessarily existent by its being/essence, that if one is not necessarily existent by his being/essence, then there is the possibility of non-existence in himself, and thus he would have needed - for his existence - a *mukhassis* (specifier), and then he would have been originated, because we do not mean by "originated" except that which, its existence is connected to the creating of something else.

ثم اعترضوا بأن الصفات لو كانت واجبة لذاتها لكانت باقية, والبقاء معنى, فيلزم قيام المعنى بالمعنى, وأجابوا بأن كل صفة فهي باقية ببقاء هو نفس تلك الصفة, وهذا كلام في غاية الصعوبة, فإن القول بتعدد الواجب لذاته مناف للتوحيد, والقول بإمكان الصفات ينافي قولهم بأن كل ممكن فهو حادث, فإن زعموا أنها قديمة بالزمان بمعنى عدم المسبوقية بالعدم, وهذا لا ينافي الحدوث الذاتي بمعنى الإحتياج إلى ذات الواجب, فهو قول بما ذهب إليه الفلاسفة من انقسام كل من القدم والحدوث إلى الذاتي والزماني, وفيه رفض لكثير من القواعد, وستأتي لهذا زيادة تحقيق

Thereafter, they objected that, the Attributes, if they are necessarily existent in their essence, then they would be *baaqiyah* (continuous), and *baqaa'* (continuance) is an idea, so it would necessitate the subsisting of an idea within another idea. They answered by saying that every attribute is *baaqiyah* (continuous) with a continuance (*baqaa'*) which is that very attribute itself, and this speech is of the utmost degree of difficulty, because the assertion that the Necessarily Existent in His Being/Essence is a plurality is negatory of Tawheed, and the assertion that the Attributes are possible (i.e. not necessarily existent) contradicts their declaration that every possible thing is originated. If they claim that the Attributes are eternal in time, meaning that they are not preceded by non-existence, and that this does not contradict their essential origin (*al-hudooth adh-dhaati*), meaning that they are in need of the Necessarily Existent Being/Essence (*Dhaat*), then this is what the philosophers had said, for they had divided *qidam* (eternity) and hudooth (origination) into "*dhaati*" (essential) and *zamaani* (temporal). In this position there is a rejection of many principles (of `Aqeedah), and more verification concerning it will be mentioned later on.

(الحي القادر العليم السميع البصير الشائي المريد)

"The Living, the All-Powerful, the All-Knowing, the All-Hearing, the All-Seeing, the One Who Wills (*Ash-Shaa'iyy*), the One Who Intends."

لأن بديهة العقل جازمة بأن محدث العالم على هذا النمط البديع, والنظام المحكم, مع ما يشتمل عليه من الأفعال المتقنة, والنقوش المستحسنة, لا يكون بدون هذه الصفات على أن أضدادها نقائص يجب تنزيه الله تعالى عنها, وأيضاً قد ورد الشرع بها, وبعضها مما لا يتوقف ثبوت الشرع عليها, فيصح التمسك بالشرع فيها كالتوحيد, بخلاف وجود الصانع ونحو ذلك مما يتوقف ثبوت الشرع عليه

(The evidence for this) is that the intellect immediately perceives and comprehends that Allaah Ta`aalaa, the Originator of the world according to this unique and wonderful way, and this perfectly balanced system and order, along with what it contains of perfected actions and excellent handicrafts. He is not without these Attributes, because their opposites (i.e. the non-existence of these Attributes) signify weaknesses, and Allaah Ta`aalaa is free from all weaknesses, all flaws, all faults.

Also, the Sharee`ah has mentioned them (these Attributes), and some of them are such that are not based upon establishment by the Sharee`ah, and it is proper to hold firmly to the Sharee`ah in these cases, like Tawheed, contrary to the existence of the Creator, etc., from those things upon which the affirmation of the Sharee`ah is based.

(ليس بعرض)

"He is not a substance."

لأنه لا يقوم بذاته, بل يفتقر إلى محل يقوّمه فيكون ممكناً, ولأنه يمتنع بقاؤه, وإلا لكان البقاء معنى قائماً به, فيلزم قيام المعنى بالمعنى, وهو محال, لأن قيام العرض بالشيء معناه أن تحيزه تابع لتحيزه, والعرض لا تحيز له بذاته, حتى يتحيز غيره بتبعيته, وهذا مبني على أن بقاء الشيء معنى زايد على وجوده, وأن القيام معناه التبعية في التحيز, والحق أن البقاء إستمرار الوجود وعدم زواله, وحقيحته: الوجود من حيث النسبة إلى الزمان الثاني

Because *a`raadh* (substances) do not subsist by themselves. Rather, they are in need of a *mahall* (locus) to subsist them, and so they are *mumkin* (possible), and also because it is impossible for a`raadh to have *baqaa'* (continuance). Otherwise, *baqaa'* (continuance) would have been an idea that subsists within (these *a`raadh*), which would have necessitated the subsisting of an idea within an idea, which is impossible, because the subsisting of (*a`raadh*) with something else, what it means is that its *tahayyuz* (having a boundary) is subsequent to the *tayahhuz* of that thing, and that *a`raadh* have no *tahayyuz* in themselves which would have allowed something else to follow them in *tahayyuz* (boundaries). The truth is that *baqaa'* (continuance) is the continuation of existence and the absence of removal, and its *haqeeqat* (reality) is its existence from the aspect of being connected to a second time.

ومعنى قولنا وجد فلم يبق: أنه حدث فلم يسمتر وجوده, ولم يكن ثابتاً في الزمان الثاني, وأن القيام هو اختصاص الناعت بالمنعوت, كما في أوصاف الباري تعالى, وأن انتفاء الأجسام في كل آن, ومشاهدة بقائها, وبتجدد الأمثال, ليس بأبعد من ذلك في الأعراض

The meaning of our saying, "it existed but did not remain," is that it was originated but its *wujood* (existence) did not continue, and it was not affirmed or established for the second time. Also, subsisting is the specification of the qualifier with the thing qualified, like how it is in the things described by Allaah Ta`aalaa. Also, bodies cease to exist at every moment of time (*fee kulli aan*), and what is observed of their *baqaa'* (continuance) and by the renewal of their similars is not more far-fetched than that in *a`raadh*.

نعم تمسكهم في قيام العرض بسرعة الحركة وبطئها ليس بتام, إذ ليس هنا شيء هو حركة وآخر هو سرعة أو بطء, بل هنا حركة مخصوصة تسمى بالنسبة إلى بعض الحركات سريعة, وبالنسبة إلى البعض بطيئة, وبهذا تبين أن ليس السرعة والبطء نوعين مختلفيه من الحركة, إذ الأنواع الحقيقية لا تختلف بالإضافات

Yes, their belief that *a`raadh* subsist with *a`raadh*, like in the case of the swiftness of movement and the slowness of movement, is incomplete, because there is not a thing which is movement and another which is swiftness or slowness; rather, there is a specified movement which is named, in relation to other movements, as being swift, and in relation to other movements as being slow. From this it becomes clear that swiftness and slowness are not two different types of movement, because true types (*anwaa`*) do not differ from each other in their relations to something else.

(ولا جسم)

"He is not a body."

لأنه مترکب ومتحیز, وذلك أمارة الحدوث

Because a body is compounded (i.e. made up of different parts) and has a boundary, and that is indicative of origination.

(ولا جوهر)

"Nor is He an atom."

أما عندنا فلأنه اسم للجزء الذي لا يتجزأ, وهو تمحيز, وجزء من الجسم, والله تعالى متعال عن ذلك, وأما عند الفلاسفة فلأنهم وإن جعلوه إسماً للموجود لا في موضوع, مجرداً كان أو متحيزاً, لكنهم جعلوه من أقسام الممكن, وأرادوا به الماهية الممكنة التي إذا وجدت كانت لا في موضوع, وأما إذا أريد بهما القائم بذاته والموجود لا في موضوع, فإنما يمتنع إطلاقها على الصانع من جهة عدم ورود الشرع بذلك, من تبادر الفهم إلى المركب والمتحيز, وذهبت المجسمة والنصارى إلى أطلاق الجسم والجوهر عليه بالمعنى الذي يجب تنزيه الله تعالى عنه

According to us, it is because it is a name for "the indivisible part" (*al-juz' alladhee laa yatajazza'*), and it has a boundary, and it is a part from a *jism* (body), and Allaah Ta`aalaa is far exalted above any of that.

According to the philosophers, then they, even though they make it (a jawhar or atom) the name of an existing thing - however, not in a subject - whether it be absolute (*mujarrad*) or having boundaries (*mutahayyiz*), however, they regard it as being one of the categories of that which is possible (*al-mumkin*), and they intend by it the possible quiddity (or essence) which, when it exists, it does not exist within a subject.

As for if what is intended by them (*jism* and *jawhar*) is the self-subsisting thing which does not exist in a subject, then it is not possible to apply it to the Creator because the Sharee`ah has not mentioned them, along with the fact that when these terms are used, the minds jumps to the conclusions of being a compound and being within a boundary.

The Mujassimmah (those who ascribe a body to Allaah Ta`aalaa) and the Nasaaraa (Christians) hold the view that *jism* and *jawhar* is to be applied to Allaah Ta`aalaa, thus giving a meaning or a concept from which Allaah Ta`aalaa is necessarily far removed.

فإن قيل: كيف صح إطلاق الموجود, والواجب, والقديم, ونحو ذلك مما لم يرد به الشرع؟

قلنا: بالإجماع, وهو من الأدلة الشرعية, وقد يقال إن الله تعالى والواجب والقديم ألفاظ مترادفة, والموجود لازم للواجب, وإذا ورد الشرع بإطلاف اسم بلغة, فهو إذن بإطلاف ما يرادفه من تلك اللغة, أو من لغة أخرى, وما يلازم معناه, وفيه نظر

If it is asked: "How is it valid to apply the terms "*Al-Mawjood*" (The Existent), "*Al-Waajib*" (The Necessarily Existent), "*Al-Qadeem*" (The Eternal), etc. to Allaah Ta`aalaa when these names have not been mentioned by the Sharee`ah?

We say: "It is taken from *ijmaa`* (consensus of the `Ulamaa), and *ijmaa`* is one of the Shar`i proofs.

It has been said that Allaah Ta`aalaa, and the names *Al-Waajib* (The Necessarily Existent), and *Al-Qadeem* (The Eternal), are synonymous, and *Al-Mawjood* (The Existent) cannot be separated from *Al-Waajib* (The Necessarily Existent). And, when the Sharee`ah applies one term of a language (to Allaah Ta`aalaa), then it makes it permissible to apply that which is synonymous to that word or approximate to it from that language or from a different language. However, there is speculation regarding this.

(ولا مصور)

"He is not something formed (*musawwar*)."

أي ذي صورة وشكل مثل صورة إنسان أو فرس, لأن تلك من خواص الأجسام, تحصل لها بواسطة الكميات والكيفيات وإحاطة الحدود والنهايات

Meaning, having a *soorah* (form), or a shape, like the form of human beings, or of a horse, because those are from the special characteristics of bodies. It occurs in them by means of quantities (*kammiyyaat*), and qualities (*kayfiyyaat*), and via being encompassed by limits and ends.

(ولا محدود)

"Nor is He limited."

أي ذي حد ونهاية

Meaning, He has no limit or end.

(ولا معدود)

"Nor is He numbered."

أي ذي عد وكثرة, يعني ليس محلاً للكميات المتصلة كالمقادير ولا المنفصلة كالأعداد, وهو ظاهر

Meaning, having a number or multiplicity, i.e. *kammiyyaat* (quantities) do not apply to Him, whether they be connected (*muttasilah*) like *maqaadeer* (magnitudes) or separated (*munfasilah*) like things that are counted, and this is clear.

(ولا متبعض ولا متجزئ)

"Nor is He portioned or divided."

أي ذي أبعاض وأجزاء

Meaning, having portions or parts (*ajzaa'*).

(ولا مترکب)

"Nor is He compounded."

منها, لما في كل ذلك من الإحتياج المنافي للوجوب, فما له أجزاء يسمى باعتبار تألفه منها مترکباً, وباعتبار انحلاله إليها متبعضاً ومتجزئاً

From such things, because all of that results in having a need, and that is negatory of *Al-Wujoob* (The Necessarily Existent). That which has parts, it is called - when they are joined together - "compounded", and when they are separated they are called "portioned" and "divided".

(ولا متناه)

"Nor does He come to an end."

لأن ذلك من صفات المقادير والأعداد

Because that is from the attributes of magnitudes and numbers.

(ولا يوصف بالمائية)

"Nor is He described with quiddity."

أي المجانسة للأشياء, لأن معنى قولنا: ما هو؟ من أي جنس هو؟ والمجانسة توجب التمايز عن المجانسات بفصول مقومة, فيلزم التركيب

Meaning, sharing the same *jins* (species) as other things, because the meaning of our statement, "What is it?" is: "Of what species is it?"

Mujaanasah (sharing the same *jins* as other things) necessitates differing from other things having the same species in certain divisions which are set up, and that necessitates composition.

(ولا بالكيفية)

"Nor is He described with quality (*kayfiyyah*)."

أي من اللون, والطعم, والرائحة, والحرارة, والبرودة, والرطوبة, واليبوسة, وغير ذلك مما هو من صفات الأجسام وتوابع المزاج والتركيب

Meaning, of colour, or taste, or smell, or heat, or coldness, or wetness, or dryness, or other than that from that which is from the attributes of bodies and which are subsequent to mixture and composition.

(ولا يتمكن في مكان)

"He is not situated in a place."

لأن التمكن عبارة عن نفوذ بعد في بعد آخر متوهم, أو متحقق يسمونه المكان, والبُعد عبارة عن امتداد قائم بالجسم, أو بنفسه, عند القائلين بوجود الخلاء, والله تعالى منزه عن الإمتداد والمقدار لاستلزامه التجزيء

Because being situated in a certain place refers to the penetration of one dimension in another, whether imagined or real. This is called "*makaan*" (place). *Bu`d* (dimension) refers to an extending subsisting within the jism (body), or by itself (*bi-nafsihi*), according to those who believe in the existence of *al-khalaa'* (the vacuum).

Allaah Ta`aalaa is far removed from extension and magnitude, because those necessitate being divided into parts.

فإن قيل: الجوهر الفرد متحيز ولا بعد فيه, وإلا لكان متجزئاً

If it is said: the singular atom (*al-jawhar al-fareed*) has a boundary (*mutahayyiz*) and yet it does not have a dimension, because if it were to have had a dimension, it would have been able to be divided (and thus would not have been a pure atom).

قلنا: المتمكن أخص من المتحيز, لأن الحيز هو الفراغ المتوهم الذي يشغله شيء ممتد أو غير ممتد, فما ذكر دليل على عدم التمكن في المكان, وأما الدليل على عدم التحيز فهو أنه لو تحيز فإما في الأزل فيلزم قدم الحيز أو لا, فيكون محلاً للحوادث, وأيضاً إما أن يساوي الحيز أو ينقص عنه فيكون متناهياً, أو يزيد عليه فيكون متجزئاً, وإذا لم يكن في مكان لم يكن في جهة, لا علو ولا سفل ولا غيرهما, لأنهما إما حدود وأطراف للأمكنة, أو نفس الأمكنة باعتبار عروض الإضافة إلى شيء آخر

We reply by saying, "That which is situated in a place (*mutamakkin*) is more specific than that which is within a boundary (*mutahayyiz*), because *al-haiz* (the boundary) is the imagined empty space which is occupied by something which has an extension or which does not have an extension.

That which has been mentioned is proof (*daleel*) that Allaah Ta`aalaa is not situated in a place. As for the proof that He is not within a boundary, then the proof is that, had He been within a boundary, then either He would have been within that boundary since eternity (*al-azal*), which would necessitate that the boundary itself is pre-eternal, not having a beginning, or not. If not, then He would have been affected by *hawaadith* (originated matters). Also, He would either have been equal to the boundary or less than if. If equal to it, He would have been finite, and if less than it, He would have been divisible. Since He is not in a place, He is also not in a direction (*jihah*), neither above nor downward nor other than those two directions, because they are either limits or extremities of places (that by which a thing is surrounded), or they are the places themselves, taking into consideration their relationship to the thing (surrounded by the places).

(ولا يجري عليه زمان)

"Time does not pass over Him."

لأن الزمان عندنا عبارة عن متجدد يقدر به متجدد آخر, وعند الفلاسفة عبارة عن مقدار الحركة, والله تعالى منزه عن ذلك

Because time (*zamaan*), according to us, refers to that which is renewed by which something else renewed is measured. According to the philosophers, it refers to the measure of movement, and Allaah Ta`aalaa is far removed from all of that.

واعلم أن ما ذكره من التنزيهات, بعضها يغني عن البعض, إلا أنه حاول التفصيل والتوضيح في ذلك, قضاء لحق الواجب في باب التنزيه, ورداً على المشبهة والمجسمة وسائر فرق الضلال والطغيان, بأبلغ وجه وآكده. فلم يبال بتكرير الألفاظ المترادفة, والتصريح بما علم بطريق الإلتزام, ثم إن مبنى التنزيه عما ذكرت على أنها تنافي وجوب الوجود لما فيها من شائبة الحدوث والإمكان, على ما أشرنا إليه, لا على ما ذهب إليه المشايخ من أن معنى العرض بحسب اللغة: ما يمتنع بقاؤه, ومعنى الجوهر: ما يتركب عنه غيره, ومعنى الجسم: ما يتركب هو عن غيره, بدليل قولهم هذا أجسم من ذاك, وأن الواجب لو تركب, فأجزاؤه إما أن تتصف بصفات الكمال, فيلزم تعدد الواجب, أو لا, فيلزم النقص والحدوث, وأيضاً وأنه تعالى لو كان مصوراً ومشكلاً ومتصفاً بالكيفية, إما أن يكون على جميع الصور والأشكال والكيفيات والمقادير, فيلزم اجتماع الأضداد, أو على بعضها وهي مستوية الأقدام في إفادة المدح والنقص, وفي عدم دلالة

المحدثات عليه فيفتقر إلى مخصص, ويدخل تحت قدرة الغير, فيكون حادثاً, بخلاف مثل العلم والقدرة, فإنها صفات كمال دل المحدثات على ثبوتها وأضدادها صفات نقصان لا دلالة على ثبوتها لأنها تمسكات ضعيفة توهن عقائد الطالبين, وتوسع مجال الطاعنين, زعماً منهم أن تلك المطالب العالية مبنية على أمثال هذه الشبهة الواهية

Know, also, that what he (Imaam an-Nasafi رحمة الله عليه) has mentioned of the things from which Allaah Ta`aalaa is far removed, some of them make the mention of others unnecessary. The reason he mentioned them despite this is because he tried to explain in detail and clarify the matter, fulfilling the rights of the Necessarily Existent (i.e. Allaah Ta`aalaa) in the matter of *tanzeeh* (declaring Allaah Ta`aalaa to be free from any and all imperfections). Also, he mentioned it as a refutation of the Mushabbihah (those who claim that Allaah Ta`aalaa resembles His creation) and the Mujassimah (those who ascribe a body to Allaah Ta`aalaa) and the rest of the *firaq* (sects) of deviation and rebellion in the more complete and emphasised manner, thus he did not care about the repetition of synonymous words, and by emphatically declaring that which is known by way of making it binding (upon the opponents).

Thereafter, the basis of *tanzeeh*, from what I have mentioned, is that all of these things which the deviated sects ascribe unto Allaah Ta`aalaa are negatory of the position of *Waajib-ul-Wujood* (The Necessarily Existent), because all of that which they ascribe contain the deficiency of *hudooth* (being originated) and possibility, as we have pointed out.

This is not according to the way the Mashaayikh had taken (to explaining this), because they said the meaning of *al-`aradh*, linguistically, is that which is impossible to endure; the meaning of *al-jawhar*, linguistically, is that which from it, other things are compounded; the meaning of *al-jism* is that which is compounded from something else, and the evidence for this is the saying, "He is *ajsam* (bulkier/has more body) than that one."

If the Necessarily Existent were to have been compounded, then His *Ajzaa'* (Parts) would either have been attributed with the attributes of perfection, which would have necessitated the plurality of Necessarily Existents, or they would not have been, and that would have necessitated lacking in something and *hudooth* (being originated).

Also, if - as they claim - Allaah Ta`aalaa were to have had a form, or shape, or attributed with qualities and magnitured, then, either He would have had to have been upon all of the forms, shapes and qualities and magnitudes, which would have necessitated the coming together of opposites, or upon some (of these forms, shapes, etc.) and they would have had to be equal in order in bringing about praise or blame, and, in the absence of proof of originated things applying to Allaah Ta`aalaa, this would have meant that He would require a *mukhassis* (determining principle), and thus would have entered under the power or capability of something else, and thus would have been originated, and He would then have been contrary to, for example, Knowledge and Power, for they are the attributes of perfection, concerning which there is evidence from the originated things that they (the Attributes of Perfection) are affirmed for Allaah Ta`aalaa. Their opposites are the attributes of imperfection which have no evidence from the originated things (that they apply to Allaah Ta`aalaa), for they are weak views which weaken the `*Aqaa'id* (beliefs) of the seekers and which widen the field for the critics who claim that those lofty issues (of `*Aqeedah*) are based on the likes of these weak ambiguities.

واحتج المخالف بالنصوص الظاهرة في الجهة والجسمية والصورة والجوارح, وبأن كل موجودين فرضاً لابد أن يكون أحدهما متصلاً بالأخر, مماساً له, أو منفصلاً عنه, مبايناً في الجهة, والله تعالى ليس حالاً ولا محلاً للعالم, فيكون مبايناً للعالم في جهة فيتحيز, فيكون جسماً أو جزء جسم مصوراً متناهياً

Those who disagree (with this position) cite as proof the nusoos which outwardly (affirm) direction (*jihah*), having a body (*jismiyyah*), having a form (*soorah*), and limbs (*jawaarih*). They mention further that each of the existing things has to - by necessity - be such that, one of two is connected to the other, in contact with it, or separate from it and cut off from it in some direction. Allaah Ta`aalaa neither resides in the world nor is He a locus for the world, so He is separate from the world in some direction and within a boundary, thus being a body (*jism*) or a part of a body, having a form and finite (this is their claim).

والجواب عنه أن ذلك وهم محض, وحكم على غير المحسوس بأحكام المحسوس, والأدلة القطعية قائمة على التنزيهات, فيجب أن يفوض علم النصوص إلى الله تعالى, على ما هو دأب السلف, إيثاراً للطريق الأسلم, أو تؤول بتأويلات صحيحة على ما اختاره المتأخرون, دفعاً لمطاعن الجاهلية, وجذباً لطبع القاصرين سلوكاً للسبيل الأحكم

The response to this is that all of (what they have claimed) is pure imagination, and passing judgement concerning things which cannot be perceived by the senses according to the judgements of those things which are perceived by the senses.

The decisive evidences are based upon *tanzeehaat* (declaring Allaah Ta`aalaa to be far removed from any and all imperfections); thus, it is necessary to that the knowledge of (the meaning of) these nusoos be left up to Allaah Ta`aalaa, as was the practice of the Salaf who had preferred to follow the safest path. Otherwise, these *nusoos* are to be interpreted with interpretations which are valid, as is the view which was chosen by the Muta'akh-khireen in order to repel the objections of the ignorant and to pull the dispositions of those who are lacking (in understanding) towards the path the wiser path.

(ولا يشبهه شيء)

"And nothing resembles Him."

أي لا يماثله, أما إذا أريد بالمماثلة الإتحاد في الحقيقة, فظاهر أنه ليس كذلك, وأما إذا أريد بها كون الشيئين بحيث يسد أحدهما مسد الآخر, أي يصلح كل لما يصلح له الآخر, فلأن شيئاً من الموجودات لا يسد مسده تعالى في شيء من الأوصاف فإن أوصافه من العلم والقدرة وغير ذلك أجل وأعلى مما في المخلوقات, بحيث لا مناسبة بينهما

قال في البداية: إن العلم منا موجود, وعرض, ومحدث, وجائز الوجود, ومتجدد في كل زمان, فلو أثبتنا العلم صفة لله لكان موجوداً وصفة وقديماً وواجب الوجود دائماً من الأزل إلى الأبد, فلا يماثله علم الخلق بوجه من الوجوه, هذا كلامه, فقد صرح بأن المماثلة عندنا إنما تثبت بالأشتراك في جميع الأوصاف, حتى لو اختلق وصف واحد انتفت المماثلة

Meaning, nothing is similar to Him. If what is meant by mumaathalah (similarity) is being one in terms of *haqeeqat* (reality), then it is clear that the matter is not as such. However, if what is meant by it is that both things are able to take each other's places, i.e. each one is capable of that which the other is capable of - then nothing from the existing things can take His place - Sub-haanahu wa Ta`aalaa - in any of His Qualities, because His Qualities, such as `*Ilm* (Knowledge), *Qudrah* (Power), etc., are loftier and higher than that which is within the created beings, so there is absolutely no comparison between Allaah Ta`aalaa and His creation.

The author of *al-Bidaayah* said: "The knowledge which we have is *mawjood* (existing), and is an `*aradh*, and is originated, and is *jaa'iz-ul-wujood* (possible to exist, i.e. not necessarily existent), and is renewed ever moment of time.

Thus, if we affirm *`Ilm* (Knowledge) as an Attribute of Allaah Ta`aalaa, then it is something existing (*mawjood*), it is an attribute, it is eternal, it is *waajib-ul-wujood* (necessarily existent), it is everlasting, from pre-eternity to eternity, and so the knowledge of the creation is not similar to His Knowledge in any aspect whatsoever."

This is his statement. He has explicitly stated that according to us, *mumaathalah* (similarity) between two things is established by them sharing together all of their qualities, so much so that if there is a difference in even one quality, then the similarity falls away.

قال الشيخ أبو المعين في التبصرة: إنا نجد أهل اللغة لا يمتنعون من القول بأن زيداً مثل عمرو في الفقه, إذا كان يساويه فيه ويسد مسده في ذلك الباب, وإن كان بينهما مخالفة بوجوه كثيرة, وما يقوله الأشعرية من أنه لا مماثلة إلا بالمساواة من جميع الوجوه فاسد لأن النبي صلى الله عليه وسلم قال: الحنطة بالحنطة, مثلاً بمثل, وأراد الإستواء به في الكل لا غير, وإن تفاوت الوزن وعدد الحبات والصلابة والرخاوة, والظاهر أنه لا مخالفة لأن مراد الأشعري المساواة من جميع الوجوه فيما به المماثلة كالكيل مثلاً, وعلى هذا ينبغي أن يحمل كلام البداية أيضاً وإلا فاشتراك الشيئين في جميع الأوصاف ومساواتهما من جميع الوجوه يدفع التعدد, فكيف يتصور التماثل لأن التماثل يقتضي التعدد والتغاير بينهما

Shaykh Abu'l Mu`een said in *at-Tabsirah*: "The experts of language do not preclude the statement that Zaid is similar to `Amr in (the knowledge of) *Fiqh*, if he is equal to him in it and is able to take his place in that particular subject, even if there are differences between them in many facets. As for what the Ash`aris say, that there is no *mumaathalah* (similarity) except if they are equal in all facets, then this is incorrect, because Nabi صلى الله عليه وسلم said: "Wheat for wheat, like for like." What he meant by that is equality in measure only, because wheat differs also in weight, and the number of grains, and hardness or tenderness.

What is clear is that there is no disagreement (between the two views), because the intended meaning of Imaam al-Ash`ari is equality in all facets in those things in which there is similarity, like in measure, for example. And upon this, it is necessary that the statement of the author of *al-Bidaayah* be interpreted also (in this same way); otherwise, the sharing of two things all of the same qualities and being equal in all facets prevents there being a plurality of things, for how would similarity be conceived, for similarity necessitates plurality and differences between them.

(ولا يخرج عن علمه وقدرته شيء)

"Nothing is outside of His *Ilm* (Knowledge) and *Qudrah* (Power)."

لأن الجهل بالبعض والعجز عن البعض نقص وافتقار إلى مخصص, مع أن النصوص القطعية ناطقة بعموم العلم وشمول القدرة فهو سبحانه بكل شيء عليم وعلى كل شيء قدير, لا كما يزعم الفلاسفة: أنه لا يعلم الجزئيات ولا يقدر على أكثر من واحد, والدهرية: أنه تعالى لا يعلم ذاته, والنظام: على أنه لا يقدر على خلق الجهل والقبح, والبلخي: على أنه لا يقدر على مثل مقدور العبد, وعامة المعتزلة: أنه لا يقدر على نفس مقدور العبد

Because ignorance of some things and being incapable of some things is an imperfection which results in a need for a determining principle, along with the fact that the decisive *nusoos* (clear texts) speak of Knowledge of all things and an Al-Encompassing Power. Allaah Sub-haanahu wa Ta`aalaa has full knowledge over everything and has full power over everything, unlike what the philosophers claim, that He does not know the particulars and that He is not capable of doing more than one thing. It is also unlike the claim of the Dahriyyah, who claimed that Allaah Ta`aalaa does not know His Essence (*Dhaat*). It is also unlike an-Nazh-zhaam, who claimed that He is not capable of creating ignorance and bad. It is also unlike al-Balkhi, who claimed that He is not capable of doing that which is within the capability of the creature (to do). It is also unlike the view of the majority of the Mu`tazilah, who claimed that He is not capable of doing that which is within the power of the creature to do.

مطلب صفات المعاني

A Discussion on Sifaat al-Ma`aani:

(وله صفات)

"And He (Allaah Ta`aalaa) has *Sifaat* (Attributes)."

ولما ثبت أنه عالم, حي, قادر, إلى غير ذلك, ومعلوم أن كلاً من ذلك يدل على معنى زائد على مفهوم الواجب, وليس الكل ألفاظاً مترادفة, وأن صدق المشتق على الشيء يقتضي ثبوت مأخذ الإشتقاق له, فثبت له صفة العلم والقدرة والحياة وغير ذلك, لا كما تزعم المعتزلة من أنه عالم لا علم له, وقادر لا قدرة له, إلى غير ذلك, فإنه محال ظاهر, بمنزلة قولنا أسود لا سواد له, وقد

نطقت النصوص بثبوت علمه وقدرته وغيرهما, ودل صدور الأفعال المتقنة على وجود علمه وقدرته, لا على مجرد تسميته عالماً وقادراً

Now that it has been affirmed that Allaah Ta`aalaa is All-Knowing (`*Aalim*), Living (*Hayy*), All-Powerful (*Qaadir*), etc., and it is known that all of that points out to a meaning or an idea which is additional to the meaning of *Al-Waajib*, and all of them are not terms that are synonymous.

Also, the truthfulnesss of what is derived from a thing necessitates the affirmation of the source from whence it was derived for it (i.e. a derivative term possesses the source from which the term is derived). Thus, the Attributes of `*Ilm*, *Qudrah*, *Hayaah* (Life), etc. are affirmed for Allaah Ta`aalaa, unlike what is claimed by the Mu`tazilah, that He is `*Aalim* (All-Knowing) without possessing `*Ilm*, and All-Powerful (*Qaadir*) without possessing power, etc., because that claim of theirs is clearly impossible, and is like us saying, "A thing is black without having any blackness."

The nusoos have affirmed His `*Ilm*, His *Qudrah*, etc., and the perfect Actions which have come from Allaah Ta`aalaa manifestly prove His `*Ilm* and His *Qudrah*, and does not simply mean that He is described as All-Knowing and All-Powerful.

وليس النزاع في العلم والقدرة التي هي من جملة الكيفيات والملكات, لما صرح به مشايخنا من أن الله تعالى حي, وله حياة أزلية, ليست بعرض ولا متسحيل البقاء, والله تعالى عالم, وله علم أزلي شامل, ليس بعرض ولا مستحيل البقاء, ولا ضروري ولا مكتسب, وكذا في سائر الصفات, بل النزاع في أنه كما أن للعالم منا علماً, هو عرض قائم به, زائد عليه, حادث فهل لصانع العلم علم, هو صفة أزلية قائمة له زائدة عليه, وكذا جميع الصفات؟

The disagreement is not regarding `*Ilm* and *Qudrah* which are from the qualities (*al-Kayfiyyaat*) and habits (*al-Malakaat*), because our Mashaayikh emphatically declared that Allaah Ta`aalaa is Ever-Living, and that He possesses eternal life (without a beginning and without an end), it is not an `*aradh* nor is it impossible for it to last forever (*baqaa'*). Allaah Ta`aalaa is All-Knowing, and He possesses eternal Knowledge which is all-encompassing, which is not an `*aradh* and which is not impossible to last forever, and which is not necessitated nor acquired, and the same is the case with the rest of the Attributes. Rather, the disagreement is regarding the fact that, just as how the the knower (`*Aalim*) amongst us has knowledge, but his knowledge is `*aradh*, subsisting with it, additional upon him, originated. So, does the Creator of `*Ilm* (Knowledge) possess `*Ilm* that is an Eternal

Attribute, subsisting with Him, additional upon Him, and is that the case with the rest of the Attributes?

فأنكره الفلاسفة والمعتزلة, وزعموا أن صفاته عين ذاته, بمعنى أن ذاته تمسى باعتبار التعلق بالمعلومات عالماً, وبالمقدورات قادراً, إلى غير ذلك, فلا يلزم تكثر في الذات ولا تعدد في القدماء والواجبات

والجواب ما سبق من أن المستحيل تعدد الذوات القديمة, وهو غير لازم, ويلزمكم كون العلم مثلاً قدرة وحياة وعالماً وحياً وقادراً وصانعاً للعلم ومعبود للخلق, وكون الواجب غير قائم بذاته إلى غير ذلك من المحالات

The philosophers and the Mu`tazilah denied this, and they claimed that His Attributes are His *Dhaat*, meaning that His *Dhaat* is called, with respect to its connection with known things, "`*Aalim*" (All-Knowing), and with respect to things over which He has power, "*Qaadir*" (All-Powerful), etc., so that (according to them) does not necessitate multiplicity in The *Dhaat* nor multiplicity (and existence of) numerous eternal beings that are necessarily existent.

The answer to this is that which has preceded, that for there to be multiplicity of Eternal *Dhawaat* (pl. of *Dhaat*, i.e. *Dhawaat* other than the *Dhaat* of Allaah Ta`aalaa) is impossible, and it is not does not follow, but your claim would result in the belief that `*Ilm* is similar to *Qudrah* and *Hayaah* (Life), (and also similar to) the All-Knowing, the Living, the All-Powerful, the Creator of `*Ilm*, the One Who is worshipped by the creation, and that the Necessarily Existent Being would not be subsisting by His *Dhaat*, and other such impossible, absurd beliefs.

(أزلية)

"He is Eternal (i.e. He possesses *Azaliyyah*)."

لا كما تزعم الكرامية من أن له صفاتم لكنها حادثة لاستحالة قيام الحوادث بذاته تعالى

Unlike what is claimed by the Karaamiyyah, that He possesses Attributes but that these Attributes are originated (came into existence), because it is impossible for things that are originated to subsist with the *Dhaat* of Allaah Ta`aalaa.

(قائمة بذاته)

"Subsistent in His *Dhaat*."

ضرورة أنه لا معنى لصفة الشيء إلا ما يقوم به , لا كما تزعم المعتزلة من أنه متكلم بكلام هو قائم بغيره , لكن مرادهم نفي كون الكلام صفة له لا إثبات كونه صفة له غير قائم بذاته

Of necessity, because of the fact taht nothing can be said to be an attribute of something unless it subsists within that thing, unlike what is claimed by the Mu`tazilah that Allaah Ta`aalaa speaks with a Speech which subsists in something other than Himself, but their intended meaning is the negation of *Kalaam* (Speech) as an Attribute of His, not the affirmation of *Kalaam* as a *Sifah* (Attribute) of Allaah Ta`aalaa but subsisting in other than His *Dhaat*.

ولما تمسكت المعتزلة بأن في إثبات الصفات إبطال التوحيد لما أنها موجودات قديمة مغايرة لذات الله تعالى , فيلزم قدم غير الله تعالى , وتعدد القدماء , بل تعدد الواجب لذاته على ما وقعت الإشارة إليه في كلام المتقدمين , والتصريح به في كلام المتأخرين , من أن واجب الوجود بالذات هو الله تعالى وصفاته , وقد كفرت النصارى بإثبات ثلاثة من القدماء , فما بال الثمانية أو أكثر , أشار إلى جوابه بقوله:

The Mu`tazilah held onto the belief that, in the affirmation of *Sifaat* (to Allaah Ta`aalaa) there is the destruction of Tawheed, because (these Attributes) are existing, eternal, different from the *Dhaat* of Allaah Ta`aalaa, and that would necessitate the eternity of something other than Allaah Ta`aalaa, and would necessitate the multiplicity of eternal beings, even the multiplicity of necessarily existent beings, as was pointed out to in the speech of the Mutaqaddimeen, and the emphatic declaration of it in the speech of the Muta'akh-khireen, that the *Waajib-ul-Wujood* (Necessarily Existent) in His *Dhaat* is Allaah Ta`aalaa and His *Sifaat* (Attributes).

The Mu`tazilah said that the Nasaaraa (Christians) became Kuffaar by affirming three eternal beings, so what about those who affirm eight or even more (eternal beings)? (Meaning that, according to them, affirming *Sifaat* for Allaah Ta`aalaa, which some say are Eight Sifaat and some say more, this would mean that there are more than eight Eternal Beings, in their claim.)

Imaam an-Nasafi رحمة الله عليه answered this by saying:

(وهي لا هو ولا غيره)

"These Attributes are not (Allaah) nor are they other than Him."

يعني أن صفات الله تعالى ليست عين الذات ولا غير الذات, فلا يلزم قدم الغير ولا تكثر القدماء

Meaning that the *Sifaat* (Attributes) of Allaah Ta`aalaa are not His *Dhaat* Itself nor are they are than The *Dhaat*; thus, it does not necessitate the eternity of anything other than Allaah Ta`aalaa and nor does it necessitate the multiplicity of eternal beings.

والنصارى وإن لم يصرحوا بالقدماء المتغايرة لكن لزمهم ذلك لأنهم أثبتوا الأقانيم الثلاثة التي هي: الوجود, والعلم, والحياة, وسموها الأب والإبن وروح القدس, وزعموا أن أقنوم العلم قد انتقل إلى بدن عيسى عليه السلام, فجوزوا الإنفكاك والإنتقال, فكانت الأقانيم ذوات متغايرة

Even though the Nasaaraa (Christians) did not explicitly state the existence of different eternal beings, however, it compelled them to affirm *al-Aqaaneem ath-Thalaathah* (The Three Persons of the Godhead), which are: Existence, Knowledge and Life, and they named these are the Father, the Son and the Holy Spirit.

They claimed that the *Uqnoom-ul-`Ilm* (The Person of the Godhead of Knowledge) transferred himself into the body of Nabi `Eesa عليه السلام. Thus, they (the Christians) believe in the possibility of separation and transferrence, and thus the *Aqaaneem* are three different beings (*dhawaat*).

ولقائل أن يمنع توقف التعدد والتكثر على التغاير, بمعنى جواز الإنفكاك للقطع بأن مراتب الأعداد من الواحد والإثنين والثلاثة إلى غير ذلك متعددة متكثرة, مع أن البعض جزء من البعض, والجزء لا يغاير الكل

Some say that it is impossible to make plurality and multiplicity dependant upon distinct entities being made, which means that it is possible for them to separate completely, so that series of numbers from one, two, three, etc., multiple, numerous, with some of them being part of others, and a part is not distinctly different fro a whole.

وأيضاً لا يتصور نزاع من أهل السنة والجماعة في كثرة الصفات وتعددها, متغايرة كانت أو غير متغايرة, فالأولى أن يقال: المستحيل تعدد ذوات قديمة لا ذات وصفات, وأن لا يجترأ على

القول بكون الصفات واجبة الوجود لذاتها, بل يقال: هي واجبة لا لغيرها, بل لما ليس عينها ولا غيرها, أعني ذات الله تعالى وتقدس, ويكون هذا مراد من قال: الواجب الوجود لذاته هو الله تعالى وصفاته, يعني أنها واجبة لذات الواجب تعالى وتقدس, وأما في نفسها فهي ممكنة, ولا استحالة في قدم الممكن إذا كان قائماً بذات القديم, واجباً له غير منفصل عنه, فليس كل قديم إلهاً حتى يلزم من وجود القدماء وجود الآلهة, لكن ينبغي أن يقال: الله تعالى قديم بصفاته, ولا يطلق القول بالقدماء لئلا يذهب الوهم إلى أن كلاً منها قائم بذاته, موصوف بصفات الألوهية, ولصعوبة هذا المقام ذهبت المعتزلة والفلاسفة إلى نفي الصفات, والكرامية إلى نفي قدمها, والأشاعرة إلى نفي غيرتها وعينيتها

Also, it was inconceiveable that there be a disagreement between the Ahlus Sunnah wal-Jamaa`ah in the issue of the multiplicity and plurality of *Sifaat* (Attributes of Allaah Ta`aalaa), as to whether they are distinctly separate from one another or not. It would have been better for it to have been said: "What is impossible is the plurality of eternal essences (*dhawaat*), not that of a *Dhaat* and *Sifaat*."

It would also be better not to be as bold as to make the statement that the *Sifaat* are necessarily existent in and of themselves, but rather to say: they are necessarily existent, not for other than themselves, but rather, for that which themselves but also not other than themselves, i.e. the *Dhaat* of Allaah Ta`aalaa.

This is the intended meaning of the one who say: The One Who is *Waajib-ul-Wujood* by His *Dhaat* is Allaah Ta`aalaa and His *Sifaat*, meaning that they (the Attributes) are necessarily existent in the *Dhaat* of He Who is Necessarily Existent, which is Allaah Ta`aalaa. As for in themselves, then it is possible, and there is no impossibility in the eternity of the possible if it subsists with the *Dhaat* of the Eternal Being, necessarily existent in Him, not separated (*munfasil*) from Him. Not every eternal being is an Ilaah, so the existence of multiple gods is not implied from the existence of multiple eternal beings; however, it is necessary to say: Allaah Ta`aalaa is *Qadeem* (Eternal) along with His *Sifaat* (Attributes). The term "eternal beings" should not be used, for it may result in some imagining that each of them (these eternals) subsists within themselves, attributed with the attributes of *Uloohiyyah*.

Due to the difficulty of this question, the Mu`tazilah and the philosophers denied the *Sifaat* (Attributes of Allaah Ta`aalaa), and the Karaamiyyah denied the eternity of the *Sifaat*, and the Ash`aris denied both that the *Sifaat* are other than Allaah and that they are His *Dhaat*.

فإن قيل: هذا النفي في الظاهر رفع للنقيضين, وفي الحقيقة جمع بينهما, لأن نفي الغيرية صريحاً مثلاً, إثبات للعينية ضمناً, وإثباتها مع نفي العينية صريحاً جمع بين النقضين, وكذا نفي العينية صريحاً جمع بينهما, لأن المفهوم من الشيء إن لم يكن هو المفهوم من الآخر فهو غيره, وإلا فهو عينه, ولا يتصور بينهما واسطة

If it is said: This negation, on the apparent, removes the two contradictories and in reality is a uniting between them, because the explicit negation of the fact that the Attributes are other than Allaah Ta`aalaa, for example, affirmed exclusively their identity with Him, and the affirmation of them along with the negation of their identity with Him explicitly is a uniting between two contradictories. Similarly also is the explicit negation of their identity with Him, it is a uniting between them, because what is understood (*mafhoom*) from a thing, if it is not what is understood from the other, then it is other than it; otherwise, it is the same thing, and it is not conceiveable that there be between them an intermediary.

قلنا: قد فسروا الغيرية بكون الموجودين بحيث يقدر ويتصور وجود أحدهما مع عدم الآخر, أي يمكن الإنفكاك بينهما, والعينية باتحاد المفهوم بلا تفاوت أصلاً, فلا يكونان نقيضين, بل يتصور بينهما واسطة, بأن يكون الشيء بحيث لا يكون مفهومه مفهوم الآخر, ولا يوجد بدونه كالجزء مع الكل, والصفة مع الذات, وبعض الصفات مع البعض, فإن ذات الله تعالى وصفاته أزلية, والعدم على الأزلي محال, والواحد من العشرة يستحيل بقاؤه بدونها, وبقاؤها بدونه, إذ هو منها, فعدمها عدمه, ووجودها وجوده, بخلاف الصفة المحدثة, فإن قيام الذات بدون تلك الصفات المعينة متصور, فتكون غير الذات, كما ذكره المشايخ

We say: They have explained *al-Ghayriyyah* (otherness) as being the existence of two things in such a manner that, the existence of one of them is determined and conceived along with the non-existence of the other, i.e. it is possible for there to be separation between them. They have explained *al-`Ayniyyah* (identity) as being the unity of what is understood (*al-mafhoom*) without there being a distinction at all, so they are not contradictory, but rather, it is conceiveable that there be an intermediary between them, such as by a thing being such that what is understood from it is not what is understood from the other, and it does not exist without it, the a *juz'* (part) with a *kull* (whole), and the attribute along with the essence, and the attributes along with other attributes.

The *Dhaat* of Allaah Ta`aalaa and His *Sifaat* are pre-eternal (having no beginning), and it is impossible for non-existence to come upon that which is pre-eternal.

It is impossible for one as a part of ten to continue without the ten, and for ten to continue without the one, because it is from it, so its non-existence is the non-existence of the other, and its existence is the existence of the other, unlike the originated attribute, because for the *Dhaat* to subsist (in Itself) without those originated attributes is conceiveable, so they are other than the *Dhaat*, as was mentioned by the Mashaayikh.

وفيه نظر, لأنهم إن أرادوا صحة الإنفكاك من الجانبين, إنتقض بالعالم مع الصانع, والعرض مع المحل, إذ لا يتصور وجود العالم مع عدم الصانع, لاستحالة عدمه, ولا وجود العرض كالسواد مثلاً بدون المحل, وهو ظاهر مع القطع بالمغايرة إتفاقاً, وإن اكتفوا بجانب واحد لزمت المغايرة بين الجزء والكل, وكذا بين الذات والصفة, للقطع بجواز وجود الجزء بدون الكل, والذات بدون الصفة, وما ذكروا من استحالة بقاء الواحد بدون العشرة ظاهر الفساد

However, there is speculation regarding this, because if what they meant is the validity of separation fro both sides, then this contradicts the case of the world along with its Creator, and the `aradh* along with its locus, because it is inconceiveable for the world to exist without the Creator existing because His existence is impossible. It is also impossible for an `aradh* to exist, like black, for example, without its locus, and that is clear, along with the fact that there must be a distinct difference (between the two entities) as a matter of agreement.

If they sufficed with one standpoint, then the existence of a distinct difference between a part and a whole is necessary, and also between *Dhaat* and *Sifah* (Attribute), as a distinction so that it is possible for a part to exist without the whole, and for the *Dhaat* to exist without the *Sifah*. As for what they have mentioned of the impossibility of the continuance of one which is a part of ten, then this is clearly unsound.

لا يقال: المراد إمكان تصور وجود كل منهما مع عدم الآخر, ولو بالفرض, وإن كان محالاً, والعالم قد يتصور موجوداً ثم يطلب بالبرهان ثبوت الصانع, بخلاف الجزء مع الكل, فإنه كما يمتنع وجود العشرة بدون الواحد يمتنع وجود الواحد من العشرة بدون العشرة, إذ لو وجد لما كان واحداً من العشرة

It is not to be said that what is meant is the possibility of conceiving the existence of each of the two of them along with the non-existence of the other, even if it be by mere supposition. Even if it is impossible, the world may by conceived of as existing, then later on the affirming of a Creator through evidence is sought for, unlike the case of the part (*juz'*) with the whole (*kull*), because just as the existence of ten without one is not possible, it it not possible for one to exist (as part of ten) without ten, because were it to exist, it would not be (in that case) one from ten.

والحاصل أن وصف الإضافة معتبر, وامتناع الإنفكاك ظاهر لأنا نقول: قد صرحوا بعدم المغايرة بين الصفات بناء على أنها لا يتصور عدمها لكونها أزلية, مع القطع بأن يتصور وجود البعض كالعلم مثلاً, ثم يطلب بالبرهان إثبات البعض الآخر, فعلم أنهم لم يريدوا هذا المعنى, مع أنه لا يستقيم في العرض مع المحل, ولو اعتبر وصف الإضافة لزم عدم المغايرة بين كل متضايفين كالأب والإبن, وكالإخوين وكالعلة مع المعلول, بل بين الغيرين لأن الغير من الأسماء الإضافية, ولا قائل بذلك

The result of this is that, the description of relationship (between the two entities) must be considered. The impossibility of separation is clear, because we say: they have explicitly declared the non-existence of the Attributes being distinctly different from one another, based on the fact that their non-existence is inconceiveable because they are pre-eternal (always having existed, without a beginning). Yet, it is certain that it is possible to conceive the existence of some of them, like Knowledge, for example, and thereafter the affirmation of the others with evidence is sought, so it is known that they had not intended this meaning, even though it does not apply in the case of the 'aradh with its *mahall* (locus).

If consideration is to be given to the description of relationship (between the two entities), then the absence of there being distinct differences between things related, like a father and son, and like two brothers, and like the cause ('*illat*) with its effect (*ma'lool*). In fact, even more two different things, because *al-ghayr* (something other) is from the nouns used for showing relationship or attribution (*al-idhaafiyyah*), and no one holds that view.

فإن قيل: لم لا يجوز أن لا يكون مرادهم أنها لا هو, بحسب المفهوم, ولا غيره بحسب الوجود, كما هو حكم سائر المحمولات بالنسبة إلى موضوعاتها, فإنه يشترط الإتحاد بينهما بحسب

الوجود, ليصح الحمل والتغاير بحسب المفهوم, ليفيد الحمل, كما في قونا: الإنسان كاتب, بخلاف قولنا: الإنسان حجر لأنه لا يصح, وقولنا: الإنسان إنسان, فإنه لا يفيد

If it is said: why is it not possible that their intended meaning could be that the Attributes are not Allaah Ta`aalaa, according to what is understood, and they are not other than Him, as far as His Existence is concerned, as is the case with the rest of the possible things in relation to their subjects. Because, there is the stipulation of unity between them as far as their existence is concerned, so that the possibility may be valid and the distinct difference may be according to what is understood, to bring about the possibility, like in our statement: "Man is a writer." Unlike our statement: "Man is a stone," because that would be incorrect, or like our statement, "Man is man," because that would be meaningless.

قلنا: إن هذا إنما يصح في مثل العالم والقادر بالنسبة إلى الذات, لا في مثل العلم والقدرة, مع أن الكلام فيه ولا في الأجزاء الغير المحمولة, كالواحد من العشرة, واليد من زيد

We say: this is only valid in the case of the Attributes of, "Al-`Aalim" (the All-Knowing), "Al-Qaadir" (the All-Powerful), in relation to the *Dhaat* of Allaah Ta`aalaa, not in the case of the attributes of *Al-`Ilm* (Knowledge) and *Al-Qudrah* (Power), despite the fact that the discussion is regarding that and not regarding parts (*ajzaa'*) which are not possible, like one from them, and "the hand of Zaid."

وذكر في التبصرة أن كون الواحد من العشرة واليد من زيد غيره مما لم يقل به أحد من المتكلمين سوى جعفر بن حارث, وقد خالف في ذلك جميع المعتزلة, وعد ذلك من جهالاته, وهذا لأن العشرة إسم لجميع الأفراد, ومتناول لكل فرد من آحاده مع أغياره فلو كان الواحد غيرها لكان غير نفسه, لأنه من العشرة, وأن تكون العشرة بدونه, وكذا لو كان يد زيد غيره, لكان اليد غير نفسها, هذا كلامه ولا يخفى ما فيه

It is mentioned in *at-Tabsirah* the argument that one from ten is other than ten and "the hand of Zaid" is other than Zaid, an opinion which was not held by any of the Mutakallimeen except for Ja`far ibn Haarith, and in that opinion of his he had gone against all of the Mu`tazilah, and this was counted as being due to his ignorance. This is because "ten" is the name given to all of the individual units and it includes each individual of the units along with the others. So, if one was other than it, then it would be other than itself, because it is part of (the unit of) ten, and that ten is formed from something besides it. The same would be the case in "the hand of Zaid is other than him," because then the hand would be other than itself, and the ludicrousness of what this argument contains is not hidden.

(وهي)

"And they-"

أي صفاته الأزلية

Meaning, the Eternal Attributes of Allaah Ta`aalaa.

(العلم)

"Are: *Al-`Ilm* (Knowledge)."

وهي صفة أزلية تنكشف المعلومات عند تعلقها بها

It is an Eternal Attribute. The things that have to do with Knowledge become unveiled when connected with this Attribute.

(والقدرة)

"And *Al-Qudrah* (Power)."

وهي صفة أزلية تؤثر في المقدورات عند تعلقها بها

It is an Eternal Attribute. It affects all that over which He has power, when connected with this Attribute.

(والحياة)

"And *Al-Hayaah* (Life)."

وهي صفة أزلية توجب صحة العلم

It is an Eternal Attribute. It necessitates the validity of Knowledge.

(والقوة)

"And *Al-Quwwah* (Power)."

وهي بمعنى القدرة

It has the meaning of *Al-Qudrah*.

(والسمع)

"And *As-Sam`* (Hearing)."

وهي صفة تتعلق بالمسموعات

It is an Attribute connected to all of that which is heard.

(والبصر)

"And *Al-Basar* (Seeing)."

وهي صفة تتعلق بالمبصرات, فتدرك إدراكاً تاماً, لا على سبيل التخيل أو التوهم ولا على طريق تأثير حاسة, ووصول هواء, ولا يلزم من قدمها قدم المسموعات والمبصرات, كما لا يلزم من قدم العلم والقدرة قدم المعلومات والمقدورات, لأنها صفات قديمة تحدث لها تعلقات بالذوات

It is an Attribute connected to all of that which is seen, so it comprehends it with a perfect comprehension, not simply by way of imagination or by use of the estimative faculty (*al-tawahhum*), nor by an effect being had on some faculty and the reaching of the air (to it). Its eternity does not imply the eternity of things that are heard or things that are seen, just as the eternity of Knowledge and Power does not imply the eternity of those things which are known or those things over which He (Allaah Ta`aalaa) has power. This is so because they are Eternal Attributes, and connections with originated things are originated for them.

(والإرادة والمشيئة)

"And *Al-Iraadah* (Intending) and *Al-Mashee'ah* (Will)."

وهما عبارتان عن صفة في الحي توجب تخصيص أحد المقدورين في أحد الأوقات بالوقوع مع استواء نسبة القدرة إلى الكل, وكون تعلق العلم تابعاً للوقوع, وفيما ذكر تنبيه على الرد على من زعم أن المشيئة قديمة, والإرادة حادثة قائمة بذات الله تعالى, وعلى من زعم أن معنى إرادة الله

تعالى فعله, أنه ليس بمكره ولا ساه ولا مغلوب, ومعنى إرادته فعل غيره أنه أمر به, كيف وقد أمر كل مكلف بالإيمان وسائر الواجبات ولو شاء لوقع؟

Both of these refer to a *Sifah* in *Al-Hayy* (The Ever Living), which necessitates the specification of one of the two alternatives over which He has power and brings it about at a particular time, despite the fact that He has full power over both of them (and all things). The connection of Knowledge with it is a consequence of its occuring.

In what has been mentioned, attention is drawn to a refutation of those who claim that *Al-Mashee'ah* is Eternal but *Al-Iraadah* is originated and subsisting by the *Dhaat* of Allaah Ta`aalaa, and also a refutation o those who claim that the meaning of *Al-Iraadah* (Allaah Ta`aalaa intending) His Action is that He is not forced nor heedless nor overcome, and that the meaning of His intending an action of other than Him is that He commanded it. How can that be, when every *mukallaf* (one who is responsible for his actions according to the Sharee`ah) has been ordered to bring *Imaan* and carry out all of the compulsory duties, and had Allaah Ta`aalaa willed it, it would have occurred?

(والفعل والتخليق)

"And *Al-Fi'l* (Doing) and *At-Takhleeq* (Creating)."

عبارة عن صفة أزلية تسمى التكوين, وسيجيء تحقيقه, وعدلَ عن لفظ الخلق لشيوع استعماله في المخلوق

This refers to an Eternal Attribute which is known as *At-Takween* (bringing into being), and its verification will be mentioned later on. Imaam an-Nasafi رحمة الله عليه avoided the usage of the word "*khalq*" (creating) due to it often being used in place of "*al-Makhlooq*".

(والترزيق)

"And *At-Tarzeeq* (providing sustenance)."

هو تكوين مخصوص صرح به, إشراة إلى أن مثل التخليق والترزيق والتصوير والإحياء والإماتة وغير ذلك مما أسند إلى الله تعالى, كل منها راجع إلى صفة حقيقية أزلية قائمة بالذات هي التكوين, لا كما زعم الأشعري من أنها إضافات وصفات للأفعال

This is the special bringing into existence which (Imaam an-Nasafi) explicitly mentioned in order to point out that such things as creating, providing sustenance, forming, giving life, giving death, etc., all of that is traced back to Allaah Ta`aalaa Alone. All of those things return to a Real Attribute which is Eternal, subsisting with the Dhaat of Allaah Ta`aalaa, and that is *At-Takween* (bringing into being). It is unlike what is assumed by the Ash`aris, that these things are *idhaafaat* (relationships) and attributes of actions (*sifaat lil-af`aal*).

(والكلام)

"And *Al-Kalaam* (Speech)."

وهي صفة أزلية عبر عنها بالنظر المسمى بالقرآن المركب من الحروف, وذلك لأن كل من يأمر وينهى ويخبر يجد من نفسه معنى, ثم يدل عليه بالعبارة أو الكتابة أو الإشارة, وهو غير العلم, إذ قد يخبر الإنسان عما لا يعلمه, بل يعلم خلافه, وغير الإرادة لأنه قد يأمر بما لا يريده, كمن أمر عبده قصداً لإظهار عصيانه وعدم امتثاله لأوامره, ويسمى هذا كلاماً نفسياً على ما أشار إليه الأخطل بقوله:

This is an Eternal Attribute which is an expression for that context composed of letters which is called "Al-Qur'aan". And that is because everyone who commands, prohibits and informs, finds within himself an idea and then points out to it by means of expressing himself or by writing or by gesturing to it, and it is other than *Al-`Ilm* (Knowledge), because a person can narrate that which he does not know (to be factual), but rather, he knows the opposite of it (to be factual). It is also not *Al-Iraadah* (Intending), because a person can command that which he does not intend, like the one who commands his slave with something but with the intention of exposing his disobedience and his failure to fulfill the commands.

This kind of speech is known as *Al-Kalaam An-Nafsi* (the speech of the heart).

Al-Akhtal referred to this by saying:

إن الكلام لفي الفؤد وإنما   جعل اللسان على الفؤاد دليلا

"True speech lies within the heart; the tongue has only been made as a guide to the heart."

وقال عمر رضي الله عنه: إني زورت في نفسي مقالة, وكثيراً ما تقول لصاحبك إن في نفسي كلاماً أريد أن أذكره لك

Hadhrat `Umar رضي الله عنه said, "I made a speech right within myself."

Often you say to your friend, "There is speech within me which I wish to mention to you."

والدليل على ثبوت صفة الكلام: إجماع الأمة وتواتر النقل عن الأنبياء عليهم السلام, أنه تعالى متكلم, مع القطع باستحالة التكلم من غير ثبوت صفة الكلام, فثبت أن لله تعالى صفات ثمانية, هي: العلم, والقدرة, والحياة, والسمع, والبصر, والإرادة, والتكوين, والكلام

The evidence for the affirmation of the Attribute of Speech is the *ijmaa`* (consensus) of the Ummah and that it has reached us through *tawaatur* (continuity in narration) from the Ambiyaa عليهم السلام themselves, that Allaah Ta`aalaa speaks, because it is certain that speaking is impossible without the attribute of speech, so it is thus affirmed that Allaah Ta`aalaa has Eight Attributes (*Sifaat*), and they are:

1. *Al-`Ilm* (Knowledge).
2. *Al-Qudrah* (Power).
3. *Al-Hayaah* (Life).
4. *As-Sam`* (Hearing).
5. *Al-Basar* (Seeing).
6. *Al-Iraadah* (Intending).
7. *At-Takween* (Bringing into being).
8. *Al-Kalaam* (Speech).

صفة كلام الله

The Speech of Allaah Ta`aalaa:

ولما كان في الثلاثة الأخيرة زيادة نزاع وخفاء, كرر الإشارة إلى إثباتها وقدمها وفصل الكلام بعض التفصيل فقال:

Due to the fact that in the last three there is additional dispute and obscurity, he repeated the gesturing towards their affirmation and their being eternal, and he explained in detail his statement, so he said:

(هو)

"He."

أي الله تعالى

Meaning, Allaah Ta`aalaa.

(متكلم بكلام هو صفة له)

"He speaks with a *Kalaam* (Speech) which is an Attribute of His."

ضرورة إمتناع إثبات المشتق للشيء من غير قيام مأخذ الإشتقاق به, وفي هذا رد على المعتزلة حيث ذهبوا إلى أنه متكلم بكلام هو قائم بغيره, ليس صفة له

Of necessity, because it is impossible to affirm the derivative of any thing without affirming the subsistence in that thing from which it is derived. In this there is a refutation of the Mu`tazilah who claimed that Allaah Ta`aalaa speaks with a Kalaam which subsists in other than Himself and which is not an Attribute of His.

(أزلية)

"It is Eternal."

ضرورة إمتناع قيام الحوادث بذاته تعالى

Of necessity, because it is impossible for originated matters to subsist with the *Dhaat* of Allaah Ta`aalaa.

(ليس من جنس الحروف والأصوات)

"It is not from the *jins* of letters and sounds."

ضرورة أنها أعراض حادثة مشروط حدوث بعضها بانقضاء البعض, لأن امتناع التكلم بالحرف الثاني بدون انقضاء الحرف الأول بديهي, وفي هذا رد على الحنابلة والكرامية القائلين بأن كلامه تعالى عرض من جنس الأصوات والحروف, ومع ذلك فهو قديم

Of necessity, because letters and sounds are *a`raadh*, originated things, the occurence of some of them being hinged on the completion of others. Because, it is impossible to speak the second letter without having completed the first letter, and this is clearly understood by the intellect. In this there is a refuation of the Hanaabilah and the Karaamiyyah who held the view that the Kalaam of Allaah Ta`aalaa is from the *jins* of sounds and letters and despite that it is Qadeem (Eternal).

(وهو)

"And It."

أي الكلام

Meaning, the Speech of Allaah Ta`aalaa.

(صفة)

"Is an Attribute."

أي معنى قائم بالذات

Meaning, it is a Meaning which subsists with the *Dhaat* of Allaah Ta`aalaa.

(منافية للسكوت)

"It is negatory of silence."

الذي هو ترك التكلم مع القدرة عليه

Silence being the leaving off of speaking despite having the ability to do so.

(والآفة)

"And (negatory of) defect."

التي هي عدم مطاوعة الآلات, إما بحسب الفطرة كما في الخرس أو بحسب ضعفها وعدم بلوغها حد القوة كما في الطفولية

Defect in this case being the lack of fitness in the instruments (of speech), either by the nature of the person as in the case of a person who is mute, or due to weakness and absence of reaching the level of ability (to speak), as in the case of babies.

فإن قيل: هذا الكلام إنما يصدق على الكلام اللفظي دون الكلام النفسي, إذ السكوت والخرس إنما ينافي التلفظ

If it is said: "This definition only applies to *al-Kalaam al-Lafzhi* (verbal speech) and not *al-Kalaam an-Nafsi* (inner speech, or the speech of the heart), because silence and muteness are negatory only of verbal speech."

قلنا: المراد السكوت والآفة الباطنيان, بأن لا يريد في نفسه التكلم أو لا يقدر على ذلك, فكما أن الكلام لفظي ونفسي, فكذا ضده, أعني السكوت والخرس

We say: "The intended meaning is silence and inner defects, such as by the person not intending in himself speech or not being able to speak. Thus, just as speech is of two types, which is *lafzhi* (verbal) and *nafsi* (inner), so too are its opposites, i.e. silence and muteness.

(والله تعالى متكلم بها, آمر به, ناه, مخبر)

"Allaah Ta`aalaa speaks with (this Attribute of Speech); He orders with it, prohibits with it, and informs with it."

يعني أنه صفة واحدة تتكثر إلى الأمر والنهي والخبر, باختلاف التعلقات كالعلم والقدرة وسائر الصفات, فإن كلاً منها صفة واحدة قديمة, والتكثر والحدوث إنما هو باعتبار التعلقات والإضافات, لما أن ذلك أليق بكمال التوحيد, ولأنه لا دليل على تكثر كل منها في نفسها

Meaning that it is one Attribute (*Sifah*) with a variety of forms for commanding, prohibiting and information, with the different types of connections such as Knowledge, and Power, and the rest of the Attributes (*Sifaat*). This is because each of them is one *Sifah* (Attribute) that is Eternal, and variety and origination are only with regards to the connections and relationships, because that is more in conformity with the perfection of Tawheed, and because there is no evidence for each Attribute having variety within Itself.

فإن قيل: هذه أقسام للكلام لا يعقل وجوده بدونها, قلنا إنه ممنوع, بل إنما يصير أحد تلك الأقسام عند التعلقات, وذلك فيما لا يزال, وأما في الأزل فلا انقسام أصلاً

If it is said: These are categories of the Speech, which it is impossible to understand Its existence without. We say: This is impossible; rather, (the Speech) becomes one of those categories only when the connections (with created things) are made. That is true of Speech which does not pass away. But in the beginning, since all of eternity there was no division whatsoever.

وذهب بعضهم إلى أنه في الأزل خبر, ومرجع الكل إليه, لأن حاصل الأمر إخبار عن استحقاق الثواب على الفعل, والعقاب على الترك, والنهي على العكس, وحاصل الإستخبار الخبر عن طلب الإعلام, وحاصل النداء الخبر عن طلب الإجابة, ورد بأنا نعلم إختلاف هذه المعاني بالضرورة, واستلزام البعض للبعض لا يوجب الإتحاد

Some of them claimed that in pre-eternity, the Speech was informing, and all (other kinds of Speech) goes back to it, because the result of *Amr* (Commanding) is information of the deserving of reward for the doing of a certain action, and punishment for the abandoning of a certain action, and vice-versa in the case of prohibiting.

فإن قيل: الأمر والنهي بلا مأمور ولا منهي سفه وعبث, والإخبار في الأزل بطريق المضي كذب محض, يجب تنزيه الله تعالى عنه

If it is said: "Commanding and prohibiting without there being someone commanded or someone being prohibited is foolishness and futility, and to say that from eternity there is *ikhbaar* (Allaah Ta`aalaa narrating) which assumes the past tense is pure falsehood from which it is necessary to declare Allaah Ta`aalaa as being free from."

قلنا: إن لم يجعل كلامه في الأزل أمراً ونهياً وخبراً فلا إشكال, وإن جعلناه فالأمر في الأزل لإيجاب تحصيل المأمور به في وقت وجود المأمور وصيرورته أهلاً لتحصيله, فيكفي وجود المأمور في علم الآمر, كما إذا قدر الرجل إبناً له فأمره بأن يفعل كذا بعد الوجود, والإخبار

بالنسبة إلى الأزل لا يتصف بشيء من الأزمنة, إذ لا ماضي ولا مستقبل ولا حال بالنسبة إلى الله تعالى, لتنزيهه عن الزمان, كما أن علمه أزلي لا يتغير بتغير الأزمان

We would respond to this by saying: "If His Speech is not made from eternity to be commanding, prohibiting and narrating, then there is no difficulty. If we make it as such (i.e. commanding, prohibiting, narrating), then prohibitinng since eternity is to make it binding upon the one who is commanded at the time of the one being commanded coming into existence and becoming fit for receiving (this command). Thus, the existence of the one commanded is sufficient in the Knowledge of the One commanding.

This is like the case of a person taking for granted that he had a son, and then commanding him to do such-and-such when he comes into existence.

Narrating since pre-eternity is not attributed with anything from the tenses, because when it comes to Allaah Ta`aalaa, there is no past tense, no future tense, no present tense, because Allaah Ta`aalaa is free from time, just as His Knowledge is Eternal and does not change with the changing of time.

القرآن كلام الله

The Qur'aan is the *Kalaam* (Speech) of Allaah Ta`aalaa:

ولما صرح بأزلية الكلام حاول التنبيه على أن القرآن أيضاً قد يطلق على هذا الكلام النفسي القديم كما يطلق على النظم المتلوّ الحادث, فقال:

When the author explicitly declared that the *Kalaam* of Allaah Ta`aalaa is Eternal, he wanted to draw attention to the fact that *Al-Kalaam An-Nafsi Al-Qadeem* (The Eternal Inner Speech) has also been referred to as "Qur'aan" just as the name "Qur'aan" has been used to refer to originated context which is read, so he said:

(والقرآن كلام الله تعالى غير مخلوق)

"The Qur'aan is the Speech of Allaah, uncreated."

وعقب القرآن الكريم بكلام الله, لما ذكره المشايخ من أنه يقال: القرآن كلام الله تعالى غير مخلوق, ولا يقال: القرآن غير مخلوق, لئلا يسبق إلى الفهم أن المؤلف من الأصوات والحروف قديم, كما ذهب إليه الحنابلة جهلاً أو عناداً, وأقام غير المخلوق مقام غير الحادث, تنبيهاً على اتحادهما, وقصداً إلى جري الكلام على وفق الحديث, حيث قال صلى الله عليه وسلم: الْقُرْآنُ كَلَامُ اللهِ تَعَالَى غَيْرُ مَخْلُوقٍ

He mentions the Qur'aan Kareem after mentioning "the *Kalaam* of Allaah", due to that which the Mashaayikh have mentioned that, the Qur'aan is the *Kalaam* of Allaah Ta`aalaa, uncreated, and it is not to be said: "The Qur'aan is uncreated," in order to avoid the understandings of people jumping to the conclusion (if it is said as such) that that which is made up of sounds and letters is eternal, which is the position that was adopted by the Hanaabilah out of ignorance (*jahl*) or obstinacy.

Imaam an-Nasafi uses the term "*ghayr makhlooq*" (uncreated) rather than using "*ghayr haadith*" (unoriginated), drawing attention to the fact that they are one and the same, and also to make his statement be in conformity with the Hadeeth of Rasoolullaah صلى الله عليه وسلم wherein he said:

"The Qur'aan is the Kalaam of Allaah Ta`aalaa, *ghayr makhlooq* (uncreated)."

ومن قال: إنه مخلوق فهو كافر بالله العظيم, وتنصيصاً على محل الخلاف بالعبارة المشهورة فيما بين الفريقين, وهو أن القرآن مخلوق أو غير مخلوق, ولهذا تترجم المسألة بمسألة خلق القرآن

And whosoever says that is is *makhlooq* (created), then he is a Kaafir in Allaah Al-`Azheem.

And also, (he had used that term) to take into account the difference between the two groups regarding the well-known text, which is that of whether the Qur'aan is created or uncreated, and for this reason the issue is to be interpreted as being the issue of "*Khalq Al-Qur'aan*" (The Creation of the Qur'aan)

وتحقيق الخلاف بيننا وبينهم يرجع إلى إثبات الكلام النفسي ونفيه, وإلا فنحن لا نقول بقدم الألفاظ والحروف, وهم لا يقولون بحدوث الكلام النفسي, ودليلنا ما مر أنه ثبت بالإجماع وتواتر النقل عن الأنبياء صلوات الله عليهم أنه متكلم, ولا معنى له سوى أنه متصف بالكلام, ويمتنع قيام اللفظي الحادث بذاته تعالى, فتعين النفسي القديم

The verification of the difference between us and them goes back to the affirmation of *Al-Kalaam An-Nafsi* or negating it; otherwise, we do not believe in the words and letters being eternal, and they do not believe in the origination of *Al-Kalaam An-Nafsi*. Our evidence is that which has passed, that it has been established by *ijmaa`* and the continuity of transmission from the Ambiyaa صلوات الله عليهم that Allaah Ta`aalaa speaks, and there is no meaning to that other than that Allaah Ta`aalaa is attributed with *Al-Kalaam*, and it is impossible for verbal speech that is originated to subsist with the *Dhaat* of Allaah Ta`aalaa, thus *Al-Kalaam An-Nafsi Al-Qadeem* has been designated as being the meaning.

وأما إستدلالهم بأن القرآن متصف بما هو من صفات المخلوق, وسمات الحدوث من التأليف والتنظيم والإنزال والتنزيل, وكونه عربياً مسموعاً فصيحاً معجزاً إلى غير ذلك, فإنما يقوم حجة على الحنابلة لا علينا, لأنا قائلون بحدوث التنظيم وإنما الكلام في المعنى القديم

The Mu`tazilah inferred that the Qur'aan is attributed with that which is from the attributes of the creation, and by marks which show its origination (*hudooth*), such as composition and arrangement, and being sent down and being revealed bit by bit, and its being in Arabic, and being heard (by the ears), and being eloquent, and being inimitable, etc.

That only acts as evidence against the Hanaabilah, not against us, because we believe that in the arrangement being originated. The discussion, however, is regarding *Al-Kalaam* in the meaning of being Eternal.

والمعتزلة لما لم يمكنهم إنكار كونه تعالى متكلماً ذهبوا إلى أنه متكلم بمعنى إيجاد الأوصات والحروف في محالها, أو إيجاد أشكال الكتابة في اللوح المحفوظ, وإن لم يقرأ على اختلاف بينهم, وأنت خبير بأن المتحرك من قامت به الحركة لا من أوجدها, وإلا لصح اتصاف الباري تعالى بالأعراض المخلوقة له, تعالى عن ذلك علواً كبيراً

Because the Mu`tazilah were unable ot deny the fact that Allaah Ta`aalaa speaks, they adopted the view that He speaks by bringing about sounds and letters in their places, or bringing about the forms of writing in *Al-Lawh Al-Mahfoozh* (The Preserved Tablet), though it may not be read, according to the differences they have among them on that point.

You know that the one who moves is the one in whom movement subsists, not the one who brings movement into into existence; otherwise, it would have been valid to describe Allaah Ta`aalaa with *a`raadh* which are created for him.

Allaah Ta`aalaa is far exalted above that.

ومن أقوى شبه المعتزلة: أنكم متفقون على أن القرآن إسم لما نقل إلينا بين دفتي المصاحف تواتراً, وهذا يستلزم كونه مكتوباً في المصاحف مقروءاً بالألسن مسموعاً بالآذان وكل ذلك من سمات الحدوث بالضرورة, فأشار إلى الجواب بقوله:

One of the strongest ambiguities of the Mu`tazilah is their claim that: "You are agreed upon the fact that the Qur'aan is a noun given to that which has been transmitted to us between the two covers of the *Mus-haf*, through continuity, and this necessitates its being written in the *Masaahif* (pl. of Mus-haf), recited upon the tongues, heard by the ears, and all of that is, by necessity, from the marks of origination."

The author responds to that by saying:

(وهو)

"And It-"

أي القرآن الذي هو كلام الله تعالى

Meaning, the Qur'aan, which is the *Kalaam* of Allaah Ta`aalaa.

(مكتوب في مصاحفنا)

"Is written in our Masaahif."

أي بأشكال الكتابة وصور الحروف الدالة عليه

Meaning, with written characters and the forms of the letters which point out to it.

(محفوظ في قلوبنا)

"Preserved in our hearts."

أي بالألفاظ المخيلة

Meaning, by verbal expressions which are imagined.

(مقروء بألسنتنا)

"Recited by our tongues."

بالحروف الملفوظة المسموعة

With the letters that are verbalised and heard.

(مسموع بآذاننا)

"Heard with our ears."

بذلك أيضاً

With that also.

(غير حال فيها)

"It does not reside in them."

أي مع ذلك ليس حالاً في المصاحف ولا في القلوب والألسنة والآذان, بل هو معنى قديم قائم بذات الله تعالى, يلفظ ويسمع بالنظم الدال عليه, ويحفظ بالنظم المخيل, ويكتب بنقوش وصور وأشكال موضوعة للحروف الدالة عليه, كما يقال: النار جوهر محرق, تذكر باللفظ وتكتب بالقلم, ولا يلزم منه كون حقيقة النار صوتاً وحرفاً

Meaning, despite that, it is not residing within the *Masaahif* or within the hearts, or the tongues or the ears. Rather, it is an Eternal Meaning which subsists with the *Dhaat* of Allaah Ta`aalaa. It is recited and heard by means of the context which indicates it, and it is preserved by the context which is imagined (in the minds) and written by marks, forms and characters that are used for the letters which point out to it, like how it is said: "The fire is a substance that burns, which is recalled by the word and written down by the pen." It is not necessitated from it that the *haqeeqat* of the fire is a sound and letter.

وتحقيقه أن للشيء وجوداً في الأعيان, ووجوداً في الأذهان, ووجوداً في العبارة, ووجوداً في الكتابة, والكتابة تدل على العبارة, وهي على ما في الأذهان, وهو على ما في الأعيان, فحيث

يوصف القرآن بما هو من لوازم القديم كما في قولنا القرآن غير مخلوق, فالمراد حقيقته الموجودة في الخارج

The verification of this is the fact that a thing (*shay'*) has an existence in substances (*a`yaan*), and an existence in the minds, and an existence in expression, and an existence in writing. The writing points out to the expression; the expression points out to that which is in the minds; the minds point out to that which exists within the *a`yaan* (substances).

Thus, when the Qur'aan is described with that which is from the things that are bound to The Eternal, like in our statement: "The Qur'aan is uncreated," then the intended meaning is its Reality which exists in external reality.

وحيث يوصف بما هو من لوازم المخلوقات والمحدثات يراد به الألفاظ المنطوقة المسموعة, كما في قولنا: قرأت نصف القرآن, أو المخيلة كما في قولنا: حفظت القرآن, أو الأشكال المنقوشة, كما في قولنا: يحرم للمحدث مس القرآن

When it is described with that which is from the things bound to the created beings and originated matters, then what is intended thereby are the words that are uttered and heard, like in our statement: "I recited half of the Qur'aan," or that which is imagined (in the minds), like in our statement: "I memorised the Qur'aan." Or the characters that are written, like in our statement: "It is prohibited for the *muhdith* (one in a state of minor impurity) to touch the Qur'aan."

ولما كان دليل الأحكام الشرعية هو اللفظ دون المعنى القديم, عرفه أئمة الأصول بالمكتوب في المصاحف, المنقول بالتواتر, وجعلوه إسماً للنظم والمعنى جميعاً, أي للنظم من حيث الدلالة على المعنى لا لمجرد المعنى

Because that which indicates to the *Shar`i Ahkaam* is the word rather than the Eternal Meaning, the A'immah of *Usool* defined it as that which is written down in the *Masaahif*, transmitted through *tawaatur* (continuity), and they applied the name (Qur'aan) to both the context and the meaning, i.e. the context from the aspect of it pointing out to the meaning, not just to the meaning.

وأما الكلام القديم الذي هو صفة الله تعالى فذهب الأشعري إلى أنه يجوز أن يسمع, ومنعه الأستاذ أبو إسحاق الإسفرايينيي, وهو اختيار الشيخ أبي منصور رحمه الله, فمعنى قوله تعالى:

As for the Eternal Speech which is an Attribute of Allaah Ta`aalaa, then Imaam al-Ash`ari held the view that it is possible to be heard, and al-Ustaadh Abu Is-haaq al-Isfaraayeeni regarded it as not being possible, and that is the chosen view of ash-Shaykh Abu Mansoor رحمة الله عليه (i.e. Imaam al-Maatureedi). Thus, the meaning of the Aayah:

$$حَتَّى يَسْمَعَ كَلَامَ اللهِ$$

{"*Until he hears the Kalaam of Allaah...*"}

يسمع ما يدل عليه, كما يقال: سمعت علم فلان, فموسى عليه السلام سمع صوتاً دالاً على ما يدل على كلام الله تعالى, لكن لما كان بلا واسطة الكتاب والملك خص باسم الكليم

He heard that which the (*Kalaam*) points out to, like how it is said: "I heard the knowledge of so-and-so."

Nabi Moosaa عليه السلام heard a voice which pointed out to the *Kalaam* of Allaah Ta`aalaa; however, because of it having been without the intermediary of a Kitaab or one of the Malaa'ikah, he was given the title "Al-Kaleem" (The one with whom Allaah Ta`aalaa spoke.)

فإن قيل: لو كان كلام الله تعالى حقيقة في المعنى القديم, مجازاً في النظم المؤلف, لصح نفيه عنه, بأن يقال: ليس النظم المنزل المعجز المفصل إلى السور والآيات كلام الله تعالى, والإجماع خلافه وأيضاً المعجز المتحدى به هو كلام الله تعالى حقيقة, مع القطع بأن ذلك إنما يتصور في النظم المؤلف المفصل إلى السور والآيات, إذ لا معنى لمعارضة الصفة القديمة

If it is said: "If the *Kalaam* of Allaah Ta`aalaa really in an Eternal Meaning, and metaphorically in a composed context, then it would have been valid to deny it from Him by saying: "The revealed, inimitable context which is divided into *Soorahs* and *Aayaat* is not the *Kalaam* of Allaah Ta`aalaa." However, *ijmaa*` opposes that statement."

An objection might also be raised that if the inimitable thing which is the object of contention is in reality the *Kalaam* of Allaah Ta`aalaa, along with absolute certainty that that is only conceiveable in the context which is composed and divided into *Soorahs* and *Aayaat*, because there would be no meaning to their opposing the Eternal Attribute (of Speech)."

قلنا: التحقيق أن كلام الله تعالى إسم مشترك بين الكلام النفسي القديم, ومعنى الإضافة: كونه صفة لله تعالى, وبين اللفظي الحادث المؤلف من السور والآيات, ومعنى الإضافة: أنه مخلوق الله تعالى ليس من تأليفات المخلوقين, فلا يصح النفي أصلاً, ولا يكون الإعجاز والتحدي إلا في كلام الله تعالى, وما وقع في عبارة بعض المشايخ من أنه مجاز فليس معناه أنه غير موضوع للنظم المؤلف, بل معناه أن الكلام في التحقيق وبالذات إسم للمعنى القائم بالنفس, وتسمية اللفظ به ووضعه لذلك, إنما هو باعتبار دلالته على المعنى, فلا نزاع لهم في الوضع والتسمية

We respond by saying: "The verification of this is that the *Kalaam* of Allaah Ta`aalaa is a name common to *Al-Kalaam An-Nafsi Al-Qadeem*, and the meaning of the *idhaafah* (attachment) here in the phrase, "*Kalaam* of Allaah", is that it is an Attribute of Allaah Ta`aalaa, and it is (also shared) with the Speech which is originated, verbally uttered, made up of *Soorahs* and *Aayaat*, and the meaning of the *idhaafah* here (in this case) is that it is from the creation of Allaah Ta`aalaa and not from the compositions of the created beings; thus, it is not valid to deny it at all.

That which is inimitable and over which they contend can only be the *Kalaam* of Allaah Ta`aalaa.

As for what has occurred in the expressions of some of the Mashaayikh, that it is *majaaz* (metaphorical), then the meaning of that is not that it is not used for the Speech that is verbally uttered and composed (of *Soorahs* and *Aayaat*). Rather, what it means is that in being verified as having a reality and in essence the Speech is a word used to mean that which subsists in the mind. As for the naming of the verbal utterance (as *Kalaam* of Allaah) and using it for that meaning, then that is due to its pointing out the meaning (of the *Kalaam* of Allaah), thus there is no dispute with them regarding the usage and the naming.

وذهب بعض المحققين إلى أن المعنى في قول مشايخنا كلام الله تعالى معنى قديم, ليس في مقابلة اللفظ, حتى يراد به مدلول اللفظ ومفهومه, بل في مقابلة العين, والمراد به ما لا يقوم بذاته كسائر الصفات, ومرادهم أن القرآن إسم اللفظ, والمعنى شامل لهما, وهو قديم, لا كما زعمت الحنابلة من قدم النظم المؤلف المرتب الأجزاء, فإنه بديهي الإستحالة, للقطع بأنه لا يمكن التلفظ بالسين من بسم الله إلا بعد التلفظ بالباء, بل بمعنى أن اللفظ القائم بالنفس ليس مرتب الأجزاء في نفسه كالقائم بنفس الحافظ, من غير ترتب الأجزاء, وتقدم البعض على البعض, والترتب إنما يحصل في التلفظ والقراءة لعدم مساعدة الآلة, وهذا هو معنى قولهم المقروء قديم,

والقراءة حادثة, وأما القائم بذات الله تعالى فلا ترتب فيه, حتى أن من سمع كلامه تعالى سمع غير مرتب الأجزاء لعدم احتياجه إلى الآلة, هذا حاصل كلامهم وهو جيد لمن تعقل لفظاً قائماً بالنفس غير مؤلف من الحروف المنطوقة أو المخيلة المشروطة وجود بعضها بعدم البعض, ولا من الأشكال المرتبة الدالة عليه

Some of the Muhaqqiqoon held the view that the meaning in the statement of our Mashaayikh is that the *Kalaam* of Allaah Ta`aalaa is Eternal Speech. It was not something that was contrasted with the verbal utterance so that it means that which is pointed out to by the verbal utterance and which is understood from it. Rather, it was used in contrast to the substance itself. The intended meaning of that was that which does not subsist by itself like the rest of the attributes. Their intended meaning is that the Qur'aan is a word used to refer to the verbal utterance, and the (Eternal) Meaning encompasses them both, and it is Eternal, unlike what was claimed by the Hanaabilah that the context which is composed and arranged of parts is eternal, because that is clearly impossible, of a certainty, because it is not possible to pronounce the *seen* in "*Bismillaah*" except after pronouncing the *baa'*. Rather, it means that the verbal utterance which subsists in the mind is not made up of parts in His self unlike how it is in the mind of the Haafiz (one who has memorised the Qur'aan), without any arrangement of parts and without any of it preceding other parts.

Arrangement only takes place in verbal utterance and recital due to the absence of help from the instrument, and this is the meaning of their statement: "That which is read is Eternal, but the recital is originated." As for that which subsists with the *Dhaat* of Allaah Ta`aalaa, then there is no arrangement in it, so much so that, the one who hears the *Kalaam* of Allaah Ta`aalaa hears it without the arrangement of parts, because Allaah Ta`aalaa has no need for the instrument (of speech).

This is the conclusion of their speech, and it is excellent for the one who understands that (the *Kalaam* of Allaah) is a verbal expression which subsists in the mind, not composed of letters that are spoken or imagine, because it is stipulated that the existence of some of them precludes the existence of others, and it is also not composed of the arranged characters which point out to it.

ونحن لا نعتقل من قيام الكلام بنفس الحافظ إلا كون صور الحروف مخزونة مرتسمة في خياله, بحيث إذا التفت إليها كان كلاماً مؤلفاً من ألفاظ مخيلة, أو نقوش مرتبة, وإذا تلفظ كان كلاماً مسموعاً

We do not conceive the speech which subsists in the mind of the one who has memorised it except as it being the forms of letters which are inscribed in his imagination, so that if he turns to them, it becomes a speech composed of imagined words, or marks that are arranged, and when he verbalises (these words) they become speech that is heard.

(والتكوين)

"And *At-Takween*."

وهو المعنى الذي يعبر عنه بالفعل والخلق والتخليق والإيجاد والإحداث والإختراع ونحو ذلك, ويفسر بإخراج المعدوم من العدم إلى الوجود

It is the meaning expressed by (words) such as doing, creating, producing, bringing into existence, originating, inventing, etc. It is explained as being the act of bringing something out from the state of non-existence into the state of existence.

(صفة الله تعالى)

"It is an Attribute of Allaah Ta`aalaa."

لإطباق العقل والنقل على أنه خالق للعالَم ومكوّن له, وامتناع إطلاق اسم المشتق على الشيء من غير أن يكون مأخذ الإشتقاق وصفاً له قائماً به

Because both logic and Narration are in agreement that Allaah Ta`aalaa is the Creator of the world and the One Who brought it into being, and because it is impossible to apply a derivative term to a thing without the source of the derivative being a description for it which subsists with it.

(أزلية)

"It is Eternal."

لوجوه:

For different reasons:

الأول أنه يمتنع قيام الحوادث بذاته تعالى لما مر

The first reason being that it is impossible for originated matters to subsist with the *Dhaat* of Allaah Ta`aalaa, as has been explained.

الثاني أنه وصف ذاته في كلامه الأزلي بأنه الخالق, فلو لم يكن في الأزل خالقاً لزم الكذب أو العدول إلى المجاز, أي الخالق فيما يستقبل, أو القادر على الخلق من غير تعذر من الحقيقة, على أنه لو جاز إطلاق الخالق عليه بمعنى القادر على الخلق لجاز إطلاق كل ما يقدر هو عليه من الأعراض

The second is that Allaah Ta`aalaa has, in His Eternal Speech described Himself as being Al-Khaaliq (The Creator). Thus, if He had not been the Creator since all eternity, then that would necessitate falsehood or resorting to *majaaz* (metaphor), i.e. The Creator of that which is to come, or The One Who has the power to create without difficulty. The reality is that were it permissible to apply the term Al-Khaaliq to Allaah Ta`aalaa in the meaning of "The One Who has the power to create," that would have permitted to apply to Allaah Ta`aalaa all of the terms having to do with *a`raadh*.

الثالث أنه لو كان حادثاً فإما بتكوين آخر فيلزم التسلسل وهو محال, ويلزم منه استحالة تكون العالم مع أنه مشاهد, وإما بدونه فيستغني الحادث عن المحدث والإحداث, وفيه تعطيل الصانع

The third reason is that were He to be originated, then either it would be through the *Takween* of another, which would necessitate the endless chain which is impossible, and it would necessitate therefrom the impossibility of the world being created, despite the fact that it (the world) is witnessed. Or, it (the origination) would be without (the *Takween* of another), and thus that which originated would be independent of an originator and of origination, and that constitutes denial of the Creator.

والرابع أنه لو حدث لحدث, إما في ذاته فيصير محلاً للحوادث, أو في غيره كما ذهب إليه أبو الهذيل من أن تكوين كل جسم قائم به فيكون كل جسم خالقاً, أو مكوناً لنفسه, ولا خفاء في استحالته

The fourth reason is that were He to have been originated, then He would have been originated either in His *Dhaat* and therefore would be a *mahall* (locus) for originated matters, or (He would have been originated) in other than (His *Dhaat*) as was the view of Abu-l Hudhail, who believed that the creating of every *jism* (body) subsists with it, so each *jism* (body) is a creator of itself or brought itself into existence, and the impossibility of this is not hidden.

ومبنى هذه الأدلة على أن التكوين صفة حقيقة كالعلم والقدرة, والمحققون من المتكلمين على أنه من الإضافات, والإعتبارات العقلية, مثل كون الصانع تعالى وتقدس قبل كل شيء, ومعه, وبعده, ومذكوراً بألسنتنا, ومعبوداً لنا, ويحيينا, ونحو ذلك

The basis of these four proofs is that *Takween* is a Real Attribute like *Al-`Ilm* and *Al-Qudrah*. The verifiers (Muhaqqiqeen) from the Mutakallimeen held the view that creating is from the *idhaafaat* (relationships) and rational expressions (*al-i`tibaaraat al-`aqliyyah*), like Allaah Ta`aalaa existing before everything, and with everything, and after everything, and mentioned by our tongues, and worshipped by us, and He gives us life, etc.

والحاصل في الأزل هو مبدأ التخليق والترزيق والإماتة والإحياء وغير ذلك, ولا دليل على كونه أي التكوين صفة أخرى سوى القدرة والإرادة, فإن القدرة وإن كانت نسبتها إلى وجود المكون وعدمه على السواء, لكن مع انضمام الإرادة يتخصص أحد الجانبين

ولما استدل القائلون بحدوث التكوين بأنه لا يتصور بدون المكون كالضرب بدون المضروب, فلو كان قديماً لزم قدم المكوّنات, وهو محال, أشار إلى الجواب بقوله:

The conclusion to be drawn from this is that from eternity He is the Beginning of the acts of producing and sustaining and of giving death and life, and there is no proof for it, i.e. *Takween*, being a different Attribute other than *Al-Qudrah* and *Al-Iraadah*, because *Al-Qudrah*, even though its relationship to the existence or non-existence of that which is brought into existence is equal, however, it is only when *Al-Iraadah* embraces one of the two sides (potentialities) that this one is specified.

Because those who believe in the origination of *Takween* use as evidence the fact that they cannot be conceived without that which has been brought into existence, like a hitter without one who is being hit, then, if it were to be eternal, it would necessitate the eternity of things that are brought into existence, which is impossible. He gestures to a response by saying:

(وهو)

"And It."

أي التكوين

Meaning, Takween.

(تكوينه تعالى للعالم وكل جزء من أجزائه, لا في الأزل بل لوقت وجوده على حسب علمه وإرادته)

"The *Takween* (creating) of the world and all of its parts by Allaah Ta`aalaa. Not since eternity, but at the time of its coming into existence, according to His *'Ilm* and *Iraadah*."

فالتكوين باق أزلاً وأبداً, والمكوَّن حادث بحدوث التعلق, كما في العلم والقدرة وغيرهما من الصفات القديمة التي لا يلزم من قدمها قدم تعلقاتها, لكون تعلقاتها حادثة, وهذا تحقيق ما يقال إن وجود العالم إن لم يتعلق بذات الله تعالى أو صفة من صفاته, لزم تعطيل الصانع واستغناء تحقق الحوادث من الموجد, وهو محال, وإن تعلق فإما أن يستلزم ذلك قدم ما يتعلق وجوده به, فيلزم قدم العالم, وهو باطل, أو لا, فليكن التكوين أيضاً مع حدوث المكوَّن المتعلق به

Creating remains from eternity to eternity, and *mukawwan* (that which is brought into being) is originated with the origination of connection (between creating and that which is created) like how it is in *Al-`Ilm* and *Al-Qurdah* and other than them from the Eternal Attributes, the eternity of which do not necessitate the eternity of the connections due to the connections being originated. This is the verification of what has been said, that the existence of the world, if it is not connected to the *Dhaat* of Allaah Ta`aalaa or an Attribute from His Attributes, that necessitates the denial of the Creator and that there is no need for verifying the fact that originated things come from One Who brought them into existence, (but these conclusions are impossible). If it is connected, then either that necessitates the eternity of that which, its existence is connected to it, which necessitates the eternity of the world, which is *baatil* (false), or not, so creating then is also eternal, even though the origination of the things which came into being is connected to it.

وما يقال من أن القول بتعلق وجود المكون بالتكوين قول بحدوثه, إذ القديم ما لا يتعلق وجوده بالغير, والحادث ما يتعلق وجوده به, ففيه نظر, لأن هذا معنى القديم والحادث بالذات على ما يقول به الفلاسفة, وأما عند المتكلمين, فالحدوث ما يكون لوجوده بداية, أي يكون مسبوقاً بالعدم, والقديم بخلافه, ومجرد تعلق وجوده بالغير لا يستلزم الحدوث بهذا المعنى, لجواز أن يكون محتاجاً إلى الغير صادراً عنه, دائماً بدوامه, كما ذهب إليه الفلاسفة فيما ادعوا قدمه من الممكنات كالهيولى مثلاً

As for what has been said, that the statement that the connection of the existence of the thing brought into existence with creating is (like) saying that it is originated because Eternal is that which, its existence is not connected to something else, and *haadith* (originated) is that which its existence is connected to something else. There is speculation regarding this, because this is the meaning of The Eternal and The Originated with the *Dhaat* as is said by the philosophers. As for the Mutakallimeen, then originated refers to those things which, their existence has a beginning, i.e. their existence was preceded by non-existence, and Eternal is contrary to that. The mere connected of its existence with something else does not necessitate origination with this meaning, due to the validity of it being muhtaaj (in need) of something else, produced from it, eternal with its eternity (i.e. the eternity of that thing), as was the view of the philosophers in their claim of the eternity of the possible things, like *hayooli* (the primary matter), for example.

نعم إذا أثبتنا صدور العالم عن الصانع بالإختيار دون الإيجاب, بدليل لا يتوقف على حدوث العالم, كان القول بتعلق وجوده بتكوين الله تعالى قولاً بحدوثه, ومن هاهنا يقال إن التنصيص على كل جزء من أجزاء العالم إشارة إلى الرد على من زعم قدم بعض الأجزاء كالهيولي, وإلا فهم إنما يقولون بقدمها بمعنى عدم المسبوقية بالعدم, لا بمعنى عدم تكوينه بالغير

Yes, when we affirm the fact that the world has come from a Creator, with choice (*ikhtiyaar*) not through necessity, with evidence that is not based on the origination of the world, then the statement that its existence is connected with the Creating of Allaah Ta`aalaa is a statement of it being originated, and from one may go on to say that it applies to every *juz'* (part) from the *ajzaa'* (parts) of the world, gesturing thereby to a refuation upon those who claim the eternity of some parts, like *al-hayooli* (the primary matter). Otherwise, then they say that those things are eternal in the meaning that, they were not preceded by non-existence, not in the meaning that they were not created by another.

والحاصل أنا لا نسلم أنه لا يتصور التكوين بدون وجود المكون, وأن وزانه معه كوزان الضرب من المضروب, فإن الضرب صفة إضافية لا يتصور بدون المضافين, أعني الضارب والمضروب, والتكوين صفة حقيقية هي مبدأ الإضافة التي هي إخراج المعدوم من العدم إلى الوجود, لا عينها, حتى لو كانت عينها على ما وقع في عبارة المشايخ, لكان القول بتحقيقها بدون المكون مكابرة وإنكاراً للضروري, فلا يندفع بما يقال من أن الضرب عرض مستحيل البقاء, فلا بد لتعلقه

بالمفعول, ووصول الألم إليه من وجود المفعول معه, إذا لو تأخر لانعدم, وهو بخلاف فعل الباري فإنه أزلي واجب الدوام, يبقى إلى وقت وجود المفعول

The conclusion is that we do not submit that creating is inconceiveable without the existence of things that are created, and that creating has the same relation to the thing created as the act of hitting has to the person or thing being hit, because hitting is a quality which shows idhaafah (relationship) and which is inconceiveable without the two things related, i.e. the hitter and the one being hit. *Takween* is a Real Attribute which is the Beginning of *idhaafah*, which is the taking of things from the state of non-existence into the state of existence, but not the relationship itself. So much so that if it were the relationship itself as has been mentioned in the texts of some of the Mashaayikh, then the statement which verifies this relationship as being true without there being a thing which was brought into existence, it would be a contention and a denial of that which is necessary. Thus, it is not to be rejected by that which has been said that, the act of hitting is an *`ardh* which is impossible to be perpetual and thus it has to be connected to a *maf`ool* (object), and the reaching of pain to him due to the existence of the maf`ool with him, because if it were delayed it would be non-existent, and that is contrary to the Actions of Allaah Ta`aalaa, because the Actions of Allaah Ta`aalaa are Eternal, Necessarily Perpetual, lasting until the coming into existence of the *maf`ool* (object).

(وهو غير المكون عندنا)

"And it (i.e. the Attribute of Creating) is not *mukawwan* (created), according to us."

لأن الفعل يغاير المفعول بالضرورة, كالضرب مع المضروب, والأكل مع المأكول, ولأنه لو كان نفس المكون لزم أن يكون المكون مكوناً مخلوقاً بنفسه, ضرورة أنه مكون بالتكوين الذي هو عينه, فيكون قديماً مستغنياً عن الصانع, وهو محال, وأن لا يكون للخالق تعلق بالعالم سوى أنه أقدم منه, وقادر عليه من غير صنع وتأثير فيه, ضرورة تكونه بنفسه, وهذا لا يوجب كونه خالقاً والعالم مخلوقاً له, فلا يصح القول بأنه خالق العالم وصانعه, هذا خلق, وأن لا يكون الله تعالى مكوناً وإما للأشياء, ضرورة أنه لا معنى للمكون إلا من قام به التكوين, والتكوين إذا كان عين المكون لا يكون قائماً بذات الله تعالى, وأن يصح القول بأن خالق سواد هذا الحجر أسود, وهذا الحجر خالق السواد, إذ لا معنى للخالق والأسود إلا من قام به الخلق والسواد, وهما واحد, فمحلهما واحد, وهذا كله تنبيه على كون الحكم بتغاير الفعل والمفعول ضرورياً

Because the action is distinctly different from the object, by necessity, like the act of hitting with the one that is hit, and the act of eating with the thing that is eaten. And because, had it been the very *mukawwan* (created thing) itself, it would have necessitated that the mukawwin (that which creates) is itself a thing that is created, of necessity due to being created with the creating which it iself is, so it would be eternal, having no need of The Creator, and that is impossible.

Secondly, it would necessitate the Creator having no connection with the world other than that He is more Eternal than it, and All-Powerful over it without creating and having an effect in it, due to it coming about through itself, and this does not necessitate Him being a Creator and the world being created by Him, and thus it would have been invalid to say that He is the Creator of the world and its Maker, and this (such a statement) is false. It would also have necessitated the invalidity of saying that Allaah Ta`aalaa is the Mukawwin (One Who brought into existence) of things, of necessity because there is no meaning of Mukawwin other than the one in Whom *Takween* (creating) subsists. And *Takween* (creating), if it is the thing created itself, then it would not subsist with the *Dhaat* of Allaah Ta`aalaa.

It would also have necessitated the validity of such a statement as, the creator of the blackness of this stone is black, and that the stone is the creator of blackness, because there is no meaning of Creator and blackness except the One in Whom creating subsists and the thing in which blackness subsists. They are one and the same and their *mahall* (locus) is one and the same. All of this is to draw attention to the fact that it is necessary to make a distinction between the action and the thing *maf`ool* (object), of necessity.

لكنه ينبغي للعاقل أن يتأمل في أمثال هذه المباحث , ولا ينسب إلى الراسخين من علماء الأصول ما يكون استحالته بديهية ظاهرة على من له أدنى تمييز , بل يطلب لكلامهم محملاً صحيحاً يصلح محلاً لنزاع العلماء, واختلاف العقلاء, فإن من قال التكوين عين المكون أراد أن الفاعل إذا فعل شيئاً فليس هاهنا إلا الفاعل والمفعول

However, it is necessary for the person with intellect to ponder over the likes of these discussions, and to not attribute to those grounded in knowledge from the *raasikheen* of the `Ulamaa of *Usool* that which is clearly impossible which is clear to the one who the lowest amount of *tamzeez* (distinguishing). Rather, a valid interpretation is sought for their speech which is fit to be a locus for the disagreements of the `Ulamaa and the disagreements of the thinkers, for the one who says that *Takween* is the same thing as the *mukawwan* intends thereby that when a doer does something, then there is not, here, except the doer (*faa`il*) and that which is done (*maf`ool*).

وأما المعنى الذي يعبر عنه بالتكوين والإيجاد ونحو ذلك, فهو أمر إعتباري يحصل في العقل من نسبة الفاعل إلى المفعول, وليس أمراً محققاً مغايراً للمفعول في الخارج, ولم يرد أن مفهوم التكوين هو بعينه مفهوم المكون ليلزم المحالات, وهذا كما يقال إن الوجود عين الماهية في الخارج, بمعنى أنه ليس في الخارج للماهية تحقق, ولعارضها المسمى بالوجود تحقق آخر, حتى يجتمعان إجتماع القابل والمقبول, كالجسم والسواد, بل الماهية إذا كانت فتكونها هو وجودها, لكنهما متغايران في العقل, بمعنى أن للعقل أن يلاحظ الماهية دون الوجود, وبالعكس, فلا يتم إبطال هذا الرأي إلا بإثبات أن تكوُّن الأشياء وصدورها عن الباري تعالى يتوقف على صلة حقيقية قائمة بالذات, مغايرة للقدرة والإرادة.

As for the meaning indicated to by terms such as *At-Takween*, *Al-Eejaad* (bringing into existence), etc., then it is a considered matter, acquired in the intellect from the connection of the doer to the object, and it is not a matter that is *muqaqqaq* (verified) as being distinctly different to the object externally. His intended meaning is not that what is understood from *At-Takween* is itself what is understood from *mukawwan* (that which is brought into existence), for that would necessitate impossibilities. This is how it is said that, *al-wujood* (that which exists) is the very *maahiyah* externally, meaning that externally (on the outside), *maahiyah* has no *tahaqquq* (verification as having a *haqeeqat*). Its opposite, termed *al-wujood*, has a different *tahaqquq* (verification), until they join together with the joining together of the accepter and the accepted, like the *jism* (body) and *sawaad* (blackness). Rather, when *maahiyat* exists, then its coming into existence (*takawwun*) is its *wujood* (existence), but they are distinctly different in the intellect, meaning that the intellect perceives the *maahiyah*, not the *wujood* (existence), and vice-versa. Thus, the nullification of this opinion cannot be complete except with affirming that the *takawwun* (coming into being) of things and their being produced by Allaah Ta`aalaa is hinged upon a real connected which subsists with the *Dhaat*, which is distinctly different from *Al-Qudrah* and *Al-Iraadah*.

والتحقيق أن تعلق القدرة على وفق الإرادة بوجود المقدور لوقت وجوده, إذا نسب إلى القدرة يسمى إيجاداً له, وإذا نسب إلى القادر يسمى الخلق والتكوين ونحو ذلك, فحقيقته كون الذات بحيث تعلقت قدرته بوجود المقدور لوقته, ثم يتحقق بحسب خصوصيات المقدورات خصوصيات الأفعال, كالترزيق والتصوير الإحياء والإماتة وغير ذلك إلى ما لا يكاد يتناهى, وأما كون كل من ذلك صفة حقيقية أزلية, فمما تفرد به بعض علماء ما وراء النهر, وفيه تكثير للقدماء

جداً, وإن لم تكن مغايرة, والأقرب ما ذهب إليه المحققون منهم, وهو أن مرجع الكل إلى التكوين, فإنه وإن تعلق بالحياة يسمى إحياء, وبالموت إماتة, وبالصورة تصويراً, وبالرزق ترزيقاً, إلى غير ذلك, فالكل تكوين, وإنما الخصوص بخصوصية التعلقات

The verification of this is the fact that the connection of *Al-Qudrah* in conformity with *Al-Iraadah* is with the existence of the thing which *Al-Qudrah* is connected to at the time of its (this thing) coming into existence. When it is connected to *Al-Qudrah*, it is termed "*Eejaad*" of it, and when it is connected to *Al-Qaadir* is it termed *Al-Khalq*, *At-Takween*, etc. So, its haqeeqat is that the *Dhaat* is such that, His *Qudrah* is connected with the existence of the thing which has come into contact with it at that time, then it is verified according to the specialities of the things which have come into contact with It like the specialities of the actions, like *At-Tarzeeq* (sustaining), *At-Tasweer* (forming), *Al-Ihyaa* (bringing to life), *Al-Imaatah* (causing to die), etc., infinitely.

As for each of those things being an Eternal Attribute, then that is from the *tafarrudaat* (obscure views) of some of the 'Ulamaa of Maa Waraa an-Nahr, and it is a view that very much implies the multiplicity of eternal beings, even if there is no distinct difference. The closest is that which the Muhaqqiqoon (verifiers) adopted, which is that all of it returns to *At-Takween*, becaues It (*At-Takween*), if it is connected to life, it is termed *Al-Ihyaa* (giving life), and if it is connected to death, it is termed *Al-Imaatah* (giving death). If it is connected to a form, it is called *At-Tasweer* (forming). If it is connected to *rizq*, it is called *At-Tarzeeq* (sustaining), etc. So all of it falls under *At-Takween*, but the *khusoos* (specifics) come about with the specifics of the connections.

الإرادة

Al-Iraadah (The Intending):

(والإرادة صفة الله تعالى أزلية قائمة بذاته)

"*Al-Iraadah* is an Eternal Attribute of Allaah Ta`aalaa that subsists with His *Dhaat*."

كرر ذلك تأكيداً وتحقيقاً لإثبات صفة قديمة لله تعالى, تقتضي تخصيص المكونات بوجه دون وجه, وفي وقت دون وقت, لا كما زعمت الفلاسفة من أنه تعالى موجب بالذات, لا فاعل

بالإرادة والإختيار, والنجارية من أنه مريد بذاته لا بصفته, وبعض المعتزلة من أنه مريد بإرادة حادثة لا في محل, والكرامية من أن إرادته حادثة في ذاته, والدليل على ما ذكرنا الآيات الناطقة بإثبات صفة الإرادة والمشيئة لله تعالى, مع القطع بلزوم قيام صفة الشيء به, وامتناع قيام الحوادث بذاته تعالى, وأيضاً نظام العالم ووجوده على الوجه الأوفق الأصلح, دليل على كون صانعه قادراً مختاراً, وكذا حدوثه, إذ لو كان صانعه موجباً بالذات لزم قدمه, ضرورة امتناع تخلف المعلول عن علته الموجبة

He repeated that for the sake of emphasis, and as a verification for the affirmation of the Eternal Attribute to Allah Ta`aalaa, because it necessitates the specification of some of the *mukawwanaat* (those things which were brought into being) with one facet instead of another, and in some times instead of other times, unlike what is claimed by the philosophers that Allaah Ta`aalaa necessitates with The *Dhaat*, and does not do through *Al-Iraadah* and *Al-Ikthiyaar* (Choice). The Najjaariyyah claimed that He intends by His *Dhaat*, not by His *Sifah* (Attribute). Some of the Mu`tazilah claimed that He intends with an *Iraadah* that is originated and which is not in a locus. The Karaamiyyah claimed that His *Iraadah* is originated in His *Dhaat*. The proof for what we mentioned are the Aayaat that speak about the affirmation of the Attribute of *Al-Iraadah* and *Al-Mashee'ah* for Allaah Ta`aalaa, with certitude of the subsistence of the Attribute of a thing with Him, and that it is impossible for originated matters to subsist with the *Dhaat* of Allaah Ta`aalaa. Also, the system of the world and its existence is in the best and most appropriate way, and that is proof that its Maker is All-Powerful, Choosing, and also that it (the world) is originated, because if its Maker were to be necessitating (things) with The *Dhaat* then what would have followed therefrom is that the world is eternal (whilst it is not), of necessity because it is impossible for the effect to lag behind the necessitating cause.

رؤية الله تعالى

Seeing Allaah Ta`aalaa:

(ورؤية الله تعالى)

"And seeing Allaah Ta`aalaa."

بمعنى الإنكشاف التام بالبصر, وهو معنى إدراك الشيء كما هو بحاسة البصر, وذلك أنا إذا نظرنا إلى البدر ثم غمضنا العين, فلا خفاء في أنه وإن كان منكشفاً لدينا في الحالين, لكن انكشافه حال النظر إليه أتم وأكمل, ولنا بالنسبة إليه حينئذ حالة مخصوصة هي المسماة بالرؤية

Meaning, with a complete unveiling (*inkishaaf*) through the faculty of sight (*basar*), and that means the perception of a thing, the way that it is, with the faculty of sight, and that is because if we look at the moon, and then we close our eyes, then it is not hidden that the moon remains unveiled in both cases (with the eyes open or closed); however, its being unveiled (not hidden) in the state of looking at it (with the eyes open) is more complete and more perfect, and at that time we, in connection to it, have a specific state which is termed "*ar-Ru'yah*" (vision).

(جائزة في العقل)

"Is logically possible."

بمعنى أن العقل إذا خلي ونفسه لم يحكم بامتناع رؤيته ما لم يقم له برهان على ذلك, مع أن الأصل عدمه, وهذا القدر ضروري, فمن ادعى الإمتناع فعليه البيان

Meaning that the intellect or logic, when acting by itself, does not judge that the Vision (of Allaah Ta`aalaa) is impossible so long as no proof against that is brought, despite the fact that the default is the absence (of Seeing Allaah Ta`aalaa), and this ruling is necessary, so the one who claims impossibility must bring forth his evidence for that claim.

وقد استدل أهل الحق على إمكان الرؤية بوجهين: عقلي وسمعي

The Ahl-ul-Haqq (People of Reality) inferred the possibility of Seeing Allaah Ta`aalaa in two ways: logically (`*aqliyy*) and through what has been heard (*sam`iyy*, i.e. that which has been heard from Rasoolullaah صلى الله عليه وسلم).

تقرير الأول: أنا قاطعون برؤية الأعيان والأعراض, ضرورة أنا نفرق بالبصر بين جسم وجسم, وعرض وعرض, ولا بد للحكم المشترك من علة مشتركة, وهي إما الوجود, أو الحدوث, أو الإمكان, إذا لا رابع يشترك بينهما, والحدوث عبارة عن الوجود بعد العدم, والإمكان عبارة عن عدم ضرورة الوجود والعدم, ولا مدخل للعدم في العلية, فتعين الوجود, وهو مشترك بين الصانع وغيره, فيصح أن يرى سبحانه من حيث تحقق علة الصحة وهي الوجود, ويتوقف امتناعها على

ثبوت كون شيء من خواص الممكن شرطاً, أو من خواص الواجب مانعاً, وكذا يصح أن ترى سائر الموجودات من الأصوات والطعوم والروائح وغير ذلك, وإنما لا ترى بناء على أن الله تعالى لم يخلق في العبد رؤيتها بطريق جري العادة لا بناء على امتناع رؤيتها

The establishment of the first proof is that we (Ahlus Sunnah wal-Jamaa`ah) have absolute certitude regarding the seeing of substances and *a`raadh*, of necessity because we differentiate, with the faculty of sight, between one body (*jism*) and another, and between one *`aradh* and another, and the common designation inevitably requires a common cause, that cause being either existence, or origination, or possibility, because there is no fourth alternative which is common (between *a`yaan* and *a`raadh*).

Hudooth (origination) is a term used to refer to coming into existence after a state of non-eixstence. *Imkaan* (possibility) is a term used to refer to the absence of the necessity of existence and non-existence. But, non-existence cannot enter into causality, and thus *wujood* (existence) is established, and this (existence) is common between The Creator and other than Him. Thus, it is valid that He - *Sub-haanahu wa Ta`aalaa* - be seen from the aspect of the verification of the cause of validity (of seeing), which is *al-wujood* (existence). The impossibility of a thing being seen is hinged on the affirmation of a thing being from the special kinds of possibilities, as a condition, or a preventor from the special kinds of necessity. Similarly, it is valid (possible) to see the rest of the things which exist such as sounds, tastes, smells, etc. The reason those things are not seen is based on the fact that Allaah Ta`aalaa has not created in the slave the vision of those things, generally. Not seeing those things is not based on them being impossible to be seen.

وحين اعترض بأن الصحة عدمية فلا تستدعي علة, ولو سلم فالواحد النوعي قد يعلل بالمختلفات كالحرارة بالشمس والنار, فلا يستدعي علة مشتركة, ولو سلم فالعدمي يصلح علة للعدمي, ولو سلم فلا نسلم اشتراك الوجود, بل وجود كل شيء عينه, أجيب بأن المراد بالعلة متعلق الرؤية, والقابل لها, ولا خفاء في لزوم كونه وجودياً, ثم لا يجوز أن يكون خصوصية الجسم أو العرض, لأنا أول ما نرى شبحاً من بعيد إنما ندرك منه هوية مّا, دون خصوصية جوهريته أو عرضيته أو إنسانيته أو فرسيته, ونحو ذلك, وبعد رؤيته برؤية واحدة متعلقة بهويته قد نقدر على تفصيله إلى ما فيه من الجواهر والأعراض, وقد لا نقدر, فمتعلق الرؤية هو كون الشيء له هوية ما, وهو المعنى بالوجود, اشتراكه ضروري, وفيه نظر, لجواز أن يكون متعلق الرؤية هو الجسمية وما يتبعها من الأعراض من غير اعتبار خصوصيته

An objection may be raised that the invalidity is non-existent, so it does not call for a cause (`illat`). And even if that were to be submitted, then one kind of thing may be caused by different things like heat is caused by the sun and by fire, so it does not call for a common cause. And even if it were to be submitted, then the non-existent is suitable as an *`illat* (cause) for the non-existent. And even if that were to be submitted, then we do not admit to the (view of) existence being a common cause, but rather the existence of each thing in itself.

To all this it is answered that the intended meaning of *`illat* (cause) is that which is connected to the vision and the one receiving the vision. It is not hidden, the necessity of being existent (*wujoodiyy*). Then, it is not valid for it to be a thing that is specific to the body or an *`aradh*, because when we see a shape from afar, we comprehend from it a certain *huwiyyah* (individuality or personality) rather than a specific substance of *`aradh*, or humanity, or being a horse, etc. After seeing it with one vision connected to its *huwiyyah* (itness), we may be able to distinguish what substances and *a`raadh* are in it, or we might not be able to. So, the connection of vision is the thing having a certain *huwiyyah* (itness), and that is the meaning of existence. Its being common is necessary, and there is speculation in this, because it is possible for the connection of the vision to be the fact that it has a body and what follows that such as *a`raadh*, without taking into consideration its particular characteristic.

وتقرير الثاني: أن موسى عليه السلام قد سأل الرؤية بقوله:

رَبِّ أَرِنِيْ أَنْظُرْ إِلَيْكَ

The establishment of the second proof is that Nabi Moosaa عليه السلام asked Allaah Ta`aalaa for a vision, saying:

{"O my Rabb, let me look unto You."}

فلو لم تكن الرؤية ممكنة لكان طلبها جهلاً بما يجوز في ذات الله تعالى وما لا يجوز, أوسفها وعبثاً وطلباً للمحال, والأنبياء منزهون عن ذلك, وأن الله تعالى قد علق الرؤية باستقرار الجبل, وهو أمر ممكن في نفسه, والمعلق بالممكن ممكن, لأن معناه الإخبار بثبوت المعلق عند ثبوت المعلق به, والمحال لا يثبت على شيء من التقادير الممكنة

وقد اعترض عليه بوجوه, أقواها: أن سؤال موسى عليه السلام كان لأجل قومه, حيث قالوا لن نؤمن لك حتى نرى الله جهرة, فسأل ليعلموا امتناعها كما علمه هو, وبأنا لا نسلم أن المعلق عليه ممكن, بل هو استقرار الجبل حال تحركه, وهو محال

If seeing Allaah Ta`aalaa were not possible, then such a request would have been something of ignorance of that which is permissible pertaining to the *Dhaat* of Allaah Ta`aalaa and that which is not permissible, or it would have been some sort of foolishness, or futility, or a request for that which is impossible. The Abmiyaa عليهم السلام are far removed from all of that. Allaah Ta`aalaa made seeing Him connected to the mountain remaining fixed in place, and that is a matter which is possible in itself, and that which is connected to a thing which is possible is itself possible, because its meaning is that of giving information regarding the affirmation of the connected thing when affirming the thing to which it is connected, and that which is impossible is not affirmed upon anything of those things the determination of which is possible.

Some objections have been raised to this. The strongest of these objections is that, Nabi Moosaa عليه السلام had asked to see Allaah Ta`aalaa for the sake of his people, because they had said, "We will not believe in you until we openly see Allaah." Thus, he asked Allaah Ta`aalaa so that they (those who asked) could know that it is impossible just as he knew that it is impossible, and because we do not admit to the thing to which it was connected being possible, because that which is was connected to was for the mountain to remain fixed in place whilst moving, which is possible.

وأجيب بأن كلاً من ذلك خلاف الظاهر, ولا ضرورة في ارتكابه, على أن القوم إن كانوا مؤمنين كفاهم قول موسى عليه السلام أن الرؤية ممتنعة, وإن كانوا كفاراً لم يصدقوه في حكم الله تعالى بالإمتناع, وأياً ما كان يكون السؤال عبثاً, والإستقرار حال التحرك أيضاً ممكن بأن يقع السكون بدل الحركة, وإنما المحال إجتماع الحركة والسكون

An answer may be given that each of these two opinions is contrary to the literal (of the Aayah) and there was no necessity for Nabi Moosaa عليه السلام (to ask), because if the people were Mu'mineen, then the statement of Nabi Moosaa عليه السلام would have sufficed them, i.e. that to see Allaah Ta`aalaa (in this Dunyaa) is impossible. If they were Kuffaar, they would still not have believed the Judgement of Allaah Ta`aalaa of it not being possible. Either way, the request would have been futile.

Remaining fixed in place whilst moving is also possible if rest occurs in place of movement, because what is impossible is for it to be both moving and still at one and the same time.

(واجبة النقل, ورد الدليل السمعي بإيجاب رؤية المؤمنين الله تعالى في دار الآخرة)

"Necessary, by *Naql*. The *sam`iyy* evidence has affirmed that the Mu'mineen will see Allaah Ta`aalaa in the abode of the Aakhirah."

أما الكتاب, فقوله تعالى:

وُجُوهٌ يَوْمَئِذٍ نَاضِرَةٌ إِلَى رَبِّهَا نَاظِرَةٌ

As for the *Aayah*, then it is:

{*"Some faces on that day will be radiant, looking at their Rabb."*}

أما السنة, فقوله عليه السلام:

إِنَّكُمْ سَتَرَوْنَ رَبَّكُمْ كَمَا تَرَوْنَ هَذَا الْقَمَرَ لَيْلَةَ الْبَدْرِ

As for the Hadeeth, then it is:

"You will see your Rabb like you see the moon on the night of the full moon."

وهو مشهور, رواه أحمد وعشرون من أكابر الصحابة رضي الله عنهم

This Hadeeth is *mash-hoor*. It has been narrated by 21 of the senior Sahaabah رضي الله عنهم.

وأما الإجماع, فهو أن الأمة كانوا مجمعين على وقوع الرؤية في الآخرة, وأن الآيات الواردة في ذلك محمولة على ظواهرها, ثم ظهرت مقالة المخالفين وشاعت شبههم وتأويلاتهم

As for *ijmaa`*, then it is the fact that all the years the Ummah has had consensus on the fact that the Muslims will see Allaah Ta`aalaa in the Aakhirah, and that the *Aayaat* that have come regarding that are to be carried upon their literal meaning.

Thereafter, the statement of the opponents appeared and became widespread, along with their *ta'weelaat* (interpretations).

وأقوى شبههم من العقليات: أن الؤية مشروطة بكون المرئي في مكان وجهة ومقابلة من الرائي, وثبوت مسافة بينهما, بحيث لا يكون في غاية القرب, ولا في غاية البعد, واتصال من الباصرة بالمرئي, وكل ذلك محال في حق الله تعالى

والجواب منع هذا الإشتراط, وإليه أشار بقوله:

Their strongest *`aqli* evidence was that to see something is stipulated by the thing which is seen being in a place and a direction and being opposite to the one who is seeing, and with there being a distance between (the one seeing and the one being seen), so that the one who is seen is neither very near nor very far, and the vision of the one who sees must connect with the one who is seen, and all of that is impossible when it comes to Allaah Ta`aalaa.

The response to this is the prevention of this stipulation, and that has been pointed out to by him saying:

فيرى لا في مكان ولا على جهة من مقابلة, ولا اتصال شعاع, ولا ثبوت مسافة بين الرائي وبين) (الله تعالى

"So Allaah Ta`aalaa will be seen, not in a place, or in an opposite direction, or with the conjunction of the rays of light, or with a distance between the one seeingi and between Allaah Ta`aalaa."

وقياس الغائب على الشاهد فاسد, وقد يستدل على عدم الإشتراط برؤية الله تعالى إياناً, وفيه نظر, لأن الكلام في الرؤية بحاسة البصر

To draw analogy (*qiyaas*) for the Unseen using that which is seen is invalid. The fact that it is not stipulated that Allaah Ta`aalaa see us (with the sense of sight) is sometimes used as evidence, but there is speculation regarding it, because the discussion is regarding Seeing Allaah Ta`aalaa with the faculty of sight.

فإن قيل: لو كان جائز الرؤية والحاسة سليمة وسائر الشرائط موجودة لوجب أن يرى, وإلا لجاز أن يكون بحضرتنا جبال شاهقة لا نراها, وأنها سفسطة, قلنا: ممنوع, فإن الرؤية عندنا بخلق الله تعالى, فلا تجب عند اجتماع الشرائط

If it is said: if the Vision is possible, and the faculty (of sight) is sound, and all of the stipulations are present and found, then it is necessary (that it is possible) that Allaah Ta`aalaa be seen; otherwise, it would be possible for there to be, in our presence, lofty mountains which we do not see, but this is sophistry. We say: It is impossible, because the Vision, according to us, comes about through Allaah Ta`aalaa creating it, so it does not become necessary when the stipulations are met.

مطلب السمعيات

A Discussion on *Sam`iyyaat*

ومن السمعيات قوله تعالى:

لَا تُدْرِكُهُ الْأَبْصَارُ وَهُوَ يُدْرِكُ الْأَبْصَارَ

From the *sam`iyyaat* (evidences based on what we have heard from Rasoolullaah صلى الله عليه وسلم) is the *Aayah*:

{*"Eyes do not perceive Him, although He perceives the eyes."*}

والواجب بعد تسليم كون الأبصار للإستغراق, وإفادته عموم السلب لا سلب العموم, وكون الإدراك هو الرؤية مطلقاً لا الرؤية على وجه الإحاطة بجوانب المرئي, أن لا دلالة فيه على عموم الأوقات والأحوال, وقد يستدل بالآية على جواز الرؤية إذ لو امتنعت لما حصل التمدح بنفيها, كالمعدوم لا يمدح بعدم رؤيته لامتناعها, وأما التمدح في أنه تمكن رؤيته, ولا يرى للتمنع والتعزز بحجاب الكبرياء, وإن جعلنا الإدراك عبارة عن الرؤية على وجه الإحاطة بالجوانب والحدود, فدلالة الآية على جواز الرؤية, بل تحققها أظهر, لأن المعنى أن الله تعالى مع كونه مرئياً لا يدرك بالأبصار لتعاليه عن التناهي والإتصاف بالحدود والجوانب

What is necessary, after admitting that the eyes (mentioned in the *Aayah*) is for *istighraaq* (inclusivity), and that the purport (of the *Aayah*) is a general negation and not a negation of perceiving in general, and that perception here is absolute vision, not vision by way of complete encompassing of all sides of the one seen. Our answer is that there is no evidence therein regarding perception that this is a general statement covering all times and all conditions.

It may be deduced from the *Aayah* the permissibility of seeing (Allaah Ta`aalaa), for had it been impossible, then there would have been no reason for commending the negation of it, just as the non-existent being is nto commended for its non-vision because it (seeing it) is impossible. But as for commendation due to it being possible to be seen, but not seen due to the preventative factors of the veils of Majesty.

If we say that perception refers to seeing by way of complete encompassing all sides and boundaries (of the thing seen), then the *Aayah* would be pointing out to the permissible of the Vision; rather, it is verified even more clearly as real, because the meaning is that Allaah Ta`aalaa, despite being able to be seen, is not perceived by the eyes due to Him being far exalted above being limited and described by boundaries and sides.

ومنها أن الآيات الواردة في سؤال الرؤية مقرونة بالإستعظام والإستنكار, والجواب أن ذلك لتعنتهم وعنادهم في طلبها, لا لامتناعها, وإلا لمنعهم موسى عليه السلا عن ذلك, كما فعل حين سألوا أن يجعل لهم آلهة فقال:

Another objection raised is the fact that the *Aayaat* mentioning the request to see Allaah Ta`aalaa are connected to glorifying Allaah Ta`aalaa and rebuking (the people of Nabi Moosaa عليه السلام, who had requested it). The response to this is: That was on account of their obstinacy and rebellious nature which drove them to ask, not because it is not possible to see Allaah Ta`aalaa. Otherwise, Nabi Moosaa عليه السلام would have stopped them from that (i.e. asking), like how he did when they asked that he make for them idols. He said to them:

بَلْ أَنتُمْ قَوْمٌ تَجْهَلُونَ

{*"You are an ignorant nation."*}

وهذا مشعر بإمكان الرؤية في الدنيا, ولهذا اختلف الصحابة رضي الله عنهم في أن النبي صلى الله عليه وسلم هل رأى ربه ليلة المعراج أم لا؟ والإختلاف في الوقوع دليل الإمكان, وأما الرؤية

في المنام فقد حكيت عن كثير من السلف, ولا خفاء في أنها نوع مشاهدة, تكون بالقلب دون العين

This is a mark of the possibility of seeing Allaah Ta`aalaa in the Dunyaa. For this reason, the Sahaabah رضي الله عنهم had differences of opinion regarding whether or not Rasoolullaah صلى الله عليه وسلم had seen Allaah Ta`aalaa on the night of the Mi`raaj. The difference of opinion regarding its occurrence proves that it is possible. As for seeing Allaah Ta`aalaa in a dream, then this has been reported from many of the Salaf, and it is obvious that it is a kind of witnessing which is done through the heart rather than through the eyes.

مطلب خلق أفعال العباد

A Discussion on the Creation of the Actions of the Slaves:

(والله تعالى خالق لأفعال العباد كلها, من الكفر والإيمان والطاعة والعصيان)

"Allaah Ta`aalaa creates all of the actions of the slaves, such as *Kufr*, *Imaan*, obedience and disobedience."

لا كما زعمت المعتزلة أن العبد خالق لأفعاله, وقد كانت بلفظ الموجد والمخترع ونحو ذلك, وحين رأى الجبائي وأتباعه أن معنى الكل واحد, وهو المخرج من العدم إلى الوجود تجاسروا على إطلاق لفظ الخالق

إحتج أهل الحق بوجوه:

Unlike the claim of the Mu`tazilah that the slave is the creator of his actions. Instead of using the term creator (*khaaliq*), they chose to use the terms "*al-moojid*" (bringing into existence), *mukhtari`* (inventing), etc. When al-Jubbaa'i and his followers saw that the meaning of all of that is the same, which is the action of bringing something from the state of non-existence into the state of existence, they became bold in using the term "*khaaliq*" (creator).

The Ahl-ul-Haqq argued against them from different angles:

الأول: أن العبد لو كانت خالقاً لأفعاله لكان عالماً بتفاصيلها, ضرورة أن إيجاد الشيء بالقدرة والإختيار لا يكون إلا كذلك, واللازم باطل, فإن المشي من موضع إلى موضع قد يشتمل على

سكنات مختلفة, وعلى حركات بعضها أسرع وبعضها أبطأ, لا شعور للماشي بذلك, وليس هذا ذهولاً عن العلم, بل لو سئل عنها لم يعلم, وهذا في أظهر أفعاله, وأما إذا تأملت في حركات أعضائه في المشي والأخذ والبطش ونحو ذلك, وما يحتاج إليه من تحريك العضلات وتمديد الأعصاب ونحو ذلك, فالأمر أظهر.

The first is that the slave, were he to be the creator of his actions, then he would know all of the details of these actions, of necessity, because bringing something into existence with power and choice cannot be except like that, and the obligation (to know all of the details) is false, because walking from one place to another can encompass numerous periods of rest, and of movements, some of them faster and some of them slower, yet the walker does not feel this. This is not because he is diverted from the knowledge of it; rather, were he to be asked about the actions he would not know, and this is the case in the most apparent of his actions. As for the case of pondering over the movements of his limbs in walking, taking, seizing, etc., and what that requires such as moving his muscles, straining his nerves, etc., then the matter is quite clear.

الثاني: النصوص الواردة في ذلك كقوله تعالى:

وَاللَّهُ خَلَقَكُمْ وَمَا تَعْمَلُونَ

The second proof is that of the nusoos which mention the opposite of their claim, like the Aayah:

{"*And Allaah created you and that which you do.*"}

أي عملكم, على أن ما مصدرية لئلا يحتاج إلى حذف الضمير, أو معمولكم على أن ما موصولة, ويشتمل الأفعال, لأنا إذا قلنا أفعال العباد مخلوقة لله تعالى للعبد, لم نرد بالفعل المعنى المصدري الذي هو إيجاد والإيقاع, أعني ما نشاهده من الحركات والسكنات مثلاً, وللذهول عن هذه النكتة قد يتوهم أن الإستدلال بالآية موقوف على كون ما مصدرية, وكقوله تعالى:

اللَّهُ خَالِقُ كُلِّ شَيْءٍ

Meaning, your deeds. The *maa* (what) in the Aayah is *masdariyyah* so that it is not necessary to omit the dhameer (pronoun). Or (the *Aayah* means): "Your deeds," in which case the *maa* is *mawsoolah*, and it encompasses the actions, because if we say the actions of the slaves are created by Allaah Ta`aalaa for the slave, we do not mean thereby the *masdari* meaning, which is that or bringing into existence (*eejaad*) or bringing to pass (*eeqaa`*), i.e. that which we witness from the movements and rests, for example. The fine point that may be forgotten is that one might imagine that drawing an inferrence from the *Aayah* is hinged upon *maa* being *masdariyyah*. And like the *Aayah*:

{*"Allaah is the Creator of everything."*}

أي ممكن بدلالة العقل, وفعل العبد شيء ممكن, وكقوله تعالى:

أَفَمَنْ يَخْلُقُ كَمَنْ لَا يَخْلُقُ

Meaning, everything possible, by the evidence of the intellect. The action of the slave is something possible. And like the *Aayah*:

{*"Is He Who creates like the one who does not create?"*}

في مقام التمدح بالخالقية, وكونها مناطاً لاستحقاق العبادة

Regarding the commendation of the Stage of *Khaaliqiyyah* (Being the Creator), and it being that which makes One deserving of `Ibaadah*.

لا يقال: فالقائل بكون العبد خالقاً لأفعاله يكون من المشركين دون الموحدين, لأنا نقول: الإشراك هو إثبات الشريك في الألوهية, بمعنى وجوب الوجود كما للمجوس, أو بمعنى استحقاق العبادة كما لعبدة الأصنام, والمعتزلة لا يثبتون ذلك, بل لا يجعلون خالقية العبد كخالقية الله تعالى, لافتقاره إلى الأسباب والآلات التي هي بخلق الله تعالى, إلا أن مشايخ ما وراء النهر قد بالغوا في تضليلهم في هذه المسألة حتى قالوا: إن المجوس أسعد حالاً منهم, حيث لا يثبتوا إلا شريكاً واحداً, والمعتزلة أثبتوا شركاء لا تحصى

It is not to be said that, the one who says that the slave creates his actions is from the Mushrikeen rather than the Muwahhideen, because we say: *Ishraak* is to declare a partner to Allaah Ta`aalaa in *Uloohiyyah*, meaning a necessarily existent partner, like the Majoos (fire-woshippers) claim, or by the meaning of being deserving of `Ibaadah*, like the idol-worshippers claim.

The Mu`tazilah do not affirm that; rather, they do not declare the khaaliqiyyah of the slave as being like the *Khaaliqiyyah* of Allaah Ta`aalaa, because the slave requires *asbaab*, and *aalaat* (instruments), which are created by Allaah Ta`aalaa. However, the Mashaayikh of Maa Waraa an-Nahr had gone to excess in their declaring as deviated (those who held that belief) in this issue, so much so that they said: The Majoos are in a better position than the (Mu`tazilah), because the Majoos only affirm one partner (unto Allaah Ta`aalaa) whereas the Mu`tazilah affirm innumerable partners.

واحتجت المعتزلة بأنا نفرق بالضرورة بين حركة الماشي وحركة المرتعش, وأن الأولى باختياره دون الثانية, وبأنه لو كان الكل بخلق الله تعالى لبطل قاعدة التكليف, والمدح والذم والثواب والعقاب وهو ظاهر

والجواب: أن ذلك إنما يتوجه على الجبرية القائلين بنفي الكسب والإختيار له أصلاً, وأما نحن فنثبته على ما نحققه إن شاء الله تعالى

The Mu`tazilah argued that we, by necessity, differentiate between the movement of the walker and the movement of the one trembling, for the movement of the first is by choice whilst the movement of the second is not, and because, if all actions of the slaves were created by Allaah Ta`aalaa, then the principle of legal responsibility (*takleef*) would fall away, as would praise, dispraise, reward, punishment, and that is clear.

The response to this statement of theirs is that, their argument should be addressed to the Jabariyyah, those who denied that (people) the power of acquisition and choice. As for us, then we affirm it according to what we shall verify, إن شاء الله تعالى.

وقد يتمسك بأنه لو كان خالقاً لأفعال العباد لكان هو القائم والقاعد والآكل والشارب والزاني والسارق إلى غير ذلك, وهذا جهل عظيم, لأن المتصف بالشيء من قام به ذلك الشيء لا من أوجده, أو لا يرون أن الله تعالى هو الخالق للسواد والبياض, وسائر الصفات في الأجسام, ولا يتصف بذلك؟ وربما يتمسك بقوله تعالى:

Another objection raised by some is that if Allaah Ta`aalaa creates the actions of people, then that would mean (according to them) that He is the One Who does the actions of standing, sitting, eating, drinking, *zinaa*, theft, and so on, and this is extreme *jahl* (ignorance), because the one who is described with a thing is the one in whom that thing subsists, not the One Who brings it into existence. Do they not see that Allaah Ta`aalaa is the Creator of both blackness and whiteness, and the rest of the qualities of bodies, and He is not described with (those qualities)? Some of them try to use as proof the Aayah:

$$\text{فَتَبَارَكَ اللهُ أَحْسَنُ الْخَالِقِينَ}$$

{"So glory be to Allaah, the Best of Creators."}

$$\text{وَإِذْ تَخْلُقُ مِنَ الطِّينِ كَهَيْئَةِ الطَّيْرِ}$$

{"And when you created from the clay the likeness of a bird..."}

والجواب: أن الخلق هاهنا بمعنى التقدير

The response is that *khalq* here has the meaning of *taqdeer* (decreeing).

(وهي)

"And it."

أي أفعال العباد

Meaning, the actions of the slaves (of Allaah Ta`aalaa).

(كلها بإرادته ومشيئته)

"All of them are by His *Iraadah* and *Mashee'ah*."

قد سبق أنهما عندنا عبارة عن معنى واحد

It has already preceded that according to us, they have one and the same meaning.

(وحكمه)

"And His Ruling."

لا يبعد أن يكون ذلك إشارة إلى خطاب التكوين

It is not unlikely that the reference here is to the *Khitaab* (Direct Command of Allaah Ta`aalaa) in creating (i.e. saying "*Kun*" (Be) and it is (*fa yakoon*.)

(وقضيته)

"And His Decree."

أي قضائه, وهو عبارة عن الفعل مع زيادة أحكام

لا يقال: لو كان الكفر بقضاء الله تعالى لوجب الرضا به, لأن الرضا بالقضاء واجب, واللازم باطل لأن الرضا بالكفر كفر, لأنا نقول: الكفر مقتضى لا قضاء, والرضا إنما يجب بالقضاء دون المقضى

Meaning, His Decree, and that refers to the action along with the rulings.

It is not to be said: "If *Kufr* is by the *Qadhaa* (Decree) of Allaah Ta`aalaa, then that necessitates that He is pleased with it, because, being pleased with the Decree of Allaah Ta`aalaa (*Ridhaa bil-Qadhaa*) is compulsory."

The obligation (suggested here) is invalid, because being pleased with Kufr is *Kufr*, because we say: *Kufr* is something decided (muqtadhaa), not a Decree (*Qadhaa*), and *Ridhaa* is compulsory in the case of *Qadhaa*, not in the case of the thing that is decided.

(وتقديره)

"And His Pre-destining."

وهو تحديد كل مخلوق بحده الذي يوجد من حسن وقبح ونفع وضر, وما يحويه من زمان ومكان, وما يترتب عليه من ثواب وعقاب, والمقصود تعميم إرادة الله وقدرته لما مر من أن الكل بخلق الله تعالى, وهو يستدعي القدرة والإرادة لعدم الإكراه والإجبار

That is the limiting of each creature to the limit within which he exists, whether it be goodness, or badness, and that which he occupies of space and time, and that which results thereby of reward and punishment. The intended meaning is the comprehensiveness of the *Iraadah* of Allaah Ta`aalaa and the *Qudrah* of Allaah Ta`aalaa, for what which has been mentioned, that all (actions) are created by Allaah Ta`aalaa, and that calls for

Al-Qudrah and *Al-Iraadah*, due to the absence of forcing and compulsion (i.e. no one can force Allaah Ta`aalaa to do anything.)

فإن قيل: فيكون الكافر مجبوراً في كفره, والفاسق في فسقه, فلا يصح تكليفهما بالإيمان والطاعة

So if it is said: "So the Kaafir is forced to commit *Kufr* and the *faasiq* is forced to commit *fisq*, and thus it is invalid for them to be burdened with the responsibility of *Imaan* and obedience."

قلنا: إنه تعالى أراد منهما الكفر والفسق باختيارهما, فلا جبر, كما أنه تعالى علم منهما الكفر والفسق بالإختيار, ولم يلزم تكليف المحال, والمعتزلة أنكروا إرادة الله تعالى للشرور والقبائح, حتى قالوا: إنه تعالى أراد من الكافر والفاسق إيمانه وطاعته, لا كفره ومعصيته, زعماً منهم أن إرادة القبيح قبيح كخلقه وإيجاده, ونحن نمنع ذلك, بل القبيح كسب القبيح والإتصاف به, فعندهم يكون أكثر ما يقع من أفعال العباد على خلاف إرادة الله تعالى, وهذا شنيع جداً

We say: Allaah Ta`aalaa Willed for them *kufr* and *fisq* by their own choice, so there was no compulsion, just as how Allaah Ta`aalaa knew that they would commit *kufr* and *fisq* by their own choice, and thus He had not made them responsible for the impossible (because they had been given choice).

The Mu`tazilah denied the *Iraadah* of Allaah Ta`aalaa for things that are evil and bad, so much so that they said: "Allaah Ta`aalaa Intends from the *Kaafir*, *Imaan*, and from the *faasiq*, obedience, not *kufr* and disobedience." They claimed this because they said that willing badness is bad, just as is creating it and bringing it into existence.

We preclude that by saying, "Rather, badness is the acquisition of badness and being described with it." According to them, most of what occurs from the actions of the slaves are contrary to the *Iraadah* of Allaah Ta`aalaa, and this is an extremely vile belief.

حكي عن عمرو بن عبيد أنه قال: ما الزمني أحد مثل ما الزمني مجوسي كان معي في السفينة, فقلت له لم لا تسلم؟ فقال: لأن الله لم يرد إسلامي, فإذا أراد الله إسلامي أسلمت, فقلت للمجوسي: إن الله تعالى يريد إسلامك, ولكن الشياطين لا يتركونك, فقال المجوسي: فأنا أكون مع الشريك الأغلب

It is narrated from `Amr ibn `Ubayd that he said: "No one had ever silenced me as well as a Majoosi (fire-worshipper) who was once with me on a ship. I said to him: "Why do you not accept Islaam?" He said: "Because Allaah Ta`aalaa has not intended Islaam for me. When Allaah intends Islaam for me, I will accept Islaam." I said to him: "Allaah Ta`aalaa intends your Islaam (i.e. for you to become Muslim), but the Shayaateen will not leave you." So the Majoosi said: "Then I will be with the more victorious partner."

وحكي أن القاضي عبد الجبار الهمداني دخل على الصاحب بن عباد وعنده الأستاذ أبو إسحاق الإسفراييني, فلما رأى الأستاذ قال: سبحان من تنزه عن الفحشاء, قال الأستاذ على الفور: سبحان من لا يجري في ملكه إلا ما يشاء

It is narrated from Qaadhi `Abdul Jabbaar al-Hamdaani that once, he visited his friend, ibn `Abbaad, and with him with al-Ustaadh Abu Is-haaq al-Isfaraayeeni. When he saw the Ustaadh, he said: "Glory be unto Him Who is free from all wickedness." Al-Ustaadh immediately replied: "Glory be unto Him in Whose Kingdom nothing transpires except what He wills."

والمعتزلة إعتقدوا أن الأمر يستلزم الإرادة, والنهي عدم الإرادة, فجعلوا إيمان الكافر مراداً وكفره غير مراد, ونحن نعلم أن الشيء قد يكون مراداً ويؤمر به, وقد يكون مراداً وينهى عنه, لحكم ومصالح يحيط بها علم الله تعالى, أو لأنه لا يسأل عما يفعل, ألا ترى أن السيد إذا أراد أن يظهر على الحاضرين عصيان عبده يأمره بالشيء ولا يريده منه

The Mu`tazilah believed that Command (*Al-Amr*) necessitates *Iraadah*, and Prohibiting (*An-Nahi*) necessiates the absence of Iraadah. Thus, they made the Imaan of the Kaafir *muraad* (intended) and his *kufr ghair muraad* (unintended).

We know that a thing can be *muraad* (intended) and commanded, and it can be *muraad* (intended) but prohibited from due to certain wisdoms and benefits which are encompassed by the Knowledge of Allaah Ta`aalaa, or because Allaah Ta`aalaa is not questioned regarding what He does. Do you not see that the master, when he intends to demonstrate to those present the disobedience of his slave, orders him to do a certain thing but does not intend that he does it?

وقد يتمسك من الجانبين بالآيات, وباب التأويل مفتوح على الفريقين

Both sides (i.e. Ahlus Sunnah wal-Jamaa`ah as well as the Mu`tazilah) hold onto the *Aayaat* (as evidence on the subject), and the door of *ta'weel* (interpretation) is open to both groups.

أفعال العباد

The Actions of the Slaves:

(وللعابد أفعال إختيارية, يثابون بها)

"The slaves have actions which they do willfully (by their own choice), which they will be rewarded for."

إن كانت طاعة

If it is obedience.

(ويعاقبون عليها)

"And punished for."

إن كانت معصية, لا كما زعمت الجبرية من أنه لا فعل للعبد أصلاً, وأن حركاته بمنزلة حركات الجمادات, لا قدرة للعبد عليها, ولا قصد ولا اختيار, وهذا باطل, لأنا نفرق بالضرورة بين حركة البطش وحركة الإرتعاش

If it is disobedience. Unlike what is claimed by the Jabariyyah, that the slave actually has no actions at all, and that his movements are like the movements of those things that are stationary - the slave has no power over it, nor intention or choice. This is *baatil* (false), because we by necessity differentiate between the movement of seizing and the movement of trembling.

ونعلم أن الأول باختياره دون الثاني, ولأنه لو لم يكن للعبد فعل أصلاً لما صح تكليفه, ولا ترتب استحقاق الثواب والعقاب على أفعاله, ولا إسناد الأفعال التي تقتضي سابقية القصد والإختيار إليه على سبيل الحقيقة, مثل صلى وصام وكتب, بخلاف مثل طال الغلام واسودّ لونه, والنصوص القطعية تنفي ذلك, كقوله تعالى:

$$\text{جَزَاءً بِمَا كَانُوا يَعْمَلُونَ}$$

We know that the first is by his choice rather than the second, and because, if the slave (of Allaah Ta`aalaa) had no actions at all, then burdening him would not have been valid, nor the deserving of reward or punishment based on his actions, nor the attribution of actions to him which necessitate prior intention and choice by way of reality, like performing Salaah, fasting, writing, etc., unlike, for example, "The boy grew tall," and: "His colour became black." (i.e. matters that are out of the person's control altogether.)

The decisive *nusoos* (texts) negate that, like the *Aayah*:

{"*A recompense for that which they used to do.*"}

وقوله تعالى:

$$\text{فَمَنْ شَاءَ فَلْيُؤْمِنْ وَمَنْ شَاءَ فَلْيَكْفُرْ}$$

And like the *Aayah*:

{"*So whosoever wills, let him believe, and whosoever wills, let him disbelieve.*"}

إلى غير ذلك

And other such (*Aayaat*).

فإن قيل: بعد تعميم علم الله تعالى وإرادته, الجبر لازم قطعاً, لأنهما إما أن يتعلقا بوجود الفعل فيجب أو بعدمه فيمتنع, ولا اختيار مع الوجوب والإمتناع

قلنا: الله تعالى يعلم, ويريد أن العبد يفعله أو يتركه باختياره, فلا إشكال

If it is said: After declaring the all-inclusiveness of the *`Ilm* and *Iraadah* of Allaah Ta`aalaa, coercion (*jabr*) is absolutely necessary, because either they are connected to bringing the actions into existence, in which case it is binding, or not bringing them into existence, in which case (doing those actions) is impossible, and the person has no choice in either case, be it binding (his performance of the action being binding) or impossibility.

We say: Allaah Ta`aalaa knows, and He intends that the slave does or leaves off using his own choice, so there is no difficulty (in understanding this).

فإن قيل: فيكون فعله الإختياري واجباً أو ممتنعاً, وهذا ينافي الإختيار

قلنا: ممنوع, فإن الوجوب بالإختيار محقق للإختيار لا مناف له, وأيضاً منقوض بأفعال الباري جل ذكره, لأن علمه وإرادته متعلقان بأفعاله, فيلزم أن يكون فعله واجباً عليه

If it is said: Then, his willfully done action must either be binding (*waajib*) or impossible (*mumtani`*), and this negates choice.

We say: That is not possible, because necessary by choice verifies choice as having a reality - it does not negate it. Also, it is contradicted by the Actions of Allaah - *Jalla Dhikruhu* - because His `*Ilm* and His *Iraadah* are connected to His Actions, and that would necessitate His Action being binding upon Him (whereas this is not the case, as nothing is binding upon Allaah Ta`aalaa).

فإن قيل: لا معنى لكون العبد فاعلاً بالإختيار إلا كونه موجداً لأفعاله بالقصد والإرادة, وقد سبق أن الله تعالى مستقل بخلق الأفعال وإيجادها, ومعلوم أن المقدور الواحد لا يدخل تحت قدرتين مستقلتين

قلنا: لا كلام في قوة هذا الكلام ومتانته, إلا أنه لما ثبت بالبرهان أن الخالق هو الله تعالى, وبالضرورة أن لقدرة العبد وإرادته مدخلاً في بعض الأفعال كحركة البطش دون البعض كحركة الإرتعاش, إحتجنا في التفصي عن هذا المضيق إلى القول بأن الله تعالى خالق كل شيء والعبد كاسب

If it is said: There is no meaning for a slave doing actions by his own choice, unless he brings those actions into existence by his own intention and will, and it has preceded that Allaah Ta`aalaa is Alone the One Who creates and brings into existence the actions (of people). It is known that a thing over which someone has power does not come under two independent powers.

We say: There is no (benefit in) discussing the strength and force of this discussion, other than that, because it has been established with evidence that the only Creator is Allaah Ta`aalaa, and by necessity the power and intending of the slave enters into some actions, like the movement of seizing, rather than some actions, like the movement of trembling. We argue, therefore, we need to get out of this constricted (position) by saying that Allaah Ta`aalaa is the Creator and the slave is an acquirer (*kaasib*).

وتحقيقه أن صرف العبد قدرته وإرادته إلى الفعل كسب, وإيجاد الله تعالى الفعل عقيب ذلك خلق, والمقدور الواحد داخل تحت قدرتين, لكن بجهتين مختلفتين, فالفعل مقدور الله تعالى بجهة الإيجاد, ومقدور العبد بجهة الكسب, وهذا القدر من المعنى ضروري, وإن لم نقدر على أزيد من ذلك في تلخيص العبارة المفصحة عن تحقيق كون فعل العبد بخلق الله تعالى وإيجاده, مع ما فيه للعبد من القدرة والإختيار.

The verification of this is that the slave expending his power and will into an action is *kasb* (acquisition), and Allaah Ta`aalaa bringing that action into existence thereafter is *khalq* (creating), so the *maqdoor* (that thing which is subject to power) enters under two powers; however, with two different direction. The action is under the Power of Allaah Ta`aalaa from the facet of *eejaad* (bringing into existence), and it is under the power of the slave from the facet of *kasb* (acquisition). This amount of the meaning is necessary, even though we are unable to go beyond that in summarising the eloquent expression regarding the verification of the slave's action being through Allaah Ta`aalaa creating it and bringing it into existence, along with that which the slave has of power and choice.

ولهم في الفرق بينهما عبارات مثل أن الكسب ما وقع بآلة, والخلق لا بآلة, والكسب مقدور وقع في محل قدرته, والخلق مقدور وقع لا في محل قدرته, والكسب لا يصح انفراد القادر به, والخلق يصح انفراد.

فإن قيل: فقد أثبتهم ما نسبتم إلى المعتزلة من إثبات الشركة.

Regarding the difference between the two thing, they have a number of different expressions, such as: *kasb* (acquisition) is that which occurs through the use of an instrument, and creating is not through the use of an instrument, and *kasb* is *maqdoor* which occurs in the *mahall* (locus) of his power, and *khalq* is *maqdoor* but does not occur in the *mahall* (locus) of his (the slave's) power. It is not valid to separate acquisition from the one who has power over it, but it is valid to do so in the case of creating.

If it is said: You have affirmed the very thing which you had attributed to the Mu`tazilah, which is the affirmation of co-partnership.

قلنا: الشركة أن يجتمع اثنان على شيء واحد وينفرد كل منهما بما هو له دون الآخر, كشركاء القرية والمحلة, وكما إذا جعل العبد خالقاً لأفعاله, والصانع خالقاً لسائر الأعراض والأجسام, بخلاف ما إذا إضيف أمر إلى شيئين بجهتين مختلفين, كأرض تكون ملكاً لله تعالى بجهة التخليق, وللعباد بجهة ثبوت التصرف, وكفعل العبد يسند إلى الله تعالى بجهة الخلق, وإلى العبد بجهة الكسب

We say: Co-partnership is that two people join together upon one thing, and each of them may separate himself from the other with that which belongs to him, like the partners of a village of place, and as would be the case if the slave were to be the creator of his actions, and the Maker being the Creator of all of the *a`raadh* and *ajsaam* (bodies), contrary to the case where one matter is attached to two things from two different facets, like how the earth is owned by Allaah Ta`aalaa from the aspect of *Takhleeq* (creating), and owned by the slaves from the aspect of the affirmation of *tasarruf* (having control over it and being able to do dealings regarding it). Also, like how the action of the slave is attributed to Allaah Ta`aalaa from the facet of creating, but attributed to the slave from the aspect of acquisition.

فإن قيل: فكيف كان كسب القبيح قبيحاً سفهاً موجباً لاستحقاق الذم والعقاب بخلاف خلقه؟

If it is said: How is it that the acquisition of badness is bad, foolishness, necessarily deserving of reproach and punishment, unlike creating it (badness)?

قلنا: لأنه قد ثبت أن الخالق حكيم, لا يخلق شيئاً إلا وله عاقبة حميدة, وإن لم نطلع عليها, فجزمنا بأن ما نستقبحه من الأفعال قد يكون له فيها حكم ومصالح, كما في خلق الأجسام الخبيثة الضارة المؤلمة, بخلاف الكاسب فإنه قد يفعل الحسن, وقد يفعل القبيح, فجعلنا كسبه للقبيح مع ورود النهي عنه, قبيحاً سفهاً موجباً لاستحقاق الذم والعقاب

We say: Because we have affirmed that The Creator is All-Wise. He does not create anything except that it has a praiseworthy ending, even though we may not yet know what the (reason) is. Thus, we emphatically declare that that which we consider to be bad from the actions may possess wisdoms and benefits, like in the creation of the *khabeeth*, harmful bodies that cause pain, unlike in the case of the *kaasib* (one who acquires), because he might do good or he might do bad. Thus, we say that the slave's acquisition of that which is bad despite having been prohibited from it is bad and foolishness deserving of reproach and punishment.

الحسن والقبيح

Goodness and Badness:

(والحسن منها)

"And the good in these-"

أي من أفعال العباد, وهو ما يكون متعلق المدح في العاجل والثواب في الآجل, والأحسن أن يفسر بما لا يكون متعلقاً للذم والعقاب, ليشمل المباح

Meaning, from the actions of the slave, and that is those actions that are connected to praise now and reward hereafter. It is best to explain it as that which is not connected to reproach and punishment, so that it may encompass the permissible actions as well.

(برضاء الله تعالى)

" - Is by the Pleasure of Allaah Ta`aalaa."

أي بإرادته من غير اعتراض

Meaning, by His Will, without any objection.

(والقبيح منها)

"And the evil in these-"

وهو ما يكون متعلق الذم في العاجل والعقاب في الآجل

And they are those actions that are connected to reproach now and punishment hereafter.

(ليس برضائه)

" - Is not by His Pleasure."

لما عليه من الإعتراض, قال الله تعالى:

وَلَا يَرْضَى لِعِبَادِهِ الْكُفْرَ

Because of the objection against it. Allaah Ta`aalaa said:

{"*And He is not pleased with kufr for His slaves...*"}

يعني أن الإرادة والمشيئة والتقدير يتعلق بالكل والرضا والمحبة والأمر لا يتعلق إلا بالحسن دون القبيح

Meaning that, *Iraadah*, *Mashee'ah* and *Taqdeer* are connected to all actions, and *Ridhaa* (Pleasure), *Mahabbah* (Love) and *Amr* (Command) are not connected except to those actions that are good, not those that are bad.

(والإستطاعة مع الفعل)

"And ability accompanies the action."

خلافاً للمعتزلة

Contrary to the belief of the Mu`tazilah.

(وهي حقيقة القدرة التي يكون بها الفعل)

"And it is the real power by which the action comes into being."

إشارة إلى ما ذكره صاحب التبصرة من أنها عرض يخلقه الله تعالى في الحيوان يفعل به الأفعال الإختيارية, وهي علة للفعل, والجمهور على أنها شرط لأداء الفعل لا علته, وبالجملة هي صفة يخلقها الله تعالى عند قصد اكتساب الفعل بعد سلامة الأسباب والآلات, فإن قصد فعل الخير خلق الله تعالى قدرة فعل الخير, وإن قصد فعل الشر خلق الله تعالى قدرة فعل الشر, فكان هو المضيع لقدرة فعل الخير, فيستحق الذم والعقاب, ولهذا ذم الكافرين بأنهم لا يستطيعون السمع, وإذا كانت الإستطاعة عرضاً وجب أن تكون مقارنة للفعل بالزمان, لا سابقة عليه, وإلا لزم وقوع الفعل بلا استطاعة وقدرة عليه, لما مر من إمتناع بقاء الأعراض

This is a reference to that which was mentioned by the author of *at-Tabsirah*, which was that ability is an `*aradh* created by Allaah Ta`aalaa in the animal, whereby the animal performs actions of choice, and it is an `*illat* (cause) for the action. The *jumhoor* (vast majority) are of the view that it is a condition for the discharging of the action and is not its `illat. In summary, it is an attribute which Allaah Ta`aalaa creates (for the slaves) at the time when they intend to acquire a certain action after the soundness of the *asbaab* (means) and instruments (*aalaat*). If the slave intends the doing of goodness, Allaah Ta`aalaa creates for him the ability to do the good deed. If he intends the doing of evil, Allaah Ta`aalaa creates for him the ability to do the evil deed. Thus, the slave himself wastes the ability to do good and therefore becomes deserving of reproach and punishment. For this reason, Allaah Ta`aalaa rebuked the Kaafireen saying that they are not capable of hearing. If ability is an `aradh, it must necessarily be connected to the action in time, not preceding it; otherwise, the occurence of the action would have taken place without the ability and power (of the slave) over it, due to what we mentioned of the impossibility of the continuity of a`raadh.

فإن قيل: لو سلم استحالة بقاء الأعراض فلا نزاع في إمكان تجدد الأمثال عقيب الزوال, فمن أين يلزم وقوع الفعل بدون القدرة؟

قلنا: إنما ندعي لزوم ذلك إذا كانت القدرة التي بها الفعل هي القدرة السابقة, وأما إذا جعلتموها المثل المتجدد المقارن فقد اعترفتم بأن القدرة التي بها الفعل لا تكون إلا مقارنة له, ثم إن إدّعيتم أنه لا بد لها من أمثال سابقة حتى لا يمكن الفعل بأول ما يحدث من القدرة, فعليكم البيان

If it is said: If the impossibility of the continuity of *a`raadh* is submitted, then there is no dispute about the possibility of similar new (*a`raadh*) coming into being after the passing (of the first), so from where comes the occurence of the action without the power (of the slave)?

We say: We claim that this is necessary if the power by which the action is carried out is the previous power. As for if you make it a similar (power) that is renewed and connected, then you have admitted that the power by which the action is carried out cannot be except connected to it. Thereafter, if you claim that there is no alternative but that there must be similar (*a`raadh*) that are previous so that the action is not possible with the first occurence of power, then upon you is to explain (why).

وأما ما يقال: لو فرضنا بقاء القدرة السابقة إلى آن الفعل إما بتجدد الأمثال, وإما باستقامة بقاء الأعراض, فالمعتزلة إما أن يقولوا بجواز الفعل أو امتناعه, فإن قالوا بجواز وجود الفعل بها في الحالة الأولى, فقد تركوا مذهبهم, حيث جوزوا مقارنة الفعل بالقدرة, وإن قالوا بامتناعه, لزم

التحكم والترجيح بلا مرجح, إذ القدرة بحالها لم تتغير, ولم يحدث فيها معنى, لاستحالة ذلك على الأعراض, فلم صار الفعل بها في الحالة الثانية واجباً, وفي الحالة الأولى ممتنعاً؟ ففيه نظر, لأن القائلين بكون الإستطاعة قبل الفعل لا يقولون بامتناع المقارنة الزمانية, وبأن حدوث كل فعل يجب أن يكون بقدرة سابقة عليه بالزمان البتة, حتى يمتنع حدوث الفعل في زمان حدوث القدرة مقرونة بجميع الشرائط, ولأنه يجوز أن يمتنع الفعل في الحالة الأولى لإنتفاء شرط أو وجود مانع, ويجب في الثانية لتمام الشرائط مع أن القدرة التي هي صفة القادر في الحالتين على السواء

As for what is said, that: If we suppose the continuity of the previous power until the time of the action, either by the renewing of similar (powers), or by the continuous recurrence of *a`raadh*. The Mu`tazilah either claim the possibility of the action or the impossibility of it. If they claim the possibility of the existence of the action with it in the first condition, then they have abandoned their Madh-hab because they would be permitting the connection of the action to power. If they say that it is not possible, then it necessarily follows that there was a making of a decision by someone and a giving of preference to one thing over another without a *murajjih* (one giving preference), because the power has not changed in the condition in which it was. But, there is no meaning in this, due to the impossibility of that in the case of *a`raadh*, so why does action become necessary with it in the second condition, but impossible? So there is speculation regarding it, because the ones who say that *istitaa`ah* (ability) comes before the action, they do not believe that it is impossible for the (power and action) to be connected in time, and nor do they say that the origination of every action necessitates that it be with a power prior to it in time altogether, so much so that it is impossible for the action to be originated in the time of the origination of the power connected to all of the stipulations.

Also, it is permissible for the action to be impossible in the first condition due to the non-fulfillment of a stipulation or due to the presence of a preventative factor, and it is necessary in the second condition due to the completion of the stipulations along with the power which is an attribute of the one possessing power in each condition.

ومن هاهنا ذهب بعضهم إلى أنه إن أريد بالإستطاعة القدرة المستجمعة لجميع الشرائط التأثير, فالحق أنها مع الفعل, وإلا فقبله, وأما امتناع بقاء الأعراض فمبنى على مقدمات صعبة البيان, وهي أن بقاء الشيء أمر محقق زائد عليه, وأنه يمتنع قيام العرض بالعرض, وأنه يمتنع قيامهما معاً بالمحل

From here, some of them adopted the view that if what is intended by *istitaa`ah* (ability) is the power that gathers to itself all of the stipulations for having the effect (*at-ta'theer*), then the reality is that it is with the action, otherwise, before it. As for the impossibility of the continuity of a`raadh, then it is based upon premises that are difficult to explain, which is that the continuity of a thing is a matter that is *muhaqqaq* (verified), extra upon it, and that it is impossible for an `*aradh* to subsist with an `*aradh*, and that it is impossible for them to subsist together in one *mahall* (locus).

ولما استدل القائلون بكون الإستطاعة قبل الفعل, بأن التكليف حاصل قبل الفعل, ضرورة أن الكافر مكلف بالإيمان, وتارك الصلاة مكلف بها بعد دخول الوقت, فلو لم تكن الإستطاعة متحققة حينئذ لزم تكليف العاجز, وهو باطل, أشار إلى الجواب بقوله:

Because those who say that *istitaa`ah* comes before the action used as evidence the fact that *takleef* is acquired prior to the action, of necessity because the Kaafir is *mukallaf* (bound) to bring *Imaan*, and the abandoner of Salaah is *mukallaf* to perform it after the entry of the time. Thus, is *istitaa`ah* were not verified as having a reality, then it would necessitate the *takleef* of one who is incapable, which is *baatil* (false). He points towards the answer by saying:

(ويقع هذا الإسم)

"And this name applies."

يعني لفظ الإستطاعة

Meaning, the term *istitaa`ah* (ability).

(على سلامة الأسباب والآلات والجوارح)

"Upon the soundness of the means, instruments and limbs."

كما في قوله تعالى:

Like in the *Aayah*:

(وَلِلَّهِ عَلَى النَّاسِ حِجُّ الْبَيْتِ مَنِ اسْتَطَاعَ إِلَيْهِ سَبِيلًا)

{"*And for Allaah, upon mankind, is (a performance of) Hajj to The House (i.e. Ka`bah), for the one who has the ability (to do so)...*"}

فإن قيل: الإستطاعة صفة المكلف, وسلامة الأسباب والآلات ليست صفة له, فكيف يصح تفسيرها بها؟

If it is said: Ability is an attribute of the *mukallaf*, and the soundness of the means and instruments is not an attribute for it, so how can explaining it with that be valid?

قلنا: المراد سلامة الأسباب له, والمكلف كما يتصف بالإستطاعة يتصف بذلك, حيث يقال هو ذو سلامة الأبسباب, إلا أنه لتركبه لا يشتق منه اسم فاعل يحمل عليه بخلاف الإستطاعة

We say: The intended meaning is the soundness of the means, and the *mukallaf*, like how he is described with ability he is described with that too, as it is said that he is the one who possesses the soundness of means. Otherwise, because this compounded expression is used, the active participle (*ism-ul-faa`il*) is not derived from it upon which it may be carried, contrary to ability (*istitaa`ah*).

(وصحة التكليف تعتمد على هذه الإستطاعة)

"The soundness of *takleef* rests upon this ability."

التي هي سلامة الأسباب والآلات, لا الإستطاعة بالمعنى الأول

Which is the soundness of the means and instruments, not *istitaa`ah* (ability) in the first meaning.

فإن أريد بالعجز عدم الإستطاعة بالمعنى الأول, فلا نسلم إستحالة تكليف العاجز, وإن أريد بالمعنى الثاني, فلا نسلم لزومه لجواز أن يحصل قبل الفعل سلامة الأسباب والآلات, وإن لم تحصل حقيقة القدرة التي بها الفعل

If what is intended by incapability is the absence of *istitaa`ah* (ability) in the first meaning, then we do not submit the impossibility of *takleef* upon the `*aajiz* (incapable one), and if the second meaning is intended, then we do not submit the permissibility that prior to the action the soundness of the means and instruments can be acquired even if the real power through which the action is done is not acquired.

وقد يجاب بأن القدرة صالحة للضدين عند أبي حنيفة رحمه الله تعالى, حتى أن القدرة المصروفة إلى الكفر هي بعينها القدرة التي تصرف إلى الإيمان ولا اختلاف إلا في التعلق, وهو لا يوجب الإختلاف في نفس القدرة, فالكافر قادر على الإيمان المكلف به, إلا أنه صرف قدرته إلى الكفر, وضيع باختياره صرفها إلى الإيمان, فاستحق الذم والعقاب, ولا يخفى أن في هذا الجواب تسليماً لكون القدرة قبل الفعل, لأن القدرة على الإيمان في حال الكفر تكون قبل الإيمان لا محالة, فإن أجيب بأن المراد أن القدرة وإن صلحت للضدين, لكنها من حيث التعلق بأحدهما لا تكون إلا معه, حتى أن ما يلزم مقارنتها للفعل هي القدرة المتعلقة بالفعل, وما يلزم مقارنتها للترك هي القدرة المتعلقة به, وأما نفس القدرة فقد تكون متقدمة متعلقة بالضدين.

Someone might respond by saying that it is possible for the power to be applicable to two things that are contrary to one another according to Imaam Abu Haneefah رحمة الله عليه, so much so that the power which a person expends in the path of *kufr* is the very same power which could have been expended in the path of *Imaan*, and there is no difference of opinion except regarding the *ta`alluq* (connection), and that does not necessitate difference of opinion regarding the power itself, because the Kaafir is capable of bringing *Imaan* which he has been made *mukallaf* of doing. However, he chooses to expend that power in the path of *kufr*, and by his own choice loses out on expending it in the path of *Imaan*, and thus becomes deserving of reproach and punishment. It is not hidden that in this response there is the submission of the fact that power comes before the action, because the power to bring *Imaan* whilst in the state of *kufr* is prior to bringing *Imaan*, obviously. If someone responds by saying that, the intended meaning is that power, even though it is possible to be applied to two contraries, but from the aspect of connect to one of those two contraries it has to be with just that one, so much so that the thing which necessarily has to be linked to the action is the power connected to the action, and that which necessarily has to be linked to leaving off is the power that is connected to it. As for the power itself, then it can be antecedent, connected to two contraries.

قلنا: هذا مما لا يتصور فيه نزاع, بل هو لغو من الكلام, فليتأمل.

We say: This is from that in which an argument cannot be perceived; rather, it is futile speech, so reflect.

التكليف بما لا يطاق

Burdening With the Impossible:

(ولا يكلف العبد بما ليس في وسعه)

سواء كان ممتنعاً في نفسه كجمع الضدين, أو ممكناً في نفسه لكن لا يمكن للعبد, كخلق الجسم. وأما ما يمتنع بناء على أن الله تعالى علم خلافه أو أراد خلافه كإيمان الكافر وطاعة العاصي, فلا نزاع في وقوع التكليف به, لكونه مقدوراً للمكلف بالنظر إلى نفسه, ثم عدم التكليف بما ليس في الوسع متفق عليه, كقوله تعالى:

لَا يُكَلِّفُ اللهُ نَفْساً إِلَّا وُسْعَهَا

"The slave of Allaah Ta`aalaa is not burdened except with that which is within his capacity."

Regardless of whether that thing be something that is impossible in itself, like joining between two contraries, or possible within itself but not possible for the slave, like creating a body. As for that which is impossible, based on the fact that Allaah Ta`aalaa knows the opposite of it or intends the opposite of it, like a Kaafir bringing *Imaan*, or a disobedient one becoming obedient, then there is no dispute regarding the fact that it is from what (the slaves of Allaah Ta`aalaa) have been made *mukallaf* (responsible for according to the Sharee`ah) due to it coming within the scope of the capability of the one who has been made *mukallaf*, and this fact can be ascertained simply by looking at (those actions). Thereafter, that there is no *takleef* (burdening) of that which is not within the capacity of people is a matter which is agreed upon (*muttafaqun `alayhi*), as the *Aayah* mentions:

{"*Allaah does not burden a soul except (with that which) it can bear.*"}

والأمر في قوله تعالى:

أَنْبِئُونِيْ بِأَسْمَاءِ هَؤُلَاءِ

للتعجيز دون التكليف, وقوله تعالى حكاية عن حال المؤمنين:

As for the Command mentioned in the *Aayah*:

{*"Inform Me of their names..."*}

This is for *ta`jeez* (to show the incapability of those being addressed), not *takleef* (burdening them with it).

As for the *Aayah* mentioning the condition of the Mu'mineen:

رَبَّنَا وَلَا تُحَمِّلْنَا مَا لَا طَاقَةَ لَنَا بِهِ

ليس المراد بالتحميل هو التكليف, بل إيصال ما لا يطاق من العوارض إليهم

{*"O our Rabb, and do not burden us with that which we have no capability for."*}

The intended meaning of *tahmeel* (placing a burden on someone) here is not *takleef* (making them responsible according to the Sharee`ah); rather, the intended meaning is the attaching to them such obstacles which are beyond what they are capable of bearing.

وإنما النزاع في الجواز, فمنعه المعتزلة بناء على القبح العقلي, وجوزه الأشعري, لأنه لا يقبح من الله تعالى شيء, وقد يستدل بقوله تعالى:

لَا يُكَلِّفُ اللَّهُ نَفْساً إِلَّا وُسْعَهَا

The dispute is regarding possibility. The Mu`tazilah said that it is not, based on *al-qubh al-`aqli* (logically bad). Imaam al-Ash`ari regarded it as being possible, because nothing which is done by Allaah Ta`aalaa is bad.

From the *Aayah*:

{*"Allaah does not burden a soul except with (that which it) can bear."*}

على نفي الجواز, وتقريره أنه لو كان جائزاً لما لزم من فرض وقوعه محال, ضرورة أن استحالة اللازم توجب استحالة الملزوم تحقيقاً لمعنى الملزوم, لكنه لو وقع لزم كذب كلام الله تعالى وهو محال, وهذه نكتة في بيان استحالة وقوع كل ما يتعلق علم الله تعالى, وإرادته واختياره بعدم وقوعه

Some have inferred the negation of possibility. Its establishment is that, had it been possible, then impossibility would not have been binding upon the supposition of its occurence, of necessity due to the fact that if the *laazim* (necessary) is impossible then of course the *malzoom* (that made necessary) is impossible as well, in verification of the meaning of the *malzoom*. However, were it to occur, that would necessitate the *Kalaam* of Allaah Ta`aalaa being false, which is impossible. This is a point in the explanation of the impossibility of the occurence of that which the Knowledge, *Iraadah* and *Ikhtiyaar* of Allaah Ta`aalaa do not intend.

وحلها: أنا لا نسلم أن كل ما يكون ممكناً في نفسه لا يلزم من فرض وقوعه محال , وإنما يجب ذلك لو لم يعرض له الإمتناع بالغير , وإلا لجاز أن يكون لزوم المحال بناء على الإمتناع بالغير , ألا يرى أن الله تعالى لما أوجد العالم بقدرته واختياره , فعدمه ممكن في نفسه , مع أنه يلزم من فرض وقوعه تخلف المعلول عن علته التامة, وهو محال؟

The solution is: We do not submit that everything which is possible in itself that, supposing this particular thing occurred, it follows that there was an impossible (as an alternative). That is only necessary were it (the impossible) not precluded by something else. Otherwise, it would be valid to say that the impossible is necessary, based on the fact that it is precluded by something else. Is it not seen that Allaah Ta`aalaa brought the world into existence by His *Qudrah* and His *Ikhtiyaar*, so its non-existence is possible in itself, even though on the supposition that it occurred, the *ma`lool* (effect) lags behind its complete `*illat* (cause), which is impossible?

والحاصل أن الممكن في نفسه لا يلزم من فرض وقوعه محال بالنظر إلى ذاته , وأما بالنظر إلى أمر زائد على نفسه فلا نسلم أنه لا يستلزم المحال

In conclusion, that which is possible in itself, the supposition that it occurred does not necessitate impossibility, by looking at its essence. As for the case of looking at a matter additional to itself, then we do not submit that it does not necessitate the impossible.

وما يوجد من الألم في المضروب عقيب ضرب إنسان, والإنكسار في الزجاج عقيب كسر) (إنسان

"And the pain which is experienced in the one who is hit after being hit by someone, and the state of being broken of glass after someone has broken it."

قيد بذلك, ليصح محلاً للخلاف في أنه هل للعبد صنع فيه أم لا؟

He restricted the statement with that, so that it be valid that there be a difference of opinion regarding whether the slave has a part in it or not.

(وما أشبهه)

"And such things."

كالموت عقيب القتل

Like death after being killed.

(كل ذلك مخلوق لله تعالى)

"All of that is created by Allaah Ta`aalaa."

لما مر من أن الخالق هو الله تعالى وحده, وأن كل الممكنات مستندة إليه بلا واسطة. والمعتزلة لما أسندوا بعض الأفعال إلى غير الله تعالى, قالوا: إن كان الفعل صادراً عن الفاعل لا بتوسط فعل آخر, فهو بطريق المباشرة, وإلا فبطريق التوليد, ومعناه أن يوجب الفعل لفاعله, فعلاً آخر, كحركة اليد توجب حركة المفتاح, فالألم متولد من الضرب, والإنكسار من الكسر, وليسا مخلوقين لله تعالى, وعندنا الكل بخلق الله تعالى

Because of what we have mentioned, that Allaah Ta`aalaa Alone is the Creator, and that all possible things are reliant upon Him without any intermediary. The Mu`tazilah attributed some actions to other than Allaah Ta`aalaa. They said: "If the action comes directly from the doer without the medium of the action of another, then that is by way of being done directly; otherwise, it is by way of *at-Tawleed* (resulting). The meaning of that is another action makes binding the action (the first action) upon the one who did it, like how the movement of the hand necessitates the movement of the key. Thus, pain results (literally, "is born from") the hit (*dharb*). The state of being broken is born from (results from) the act of breaking, and they are not created by Allaah Ta`aalaa, according to the Mu`tazilah. According to us, everything is created by Allaah Ta`aalaa.

(لا صنع للعبد في تخليقه)

"The slave has no part in its creation."

والأولى أن لا يقيد بالتخليق, لأن ما يسمونه متولدات لا صنع للعبد فيه أصلاً, أما التخليق فلاستحالته من العبد, وأما الإكتساب فلاستحالة اكتساب العبد ما ليس قائماً بمحل القدرة, ولهذا لا يتمكن العبد من عدم حصولها, بخلاف أفعاله الإختيارية

It would have been better not to have restricted the statement by saying "creation", because that which they term *mutawallidaat* (things that are born from others), the slave has no part in (the creation of) those things either, at all. As for creating, then it is because it is impossible to come from the slave. As for *iktisaab* (acquisition), then because it is impossible for the slave to acquire that which is not subsisting in the locus of his power. For this reason, it is not possible for the slave to not attain it, unlike the actions which are done by him by his own choice.

الأجل

The Appointed Term:

(والمقتول ميت بأجله)

"The one who is killed dies according to his appointed term."

أي الوقت المقدر لموته, لا كما زعم بعض المعتزلة من أن الله قد قطع عليه الأجل, لنا أن الله تعالى قد حكم بآجال العباد على ما علم من غير تردد, بآية:

Meaning, at the time decreed for his death, unlike what is claimed by the Mu`tazilah, that Allaah Ta`aalaa cut short his appointed term. We say that Allaah Ta`aalaa has decided the appointed terms of His slaves according to His Knowledge, without any hesitance, like in the *Aayah*:

فَإِذَا جَاءَ أَجَلُهُمْ لَا يَسْتَأْخِرُونَ سَاعَةً وَلَا يَسْتَقْدِمُونَ

{"*So when their appointed term comes, they can neither delay it for a moment and nor can they bring it nearer.*"}

واحتجت المعتزلة بالأحاديث الواردة في أن بعض الطاعات تزيد في العمر, وبأنه لو كان ميتاً بأجله لما استحق القاتل ذماً ولا عقاباً ولا دية ولا قصاصاً, إذ ليس موت المقتول بخلقه ولا بكسبه

The Mu`tazilah argued based on the *Ahaadeeth* that are reported concerning certain acts of obedience which results in the lifespan of the person being increased, and they argued that, if the person (who is killed) dies according to his *ajal* (appointed term), then he is not deserving of reproach, nor punishment, nor blood-money, nor retribution (*qisaas*), because the death of the one who is killed had not occurred by the creating of the killer nor by his acquisition.

والجواب عن الاول: أن الله تعالى كان يعلم أنه لو لم يفعل هذه الطاعة لكان عمره أربعين سنة, لكنه علم أنه يفعلها فيكون عمره سبعين سنة, فنسبت هذه الزيادة إلى تلك الطاعة, بناء على علم الله تعالى أنه لولاها لما كانت تلك الزيادة

The answer to the first argument of theirs is as follows: Allaah Ta`aalaa already knew (in His Eternal Knowledge) that if the slave were to not perform these certain acts of obedience, his lifespan would have been 40 years, but He knows that the slave will do those acts (and make those *Du`aas*) which will result in his lifespan being 70 years, (so Allaah Ta`aalaa has already decreed that the person will live for 70 years, and thus the person in reality is not extending his lifespan because it was already decreed that he would carry out such actions as would result in him dying at the age of 70), so this increase is attributed to those acts of obedience based on the fact that Allaah Ta`aalaa knew that if the person had not done these actions, there would not have been that increase.

وعن الثاني: أن وجوب العقاب والضمان على القاتل تعبدي, لارتكابه المنهي وكسبه الفعل الذي يخلق الله تعالى عقيبه الموت بطريق جري العادة, فإن القتل فعل القاتل كسباً, وإن لم يكن له خلقاً, والموت قائم بالميت مخلوق لله تعالى, لا صنع فيه للعبد, تخليقاً ولا اكتساباً, ومبنى هذا على أن الموت وجودي, بدليل قوله تعالى:

The second argument of theirs is answered as follows: The necessity of punishment and accountability upon the killer is linked up with servitude unto Allaah Ta`aalaa (i.e. *amr ta`abbudi*), due to his perpetrating that which is prohibited and acquiring the action which Allaah Ta`aalaa has created death after it according to the customary way, because killing is an action of the killer that is acquired, even though it is not created by him. Death subsists with the dead person and is created by Allaah Ta`aalaa, and the slave has no part in (creating) it, neither in creating it nor in acquiring it. The basis of this is that death is *wujoodi* (existential). The proof for this is the *Aayah*:

خَلَقَ الْمَوْتَ وَالْحَيَاةَ

{"He created death and life."}

والأكثرون على أنه عدمي, ومعنى خلق الموت قدره

Most are of the view that by default it is non-existent. The meaning of "created death" is "decreed it".

(والأجل واحد)

"The appointed term is only one."

لا كما زعم الكعبي أن للمقتول أجلين: القتل, والموت, وأنه لو لم يقتل لعاش إلى أجله الذي هو للموت, ولا كما زعمت الفلاسفة أن للحيوان أجلاً طبيعياً وهو وقت موته بتحلل رطوبته وانطفاء حرارته الغريزيتين, وآجالاً إخترامية على خلاف مقتضى طبيعته بحسب الآفات والأمراض

Unlike what was claimed by al-Ka`bi, that the person who is killed has two *ajals* (appointed terms): one is the appointed term of being killed and the other is the appointed term of dying, and that, if he does not get killed he will live until the appointed term of dying (which might be 70 years, for example), but if he does get killed then he will be dying at his appointed term of being killed (which might be at the age of 24, for example). It is also not like what was claimed by the philosophers, that the animals have a "natural appointed term" which is the time for their death through the dissolution of its moisture and the extinguishing of its heat, both of which are implanted with it, and other appointed terms which cut off (its life) contrary to the requirement of its nature, through afflictions and sicknesses.

الرزق

The Sustenance:

(والحرام رزق)

"That which is *haraam* is (also) *rizq*."

لأن الرزق إسم لما يسوقه الله تعالى إلى الحيوان فيأكله, وذلك قد يكون حلالاً وقد يكون حراماً, وهذا أولى من تفسيره بما يتغذى به الحيوان لخلوه عن معنى الإضافة إلى الله تعالى, مع أنه معتبر في مفهوم الرزق, وعند المعتزلة: الحرام ليس برزق, لأنهم فسروه تارة بمملوك يأكله المالك, وتارة بما لا يمتنع من الإنتفاع به, وذلك لا يكون إلا حلالاً, لكن يلزم على الأول أن لا يكون ما يأكله الدواب رزقاً, وعلى الوجهين أن من أكل الحرام طول عمره لم يرزقه الله تعالى أصلاً, ومبنى هذا الإختلاف على أن الإضافة إلى الله تعالى معتبرة في معنى الرزق, وأنه لا رازق إلا الله وحده, وأن العبد يستحق الذم والعقاب على أكل الحرام, وما يكون مستنداً إلى الله تعالى لا يكون قبيحاً, ومرتكبه لا يستحق الذم والعقاب

Because *rizq* is a term for that which Allaah Ta`aalaa sends the way of the animal, so he consumes it, and that can be *halaal* or it can be *haraam*. This is better than explaining it as "that which the animal derives nourishment from," because that definition is devoid of attributing (the appointing of the rizq) to Allaah Ta`aalaa, despite the fact that He must be considered in the understanding of *rizq*. According to the Mu`tazilah, that which is *haraam* is not *rizq*, because they explain it sometimes as something possessed which is eaten by the possessor, and sometimes as that which it is possible to benefit from, and that cannot be except something *halaal*. However, the first necessitates that what is eaten by the animal is not *rizq*, and both definitions of theirs leads to the conclusion that if a person eats *halaal* his entire life, then Allaah Ta`aalaa has never granted him *rizq*. The basis of this *ikhtilaaf* is that attributing (the *rizq*) to Allaah Ta`aalaa is considered in the meaning and understanding of *rizq*, and that there is no Raaziq except Allaah Ta`aalaa, and that the slave becomes deserving of reproach and punishment if he consumes haraam, and that whatever is attributed to Allaah Ta`aalaa cannot be bad and thus the one who does it is not deserving of reproach or punishment.

والجواب: أن ذلك لسوء مباشرة أسبابه باختياره

The response to this is that (the person) has made a wrong contact with the causes of the action through his own choice.

(وكل يستوفي رزق نفسه, حلالاً كان أو حراماً)

"Every person finishes up his own rizq, whether it be halaal or haraam."

لحصول التغذي بهما جميعاً

Due to nourishment being attained through either of them.

(ولا يتصور أن لا يأكل إنسان رزقه أو يأكل غيره رزقه)

"It is inconceiveable for a person to not consume his rizq or for another to consume his rizq."

لأن ما قدره الله تعالى غذاء لشخص يجب أن يأكله, ويمتنع أن يأكله غيره, وأما بمعنى الملك فلا يمتنع

Because that which Allaah Ta`aalaa has decreed as being nourishment for an individual, it is necessary that he consumes it, and it is impossible for it to be consumed by another. As for the meaning of ownership, then that is not impossible.

الضلال والهدى من الله

Deviation and Guidance Comes from Allaah Ta`aalaa:

(والله تعالى يضل من يشاء ويهدي من يشاء)

"Allaah Ta`aalaa misguides whomsoever He wishes to and guides whomsoever He wishes to."

بمعنى خلق الله الضلالة والإهتداء, لأنه الخالق وحده, وفي التقييد بالمشيئة إشارة إلى أنه ليس المراد بالهداية بيان طريق الحق, لأنه عام في حق الكل, ولا الإضلال هو عبارة عن وجدان العبد ضالاً أو تسميته ضالاً, إذا لا معنى لتعليق ذلك بمشيئة الله تعالى

Meaning that Allaah Ta`aalaa created both *Dhalaalah* (Deviation) and *Hidaayah* (Guidance), because He Alone is the Creator. In it being restricted with *Al-Mashee'ah* there is the indication that the intended meaning of *Hidaayah* here is not explaining the *Tareeq-ul-Haqq* (The Path of Truth), because that is `aam* (general) in the case of each and every person. *Idhlaal* (causing to go astray) here does not refer to "finding the slave astray" or "naming him as being astray," because there is no meaning of that being connected to the *Mashee'ah* of Allaah Ta`aalaa.

نعم, قد تضاف الهداية إلى النبي عليه الصلاة والسلام مجازاً بطريق التسبب, كما تسند إلى القرآن, وقد يسند الإضلال إلى الشيطان مجازاً كما يسند إلى الأصنام, ثم المذكور في كلام المشايخ أن الهداية عندنا خلق الإهتداء, ومثل هداه الله تعالى فلم يهتد, مجاز عن الدلالة والدعوة إلى الإهتداء, وعند المعتزلة بيان طريق الصواب, وهو باطل لقوله تعالى:

Yes, Hidaayah can be attributed to Rasoolullaah صلى الله عليه وسلم in a *majaaz* (metaphorical) way, by way of *tasabbub* (causation), like how it is attributed to the Qur'aan. *Idhlaal* (leading astray) can be attributed to Shaytaan in a metaphorical way like how it is attributed to the idols. Thereafter, that which is mentioned in the discussion of the Mashaayikh is that according to us, Hidaayah is the creating of being guided, and for example, "Allaah guided him but he was not guided," these are metaphorically referring to indicating the way and calling towards being guided. According to the Mu`tazilah, it is an explanation of the correct path, and that is *baatil* due to the *Aayah*:

إِنَّكَ لَا تَهْدِيْ مَنْ أَحْبَبْتَ

{*"You do not guide those whom you love..."*}

ولقوله عليه السلام:

And because of the *Hadeeth*:

اللهُمَّ اهْدِ قَوْمِيْ

"O Allaah, guide my people."

مع أنه بين الطريق ودعاهم إلى الإهتداء, والمشهور أن الهداية عند المعتزلة: هي الدلالة الموصولة إلى المطلوب, وعندنا: الدلالة على طريق يوصل إلى المطلوب, سواء حصل الوصول والإهتداء أو لم يحصل

Despite the fact that he clearly showed the way and called them towards guidance. It is well-known that according to the Mu`tazilah, *Hidaayah* is defined as: "guidance that leads to the objective." According to us, it is defined as: "Guidance towards the path which leads to the objective, regardless of whether (the person) reaches it and is guided or not."

الصلاح والأصلح

That Which is Good and That Which is Better:

(وما هو الأصلح للعبد فليس ذلك بواجب على الله تعالى)

"It is not binding upon Allaah Ta`aalaa to do that which is best for the slave."

وإلا لما خلق الكافر الفقير المعذب في الدنيا والآخرة, ولما كان له منة على العباد, واستحقاق شكر في الهداية وإفاضة أنواع الخيرات لكونها أداء للواجب, ولما كان امتنان الله على النبي عليه السلام فوق امتنانه على أبي جهل لعنه الله, إذ فعل بكل منهما غاية مقدوره من الأصلح له, ولما كان سؤال العصمة والتوفيق وكشف الضراء والبسط في الخصب والرخاء معنى, لأن ما لم يفعله في حق كل واحد فهو مفسدة له, يجب على الله تعالى تركها, ولما بقي في قدرة الله تعالى بالنسبة إلى مصالح العباد شيء, إذ قد أتى بالواجب

Had this not been the case, then Allaah Ta`aalaa would not have created the Kaafir who is poor and who undergoes punishment in this Dunyaa and the Aakhirah, and He would not have a Favour to His slaves and deserved gratitude for granting *Hidaayah* and for bestowing different kinds of goodness due to it being simply the discharging of something that is binding (upon Him). Also, in that case the Favour shown by Allaah Ta`aalaa to Rasoolullaah صلى الله عليه وسلم would not have been more thant the Favour shown to Abu Jahl لعنة الله عليه, because He would then have done with each of them the utmost of what is within His Power of what is best for (each of them). Also, had it been the case, then there would have been no meaning in asking for *`ismat* (protection from sin, in the case of the Ambiyaa) and for *tawfeeq*, and for the removal of difficulties, and for the granting of abundance in fruitfulness and ease, for in such a case, whatever Allaah Ta`aalaa would not have done (of granting what is best) in the case of each person would have been a corruption for that person from which it is necessary that Allaah Ta`aalaa does not do so, and nothing of the matters that are best for the slaves would then have remained in the Power of Allaah Ta`aalaa because He would have done that which is binding upon Him.

ولعمري إن مفاسد هذا الأصل, أعني وجوب الأصلح, بل أكثر أصول المعتزلة أظهر من أن يخفى, وأكثر من أن يحصى, وذلك لقصور نظرهم في المعارف الإلهية, ورسوخ قياس الغائب على الشاهد في طباعهم, وغاية تشبيههم في ذلك أن ترك الأصلح يكون بخلاً وسفهاً

And by my life, the corruption caused by this principle, i.e. that it is binding upon Allaah Ta`aalaa to do what is best for the slaves, or in fact, the corruption caused by most of the principles of the Mu`tazilah is much too clear to be hidden and far too many to be ennumerated, and that is due to the deficiency of their consideration of the various kinds of knowledge relating to Allaah Ta`aalaa, and because by their nature they are adamant on doing *qiyaas* on that which is not seen by using that which is seen. The extreme stubborness which they have in holding onto this position is due to their belief that for Allaah Ta`aalaa to not do that which is best (for people) would be niggardliness and foolishness.

وجوابه: أن منع ما يكون حق المانع, وقد ثبتت بالأدلة القاطعة كرمه وحكمته ولطفه وعمله بالعواقب يكون محض عدل وحكمة, ثم ليت شعري ما معنى وجوب الشيء على الله تعالى؟ إذ ليس معناه استحقاق تاركه الذم والعقاب, وهو ظاهر, ولا لزوم صدوره عنه بحيث لا يتمكن من الترك بناء على استلزامه محالاً من سفه أو جهل أو عبث أو بخل أو نحو ذلك, لأنه رفض لقاعدة الإختيار, وميل إلى الفلسفة الظاهرة العوار

The response to this is that prevention is done by the One Who has the right to prevent, and it has been affirmed through the decisive evidences the Generosity, Wisdom and Kindness of Allaah Ta`aalaa, and His acting according to the end results is pure Justice and Wisdom. Thereafter, what is the meaning of a thing being binding upon Allaah Ta`aalaa? Because in this case it cannot mean the one who abandons it becomes worthy of reproach and punishment, and this is clear. It also does not mean that Allaah Ta`aaala is incapable of not doing it and thus it has to be done by Him because otherwise it would result in foolishness, or ignorance, or futility, or niggadliness, etc., which is impossible. Such a belief entails rejection of the principle of *Al-Ikhtiyaar* (Allaah Ta`aalaa does whatever He wishes), and it inclines towards the beliefs of the philosophers, the reprehensibility of which is clear.

عذاب القبر

Punishment in the Grave:

(وعذاب القبر للكافرين وبعض عصاة المؤمنين)

"`Adhaab` in the `qabr` for the Kaafirs and for some of the disobedient ones among the Mu'mineen (is affirmed)."

خص البعض لأن منهم من لا يريد الله تعالى تعذيبه فلا يعذب

The reason he says "some" is because with regards to the sinners (from the Muslims), there are those whom Allaah Ta`aalaa might not intend to punish and thus they are not punished.

(وتنعيم أهل الطاعة في القبر بما يعلمه الله تعالى ويريده)

"And the granting of delights to the people of obedience in the `qabr`, according to what is Known and Intended by Allaah Ta`aalaa (is affirmed)."

وهذا أولى مما وقع في عامة الكتب من ال إقتصار على إثبات عذاب القبر دون تنعيمه بناء على أن النصوص الواردة فيه أكثر, وعلى أن عامة أهل القبور كفار وعصاة, فالتعذيب بالذكر أجدر

This is better than what has been mentioned in most of the Kitaabs, wherein they restrict it to affirming `adhaab` in the `qabr` but not affirming the granting of pleasure and delight (to the Muslims who were obedient unto Allaah Ta`aalaa), because of the fact that the nusoos which affirm `adhaab` in the `qabr` are greater in number, and because of the people of the graves are Kaafirs and disobedient Muslims, so to mention the `adhaab` is more appropriate.

سؤال القبر

The Questioning in the Grave:

(وسؤال منكر ونكير)

"And the questioning by Munkar and Nakeer-"

وهما ملكان يدخلان القبر فيسألان العبد عن ربه وعن دينه وعن نبيه, قال السيد أبو شجاع: إن للصبيان سؤالاً, وكذا الأنبياء عند البعض

They are two Malaa'ikah who enter the *qabr* and ask the slave regarding his Rabb, his Deen and his Nabi صلى الله عليه وسلم.

Sayyid Abu Shujaa` said: "The children will also be questioned, and even the Ambiyaa according to some."

(ثابت)

"Is affirmed."

كل من هذه الأمور

All of these matters.

(بالدلائل السمعية)

"With evidences that are *sam`iyy* (i.e. heard from Rasoolullaah صلى الله عليه وسلم)."

لأنها أمور ممكنة أخبر بها الصادق على ما نطقت به النصوص, قال الله تعالى:

النَّارُ يُعْرَضُونَ عَلَيْهَا غُدُوًّا وَعَشِيًّا وَيَوْمَ تَقُومُ السَّاعَةُ أَدْخِلُوا آلَ فِرْعَوْنَ أَشَدَّ الْعَذَابِ

Because they are matters which are possible and which the Truthful One (i.e. Nabi صلى الله عليه وسلم) has informed us about concerning the things spoken of in the nusoos. Allaah Ta`aalaa said:

{"*The Fire, to which they will be exposed morning and evening, and on the Day when the Hour shall arise, (it shall be said) "Bring in the people of Fir`own for the severest `adhaab."*"}

وقال الله تعالى:

أُغْرِقُوا فَأُدْخِلُوا نَاراً

And Allaah Ta`aalaa said:

{"*They were drowned and made to enter the Fire.*"}

وقال النبي صلى الله عليه وسلم:

إِسْتَنْزِهُوْا مِنَ الْبَوْلِ, فَإِنَّ عَامَّةَ عَذَابِ الْقَبْرِ مِنْهُ

Nabi صلى الله عليه وسلم said:

"Avoid contact with urine, because most of the `*adhaab* in the *qabr* is due to it."

وقال عليه السلام: قوله تعالى:

يُثَبِّتُ اللهُ الَّذِينَ آمَنُوْا بِالْقَوْلِ الثَّابِتِ فِي الْحَيَاةِ الدُّنْيَا وَفِي الْآخِرَةِ

نزلت في عذاب القبر, إذا قيل له من ربك؟ وما دينك؟ ومن نبيك؟ فيقول ربي الله وديني الإسلام ونبيّي محمد عليه السلام

Rasolullaah صلى الله عليه وسلم said regarding the Aayah:

{"*Allaah establishes those who have Imaan with the Established Word in the life of the Dunyaa and in the Aakhirah...*"}

It was revealed regarding the `*adhaab* of the *qabr*, when it is said to (the person): Who is your Rabb? And what is your Deen? And who is your Nabi? So he will say: My Rabb is Allaah, and my Deen is Islaam, and my Nabi is Muhammad صلى الله عليه وسلم.

وقال النبي عليه الصلاة والسلام: إِذَا قُبِرَ الْمَيِّتُ أَتَاهُ مَلَكَانِ أَسْوَدَانِ أَزْرَقَانِ عَيْنَاهُمَا, يُقَالُ لِأَحَدِهِمَا مُنْكَرٌ وَالْآخَرُ نَكِيْرٌ

إلى آخر الحديث

Rasoolullaah صلى الله عليه وسلم said:

"When the *mayyit* is buried, two Malaa'ikah come to him who are black with blue eyes. One of them is called Munkar and the other is Nakeer."

Until the end of the Hadeeth.

وقال النبي عليه الصلاة والسلام: الْقَبْرُ رَوْضَةٌ مِنْ رِيَاضِ الْجَنَّةِ أَوْ حُفْرَةٌ مِنْ حُفَرِ النِّيْرَانِ

Rasoolullaah صلى الله عليه وسلم said:

"The qabr is a Garden from the Gardens of Jannah, or a pit from the pits of the Fires."

وبالجملة: الأحاديث الواردة في هذا المعنى وفي كثير من أحوال الآخرة, متواترة المعنى, وإن لم يبلغ آحادها حد التواتر

وأنكر عذاب القبر بعض المعتزلة والروافض, لأن الميت جماد لا حياة له ولا إدراك, فتعذيبه محال

In summary, the *Ahaadeeth* that are narrated concerning this meaning and regarding many of the states of the *Aakhirah* are *mutawaatir* in terms of meaning, even if the individual *Ahaadeeth* do not reach the level of *tawaatur*.

The ʿ*adhaab* in the *qabr* has been rejected by the Muʿtazilah and the Rawaafidh, because they say that the *mayyit* is a solid body in which there is no life and no comprehension, and thus punishing it is impossible.

والجواب: أنه يجوز أن يخلق الله تعالى في جميع الأجزاء أو في بعضها نوعاً من الحياة, قدر ما يدرك ألم العذاب أو لذة التنعيم, وهذا لا يستلزم إعادة الروح إلى بدنه, ولا أن يتحرك ويضطرب, أو يرى أثر العذاب عليه, حتى أن الغريق في الماء أو المأكول في بطون الحيوانات أو المصلوب في الهواء, يدعب وإن لم نطلع عليه, ومن تأمل في عجائب ملكه تعالى وملكوته وغرائب قدرته وجبروته, لم يستبعد أمثال ذلك فضلاً عن الإستحالة

The response to this is that it is possible that Allaah Taʿaalaa can create a kind of life in all of the parts of the body or in some of them, an amount by which the pain of ʿ*adhaab* can be felt, or pleasure can be experienced, and this does not necessitate that the *Rooh* returns to the body, nor does it necessitate that the body will move or shake or that the effects of the ʿ*adhaab* will be seen on it, so much so that the one who drowns in water or who is eaten by animals and is in their stomachs, or the one who is crucified in the air, all of them are punished (if they were Kaafirs) even if we are not aware of it. The one who ponders over the amazing matters of the Kingdom of Allaah Ta`aalaa and the Heavens and the marvels of His Power and His Might will not consider such things to be far-fetched, let alone impossible.

واعلم أنه لما كان لما أحوال القبر مما هو متوسط بين أمر الدنيا والآخرة, أفردها بالذكر, ثم اشتغل ببيان حقيقة الحشر وتفاصيل ما يتعلق بأمور الآخرة, ودليل الكل أنها أمور ممكنة, أخبر بها الصادق, ونطق بها الكتاب والسنة, فتكون ثابتة, وصرح بحقية كل منهما تحقيقاً وتوكيداً واعتناء بشأنه فقال:

Know that, because the states of the *qabr* are in-between the affairs of the Dunyaa and the affairs of the Aakhirah, he singled it out with mention and then engaged in explaining the haqeeqat of the resurrection and gathering (of people on the Day of Qiyaamah), and in explaining the details connected the matters of the Aakhirah. The evidence for each one is that they are matters that are possible, and which we have been informed of by the Truthful One (Rasoolullaah صلى الله عليه وسلم) and which are spoken of the the Qur'aan and the Sunnah, so they are affirmed. He emphatically declared that each of them is Haqq as a verification and emphasis, due to the importance of its status, so he said:

البعث

The Resurrection:

(والبعث)

"And the Resurrection."

وهو أن يبعث الله تعالى الموتى من القبور, بأن يجمع أجزاءهم الأصلية ويعيد الأرواح إليها

Which is that Allaah Ta`aalaa resurrects the dead from their graves, by gathering the original parts of their bodies and returning their *Arwaah* to them.

(حق)

"Is *Haqq* (True)."

لقوله تعالى:

﴿ثُمَّ إِنَّكُمْ يَوْمَ الْقِيَامَةِ تُبْعَثُونَ﴾

وقوله تعالى:

﴿قُلْ يُحْيِيهَا الَّذِي أَنشَأَهَا أَوَّلَ مَرَّةٍ﴾

Because Allaah Ta`aalaa said:

{"Then on the Day of Qiyaamah, you will be resurrected."}

And Allaah Ta`aalaa said:

{"Say: The One Who created it the first time will bring it (back to) life..."}

إلى غير ذلك من النصوص القاطعة الناطقة بحشر الأجساد، وأنكره الفلاسفة بناء على امتناع إعادة المعدوم بعينه، وهو مع أنه لا دليل لهم عليه يعتد به غير مضر بالمقصود، بأن مرادنا أن الله تعالى يجمع الأجزاء الأصلية للإنسان، ويعيد روحه إليه سواء سمي ذلك إعادة المعدوم بعينه أو لم يسم، بهذا سقط ما قالوا إنه لو أكل إنسان إنساناً بحيث صار جزءاً منه فتلك الأجزاء إما أن تعاد فيهما وهو محال أو في أحدهما، فلا يكون الآخر معاداً بجميع أجزائه، وذلك لأن المعاد إنما هو الأجزاء الأصلية الباقية من أول العمر إلى آخره، والأجزاء المأكولة فضلة في الآكال لا أصلية

And others from the decisive *nusoos* which speak about the gathering of the bodies (on the Day of Qiyaamah). The philosophers denied it based on their claim that it is impossible to restore that which is non-existent with its substance is impossible, despite the fact that there have no evidence to stand on other than harming the purpose, because our intended meaning is that Allaah Ta`aalaa will gather the original parts of the human being and return the *Rooh* to it regardless of whether that is termed the restoration of the non-existent thing with its substance or not. In this way their claim falls away, which is that if one person eats up another person so that he becomes a part of the one who ate him, then those parts must be restored in both of them, and that is impossible, or in one of them only, and thus the other is not restored with all of his parts. This claim of theirs falls away because the restored parts are the original parts continuing from the beginning of one's life until its end, and the parts that are eaten are superflous in the eater and are not from his original parts (*al-ajzaa' al-asliyyah*).

فإن قيل: هذا قول بالتناسخ, لأن البدن الثاني ليس هو الأول, لما ورد في الحديث من أن أهل الجنة جرد مرد مكحلون, وأن الجهنمي ضرسه مثل جبل أحد, ومن هاهنا قال من قال: ما من مذهب إلا وللتناسخ فيه قدم راسخ

If it is said: This statement entails reincarnation, because the second body is not the first body, because it has been narrated in the Hadeeth that the people of Jannah will have no hair on their body, will be beardless and will be adorned with *kuhl*, and that the molar tooth of the Jahannami is like the mountain of Uhud. It is for this reason some said: "There is no *Madh-hab* except that reincarnation has a firm footing in it."

قلنا: إنما يلزم التناسخ لو لم يكن البدن الثاني مخلوقاً من الأجزاء الأصلية للبدن الأول, وإن سمي مثل ذلك تناسخاً, كان نزاعاً في مجرد الإسم, ولا دليل على استحالة إعادة الروح إلى مثل هذا البدن, بل الأدلة قائمة على حقيته سواء سمي تناسخاً أم لا

We reply: It would only have entailed reincarnation had the second body not have been created from the original parts of the first body. If that is termed reincarnation, the dispute is only in the name, and there is no evidence for the impossibility of the *Rooh* returning to such a body. Rather, the proofs rest on the fact of its reality, whether it is called reincarnation or not.

الميزان

The Scale:

(والوزن حق)

"And the weighing (of deeds) is *Haqq*."

لقوله تعالى:

وَالْوَزْنُ يَوْمَئِذٍ الْحَقُّ

Because Allaah Ta`aalaa said:

{"*And the weighing (of deeds) on that day is Haqq.*"}

والميزان عبارة عما يعرف به كيفية مقادير الأعمال, والعقل قاصر عن إدراك كيفيته, وأنكره المعتزلة لأن الأعمال أعراض, وإن أمكن إعادتها لم يمكن وزنها, ولأنها معلومة لله تعالى فوزنها عبث

The *Meezaan* (scale of deeds) refers to that thing by which the amounts of the deeds are known. The intellect falls short in comprehending the manner in which it works. The Mu`tazilah denied it because deeds are *a`raadh* (i.e. they have no physical form) and even if they were restored, they would not be able to be weighed. And also, they are already known to Allaah Ta`aalaa so to weigh them is futile.

والجواب: أنه قد ورد في الحديث أن كتب الأعمال هي التي توزن فلا إشكال, وعلى تقدير تسليم كون أفعال الله تعالى معللة بالأغراض, لعل في الوزن حكمة لا نطلع عليها, وعدم اطلاعنا على الحكمة لا يوجب العبث

The response to this is that it has already been mentioned in the Ahaadeeth that it is the books of deeds that will be weighed, so there is no *ishkaal*. Because we submit that the Actions of Allaah Ta`aalaa have purposes, we say that perhaps there is in the weighing of deeds a wisdom which we have not yet discovered, but our not yet having discovered the wisdom behind it does not mean that it is futile.

الكتاب

The Book of Deeds:

(والكتاب)

"And the book of deeds-"

المثبت فيه طاعات العباد ومعاصيهم, يؤتى للمؤمنين بأيمانهم وللكفار بشمائلهم ووراء ظهورهم

In which is recorded the good and bad deeds of the slaves of Allaah Ta`aalaa. It is given to the Mu'mineen in their right hands and to the Kuffaar in their left and behind their backs.

(حق)

"Is Haqq."

لقوله تعالى:

وَنُخْرِجُ لَهُ يَوْمَ الْقِيَامَةِ كِتَاباً يَلْقَاهُ مَنْشُوراً

Because Allaah Ta`aalaa said:

{"*And We will bring out for him on the Day of Qiyaamah a book which he will find wide open.*"}

وقال تعالى:

فَأَمَّا مَنْ أُوتِيَ كِتَابَهُ بِيَمِينِهِ فَسَوْفَ يُحَاسَبُ حِسَاباً يَسِيراً

And Allaah Ta`aalaa said:

{"*As for the one who will be given his Kitaab in his right hand, then he will be given an easy hisaab (reckoning).*"}

وسكت المصنف عن ذكر الحساب إكتفاء بالكتاب, وأنكره المعتزلة زعماً منهم أنه عبث, والجواب ما مر

The author has kept silent regarding mentioning the *Hisaab* by sufficing on mentioning the books of deeds. The Mu`tazilah rejected it, claiming that it is futile, and the refutation against them is what has already preceded.

سؤال الله تعالى للعباد

The Questioning of the Slaves by Allaah Ta`aalaa:

(والسؤال حق)

"And the questioning is *Haqq*."

لقوله تعالى:

لَنَسْأَلَنَّهُمْ أَجْمَعِينَ

Because of the *Aayah*:

{"*And We will question all of them.*"}

ولقوله عليه السلام:

إنَّ اللهَ يُدْنِي الْمُؤْمِنَ فَيَضَعُ عَلَيْهِ كَنَفَهُ وَيَسْتُرُهُ, فَيَقُولُ: أَتَعْرِفُ ذَنْبَ كَذَا؟ أَتَعْرِفُ ذَنْبَ كَذَا؟ فَيَقُولُ: نَعَمْ أَيْ رَبِّ, حَتَّى إِذَا قَرَّرَهُ بِذُنُوبِهِ وَرَأَى فِي نَفْسِهِ أَنَّهُ هَلَكَ, قَالَ: سَتَرْتُهَا عَلَيْكَ فِي الدُّنْيَا وَأَنَا أَغْفِرُهَا لَكَ الْيَوْمَ, فَيُعْطَى كِتَابَ حَسَنَاتِهِ, وَأَمَّا الْكُفَّارُ وَالْمُنَافِقُونَ, فَيُنَادَى بِهِمْ عَلَى رُؤُوسِ الْخَلَائِقِ: هَؤُلَاءِ الَّذِينَ كَذَبُوا عَلَى رَبِّهِمْ, أَلَا لَعْنَةُ اللهِ عَلَى الظَّالِمِينَ

And the *Hadeeth*:

"Allaah will bring the Mu'min near and will cover him, and will say to him: "Do you know such-and-such a sin? Do you know such-and-such a sin?" He will say: "Yes, O my Rabb." Until when (Allaah Ta`aalaa) has made him admit to all of his sins, and he (this person) thinks that he is going to be destroyed, (Allaah Ta`aalaa) says to him: "I concealed (these sins) for you in the Dunyaa and I forgive them for you today." He will then be given his book of good deeds.

As for the Kuffaar and Munaafiqeen, then it shall be proclaimed regarding them in the presence of all of creation: "These are the ones who denied their Rabb. Indeed, the Curse of Allaah is upon the *zhaalimeen* (wrong-doers)."

الحوض

The *Hawdh-e-Kawthar*.

(والحوض حق)

"The *Hawdh* is *Haqq*."

لقوله تعالى:

إِنَّا أَعْطَيْنَاكَ الْكَوْثَرَ

Because of the *Aayah*:

{*"Indeed, We have given you Al-Kawthar."*}

ولقوله عليه السلام:

حَوْضِيْ مَسِيْرَةُ شَهْرٍ, وَمَاؤُهُ أَبْيَضُ مِنَ اللَّبَنِ, وَرِيْحُهُ أَطْيَبُ مِنَ الْمِسْكِ, وَكِيْزَانُهُ كَنُجُوْمِ السَّمَاءِ, مَنْ يَشْرَبُ مِنْهَا فَلَا يَظْمَأُ أَبَداً

And the *Hadeeth*:

"My *Hawdh* is a month's journey long. Its water is whiter than milk. It is more fragrant than musk. Its cups are like the stars in the sky. The one who drinks from it will never again become thirsty."

والأحاديث فيه كثيرة

The *Ahaadeeth* concerning it are many.

الصراط

The Bridge Over Jahannam:

(والصراط حق)

"The bridge over Jahannam is *Haqq*."

وهو جسر ممدود على متن جهنم, أدق من الشعر وأحد من السيف, يعبره أهل الجنة, ويزل به أقدم أهل النار, وأنكره أكثر المعتزلة لأنه لا يمكن العبور عليه, وإن أمكن فهو تعذيب للمؤمنين

It is a bridge extended over the middle of Jahannam. It is finer than a hair and sharper than a sword. The people of Jannah will cross it and the feet of the people of Jahannam will slip on it. It is denied by most of the Mu`tazilah because they claim it would not be possible to cross it, and even if it were possible it would be a form of punishment for the Mu'mineen.

والجواب أن الله تعالى قادر على أن يمكن من العبور عليه ويسهله على المؤمنين, حتى أن منهم من يجوزه كالبرق الخاطف, ومنهم كالريح الهابة, ومنهم كالجواد, إلى غير ذلك مما ورد في الحديث

The response to their claim is that Allaah Ta`aalaa is All-Powerful, and for Him to grant (people) the ability to cross over it and to make it easy for the Mu'mineen is easy, so much so that from the Mu'mineen, some will cross it as quickly as swift lightning, and others like a gust of wind, and some like a fast horse, and so on as is mentioned in the *Ahaadeeth* (concerning this).

الجنة والنار

Jannah and Jahannam:

(والجنة حق والنار حق)

"Jannah is *Haqq* and Jahannam is *Haqq*."

لأن الآيات والأحاديث الواردة في شأنهما أشهر من أن تخفى, وأكثر من أن تحصى

وتمسك المنكرون بأن الجنة موصوفة بأن عرضها كعرض السموات والأرض, وهذا في عالم العناصر محال, وفي عالم الأفلاك إدخال عالم في عالم, أو عالم آخر خارج عنه, مستلزم لجواز الخرق والإلتئام, وهو باطل

Because the *Aayaat* and *Ahaadeeth* concerning them are too apparent to be hidden and are innumerable.
Those who deny it use as evidence the fact that Jannah is described with the description that its width is like the width of the heavens and the earth, and in the world of elements that is an impossibility, and in the world of spheres the insertion of one world into world or into a world outside of it necessitates the passing through an opening and its joining together again, and that is false.

قلنا: هذا مبني على أصلكم الفاسد, وقد تكلمنا عليه في موضعه

We say: This is based on your corrupt principles, and we have discussed (that issue) in its place.

(وهما)

"And they."

أي الجنة والنار

Meaning, Jannah and Jahannam.

(مخلوقتان)

"Have already been created."

الآن

They are existing right now.

(موجودتان)

"Existing."

تكرير وتوكيد, وزعم أكثر المعتزلة أنهما إنما تخلقان يوم الجزاء, ولنا قصة آدم عليه السلام وإسكانهما الجنة, والآيات الظاهرة في إعدادهما مثل

أُعِدَّتْ لِلْمُتَّقِيْنَ

و

أُعِدَّتْ لِلْكَافِرِيْنَ

This is a repetition for the sake of emphasis. The majority of the Mu`tazilah claimed that Jannah and Jahannam will only be created on the Day of Qiyaamah. For us, we have as evidence the story of Nabi Aadam عليه السلام and Hadhrat Hawwaa عليها السلام and their living in Jannah. Also, the Aayaat which clearly mention that they have been prepared, such as:

{"It (Jannah) has been prepared for the Muttaqeen."}

And:

{"It (Jahannam) has been prepared for the Kaafireen."}

إذ لا ضرورة في العدول عن الظاهر, فإن عورض بمثل قوله تعالى:

تِلْكَ الدَّارُ الْآخِرَةُ نَجْعَلُهَا لِلَّذِينَ لَا يُرِيدُونَ عُلُوًّا فِي الْأَرْضِ وَلَا فَسَاداً

There is no need to move away from the apparent. If a person moves away from the apparent on the basis of the *Aayah*:

{"That is the Abode of the Aakhirah which We will make for those who do not desire an exalted place in the earth nor corruption..."}

قلنا: يحتمل الحال والإستمرار, ولو سلم فقصة آدم تبقى سالمة عن المعارض

We say: This carries the possibility of present tense and present continuous. And even if it were to be admitted, then the story of Nabi Aadam عليه السلام remains free from any opposing factors.

قالوا: لو كانتا موجودتين الآن لما جاز هلاك أكل الجنة لقوله تعالى:

أُكُلُهَا دَائِمٌ

لكنّ اللازم باطل لقوله تعالى:

كُلُّ شَيْءٍ هَالِكٌ إِلَّا وَجْهَهُ

They claimed: If Jannah and Jahannam already exist, then the destruction of the food of Jannah would not be possible, because Allaah Ta`aalaa said:

{"Its food is everlasting (daa'im)..."}

However, we reply by saying that the *laazim* (necessary conclusion if the food is everlasting) is false, because Allaah Ta`aalaa said:

{"Everything shall perish except His Wajh."}

قلنا: لا خفاء في أنه لا يمكن دوام أكل الجنة بعينه, وإنما المراد بالدوام أنه إذا فني منه شيء جيء ببدله, وهذا لا ينافي الهلاك لحظة, على أن الهلاك لا يستلزم الفناء, بل يكفي الخروج عن الإنتفاع به, ولو سلم فيجوز أن يكون المراد أن كل شيء ممكن فهو هالك في حد ذاته, بمعنى أن الوجود الإمكاني بالنظر إلى الوجود الواجبي بمنزلة العدم

We say: It is not hidden that it is not possible for the food of Jannah to be everlasting in its substance. Rather, the intended meaning of *dawaam* (everlasting) is that when any part of it is completed, a substitution is brought, and this does not negatory of a destruction for a time (i.e. when the *Soor* is blown before the Day of Qiyaamah), because that kind of destruction does not necessitate annihilation; rather, not being able to derive benefit from it is sufficient. Even if it were admitted, then it is possible that the intended meaning is that every possible thing, for it perishes within the limit of its essence, meaning that *al-wujood al-imkaani* (possible existence), when considered from the perspective of *Al-Wujood Al-Waajibi* (Necessary Existence), is in the category of non-existence.

(باقيتان لا تفنيان ولا يفنى أهلها)

أي دائمتان لا يطرأ عليهما عدم مستمر لقوله تعالى في حق الفريقتين:

خَالِدِيْنَ فِيْهَا أَبَداً

"Lasting forever. They will not come to an end and nor will their inhabitants come to an end."

Meaning, everlasting, and over them no continuous non-existence shall pass, becaus Allaah Ta`aalaa said regarding both groups:

{"They shall be therein forever."}

وأما ما قيل من أنهما تهلكان ولو لحظة تحقيقاً لقوله تعالى:

كُلُّ شيْءٍ هَالِكٌ إلَّا وَجْهَهُ

فلا ينافي البقاء بهذا المعنى, على أنك قد عرفت أنه لا دلالة في الآية على الفناء, وذهبت الجهمية إلى أنهما يفنيان ويفنى أهلهما, وهو قول باطل, مخالف للكتاب والسنة والإجماع, ليس عليه شبهة, فضلاً عن حجة

As for what is said, that they will be destroyed even if for a moment, as a verification of the *Aayah*:

{*"Everything shall perish except His Wajh."*}

This is not negatory of *baqaa'* (continuity) with this meaning, because you know that nothing in the *Aayah* points out to annihilation.

The Jahmiyyah adopted the view that they will be annihilated as will their inhabitants, and that is a *baatil* view which opposes the Qur'aan, the Sunnah and *ijmaa`*. There is no doubt regarding (it being *baatil*), let alone it being an evidence.

الكبائر

The Major Sins:

(والكبيرة)

"And the major sins."

قد اختلفت الروايات فيها, فروي عن ابن عمر رضي الله عنهما أنها تسعة: الشرك بالله, وقتل النفس بغير حق, وقذف المحصنة, والزنا, والفرار من الزحف, والسحر, وأكل مال اليتيم, وعقوق الوالدين المسلمين, والإلحاد في الحرم

The narrations differ concerning them. It is narrated from Hadhrat `Abdullaah ibn `Umar رضي الله عنهما that they are nine:
1. *Shirk*
2. Killing a person without any right
3. Accusing a chaste woman
4. *Zinaa*
5. Fleeing from the battlefield
6. *Sihr*
7. Eating the wealth of an orphan
8. Disobedience to Muslim parents

9. Contravening the limits of the *Haram*

وزاد أبو هريرة: أكل الربا

وزاد علي رضي الله عنه: السرقة وشرب الخمر

وقيل: كل ما كان مفسدته مثل مفسدة شيء مما ذكر أو أكثر منه

Hadhrat Abu Hurayrah رضي الله عنه added: "Consuming *ribaa*."

Hadhrat `Ali رضي الله عنه added: "Theft and drinking alcohol."

It has also been said: Every such thich which has a corruption like the corruption of the mentioned (major sins), or more than it (is also a major sin).

وقيل: كل ما توعد عليه الشرع بخصوصه

It has also been said: (A major sin is every such sin which) the Sharee`ah has specifically warned against.

وقيل: كل معصية أصر عليها العبد فهي كبيرة, وكل ما استغفر عنها فهي صغيرة

It has also been said: Every sin which the person persists on is a major sin, and every sin he makes *istighfaar* from is a minor sin.

وقال صاحب الكفاية: الحق أنهما إسمان إضافيان لا يعرفان بذاتيهما, فكل معصية إذا أضيفت إلى ما فوقه فهي صغيرة, وإن أضيفت إلى ما دونها فهي كبيرة, والكبيرة المطلقة هي الكفر, إذ لا ذنب أكبر منه

The author of *al-Kifaayah* said: "The truth is that they are relative terms that are not known in and of themselves. Thus, every sin if it is compared to what is above it, then it is minor, and if it is compared to what is below it, then it is major. And the absolute greatest sin is *Kufr*, because there is no sin worse than it.

وبالجملة: المراد هاهنا أن الكبيرة التي هي غير الكفر

In summary: The intended meaning here is that *kabeerah* (major sins) are those other than *Kufr*.

(لا تخرج العبد المؤمن من الإيمان)

"Does not take the person who is a Mu'min out of *Imaan*."

لبقاء التصديق الذي هو حقيقة الإيمان, خلافاً للمعتزلة, حيث زعموا أن مرتكب الكبيرة ليس بمؤمن ولا كافر, وهذا هو المنزلة بين المنزلتين, بناء على أن الأعمال عندهم جزء من حقيقة الإيمان

Because *tasdeeq* (assent), which is the *haqeeqat* of *Imaan*, remains. This is contrary to the belief of the Mu'tazilah, who claimed that the person who commits a major sin is neither a Mu'min nor a Kaafir, but that he is in what is known as *al-Manzilah baynal Manzilatayn* (the stage between the two stages of *Imaan* and *Kufr*), based on the fact that deeds, according to them, are a part of the *haqeeqat* of *Imaan*.

(ولا تدخله)

"And it does not enter him."

أي العبد المؤمن

(في الكفر)

Meaning, the Mu'min.

"Into *Kufr*."

خلافاً للخوارج, فإنهم ذهبوا إلى أن مرتكب الكبيرة بل الصغيرة أيضاً كافر, وأنه لا واسطة بين الكفر والإيمان

Contary to the Khawaarij, because they claimd that the person who commits a major sin, or rather, even a minor sin, is a Kaafir, and that there is no middle road between *Kufr* and *Imaan*.

لنا وجوه:

We argue against their claims from different angles:

الأول: ما سيجيء من أن حقيقة الإيمان هو التصديق القلبي, فلا يخرج المؤمن عن الإتصاف به إلا بما ينافيه, ومجرد الإقدام على الكبيرة لغلبة شهوة أو حمية أو أنفة أو كسل, خصوصاً إذا اقترن به خوف العقاب ورجاء العفو والعزم على التوبة, لا ينافيه, نعم, إذا كان بطريق الإستحلال والإستخفاف كان كفراً لكونه علامة للتكذيب, ولا نزاع في أن من المعاصي ما جعله الشارع أمارة للتكذيب, وعلم كونه كذلك بالأدلة الشرعية كسجود للصنم, وإلقاء المصحف في القاذورات, والتلفظ بكلمات الكفر, ونحو ذلك مما يثبت بالأدلة أنه كفر

The first is that which shall be mentioned, which is that the *haqeeqat* of *Imaan* is *at-tasdeeq al-qalbi* (assent of the heart). Thus, nothing expels a Mu'min from being described with it except that which is negatory of it, and the mere perpetration of a major sin due to the person being overpowered by desire, or anger, or indignation, or laziness, is not negatory of Imaan, especially if it is tied to fear of being punished by Allaah Ta`aalaa and hoping for the forgiveness of Allaah Ta`aalaa and having a resolve to make *tawbah*. It is not negatory of it. Yes, if the person does istihlaal (regards the sins as being permissible) or regards them as being insignificant, then that is *Kufr*, because that is a sign of rejection, and there is no dispute regarding the fact that the Sharee`ah has branded some sins as being a sign of rejection (i.e. that the person rejects Allaah Ta`aalaa), and it is known as being such through Shar`i evidences, such as making *sujood* to an idol, or throwing the *Mus-haf* into dirt, or uttering words of *Kufr*, etc., because all of that has been established through the proofs of the Sharee`ah that it is *Kufr*.

وبهذا ينحل ما قيل: أن الإيمان إذا كان عبارة عن التصديق والإقرار, ينبغي أن لا يصير المقر المصدق كافراً بشيء من أفعال الكفر وألفاظه, ما لم يتحقق منه التكذيب أو الشك

With this, that which had been said is solved, that if Imaan refers to assent and admission, then the the one who admits and assents (to *Imaan*) should not become a Kaafir through any of the actions or statements of *Kufr* so long as rejection or doubt has not been come from him.

الثاني: الآيات والأحاديث الناطقة بإطلاق المؤمن على العاصي كقوله تعالى:

يَٰٓأَيُّهَا ٱلَّذِينَ ءَامَنُواْ كُتِبَ عَلَيْكُمُ ٱلْقِصَاصُ فِى ٱلْقَتْلَى

وقوله تعالى:

يَا أَيُّهَا الَّذِينَ آمَنُوا تُوبُوا إِلَى اللهِ تَوْبَةً نَصُوحاً

The second point is the *Aayaat* and *Ahaadeeth* which unrestrictedly uses the term Mu'min upon one who is disobedient as well, like in the *Aayah*:

{"O you who have Imaan, qisaas has been prescribed upon you for the slain."}

And the *Aayah*:

{"O you who have Imaan, turn to Allaah with a sincere repentance."}

وقوله تعالى:

وَإِنْ طَائِفَتَانِ مِنَ الْمُؤْمِنِينَ اقْتَتَلُوا

الآية

And the *Aayah*:

{"And if two groups from the Mu'mineen fight one another..."}

وهي كثيرة

And there are many like this.

الثالث: إجماع الأمة من عصر النبي عليه السلام إلى يومنا هذا, بالصلاة على من مات من أهل القبلة من غير توبة, والدعاء والإستغفار لهم مع العلم بارتكابهم الكبائر, بعد الإتفاق على أن ذلك لا يجوز لغير المؤمن

واحتجت المعتزلة بوجهين:

The third point is the *ijmaa`* of the Ummah from the time of Nabi صلى الله عليه وسلم until the present day, of performing *Janaazah Salaat* for the person who dies who is from the Ahl-ul-Qiblah, even if he had not made *tawbah*, and that *Du`aa* and *istighfaar* is made on his behalf despite knowing that he had perpetrated major sins, and along with the unanimous agreement that this is not permissible in the case of a Kaafir.

The Mu`tazilah argue from two facets:

الأول: أن الأمة بعد اتفاقهم على أن مرتكب الكبيرة فاسق إختلفوا في أنه مؤمن؟ وهو مذهب أهل السنة والجماعة, أو كافر؟ وهو قول الخوارج, أو منافق؟ وهو قول الحسن البصري, فأخذنا المتفق عليه, وتركنا المختلف فيه, وقلنا: هو فاسق, ليس بمؤمن ولا كافر ولا منافق

والجواب أن هذا إحداث للقول المخالف لما أجمع عليه السلف من عدم المنزلة بين المنزلتين, فيكون باطلاً

The first is that, even though the *Ummah* has *ittifaaq* that the person who perpetrates major sins is a faasiq, they differed regarding whether he is a Mu'min, which is the Madh-hab of Ahlus Sunnah wal-Jamaa`ah, or a Kaafir, which is the view of the Khawaarij, or a Munaafiq, which is the view of Imaam Hasan al-Basri. We took the view that is agreed upon and abandoned that which is differed regarding, and we said: He is a faasiq. He is neither a Mu'min, nor a Kaafir, nor a Munaafiq.

والثاني: أنه ليس بمؤمن لقوله تعالى:

أَفَمَنْ كَانَ مُؤْمِناً كَمَنْ كَانَ فَاسِقاً

جعل المؤمن مقابلاً للفاسق, وقوله عليه السلام: لَا يَزْنِيْ الزَانِيْ حِيْنَ يَزْنِيْ وَهُوَ مُؤْمِنٌ

وقوله عليه الصلاة والسلام: لَا إِيْمَانَ لِمَنْ لَا أَمَانَةَ لَهُ

The second is that he is not a Mu'min on account of the *Aayah*:

{"*Is the one who is a Mu'min like the one who is a faasiq?*"}

Allaah Ta`aalaa has made a Mu'min opposite to a faasiq. And also because of the *Hadeeth*:

"The *zaani* does not commit *zinaa* whilst he is a Mu'min."

And because of the *Hadeeth*:

"There is no *Imaan* for the one who is devoid of trustworthiness."

ولا كافر لما تواتر من أن الأمة كانوا لا يقتلونه, ولا يجرون عليه أحكام المرتدين, ويدفنونه في مقابر المسلمين

والجواب أن المراد بالفاسق في الآية هو الكافر, فإن الكفر من أعظم الفسوق, والحديث وارد على سبيل التغليظ, والمبالغة في الزجر عن المعاصي, بدليل الآيات والأحاديث الدالة على أن الفاسق مؤمن, حتى قال عليه السلام لأبي ذر لما بالغ في السؤال:

But they said that the one who commits major sins is not a Kaafir, because it is known through tawaatur that the *Ummah* did not kill such people and nor did they apply upon them the laws of the Murtaddeen, and also, they used to bury them in the graveyards of the Muslims.

The response is that the intended meaning of faasiq in the *Aayah* is "Kaafir", because *Kufr* is the greatest form of *fisq*, and the *Hadeeth* gives the meaning of *taghleezh* (showing how severe the crime is) and *mubaalaghah* in order to keep the Ummah away from sins, with the evidence of the *Aayaat* and *Ahaadeeth* which prove that the faasiq is a Mu'min, so much so that Rasoolullaah صلى الله عليه وسلم said to Hadhrat Abu Dharr رضي الله عنه when he went to excess in questioning:

وَإِنْ زَنَى وَإِنْ سَرَقَ عَلَى رَغْمِ أَنْفِ أَبِيْ ذَرٍّ

"Even if (the person) commits *zinaa* and steals, in spite of Abu Dharr."

واحتجت الخوارج بالنصوص الظاهرة في أن الفاسق كافر, كقوله تعالى:

وَمَنْ لَمْ يَحْكُمْ بِمَا أَنْزَلَ اللهُ فَأُولَئِكَ هُمُ الْكَافِرُوْنَ

وقوله تعالى:

وَمَنْ كَفَرَ بَعْدَ ذَلِكَ فَأُولَئِكَ هُمُ الْفَاسِقُوْنَ

The Khawaarij used as evidence the nusoos which on the apparent gives the meaning of a faasiq being a Kaafir, such as the *Aayah*:

{"And whosoever does not rule by what Allaah has revealed, they are the Kaafiroon."}

And the *Aayah*:

{"And whosoever commits Kufr after there, they are the Faasiqoon."}

وكقوله عليه السلام:

مَنْ تَرَكَ الصَّلَاةَ مُتَعَمِّداً فَقَدْ كَفَرَ

And the *Hadeeth*:

"Whosoever leaves off *Salaah* intentionally has committed *Kufr*."

وفي أن العذاب مختص بالكافر, كقوله تعالى:

أَنَّ الْعَذَابَ عَلَى مَنْ كَذَّبَ وَتَوَلَّى

And also on account of the fact that `adhaab has been made *khaas* for the Kaafir, like in the *Aayah*:

{"The `Adhaab is upon the one who rejects and turns away (from the Haqq)."}

وقوله تعالى:

لَا يَصْلَاهَا إِلَّا الْأَشْقَى الَّذِيْ كَذَّبَ وَتَوَلَّى

And the *Aayah*:

{"None shall burn in it except the most wretched. The one who rejected and turned away (from the Haqq)."}

وقوله تعالى:

إِنَّ الْخِزْيَ الْيَوْمَ وَالسُّوْءَ عَلَى الْكَافِرِيْنَ

And the *Aayah*:

{"Indeed, disgrace and punishment will be upon the Kaafireen today."}

إلى غير ذلك

And other such *Aayaat*.

والجواب: أنها متروكة الظاهر للنصوص الناطقة على أن مرتكب الكبيرة ليس بكافر والإجماع المنعقد على ذلك على ما مر, والخوارج خوارج عما انعقد عليه الإجماع, فلا اعتداد بهم

The response to them is that the apparent meaning is left off due to the nusoos which prove that the perpetrator of major sins is not a Kaafir, and because of the *ijmaa`* which has been established upon that issue, as has been mentioned. The Khawaarij as Khawaarij (literally: those who have left) from that upon which *ijmaa`* was established, so no attention is paid to them.

(والله لا يغفر أن يشرك به)

"Allaah does not forgive that *Shirk* is done concerning Him."

بإجماع المسلمين, لكنهم اختلفوا في أنه هل يجوز عقلاً أم لا؟ فذهب بعضهم إلى أنه يجوز عقلاً, وإنما علم عدمه بدليل السمع, وبعضهم إلى أنه يمتنع عقلاً, لأن قضية الحكمة التفرقة بين المسيء والمحسن, والكفر نهاية في الجناية, لا يحتمل الإباحة, ورفع الحرمة أصلاً فلا يحتمل العفو ورفع الغرامة, وأيضاً الكافر يعتقده حقاً ولا يطلب له عفواً ومغفرة, فلم يكن العفو عنه حكمة, وأيضاً هو اعتقاد الأبد فيوجب جزاء الأبد, وهذا بخلاف سائر الذنوب

This is by the *ijmaa`* of the Muslims. However, they differed regarding whether it is possible for him to be forgiven, logically, or not? Some of them said that logically it is possible, but it is known through the *sam`iyy* evidences that he will not be forgiven. Some of them said that logically it is impossible, because wisdom demands a distinction between the one who does evil and the one who does god, and *Kufr* is the greatest crime which carries no possibility of permissibility or original removal of prohibition, and thus it does not carry the possibility of forgiveness and being cleared of the penalty. Also, the Kaafir believes the *Kufr* to be *Haqq* and thus will not seek forgiveness for it, and thus forgiving him is not consistent with *Hikmah* (Wisdom). Also, it is an eternal belief and thus necessitates an eternal punishment, and this is contrary to all (other) sins.

(ويغفر ما دون ذلك لمن يشاء من الصغائر والكبائر)

"But He forgives besides (*Shirk*) whatever He wills, from the minor sins and major sins."

مع التوبة أو بدونها خلافاً للمعتزلة, وفي تقرير الحكم ملاحظة للآية الدالة على ثبوته, والآيات والأحاديث في هذا المعنى كثيرة, والمعتزلة يخصصونها بالصغائر وبالكبائر المقرونة بالتوبة, وتمسكوا بوجهين:

With or without *tawbah*, unlike the Mu`tazilah. In the statement of this ruling consideration is given to the *Aayah* which points out to its affirmation, and the *Aayaat* and *Ahaadeeth* in this meaning are many, and the Mu`tazilah make it *khaas* for the minor sins, and which major sins provided they are coupled with tawbah, and they used as evidence two facets:

الأول: الآيات والأحاديث الواردة في وعيد العصاة

The first is the *Aayaat* and *Ahaadeeth* mentioning the threat for the disobedient ones.

والجواب: أنها على تقدير عمومها, إنما تدل على الوقوع دون الوجوب, وقد كثرت النصوص في العفو, فيخصص المذنب المغفور عن عموميات الوعيد, وزعم بعضهم أن الخلف في الوعيد كرم, فيجوز من الله تعالى, والمحققون على خلافه, كيف وهو تبديل للقول وقد قال الله تعالى:

مَا يُبَدَّلُ الْقَوْلُ لَدَيَّ

The response to this first claim of theirs is that, on the supposition that (these *Aayaat* and *Ahaadeeth*) are general, then they indicate that (forgiveness) may take place, not that it necessarily takes place. And, the nusoos regarding forgiveness are many, so the sinner who is forgiven is excluded from the generality of the threat. Some of them claimed that the non-fulfillment of a threat is generosity, so it is possible (to come from) Allaah Ta`aalaa. The Muhaqqiqoon state the opposite of this, and they say, "How? That would be changing the Word (of Allaah Ta`aalaa), whereas Allaah Ta`aalaa said:

{"The Word by Me does not change."}

الثاني: أن المذنب إذا علم أنه لا يعاقب على ذنبه كان ذلك تقريراً له على الذنب, وإغراء للغير عليه, وهذا ينافي كحمة إرسال الرسل

The second argument of the Mu`tazilah is that the sinner, if he knows that he will not be punished, that will encourage him to sin and incite others (as well) to sin, and this is negatory of the Wisdom of the Rusul being sent.

والجواب: أنه مجرد جواز العفو لا يوجب ظن عدم العقاب, فضلاً عن العلم, كيف والعمومات الواردة في الوعيد المقرونة بغاية من التهديد ترجح جانب الوقوع بالنسبة إلى كل واحد؟ وكفى به زاجراً

The response to this second argument of theirs is that the mere possibility of forgiveness does not necessitate the thought of the absence of punishment, let alone the knowledge (of such a thing). How so, when the generality in the threat which is coupled to the declaration that punishment will occur, thus giving *tarjeeh* to the possibility of occurence to each individual case? And that is sufficient as a deterrant.

(ويجوز العقاب على الصغيرة)

"And punishment for a minor sin is permissible."

سواء إجتنب مرتكبها الكبيرة أم لا, لدخولها تحت قوله تعالى:

وَيَغْفِرُ مَا دُونَ ذَلِكَ لِمَنْ يَشَاءُ

Regardless of whether the person stayed away from major sins or not, because of it coming under the *Aayah*:

{"*And He forgives what is less than that for whomsoever He wills.*"}

ولقوله تعالى:

لَا يُغَادِرُ صَغِيرَةً وَلَا كَبِيرَةً إِلَّا أَحْصَاهَا

والإحصاء إنما يكون بالسؤال والمجازاة, إلى غير ذلك من الآيات والأحاديث

{"*He doe not pass by a small sin or a major sin except that He counts it.*"}

Ihsaa (counting) takes place with questioning and recompensing. There are other such *Aayaat* and *Ahaadeeth*.

وذهب بعض المعتزلة إلى أنه إذا اجتنب الكبائر لم يجز تعذيبه, لا بمعنى أنه يمتنع عقلاً بل بمعنى أنه لا يجوز أ, يقع لقيام الأدلة السمعية على أنه لا يقع, لقوله تعالى:

إِنْ تَجْتَنِبُوا كَبَائِرَ مَا تُنْهَوْنَ عَنْهُ نُكَفِّرْ عَنْكُمْ سَيِّئَاتِكُمْ

The Mu`tazilah held the view that if a person abstains from major sins, then to punish him is not permissible. Not in the meaning that it is not possible logically, but in the meaning that it cannot occur due to the *sam`iyy* evidences pointing out to the fact that it will not occur, such as the *Aayah*:

{"*If you abstain from the kabaa'ir (major sins) from which you were prohibited, We shall expiate from you your sins.*"}

وأجيب: بأن الكبيرة المطلقة هي الكفر, لأنه الكامل, وجمع الإسم بالنظر إلى أنواع الكفر, وإن كان الكل ملة واحدة في الحكم, أو إلى أفراده القائمة بأفراد المخاطبين, على ما تشهد من قاعدة أن مقابلة الجمع بالجمع تقتضي انقسام الآحاد بالآحاد, كقولنا ركب القوم دوابهم ولبسوا ثيابهم

The response to this is that the absolute largest sin is *Kufr*, because it is the most complete sin. The reason the word is used in plulral form in the *Aayah* is to refer to all the different kinds of *Kufr*, even though all of them are of one degree in terms of the ruling, or the statement is of individual sins subsisting in the ones addressed. This is according to what is testified to by the principle that putting a plural alongside a plural necessitates the separation of the units into units, like how we say, "The people rode their animals are wore their garments."

(والعفو عن الكبيرة)

"**And forgiveness for major sins.**"

هذا مذكور فيما سبق, إلا أنه أعاده ليعلم أن ترك المؤاخذة على الذنب يطلق عليه لفظ العفو, كما يطلق عليه لفظ المغفرة, وليتعلق به قوله:

This is mentioned in that which has preceded. However, he repeated it here so that it may be known that when punishment for the sin is left, the term `*Afw* (pardon) is generally used, just as the term *Maghfirah* is generally used, and connected to it is his statement:

(إذا لم تكن عن استحلال, والإستحلال كفر)

"If it is not accompanied by *istihlaal* ("Halaalizing" of sins), for *istihlaal* is *Kufr*."

لما فيه من التكذيب المنافي للتصديق, وبهذا تؤول النصوص الدالة على تخليد العصاة في النار, أو على سلب اسم الإيمان عنهم

Because *istihlaal* is negatory of *tasdeeq* (assent). In this manner the *nusoos* which point out to the disobedient ones being forever in the Fire of Jahannam or the removal of *Imaan* from them, are interpreted.

الشفاعة والخلود في النار

Intercession, and Eternity in the Fire:

(والشفاعة ثابتة للرسل بالأخبار في حق أهل الكبائر)

"*Shafaa'ah* (Intercession) by the Rusul is affirmed with the narrations regarding the perpetrators of major sins."

بالمستفيض من الأخبار, خلافاً للمعتزلة, وهذا مبني على ما سبق من جواز العفو والمغفرة بدون الشفاعة, فالشفاعة أولى, وعندهم لما لم يجز لم تجز

لنا قوله تعالى:

وَاسْتَغْفِرْ لِذَنبِكَ لِلْمُؤْمِنِينَ وَالْمُؤْمِنَاتِ

By the narrations which are widely spread. This is contrary to the view of the Mu`tazilah. This is based on what has preceded from the permissibility of `*Afw* and *Maghfirah* without *Shafaa'ah*, so with *Shafaa'ah* they are even more (likely to be forgiven). According to the Mu`tazilah, when it (`*Afw*) is not permissible, then neither is intercession.

We have as proof the *Aayah*:

{"*And seek forgiveness for your sin and for the Mu'mineen and Mu'minaat...*"}

وقوله تعالى:

فَمَا تَنْفَعُهُمْ شَفَاعَةُ الشَّافِعِيْنَ

And the *Aayah*:

{"*So the intercession of the interceders did not benefit them.*"}

فإن أسلوب هذا الكلام يدل على ثبوت الشفاعة في الجملة, وإلا لما كان لنفي نفعها عن الكافرين عند القصد إلى تقبيح حالهم وتحقيق بأسهم معنى, لأن مثل هذا المقام يقتضي أن يوسموا بما يخصهم, لا بما يعمهم وغيرهم, وليس المراد أن تعليق الحكم بالكافر يدل على نفيه عما عداه, حتى يرد عليه أنه إنما يقوم حجة على من يقول بمفهوم المخالفة

This kind of statement points out to the affirmation of *Shafaa`ah* in general; otherwise, there would be no meaning in negating the benefit in it for the Kaafireen, when the purpose is to make vile their condition and verify as certain their evil, because the likes of this position necessitates that they (the Kuffaar) be stamped with something that is characteristic of them, not with that which is general for them and other than them. The intended meaning is not that the connecting the ruling with the Kaafir points out to it not being connected with anyone else, so much so that this only stands as an argument against those who take the understanding that Allaah does not carry out (that which He has threatened).

وقوله عليه السلام: شَفَاعَتِيْ لِأَهْلِ الْكَبَائِرِ مِنْ أُمَّتِيْ

And the *Hadeeth*:

"My *Shafaa`ah* is for the perpetrators of major sins from my *Ummah*."

وهو مشهور, بال الأحاديث في باب الشفاعة متواترة المعنى

This is *Mash-hoor*. Rather, the *Ahaadeeth* concerning *Shafaa`ah* are *mutawaatir* in terms of meaning.

واحتجت المعتزلة بمثل قوله تعالى:

وَاتَّقُوْا يَوْماً لَا تَجْزِيْ نَفْسٌ عَنْ نَّفْسٍ شَيْئاً وَلَا يُقْبَلُ مِنْهَا شَفَاعَةٌ

وقوله تعالى:

مَا لِلظَّالِمِينَ مِنْ حَمِيمٍ وَلَا شَفِيعٍ يُطَاعُ

The Mu`tazilah used as evidence the *Aayah*:

{"Fear the day in which no soul shall avail another, nor will any intercession be accepted from it."}

And the *Aayah*:

{"The Zhaalimeen (oppressors; tyrants; wrong-doers) shall have no friend nor any intercessor who shall be obeyed."}

والجواب بعد تسليم دلالتها على العموم في الأشخاص والأزمان والأحوال: أنه يجب تخصيصها بالكفار, جمعاً بين الأدلة, ولما كان أصل العفو والشفاعة ثابتاً بالأدلة القطعية من الكتاب والسنة والإجماع, قالت المعتزلة بالعفو عن الصغائر مطلقاً وعن الكبائر بعد التوبة, وبالشفاعة لزيادة الثواب, وكلاهما فاسد:

The answer, after submitting that it applies in general to persons, times and conditions, is that: it is specific to the Kuffaar, as a joining between the evidences. Because the foundations of `*Afw* and *Shafaa`ah* is established with decisive proofs from the Qur'aan and the Sunnah and *ijmaa`*, the Mu`tazilah said that `*Afw* is from the minor sins, unrestrictedly, and from the major sins after *tawbah*, and with *Shafaa`ah* there is an increase in reward, and both of their (views) are corrupt.

أما الأول: فلأن التائب ومرتكب الصغيرة المجتنب عن الكبيرة لا يستحقان العذاب عندهم, فلا معنى للعفو

وأما الثاني: فلأن النصوص دالة على الشفاعة, بمعنى طلب العفو عن الجناية

As for the first, then it is because the one who makes *tawbah* and the one who commits minor sins and abstains from major sins is not deserving of punishment, according to them. If that is the case, then what is the purpose of `Afw?

As for the second, then it is because the nusoos point out to *Shafaa`ah*, in the meaning of seeking *`Afw* from crimes perpetrated.

(وأهل الكبائر من المؤمنين لا يخلدون في النار)

"The Mu'mineen who are perpetrators of major sins will not be forever in the Fire of Jahannam."

وإن ماتوا من غير توبة, لقوله تعالى:

فَمَنْ يَعْمَلْ مِثْقَالَ ذَرَّةٍ خَيْراً يَرَهُ

Even if they die without *tawbah*, because of the *Aayah*:

{*"So whosoever does good equal in weight to an atom shall see it."*}

ونفس الإيمان عمل خير, لا يمكن أن يرى جزاءه قبل دخول النار, ثم يدخل النار فيخلد, لأنه باطل بالإجماع, فتعين الخروج من النار, ولقوله تعالى:

Imaan itself is the doing of good, and it is not possible to see its recompense prior to entry into the Fire of Jahannam, and then he enters the Fire and is in it forever. Because their view is *baatil* according to *ijmaa`*, Imaam an-Nasafi specifically mentioned exiting from the Fire of Jahannam. And because of the *Aayah*:

وَعَدَ اللهُ الْمُؤْمِنِينَ وَالْمُؤْمِنَاتِ جَنَّاتٍ تَجْرِي مِنْ تَحْتِهَا الْأَنْهَارُ

ولقوله تعالى:

إِنَّ الَّذِينَ آمَنُوا وَعَمِلُوا الصَّالِحَاتِ كَانَتْ لَهُمْ جَنَّاتُ الْفِرْدَوْسِ نُزُلاً

{*"Allaah has promised the Mu'mineen and the Mu'minaat Jannaat (Gardens) beneath which rivers flow..."*}

And the *Aayah*:

{*"Indeed, those who have Imaan and do good deeds, they will have Jannaat-ul-Firdows as their resting place."*}

إلى غير ذلك من النصوص الدالة على كون المؤمن من أهل الجنة مع ما سبق من الأدلة القاطعة على أن البعد لا يخرج بالمعصية عن الإيمان, وأيضاً الخلود في النار من أعظم العقوبات, وقد جعل جزاء الكفر الذي هو أعظم الجنايات, فلو جزي به غير الكافر كان زيادة على قدر الجناية فلا يكون عدلاً

There are other such nusoos which point out to the fact that the Mu'min is from the people of Jannah, along with what has preceded from the decisive proofs that a person does not exit *Imaan* on account of disobedience. Also, eternity in Jahannam is the greatest of punishments, and thus it has been made the recompense for *Kufr* which is the worst of crimes. Thus, if other than a Kaafir were recompensed with it, it would be above the level of the crime and thus would not be just.

وذهبت المعتزلة إلى أن من أدخل النار فهو خالد فيها, لأنه إما كافر أو صاحب كبيرة مات بلا توبة, إذ المعصوم والتائب وصاحب الصغيرة إذا اجتنبوا ليسوا من أهل النار, على ما سبق من أصولهم, والكافر مخلد بالإجماع, وكذا صاحب الكبيرة بلا توبة, لوجهين:

The Mu`tazilah held the view that whosoever enters Jahannam will be in it forever, because he is either a Kaafir or a perpetrator of major sins without tawbah, because those who are *ma`soom* (protected from sins, i.e. the Ambiyaa), and the one who makes *tawbah*, and the one who committed minor sins but not major sins, they are not from the people of Jahannam, according to what has preceded from their principles. The Kaafir is forever in Jahannam according to *ijmaa`*, and the same goes for the perpetrator of major sins without *tawbah* (according to them), due to two facets:

أحدهما: أنه يستحق العذاب وهو مضرة خالصة دائمة, فينافي استحقاق الثواب الذي هو منفعة خالصة دائمة

The first is that he deserves such an `*Adhaab* as a genuine everlasting harm to him, but that is negatory of him deserving reward which is a genuine everlasting benefit for him.

والجواب: منع قيد الدوام, بل منع الإستحقاق بالمعنى الذي قصدواه, وهو الإستيجاب, وإنما الثواب فضل منه والعذا عدل فإن شاء عفا وإن شاء عذبه مدة, ثم يدخله الجنة

The response to this is to preclude the restriction of the meaning of "everlasting". Rather, precluding the meaning of "deserving" with the meaning which they intend, which is "being necessary". But reward is a Virtue from Him and punishment is Justice; so if He wills, He pardons and if He wills, He punishes the person for a time and thereafter enters him into Jannah.

الثاني: النصوص الدالة على الخلود كقوله تعالى:

The second is the *nusoos* which point out to being eternally in Jahannam, like the *Aayah*:

وَمَنْ يَقْتُلْ مُؤْمِناً مُتَعَمِّداً فَجَزَاؤُهُ جَهَنَّمُ خَالِداً فِيهَا

{"*And whosoever kills a Mu'min intentionally, then his recompense is Jahannam, to remain forever therein.*"}

وقوله تعالى:

وَمَنْ يَعْصِ اللهَ وَرَسُولَهُ وَيَتَعَدَّ حُدُودَهُ يُدْخِلْهُ نَاراً خَالِداً فِيهَا

وقوله تعالى:

مَنْ كَسَبَ سَيِّئَةً وَأَحَاطَتْ بِهِ خَطِيئَتُهُ فَأُولَئِكَ أَصْحَابُ النار هُمْ فِيهَا خَالِدُونَ

And the *Aayah*:

{"*And whosoever disobeys Allaah and His Rasool and transgresses His Hudood (the limits set by Him), He will enter him into the Fire, to abide therein forever.*"}

And the *Aayah*:

{"*Whosoever earns sin and his sins encompass him, then they are the people of the Fire. They shall abide therein forever.*"}

والجواب: أن قاتل المؤمن لكون مؤمناً لا يكون إلا الكافر, وكذا من تعدى جميع الحدود, كذا من أحاطت به خطيئته, وشملته من كل جانب, ولو سلم فالخلود قد يستعمل في المكث الطويل, كقولهم سجن مجلد, ولو سلم فمعارض بالنصوص الدالة على عدم الخلود كما مر

The response to them is that the one who kills the Mu'min on account of him being a Mu'min would only be a Kaafir (i.e. no Muslim would do such a thing), and the same goes for the one who transgresses all of the *Hudood* of Allaah and the one whose sins completely encompass him and surround him from every side. And even if it is submitted, then "*khulood*" eternity" is also used to refer to a lengthy period of time, like the statement: "perpetual imprisonment". And even if it is submitted, then still it is opposed by the nusoos which point out to the absence of eternity (for those who are Muslim) as has preceded.

مطلب الإيمان

The Meaning of *Imaan*:

(والإيمان)

"And *Imaan*."

في اللغة: التصديق, أي إذعان حكم المخبر وقبوله وجعله صادقاً, إفعال من الأمن, كأن حقيقة آمن به: آمنه من التكذيب والمخالفة يتعدى باللام كما في قوله تعالى حكاية:

وَمَا أَنْتَ بِمُؤْمِنٍ لَنَا

أي بمصدق, وبالباء كما في قوله عليه السلام:

الإِيْمَانُ أَنْ تُؤْمِنَ بِاللهِ

الحديث

Linguistically, it refers to *tasdeeq* (assent), i.e. acknowleding the judgement of the One Who informs, and accepting it, and considering it to be true. The word is on *Baab If`aal* from the word "*al-Amn*", as though the *haqeeqat* of "He brought *Imaan*" is: "He kept it safe from rejection and opposition."

It is *muta`addi* when there is a *laam*, like in the *Aayah*:

{"*And you are not a believer in us.*"}

Meaning, one who believes what we say to be true. It is also *muta`addi* with a *baa*, like in the *Hadeeth*:

"*Imaan* is that you believe in Allaah."

أي تصديق, وليس حقيقة التصديق أن يقع في القلب نسبة الصدق إلى الخبر أو المخبر من غير إذعان وقبول, بل هو إذعان وقبول لذلك, بحيث يقع عليه اسم التسليم على ما صرح به الإمام الغزالي

Meaning, that you assent to. The *haqeeqat* of *tasdeeq* is not that there occurs in the heart the relation of truthfulness to the narration or to the one narrating without there being acknowledgement and acceptance. Rather, it is acknowledgement and acceptance of it, in such a manner that the term "submitting" (*at-Tasleem*) can be applied to it, as was emphatically declared by Imaam al-Ghazaali رحمة الله عليه.

وبالجملة: هو المعنى الذي يعبر عنه بالفارسية بِگْرويدَنْ, وهو معنى التصديق المقابل للتصور, حيث يقال في أوائل علم الميزان: العلم إما تصور, وإما تصديق, صرح بذلك رئيسهم ابن سينا, ولو حصل هذا المعنى لبعض الكفار, كان إطلاق إسم الكافر عليه من جهة أن عليه شيئاً من أمارات التكذيب والإنكار, كما إذا فرضنا أن أحداً صدق بجميع ما جاء به النبي عليه السلام وسلمه وأقرّ به وعمل, ومع ذلك شد الزنار بالإختيار, أو سجد للصنم بالإختيار, نجعله كافراً, لما أن النبي عليه السلام جعل ذلك علامة التكذيب والإنكار, وتحقيق هذا المقام على ما ذكرت يسهل لك التطريق إلى حل كثير من الإشكالات الموردة في مسألة الإيمان

In summary: it has the meaning which is referred to by the Faarsi (Persian) word: "*Girawidan*" (i.e. to believe in, confide in, follow, admire, love). It has the meaning of *at-Tasdeeq*, which is opposite to *at-Tasawwur* (conception), just as it is said in the first principles of the science of logic: "Knowledge is either conception (*tasawwur*) or assertion (*tasdeeq*)." That has been declared by their leader (the head of the logicians), ibn Sinaa.

Even though this meaning applied to some of the Kuffaar, the term Kaafir was applied to them from the aspect that the person has signs of denial and rejection (of the *Haqq*), like how if we were to suppose that someone assented to all of what was brought by Nabi صلى الله عليه وسلم and admits to it and acts according to it, but despite that he willingly wears the *zunnaar* (the belt worn by the Dhimmis to distinguish themselves from the Muslims) or willingly makes *sujood* to an idol, then we will declare him to be a Kaafir, because Nabi صلى الله عليه وسلم has declared that as being a sign of denial and rejection (of the *Haqq*). The verification of this position according to what has been mentioned facilitates for you the path towards solving most of the ishkaalaat which arise in the issue of *Imaan*.

وإذا عرفت حقيقة معنى التصديق, فاعلم أن الإيمان في الشرع

Once you know what is the *haqeeqat* of the meaning of *tasdeeq*, then know that *Imaan*, according to the Sharee`ah is:

(هو التصديق بما جاء به النبي صلى الله عليه وسلم من عند الله تعالى)

"It is *tasdeeq* of that which Nabi صلى الله عليه وسلم brought from Allaah Ta`aalaa."

أي تصديق النبي عليه السلام بالقلب في جميع ما علم بالضرورة مجيئه به عن عند الله تعالى إجمالاً, وأنه كاف في الخروج عن عهدة الإيمان, ولا تنحط درجته عن الإيمان التفصيلي, فالكشرك المصدق بوجود الصانع وصفاته, لا يكون مؤمناً إلا بحسب اللغة دون الشرع, لإخلاله بالتوحيد, وإليه الإشارة بقوله تعالى:

وَمَا يُؤْمِنُ أَكْثَرُهُم بِاللَّهِ إِلَّا وَهُم مُّشْرِكُونَ

Meaning, assenting in general to everything that Nabi صلى الله عليه وسلم brought, with the heart, in all of that which must be known of necessity that he brought it from Allaah Ta`aalaa, and this is sufficient to take a person into the fold of *Imaan*. This kind of *Imaan* is not less in rank than *al-Imaan at-Tafseeli* (detailed *Imaan*).

The Mushrik who assents to the existence of a Creator and His Attributes, he is not a Mu'min except according to the linguistic meaning, not according to the Sharee`ah, because he falls short of Tawheed. This is referred to in the *Aayah*:

{"And most of them do not believe in Allaah except that they are Mushrikoon."}

(والإقرار به)

أي باللسان, إلا أن التصديق ركن لا يحتمل السقوط أصلاً, والإقرار قد يحتمله كما في حالة الإكراه

"And admitting to it."

Meaning, with the tongue. However, *tasdeeq* is a pillar that does not carry the possibility of falling at all, but *iqraar* (admitting) does, like in the state of coercion (being forced to utter words of *Kufr*).

فإن قيل: قد لا يبقى التصديق كما في حالة النوم والغفلة

قلنا: التصديق باق في القلب, والذهول إنما هو عن حصوله, ولو سلم, فالشارع جعل المحقق الذي لم يطرأ عليه ما يضاده في حكم الباقي, حتى كان مؤمن إسماً لمن آمن في الحال, أو في الماضي ولم يطرأ عليه ما هو علامة التكذيب

If it is said: *Tasdeeq* does not always remain, like in the states of sleep and heedlessness.

We say: *Tasdeeq* remains in the heart, and the neglect is only a neglect of realising it. And even if it is submitted, then the Sharee`ah considers that the kind of *Imaan* which has been verified is that against which there has not occurred any ruling that is contrary to it, so much so that Mu'min is a term used for the one who has *Imaan* right now, or in the past, and there has not issued from him any sign of denial (of the *Haqq*).

هذا الذي ذكره من أن الإيمان هو التصديق والإقرار, مذهب بعض العلماء, وهو اختيار الإمام شمس الأئمة, وفخر الإسلام رحمهما الله, وذهب جمهور المحققين إلى أنه التصديق بالقلب, وإنما الإقرار شرط لإجراء الأحكام في الدنيا, لما أن التصديق بالقلب أمر باطن لا بد له من علامة, فمن صدق بقلبه ولم يقر بلسانه فهو مؤمن عند الله وإن لم يكن مؤمناً في أحكام الدنيا, ومن أقر بلسانه ولم يصدق بقلبه كالمنافق, فبالعكس, وهذا هو اختيار الشيخ أبي منصور رحمه الله تعالى, والنصوص معاضدة لذلك, قال الله تعالى:

This which has been mentioned, that *Imaan* is *tasdeeq* and *iqraar*, it is the *Madh-hab* of some of the `Ulamaa, and it is the chosen view of Imaam *Shams-ul-A'immah* (i.e. Imaam as-Sarakhsi) and *Fakhr-ul-Islaam* (i.e. Imaam al-Bazdawi) رحمة الله عليهما. The majority of the Muhaqqiqoon held the view that it is *tasdeeq* with the heart, and that *iqraar* is only a stipulation in order to receieve the *Ahkaam* (of the Muslims upon the person) in the Dunyaa, because *tasdeeq* with the heart is a matter that is hidden and requires some sign. Thus, the one who assents with his heart but does not admit (do *iqraar*) with his tongue, then he is a Mu'min to Allaah Ta`aalaa, even though he will not be seen as a Mu'min in terms of the *Ahkaam* of the Dunyaa. As for the one who does *iqraar* with his tongue but not *tasdeeq* with his heart, like the Munaafiqeen, then they are the opposite. This is the chosen view of ash-Shaykh Abu Mansoor (i.e. Imaam al-Maatureedi) رحمة الله عليه. The *nusoos* are opposite to that. Allaah Ta`aalaa said:

أُولَٰئِكَ كَتَبَ فِيْ قُلُوْبِهِمُ الْإِيْمَانَ

وقال تعالى:

وَقَلْبُهُ مُطْمَئِنٌّ بِالْإِيْمَانِ

{*"They are those in whose hearts Allaah as written Imaan."*}

And the *Aayah*:

{*"And his heart is mutma'inn (has itminaan, i.e. calm, contented, firmly established, unshaken) with Imaan."*}

وقال تعالى:

وَلَمَّا يَدْخُلِ الْإِيْمَانُ فِيْ قُلُوْبِكُمْ

And the *Aayah*:

{*"But Imaan has not yet entered your hearts."*}

وقال عليه السلام:

يَا مُثَبِّتَ الْقُلُوْبِ ثَبِّتْ قَلْبِيْ عَلَى دِيْنِكَ وَطَاعَتِكَ

And the *Hadeeth*:

"O Muthabbit (One Who makes firm) of the hearts, make my heart firm upon Your Deen and Your Obedience."

وقال عليه السلام لأسامة حين قتل من قال لا إله إلا الله:

هَلَّا شَقَقْتَ عَلَى قَلْبِهِ؟

And the Hadeeth wherein Rasoolullaah صلى الله عليه وسلم says to Hadhrat Usaamah ibn Zaid رضي الله عنه after he killed a person who had said *Laa Ilaaha Illallaah*:

"Did you open his heart?"

فإن قلتَ: نعم, الإيمان هو التصديق لكن أهل اللغة لا يعرفون منه إلا التصديق باللسان, والنبي عليه السلام وأصحابه كانوا يقنعون من المؤمنين بكلمة الشهادة, ويحكمون بإيمانه من غير استفسار عما في قلبه

قلتُ: لا خفاء في أن المعتبر في التصديق عمل القلب, حتى لو فرضنا عدم وضع لفظ التصديق لمعنى, أو وضعه لمعنى غير التصديق القلبي, لم يحكم أحد من أهل اللغة والعرف بأن المتلفظ بكلمة صدقت مصدق للنبي عليه السلام ومؤمن به, ولهذا صح نفي الإيمان عن بعض المقرين باللسان, قال الله تعالى:

If you say: Yes, *Imaan* is *tasdeeq*; however, the linguists do not recognise from him except *tasdeeq* with the tongue. Nabi صلى الله عليه وسلم and his Sahaabah were content from the Mu'mineen (that they utter) the *Kalimah Shahaadah*, and they would judge them as being Mu'mineen without any questioning about what is in their hearts.

I (i.e Imaam at-Taftaazaani) say: It is not hidden that what is considered in *tasdeeq* is the action of the heart, so much so that, were we to suppose the absence of the usage of the word *tasdeeq* as having (this meaning), or had a meaning other than *tasdeeq* with the heart, then none of the linguists and those who know *`Urf* (the customary usage of words) would rule that the person who verbally utters the words "I assent" is one who assents to Nabi صلى الله عليه وسلم and believes in him. For this reason, the negation of *Imaan* even from some of those who do *iqraar* with the tongue is valid. Allaah Ta`aalaa says:

وَمِنَ النَّاسِ مَنْ يَقُولُ آمَنَّا بِاللَّهِ وَبِالْيَوْمِ الْآخِرِ وَمَا هُمْ بِمُؤْمِنِينَ

{"*And from mankind is he who says: "We believe in Allaah and in the Last Day," but they are not Mu'mineen.*"}

وقال تعالى:

قَالَتِ الْأَعْرَابُ آمَنَّا قُلْ لَمْ تُؤْمِنُوا وَلَٰكِنْ قُولُوا أَسْلَمْنَا

And the *Aayah*:

{"*The A`raab (Bedouins) say: "We have believed." Say: "You have not believed, but rather say: "We have submitted."*"}

وأما المقر باللسان وحده فلا نزاع في أنه يسمى مؤمناً لغة، ويجري عليه أحكام الإيمان ظاهراً، وإنما النزاع في كونه مؤمناً فيما بينه وبين الله تعالى, والنبي عليه السلام ومن بعده كما كانوا يحكمون بإيمان من تكلم بكلمة الشهادة، كانوا يحكمون بكفر المنافق، فدل على أنه لا يفكي في الإيمان فعل اللسان، وأيضاً الإجماع منعقد على إيمان من صدق بقلبه، قصد الإقرار باللسان ومنعه منه مانع من الخرس ونحوه, فظهر أن ليس حقيقة الإيمان مجرد كلمتي الشهادة على ما زعمت الكرامية

As for the one who just does *iqraar* with his tongue alone, then there is no dispute that he is termed a Mu'min linguistically and that the *Ahkaam* of *Imaan* are passed upon him externally. Rather, the dispute is regarding him being a Mu'min between him and Allaah Ta`aalaa. Nabi صلى الله عليه وسلم and those who came after him, just as they used to rule that the one who speaks the *Kalimah Shahaadah* is a Mu'min, they used to rule that the Munaafiq is a Kaafir, and this proves that when it comes to *Imaan*, mere admitting with the tongue is insufficient. Also, *ijmaa`* has been established regarding the *Imaan* of thee one who assents with his heart and who wished to admit with his tongue but was prevented by some preventative factor, such as being mute, etc. Thus, it is clear that the *haqeeqat* of *Imaan* is not simply the verbal utterance of the two *Kalimahs* of *Shahaadah* as was claimed by the Karraamiyyah (i.e. verbal utterance without actually believing in it).

زيادة الإيمان ونقصانه

The Increase and Decrease of *Imaan*:

ولما كان مذهب جمهور المتكلمين والفقهاء على أن الإيمان تصديق بالجنان, وإقرار باللسان, وعمل بالأركان, كما أشار إلى نفي ذلك بقوله:

(فأما الأعمال)

أي الطاعات

Because the *Madh-hab* of the majority of the Mutakallimeen and the Fuqahaa was that *Imaan* is *tasdeeq* with the heart and admission with the tongue and the performance of the pillars of Islaam, (Imaam an-Nasafi) hints to the negation of that by saying:

"As for deeds."

Meaning, good deeds.

(فهي تتزايد في نفسها, والإيمان لا يزيد ولا ينقص)

"Then they increase in and of themselves, but *Imaan* does not increase or decrease."

فهاهنا مقامان:

الأول: أن الأعمال غير داخلة في الإيمان, لما مر من أن حقيقة الإيمان هو التصديق, ولأنه قد ورد في الكتاب والسنة عطف الأعمال على الإيمان, كقوله تعالى:

So here, there are two positions:

The first is that *a`maal* are not part of *Imaan*, due to what has preceded that the *haqeeqat* of *imaan* is *tasdeeq*, and because in the Qur'aan and the Sunnah *a`maal* have been joined to *Imaan*, like in the *Aayah*:

إِنَّ الَّذِينَ آمَنُوا وَعَمِلُوا الصَّالِحَاتِ

{"*Indeed, those who have Imaan and do good deeds.*"}

مع القطع بأن العطف يقتضي المغايرة, وعدم دخول المعطوف في المعطوف عليه, وورد أيضاً جعل الإيمان شرط صحة الأعمال, كما في قوله تعالى:

Along with certitude that `atf` (coupling) necessitates that they (*Imaan* and *A`maal*) are distinctly different, and that the *ma`toof* does not enter the *ma`toof `alayhi* (the coupled thing does not enter into the thing it is coupled to). It has also been narrated that *Imaan* is a condition for the validity of *a`maal*, like in the *Aayah*:

وَمَنْ يَعْمَلْ مِنَ الصَّالِحَاتِ مِنْ ذَكَرٍ أَوْ أُنْثَى وَهُوَ مُؤْمِنٌ

{"*And whosoever does good works, (be they) male or female, whilst being Mu'min...*"}

مع القطع بأن المشروط لا يدخل في الشرط لامتناع اشتراط الشيء بنفسه, وورد أيضاً إثبات الإيمان لمن ترك بعض الأعمال, كما في قوله تعالى:

Along with certitude that the conditioned thing does not enter into the condition due to the impossibility of a thing being conditioned by itself. It has also been narrated that *Imaan* is affirmed for the one who leaves off some *a`maal*, like in the *Aayah*:

وَإِنْ طَائِفَتَانِ مِنَ الْمُؤْمِنِيْنَ اقْتَتَلُوا

{"*And if two groups from the Mu'mineen fight one another...*"}

على ما مر, مع القطع بأنه لا يتحقق الشيء بدون ركنه, ولا يخفى أن هذه الوجوه إنما تقوم حجة على من يجعل الطاعات ركناً من حقيقة الإيمان, بحيث إن تاركها لا يكون مؤمناً, كما هو رأي المعتزلة, لا على مذهب من ذهب إلى أنها ركن من الإيمان الكامل, بحيث لا يخرج تاركها عن حقيقة الإيمان, كما هو مذهب الشافعي, وقد سبق تمسكات المعتزلة بأجوبتها فيما سبق

According to what has preceded, and with certitude that nothing is verified as real without its *rukn* (fundamental element). It is not hidden that these points of argument are only valid points against the one who makes acts of obedience a *rukn* for the *haqeeqat* of *Imaan*, in such a manner that the one who leaves them off is not a Mu'min, as was the belief of the Mu`tazilah, not according to the *Madh-hab* of those who believed that it is a *rukn* for

Kaamil (complete) *Imaan*, such that the one who abandons it does not exit from Imaan, as was the *Madh-hab* of Imaam ash-Shaafi`ee رحمة الله عليه. The arguments of the Mu`tazilah, along with the answers to them, have already preceded.

المقام الثاني: أن حقيقة الإيمان لا تزيد ولا تنقص, لما مر من أنه التصديق القلبي الذي بلغ حد الجزم والإذعان, وهذا لا يتصور فيه زيادة ولا نقصان, حتى أن من حصل له حقيقة التصديق, فسواء أتى بالطاعات أو ارتكب المعاصي, فتصديقه باق على حاله لا تغير فيه أصلاً, والآيات الدالة على زيادة الإيمان محمولة على ما ذكره أبو حنيفة رحمه الله تعالى, من أنهم كانوا آمنوا في الجملة, ثم يأتي فرض بعض فرض فكانوا يؤمنون بكل فرض خاص

The second position is that the *haqeeqat* of *Imaan* does not increase or decrease, due to what has preceded that it is *tasdeeq* with the heart which reaches the level of certitude and acknowledement, and this is not conceiveable as having an increase or decrease, such that the one who attains the *haqeeqat* of *tasdeeq* (assent), regardless of whether he performs good doods or perpetrates evil deeds, his *tasdeeq* remains upon its same condition, completely unchanged. The *Aayaat* which point out to increase in Imaan are carried upon the meaning which was mentioned by Imaam Abu Haneefah رحمة الله عليه. He said that they (Sahaabah-e-Kiraam) brought *Imaan* in general, and thereafter, one *fardh* came after another, and they brought *Imaan* with each specific *fardh* as it came.

وحاصله: أنه كان يزيد بزيادة ما يجب الإيمان به, وهذا لا يتصور في غير عصر النبي صلى الله عليه وسلم, وفيه نظر, لأن الإطلاع على تفاصيل الفرائض ممكن في غير عصر النبي صلى الله عليه وسلم

The summary of this is that it used to increase with the increase of that which it is necessary to bring *Imaan* in, and this is inconceivable in other than the era of Nabi صلى الله عليه وسلم. There is speculation in this, however, because it is possible for a person to only learn the details of the *faraa'idh* later on (i.e. such as a new Muslim), which can take place outside of the era of Nabi صلى الله عليه وسلم.

والإيمان واجب إجمالاً فيما علم إجمالاً, وتفصيلاً فيما علم تفصيلاً, ولا خفاء في أن التفصيلي أزيد بل أكمل, وما ذكر من أن الإجمال لا ينحط عن درجته فإنما هو في الإتصاف بأصل الإيمان

Imaan is binding in general for that which is known in general, and in detail in that which is known in detail. And it is not hidden that *tafseeli* (*Imaan* in detail) is more complete (than *Imaan* in general). As for what has been mentioned, that *Imaan* in general is not less in rank, then this is with regards to being attributed with the actual *Imaan* itself.

وقيل: إن الثبات والدوام على الإيمان زيادة عليه في كل ساعة, وحاصله: أنه يزيد بزيادة الأزمان لما أنه عرض لا يبقى إلا بتجدد الأمثال, وفيه نظر, لأن حصول المثل بعد انعدام الشيء لا يكون من الزيادة في شيء, كما في سواد الجسم مثلاً

It has been said: steadfastness and continuity upon *Imaan* increases upon it every moment. Its summary is that it increases with the increase of time because of it being an `*aradh*, thus not continuing except with the renewal of its likenesses. There is speculation regarding this, however, because the occurence of a likeness after the non-existence of a thing is not an increase in that thing at all, as is the case in the blackness of a body, for example.

وقيل: المراد زيادة ثمرته, وإشراق نوره وضيائه في القلب, فإنه يزيد بالأعمال وينقص بالمعاصي, ومن ذهب إلى أن الأعمال من الإيمان فقبوله الزيادة والنقصان ظاهر, ولهذا قيل: إن هذه المسألة فرع مسألة كون الطاعات من الإيمان

It has been said that the intended meaning is the increase of its fruits, and the shining of its *Noor* and brilliance in the heart, because it increases with good deeds and decreases with disobedience. As for those who claim that *a`maal* are part of *Imaan*, then in that case, its acceptance of increase and decrease is quite apparent. For this reason it has been said: This issue is a branch issue of acts of obedience being part of *Imaan*.

وقال بعض المحققين: لا نسلم أن حقيقة التصديق لا تقبل الزيادة والنقصان, بل تتفاوت قوة وضعفاً, للقطع بأن تصديق آحاد الأمة ليس كتصديق النبي عليه السلام, ولهذا قال إبراهيم عليه السلام:

وَلَٰكِن لِّيَطْمَئِنَّ قَلْبِي

Some of the Muhaqqiqeen said: We do not submit that the *haqeeqat* of *tasdeeq* does not accept increase or decrease, but it varies in strength or weakness, due to the fact that the *tasdeeq* of the individual members of the *Ummah* is not like the *tasdeeq* of Nabi صلى الله عليه وسلم. For this reason, Nabi Ibraaheem عليه السلام said:

{*"But rather, so that my heart has itminaan."*}

بقي هاهنا بحث آخر, وهو أن بعض القدرية ذهب إلى أن الإيمان هو المعرفة, وأطبق علماؤنا على فساده لأن أهل الكتاب كانوا يعرفون نبوة محمد صلى الله عليه وسلم كما يعرفون أبناءهم, مع القطع بكفرهم لعدم التصديق, ولأن من الكفار من كان يعرف الحق يقيناً وإنما كان ينكر عناداً واستكباراً, قال الله تعالى:

وَجَحَدُوا بِهَا وَاسْتَيْقَنَتْهَا أَنفُسُهُمْ

There remains here another subject for discussion, and that is: some of the Qadariyyah adopted the view that *Imaan* is *Ma`rifah*, but our `Ulamaa were unanimous regarding the corruption of this belief, because the Ahl-ul-Kitaab had *Ma`rifat* (recognition) of the *Nubuwwah* of Rasoolullaah صلى الله عليه وسلم just as they recognised their own sons, but despite this, remained as Kaafirs because they did not do *tasdeeq*. And also, because of the fact that from the Kuffaar were those who recognised the *Haqq* as being absolutely certain, but they rejected it out of rebelliousness and arrogance. Allaah Ta`aalaa said:

{*"They denied it but their souls knew it to be the truth."*}

فلا بد من بيان الفرق بين معرفة الأحكام واستيقانها, وبين التصديق بها واعتقادها, ليصح كون الثاني إيماناً دون الأول

Thus, it is necessary to explain the difference between *Ma`rifat* (recognition) of the *Ahkaam* and knowing it to be true, and between doing *tasdeeq* of it and believing in it, in order to understand that the second (category) is *Imaan*, but not the first.

والمذكور في كلام بعض المشايخ: أن التصديق عبارة عن ربط القلب على ما علم من أخبار المخبر, وهو أمر كسبي, يثبت باختيار المصدق, ولذا يثاب عليه ويجعل رأس العبادات, بخلاف المعرفة, فإنها ربما تحصل بلا كسب, كمن وقع بصره على جسم فحصل له معرفة أنه جداراً أو حجر, وهذا ما ذكره بعض المحققين من أن التصديق هو أن تنسب باختيارك الصدق إلى المخبر, حتى لو وقع ذلك في القلب من غير اختيار لم يكن تصديقاً, وإن كان معرفة, وهذا مشكل, لأن التصديق من أقسام العلم, وهو من الكيفيات النفسانية دون الأفعال الإختيارية, لأنا إذا تصورنا النسبة بين الشيئين, وشككنا في أنها بالإثبات أو النفي, ثم أقيم البرهان على ثبوتها, فالذي يحصل لنا هو الإذعان والقبول لتلك النسبة, وهو معنى التصديق والحكم والإثبات والإيقاع

It is mentioned in the discussions of some of the Mashaayikh that *tasdeeq* refers to the heart being tied to what is known from the narrations of the Mukhbir (One Who has informed), and that is a matter that is acquired, which is affirmed by the choice of the one who does *tasdeeq*. For this reason, he is rewarded for it and it was made the pinnacle of `Ibaadaat, contrary to *Ma`rifah*, because *Ma`rifah* can sometimes come without acquisition, like the one whose gaze falls on a body and he gains *Ma`rifah* that it is a wall or a stone. This is what was mentioned by some of the Muhaqqiqeen, that *tasdeeq* is that you - of your own free will - ascribe truthfulness of the Mukhbir (One Who informs), so much so that if this occurs in the heart not of your own choice it will not be *tasdeeq*, although it will be regarded as *Ma`rifah*, and this is difficult, because *tasdeeq* is from the categories of knowledge, and that is from the qualities of the soul rather than the voluntary actions, because when we conceive the connection between two things and doubt whether it is to be affirmed or denied, and thereafter evidence is established upon its affirmation then that which occurs within us is the acknowledgement and acceptance of that connection, and that is the meaning of *tasdeeq*, and hukm (judgement), and affirmation and realisation (*eeqaa`*).

نعم, تحصيل تلك الكيفية يكون بالإختيار في مباشرة الأسباب, وصرف النظر ورفع الموانع ونحو ذلك, وبهذا الإعتبار يقع التكليف بالإيمان, وكان هذا هو المراد بكونه كسباً إختيارياً, ولا تكفي المعرفة في حصول التصديق, لأنها قد تكون بدون ذلك, نعم, يلزم أن تكون المعرفة اليقينية المكتسبة بالإختيار تصديقاً, ولا بأس بذلك, لأنه حينئذ يحصل المعنى الذي يعبر عنه بالفارسية بكرويدن, وليس الإيمان والتصديق سوى ذلك, وحصوله للكفار المعاندين المستكبرين محال,

وعلى تقدير الحصول فتكفيرهم يكون بإنكارهم باللسان, وإصرارهم على العناد والإستكبار, وما هو من علامات التكذيب والإنكار

Yes, those qualities are arrived at through choice by coming into contact with the *asbaab*, and with the use of speculation, and with the removal of the preventative factors, etc. With this being taken into consideration, the imposition of being responsible to bring *Imaan* occurs, and this is the intended meaning of it being something that is acquired by choice. *Ma`rifah* is not sufficient for the attainment of *tasdeeq*, because it can be without that. Yes, it is necessary that the convinced *Ma`rifah* that is acquired by choice be tasdeeq, and there is no harm with that, because in that case the meaning is attained which is referred to in Farsi by "*Girawidan*", because *Imaan* and *tasdeeq* is not other than that. Its attainment by the rebellious, arrogant Kuffaar is impossible. Even supposing it were to be attained, then *takfeer* would still be made of them due to their rejecting it with the tongue and their persistence upon rebelliousness and arrogance and that which is from the signs of denial and rejection.

(والإيمان والإسلام واحد)

"Imaan and Islaam is one."

لأن الإسلام هو الخضوع والإنقياد بمعنى قبول الأحكام, والإذعان, وذلك حقيقة التصديق على ما مر, ويؤيده قوله تعالى:

فَأَخْرَجْنَا مَنْ كَانَ فِيهَا مِنَ الْمُؤْمِنِينَ فَمَا وَجَدْنَا فِيهَا غَيْرَ بَيْتٍ مِّنَ الْمُسْلِمِينَ

وبالجملة: لا يصح في الشرع الحكم على أحد بأنه مؤمن وليس بمسلم, أو مسلم وليس بمؤمن, ولا نعني بوحدتها سوى هذا

Because Islaam is to submit and surrender (to Allaah Ta`aalaa), in the meaning of accepting the *Ahkaam*, and that is the *haqeeqat* of *tasdeeq* as has preceded, and this view is strengthened by the *Aayah*:

{"*So We took out from it those that were from the Mu'mineen, and We did not find therein other than one house of Muslimeen.*"}

In summary: According to the Sharee'ah, it is not valid to pass ruling upon a person that he is a Mu'min but not a Muslim, or a Muslim but not a Mu'min, and this is what we mean by the two (Imaan and Islaam) being the same.

وظاهر كلام المشايخ: أنهم أرادوا عدم تغايرهما, بمعنى أنه لا ينفك أحدهما عن الآخر, لا الإتحاد بحسب المفهوم لما ذكر في الكفاية, من أن الإيمان هو تصديق الله تعالى فيما أخبر به من أوامره ونواهيه, والإسلام هو الإنقياد والخضوع لألوهيته تعالى, وذا لا يتحقق إلا بقبول الأمر والنهي, فالإيمان لا ينفك عن الإسلام حكماً فلا يتغايران, ومن أثبت التغاير يقال له: ما حكم من آمن ولم يسلم؟ أو أسلم ولم يؤمن؟ فإن أثبت لأحدهما حكماً ليس بثابت للآخر منهما فبها ونعمت, وإلا فقد ظهر بطلان قوله

فإن قيل: قوله تعالى:

قَالَتِ الْأَعْرَابُ آمَنَّا قُلْ لَمْ تُؤْمِنُوا وَلَٰكِنْ قُولُوا أَسْلَمْنَا

صريح في تحقيق الإسلام بدون الإيمان

The apparent of the discussion of the Mashaayikh is that what they had intended is that the two are not distinctly different, meaning that one is not separate from the other. However, they did not mean that they are the same in terms of what is understood from them, as was mentioned in *al-Kifaayah*, that *Imaan* is *tasdeeq* of Allaah Ta`aalaa in that which He has informed us from His Commands and His Prohibitions, and Islaam is to surrender and submit to the *Uloohiyyah* of Allaah Ta`aalaa. Thus, it is not verified except with the acceptance of the Command and Prohibition. Thus, *Imaan* does not separate from Islaam in terms of ruling, so they are not distinctly different. As for the one who says they are distinctly different from one another, it is said to him: What is the ruilng regarding one who brings Imaan but not Islaam? Or Islaam but not Imaan? If he establishes for one of them a ruling that is not affirmed in the other, then good, but if not, then the invalidity of his statement becomes manifest.

If it is said: The *Aayah*:

{"The Bedouins say: "We have believed." Say: "You have not believed, but rather, say: "We have submitted."}

This is clear in the verification of Islaam without Imaan.

قلنا: المراد به أن الإسلام المعتبر في الشرع لا يوجد بدون الإيمان, وهو في الآية بمعنى الإنقياد الظاهر من غير انقياد الباطن, بمنزلة المتلفظ بكلمة الشهادة من غير تصديق في باب الإيمان

فإن قيل: قوله عليه السلام: أَنْ تَشْهَدَ أَنْ لَا إِلَهَ إِلَّا اللهُ, وَأَنَّ مُحَمَّداً رَسُولُ اللهِ, وَتُقِيمُ الصَّلَاةَ وَتُؤْتِيَ الزَّكَاةَ وَتَصُومَ رَمَضَانَ وَتَحُجَّ الْبَيْتَ إِنِ اسْتَطَعْتَ إِلَيْهِ سَبِيلاً

دليل على أن الإسلام هو الأعمال, لا التصديق القلبي

We say: The intended meaning of it is that the Islaam which is considered in the Sharee`ah is not found without Imaan, and in the *Aayah*, the meaning of "Islaam" is that of outward surrender without the inner self having submitted (to the Deen of Allaah Ta`aalaa), similar to the one who merely outwardly pronounces the *Kalimah* of *Shahaadah* without *tasdeeq*, (as seen in the) chapter on Imaan.

If it is said: The *Hadeeth*: "(Imaan is that) you testify that there is no Ilaah except Allaah, and that Muhammad is the Rasool of Allaah, and you establish Salaah, and you give Zakaah, and you fast (the month of) Ramadhaan and you perform Hajj to The House (i.e. Ka`bah) if you are able to do so."

This is evidence that Islaam is *a`maal*, not *tasdeeq* with the heart.

قلنا: المراد أن ثمرات الإسلام وعلاماته ذلك, كما قال عليه السلام لقوم وفدوا عليه: أَتَدْرُونَ مَا الْإِيمَانُ بِاللهِ وَحْدَهُ؟ فَقَالُوا: اللهُ وَرَسُولُهُ أَعْلَمُ, قَالَ: شَهَادَةُ أَنْ لَا إِلَهَ إِلَّا اللهُ, وَأَنَّ مُحَمَّداً رَسُولُ اللهِ, وَإِقَامُ الصَّلَاةِ وَإِيتَاءُ الزَّكَاةِ وَصَوْمُ رَمَضَانَ وَأَنْ تُعْطُوا مِنَ الْمَغْنَمِ الْخُمُسَ

وكما قال صلى الله عليه وسلم: الْإِيمَانُ بِضْعٌ وَسَبْعُونَ شُعْبَةً, أَعْلَاهَا قَوْلُ لَا إِلَهَ إِلَّا اللهُ, وَأَدْنَاهَا إِمَاطَةُ الْأَذَى عَنِ الطَّرِيقِ

We say: The intended meaning is the fruits and signs of Islaam, like Nabi صلى الله عليه وسلم said to some people who had come as a delegation to him: "Do you know what is Imaan in Allaah Alone?" They said: "Allaah and His Rasool know best." He said: "The testification that there is no Ilaah except Allaah, and that Muhammad is the Rasool of Allaah, and the establishment of Salaah, the giving of Zakaah, the fasting of Ramadhaan and that you give from the spoils of war a fifth."

And like the *Hadeeth*: "*Imaan* is seventy-some branches: the highest is to say *Laa Ilaaha Illallaah*, and the lowest is the removal of harm from the road."

(وإذا وجد من العبد التصديق والإقرار صح له أن يقول: أنا مؤمن حقاً)

"When *tasdeeq* and *iqraar* are both found within a slave, it is valid for him to say: "I am a true Mu'min."

لتحقيق الإيمان له

Due to the verification of Imaan for him.

(ولا ينبغي أن يقول: أنا مؤمن إن شاء الله)

"And it is not appropriate for him to say: "I am a Mu'min *In Shaa Allaah* (if Allaah wills)."

لأنه إن كان للشك فهو كفر لا محالة, وإن كان للتأديب وإحالة الأمور إلى مشيئة الله تعالى أو للشك في العاقبة والمآل لا في الآن والحال, أو للتبرك بذكر الله تعالى, أو التبري عن تزكية نفسه والإعجاب بحاله, فالأولى تركه, لما أنه يوهم بالشك, ولهذا قال: ولا ينبغي, دون أن يقول: ولا يجوز, لأنه إذا لم يكن للشك فلا معنى لنفي الجواز, كيف وقد ذهب إليه كثير من السلف حتى الصحابة والتابعين؟ وليس هذا مثل قولك: أنا شاب إن شاء الله, لأن الشباب ليس من الأفعال المكتسبة, ولا مما يتصور البقاء عليه في العاقبة والمآل, ولا مما يحصل به تزكية النفس والإعجاب, بل مثل قولك أنا زاهد متق إن شاء الله

Because if he says so out of doubt, then it is clear-cut *Kufr*, and if it out of (what he perceives as) respect and the relegation of matters to the *Mashee'at* of Allaah Ta`aalaa, or on account of doubt regarding what his final status will be and his outcome in the end rather than the here and now, or out of *tabarruk* with the *Dhikr* of Allaah Ta`aalaa, or to free himself from regarding himself as being purified and being amazed at his condition, then still it is better to not make this statement (i.e. to say that he is a Mu'min "*In Shaa Allaah*"), because it gives the impression of doubt. For this reason, Imaam an-Nasafi chose to use the term "it is not appropriate" rather than saying, "it is not permissible," because if it is not on account of doubt then there is no meaning for the denial of permissibility. How so, when many of the Salaf, even the Sahaabah and Taabi`een, had used this term? This is not like a person saying, "I am a youth *In Shaa Allaah*," because youth is not from the actions that are acquired, nor from that which is possible to continue and remain in the end and the final outcome, nor is it that by which regarding oneself as being purified and being amazed at one's condition occurs. Rather, it is like your statement, "I am a *zaahid, mutaqqi In Shaa Allaah*."

وذهب بعض المحققين إلى أن الحاصل للعبد هو حقيقة التصديق الذي به يخرج عن الكفر, لكن التصديق في نفسه قابل للشدة والضعف, وحصول التصديق الكامل المنجي المشار إليه بقوله تعالى:

أُولَٰئِكَ هُمُ الْمُؤْمِنُونَ حَقًّا لَهُمْ دَرَجَاتٌ عِندَ رَبِّهِمْ وَمَغْفِرَةٌ وَرِزْقٌ كَرِيمٌ

إنما هو في مشيئة الله تعالى

Some of the Muhaqqiqeen held the view that what is attained by the slave is the *haqeeqat* of *tasdeeq* by which he exits from *Kufr*, however, *tasdeeq* in itself accepts strength and weakness, and the attainment of complete, perfect *tasdeeq* which saves one (from `Adhaab), which is referred to in the *Aayah*:

{"*Those are truly Mu'minoon; they have ranks with their Rabb, and Maghfirah, and a generous sustenance.*"}

It is in the *Mashee'at* of Allaah Ta`aalaa (i.e. the attainment of that perfect, complete *tasdeeq*).

ولما نقل عن بعض الأشاعرة أنه يصح أن يقال: أنا مؤمن إن شاء الله, بناء على أن العبرة في الإيمان والكفر والسعادة والشقاوة بالخاتمة, حتى أن المؤمن السعيد من مات على الإيمان, وإن كان طول عمره على الكفر والعصيان, وأن الكافر الشقي من مات على الكفر نعوذ بالله, وإن كان طول عمره على التصديق والطاعة, على ما أشار إليه بقوله تعالى في حق إبليس:

وَكَانَ مِنَ الْكَافِرِينَ

It is narrated from some of the Ashaa`irah that it is valid to say: "I am a Mu'min *In Shaa Allaah*," based on the fact that the real account of *Imaan*, *Kufr*, happiness and misery is made at the end of a person's life, so much so that the Mu'min who is happy is the one who dies upon *Imaan* even if his entire life had been spent in *Kufr* and disobedience, and the wretched Kaafir is the one who dies upon *Kufr* even if the entirety of his life had been spent in *tasdeeq* in obedience. This is referred to in the *Aayah* regarding Iblees:

{*"And he was one of the Kaafireen."*}

وبقوله عليه السلام:

السَّعِيْدُ مَنْ سَعَدَ فِيْ بَطْنِ أُمِّهِ وَالشَّقِيُّ مَنْ شَقِيَ فِيْ بَطْنِ أُمِّهِ

And the *Hadeeth*:

"The happy is he he who was happy in his mother's womb, and the wretched one is he who was wretched in his mother's womb." (i.e. it had already been decreed at that time whether he would die upon *Kufr* or die upon *Imaan*.)

أشار إلى إبطال ذلك بقوله:

(والسعيد قد يشقى)

بأن يرتد بعد الإيمان نعوذ بالله

(والشقي قد يسعد)

بأن يؤمن بعد الكفر

He hints to the invalidity of that statement by saying:

"The happy one can become wretched."

By becoming a Murtadd after having had *Imaan*, and we seek refuge with Allaah Ta`aalaa from that.

"And the wretched one can become happy."

By bringing *Imaan* after having been a Kaafir.

(والتغيير يكون على السعادة والشقاوة, دون الإسعاد والإشقاء, وهما من صفات الله تعالى)

لما أن الإسعاد تكوين السعادة, والإشقاء تكوين الشقاوة

"The changing is in happiness and misery, not in making happy and making miserable, because those (making happy and making miserable) is from the *Sifaat* of Allaah Ta`aalaa."

Because making happy is the creating of happiness, and making miserable is the creating of misery.

(ولا تغير على الله تعالى ولا على صفاته)

"No change comes upon Allaah Ta`aalaa, nor upon His *Sifaat*."

لما مر من أن القديم لا يكون محلاً للحوادث, والحق أنه لا خلاف في المعنى, لأنه إن أريد بالإيمان والسعادة مجرد حصول المعنى فهو حاصل في الحال, وإن أريد به ما يترتب عليه النجاة والثمرات فهو في مشيئة الله تعالى, لا قطع بحصوله في الحال, فمن قطع بالحصول أراد الأول, ومن فوض إلى المشيئة أراد الثاني

Due to what has preceded, that One Who is Qadeem (Eternal) is not a locus for originated matters. The truth is that there is no difference of opinion regarding the meaning, because if what is intended is by *Imaan* and happiness is merely the attainment of the meaning then that is attained in the present already, and if what is intended by it is that thing from which salvation and fruitful works result, then that is in the *Mashee'at* of Allaah Ta`aalaa, and there is no certainty in obtaining it in the present. Thus, the one who states the attainment of it now refers to the first definition, and the one who hands the matter over to Allaah Ta`aalaa means the second definition.

الرسالة

The *Risaalat*:

(وفي إرسال الرسل)
جمع رسول, فعول من الرسالة, وهي سفارة العبد بين الله تعالى وبين ذوي الألباب من خليقته, ليزيح بها عللهم فيما قصرت عنه عقولهم من مصالح الدنيا والآخرة, وقد عرفت معنى الرسول والنبي في صدر الكتاب

(حكمة)

"In the sending of the Rusul-"

Rusul is the plural of Rasool, and it is on the scale of "*Fa`ool*", from the noun "*ar-Risaalah*" (The Message), and it refers to the sending of one of the slaves of Allaah Ta`aalaa between Him and the intelligent ones from His creation, so that He may remove thereby their defects in those matters wherein their intellects were deficient, from the benefits of the Dunyaa and the Aakhirah. You know the meaning of Rasool and Nabi from the beginning of the Kitaab.

"There is *Hikmah* (Wisdom)."

أي مصلحة وعاقبة حميدة, وفي هذا إشارة إلى أن الإرسال واجب لا بمعنى الوجوب على الله تعالى, بل بمعنى أن قضية الحكمة تقتضيه لما فيه من الحكم والمصالح وليس بممتنع, كما زعمت السمنية والبراهمية, ولا بممكن يستوي طرفاه, كما ذهب إليه بعض المتكلمين

That is, a beneficial and praiseworthy outcome. In this there is a reference to the fact that the sending of the Rusul is *Waajib*. Not *Waajib* from the facet of it being binding upon Allaah Ta`aalaa (because nothing is binding upon Allaah Ta`aalaa), but rather, from the mmeaning that *Hikmah* necessitates it due to what it contains of wisdoms and benefits, and it is not impossible as was claimed by the Sumaniyyah and the Baraahimiyyah, nor is it merely a "possibility" with both alternatives (of the possible thing) being equal as was claimed by some of the Mutakallimeen.

إرسال الرسل

The Sending of the Rusul:

ثم أشار إلى وقوع الإرسال وفائدته وطريق ثبوته وتعيين بعض من ثبتت رسالته, فقال:

Thereafter, he alludes to the occurence of the sending of the Rusul and the benefit of it and the method of affirming it and the designation of some the *Rilaasat* of whom is affirmed, by saying:

(وقد أرسل الله رسلاً من البشر إلى البشر, مبشرين)

لأهل الإيمان والطاعة بالجنة والثواب

"And Allaah sent Rusul to mankind from mankind, as bearers of glad-tidings."

To the people of *Imaan* and obedience, the glad-tidings of Jannah and reward.

(ومنذرين)

لأهل الكفر والعصيان بالنار والعقاب, فإن ذلك مما لا طريق للعقل إليه, وإن كان فبأنظار دقيقة لا يتيسر إلا لواحد بعد واحد

"And warners."

To the people of *Kufr* and disobedience, with the warnings of Jahannam and punishment, because those are matters which the intellect by itself has no way of arriving at (i.e. had the Rusul not been sent with the message). And even if the intellects were to have a way, it would be by minute speculations which would not be easy for individuals one by one.

(ومبينين ما يحتاجون إليه من أمور الدنيا والدين)

فإنه تعالى خلق الجنة والنار, وأعد فيهما الثواب والعقاب, وتفاصيل أحوالهما, وطريق الوصول إلى الأول, والإحتراز عن الثاني, مما لا يستقل به العقل, وكذا خلق الأجسام النافعة والضارة, ولم يجعل للعقول والحواس الإستقلال بمعرفتهما, وكذا جعل القضايا منها ما هي ممكنات, لا طريق إلى الجزم بأحد جانبيه, ومنها ما هي واجبات أو ممتنعات لا يظهر للعقل إلا بعد نظر دائم وبحث كامل, بحيث لو اشتغل الإنسان به لتعطل أكثر مصالحه فكان من فضل الله تعالى ورحمته, إرسال الرسل لبيان ذلك, كما قال تعالى:

وَمَا أَرْسَلْنَاكَ إِلَّا رَحْمَةً لِّلْعَالَمِينَ

"And as explainers, explaining to the people that which they require from the affairs of the Dunyaa as well as the Deen."

Because Allaah Ta`aalaa created Jannah and Jahannam, and He prepared reward in Jannah and punishment in Jahannam. The details of their states and the method of arriving at the first and avoiding the latter, these are issues which the intellect alone cannot arrive at. Similarly, Allaah Ta`aalaa the bodies that are beneficial and the bodies that are harmful, and He did not make for the intellects and sensory faculties the ability to independantly recognise them. Similarly, He made the propositions, from them being those that are possibilities, and there is no way to know with certainty either of its two alternatives (i.e. which one is right). From these propositions are those that are necessary (*waajibaat*) and those that are impossibilities; they are not apparent to the intellect except after endless speculation and complete research, so much so that if a person were to spend his time in it, he would deprive himself from most of their benefits. Thus, it is from the *Fadhl* of Allaah Ta`aalaa and His *Rahmah*, that He had sent Rusul to explain and clarify that, as Allaah Ta`aalaa said:

{*"And We have not sent you except as a Rahmah to the worlds."*}

المعجزة

The Miracles of the Ambiyaa:

(وأيدهم)

أي الأنبياء

"And He aided them."

Meaning, the Ambiyaa.

(بالمعجزات الناقضات للعادات)

"With *mu`jizaat* (miracles) that contradict the customary way of things."

جمع معجزة, وهي أمر يظهر بخلاف العادة على يد مدعي النبوة عند تحدي المنكرين على وجه يعجز المنكرين عن الإتيان بمثله, وذلك لأنه لولا التأييد بالمعجزات لما وجب قبول قوله, ولما بان الصادق في دعوى الرسالة عن الكاذب, وعند ظهور المعجزة يحصل الجزم بصدقه بطريق جري العادة بأن الله تعالى يخلق العلم بالصدق عقيب ظهور المعجزة, وإن كان عدم خلق العالم ممكناً في نفسه, وذلك كما إذا ادعى أحد بمحضر من الجماعة أنه رسول هذا الملك إليهم, ثم قال للملك: إن كنت صادقاً فخالف عادتك وقم من مكانك ثلاث مرات, ففعل, يحصل

للجماعة علم ضروري عادي بصدقه في مقالته, وإن كان الكذب ممكناً في نفسه, فإن الإمكان الذاتي بمعنى التجويز العقلي لا ينافي حصول العلم القطعي, كعلمنا بأن جبل أحد لم ينقلب ذهباً مع إمكانه في نفسه, فكذا هاهنا يحصل العلم بصدقه, بموجب العادة, لأنها أحد طرق العلم القطعي, كالحس, ولا يقدح في ذلك العلم إحتمال كون المعجزة من غير الله أو كونها لا لغرض التصديق, أو كونها لتصديق الكاذب, إلى غير ذلك من الإحتمالات, كما لا يقدح في العلم الضروري الحسي بحرارة النار إمكان عدم الحرارة للنار, بمعنى أنه لو قدر عدمها لم يلزم منه محال

Mu`jizaat* is the plural of *mu`jizah, and it refers to a matter that manifests contrary to the customary way of things, upon the hand of one who is a claimant of *Nubuwwah*, at the time the rejectors challenge them, and it occurs in such a way that the rejectors are incapable of coming with the likes of it. That is because had it not been for this assistance with *mu`jizaat*, then the acceptance of his statement would not have been waajib, and the truthful one in the claim of *Risaalah* would not have been clearly distinguishable from the liar. When the *mu`jizah* occurs, absolute certitude is attained regarding his truthfulness in the customary way whereby Allaah Ta`aalaa creates knowledge of his truthfulness after the appearance of the *mu`jizah*, even though the absence of the creating of the knowledge is possible in itself. It is like the case of one who claims in the presence of a group of people that he is the messenger of a particular king to them. Thereafter, he says to the king, "If I am truthful, then do contary to your usual habit, and rise from your seat three times." The king does so, and that results in the group attaining the necessary, customary knowledge of his truthfulness in what he has said. If lying is possible in itself - because the essential possibility means the logical permissibility - it would not preclude the attainment of absolute knowledge, like our knowledge that the mountain of Uhud did not turn into gold despite that being possible in itself. Similarly here, attainment of knowledge of his truthfulness occurs because the customary way necessitates this, because it is one of the paths of absolute knowledge, like the senses are. The possibility that the *mu`jizah* could have come from other than Allaah Ta`aalaa does not detract or its being for other than the purpose fo *tasdeeq*, or its being for the *tasdeeq* of a liar, and other than that from the possibilites, just as the necessary, sensory knowledge regarding the heat of fire is not harmed by the fact that it is possible for fire to not be hot. Meaning that, if its non-existence were supposed, it would still not follow that it is impossible.

(وأول الأنبياء آدم عليه السلام, وآخرهم محمد صلى الله عليه وسلم)

"The first of the Ambiyaa is Aadam عليه السلام and the last of them is Muhammad صلى الله عليه وسلم."

أما نبوة آدم عليه السلام فبالكتاب الدال على أنه قد أمر ونهي, مع القطع بأنه لم يكن في زمنه نبي آخر, فهو بالوحي لا غير, وكذا بالسنة والإجماع, فإنكار نبوته على ما نقل عن البعض يكون كفراً

وأما نبوة محمد صلى الله عليه وسلم, فلأنه ادَّعى النبوة وأظهر المعجزة, أما دعوى النبوة فقد علم بالتواتر, وأما إظهار المعجزة فلوجهين:

As for the *Nubuwwat* of Nabi Aadam عليه السلام, then it is established through the Kitaab itself, because it points out to the fact that he was given Commands and Prohibitions, along with the fact that in his time there was no other Nabi, so it was through *Wahi* only, nothing else. Similarly, the Sunnah and *ijmaa`* affirm it as well. Thus, rejection of his *Nubuwwah* is *Kufr* according to some of the `Ulamaa.

As for the *Nubuwwah* of Rasoolullaah صلى الله عليه وسلم, then it is because he claimed *Nubuwwah* and manifested *mu`jizaat*. As for the claim of *Nubuwwah*, then it is known through *tawaatur*, and as for the manifestation of *mu`zijaat*, then for two facets:

إحداهما: أنه أظهر كلام الله تعالى وتحدى به البلغاء مع كمال بلاغتهم, فعجزوا عن معارضة أقصر سورة منه, مع تهالكهم على ذلك حتى خاطروا بمهجتهم, وأعرضوا عن المعارضة بالحروف إلى المقارعة بالسيوف, ولم ينقل عن أحد منهم – مع توفر الدواعي – الإتيان بشيء مما يدانيه, فدل ذلك قطعاً على أنه من عند الله تعالى, وعلم به صدق دعوى النبي علماً عادياً, لا يقدح فيه شيء من الإحتمالات العقلية, على ما هو شأن سائر العلوم العادية

The first is that he manifested the *Kalaam* of Allaah Ta`aalaa and with It he challenged the most eloquent of the Arabs with their perfection in the science of *Balaaghah*, yet they were incapable of opposing the shortest *Soorah* of the Qur'aan despite applying themselves to this task until they risked their minds. When they were incapable of opposing It with words they turned to opposing it with swords. It is not narrated from any of them - despite the many claims - that any of them brought anything which is even close to the shortest *Soorah* in the Qur'aan. That proves decisively that it is from Allaah

Ta`aalaa, and with it the truthfulness of the claim of Nabi صلى الله عليه وسلم is known with a knowledge that is customary and which is not detracted from by the logical possibilities such as are found in the rest of the customary knowledge.

وثانيهما: أنه نقل عنه من الأمور الخارقة للعادة ما بلغ القدر المشترك منه, أعني ظهور المعجزة حد التواتر, وإن كانت تفاصيلها آحاداً, كشجاعة علي رضي الله عنه, وجود حاتم, فإن كلاً منهما ثبت بالتواتر, وإن كان تفاصيلها آحاداً, وهي مذكورة في كتاب السير, وقد يستدل أرباب البصائر على نبوته بوجهين:

The second (facet) is that there has been reported about Rasoolullaah صلى الله عليه وسلم so many matters that break the customary way of things (i.e. miracles) that they reach the rank sharing with it, i.e. the evident *mu`jizah*, the level of *tawaatur*, even though the details are individuals (*Aahaad*), like the bravery of Hadhrat `Ali رضي الله عنه, and the generosity of Haatim. Each of them are affirmed through *tawaatur*, even though their details are *Aahaad* (solitary reports). They are mentioned in the books of *Seerah*. The people of insight deduced his *Nubuwwah* from two standpoints:

أحدهما: ما تواتر من أحواله قبل النبوة, وحال الدعوة, وبعد تمامها, وأخلاقه العظيمة, وأحكامه الحكيمة, وإقدامه حيث تحجم الأبطال, ووقوفه بعصمة الله تعالى في جميع الأحوال, وثباته على حاله لدى الأهوال, بحيث لم تجد أعداؤه مع شدة عداوتهم وحرصهم على الطعن فيه مطعناً, ولا إلى القدح فيه سبيلاً, فإن العقل يجزم بامتناع اجتماع هذه الأمور في غير الأنبياء, وأن يجمع الله هذه الكمالات في حق من يعلم أنه يفتري عليه, ثم يمهله ثلاثاً وعشرين سنة, ثم يظهر دينه على سائر الأديان, وينصره على أعدائه, ويحيي آثاره بعد موته إلى يوم القيامة

Firstly, that which is narrated by *tawaatur* from his conditions even prior to *Nubuwwah*, and during the time of *Da`wah*, and after its completion, and regarding his great *akhlaaq*, and his wise rulings, and his going forth at times when even the heroes held back, and his conviction in the Protection of Allaah Ta`aalaa during all conditions, and his remaining firm upon his condition despite the prevailing terrors, and thus his enemies, despite their severe animosity towards it and their desire to slander him could not find a place to slander him, nor a way towards detracting from him. That is because the intellect has certitude regarding the impossibility for all of these matters to be together in other than the Ambiyaa, and also that it is impossible that Allaah Ta`aalaa would gather all of these perfections in one whom He knows is fabricating against him, and then giving him respite for 23 years, and then making his Deen reign supreme over all other religions, and granting him victory over his enemies, and granting life to his *Aathaar* after his demise until the Day of Qiyaamah.

وثانيهما: أنه ادَّعى ذلك الأمر العظيم بين أظهر قوم لا كتاب لهم ولا حكمة معهم, وبيّن لهم الكتاب والحكمة, وعلَّمهم الأحكام والشرائع, ونوَّر العلم بالإيمان والعمل الصالح, وأظهر الله دينه على الدين كله كما وعده, ولا معنى للنبوة والرسالة سوى ذلك, وإذا ثبتت نبوته, وقد دل كلامه وكلام الله تعالى المنزل عليه أنه خاتم النبيين, وأنه المبعوث إلى كافة الناس, بل إلى الجن والإنس ثبت أنه آخر الأنبياء عليهم السلام, وأن نبوته لا تختص بالعرب كما زعم بعض النصارى

The second is that Rasoolullaah صلى الله عليه وسلم claimed that great matter (i.e. *Nubuwwah*) among a people who were without a Kitaab and without *Hikmah*, and he then taught them the Kitaab and *Hikmah*, and he taught them the *Ahkaam* and the *Sharaa'i`*, and he illuminated the `*Ilm* with *Imaan* and good deeds, and Allaah Ta`aalaa made his Deen reign supreme over all other religions as He had promised. There is no meaning of *Nubuwwah* and Risaalah besides that. And, when his *Nubuwwah* is affirmed, and his speech as well as the Speech of Allaah Ta`aalaa revealed to him prove that he is the *Khaatam-un-Nabiyyeen* (Seal of the Ambiyaa), and that he has been sent to all of mankind, in fact, to all of the Jinn as well along with mankind, it is affirmed that he is the last of the Ambiyaa and that his *Nubuwwah* is not exclusive to the Arabs as was claimed by the Christians.

نزول عيسى

The Descension of Nabi `Eesa عليه السلام:

فإن قيل: قد روي في الحديث نزول عيسى عليه السلام بعده

قلنا: نعم, لكنه يتابع محمداً عليه السلام, لأن شريعته قد نسخت فلا يكون إليه وحي ولا نصب أحكام, بل يكون خليفة رسول الله عليه السلام, ثم الأصح أنه يصلي بالناس ويؤمهم, ويقتدي به المهدي, لأنه أفضل فإمامته أولى

If it is said: It has been narrated in the *Hadeeth* the descension of Nabi `Eesa عليه السلام after him.

We say: Yes; however, he will follow Rasoolullaah صلى الله عليه وسلم because his own Sharee'ah has been abrogated, and he will not receive Wahi nor any new *Ahkaam*. Instead, he will be the Khaleefah of Rasoolullaah صلى الله عليه وسلم. Thereafter, the most correct view is that he will be the Imaam for the people, leading them in Salaah, and the Mahdi will follow him in Salaah, because he (Nabi `Eesa عليه السلام) is more virtuous and thus his *Imaamat* is better.

مطلب عدد الأنبياء

A Discussion on the Number of Ambiyaa:

(وقد روي بيان عدتهم في بعض الأحاديث)

"The amount of Ambiyaa has been mentioned in some *Ahaadeeth*."

على ما روي أن النبي عليه السلام سئل عن عدد الأنبياء فقال: مِائَةُ أَلْفٍ وَأَرْبَعُ وَعِشْرُوْنَ أَلْفاً

It is narrated that Nabi صلى الله عليه وسلم was asked regarding the number of Ambiya, so he said: "124,000."

وفي رواية: مِائَتَا أَلْفٍ وَأَرْبَعُ وَعِشْرُوْنَ أَلْفاً

In another narration it appears: "224,000."

والأولى أن لا يقتصر على عدد في التسمية فقد قال الله تعالى: مِنْهُمْ مَنْ قَصَصْنَا عَلَيْكَ وَمِنْهُمْ مَنْ لَمْ نَقْصُصْ عَلَيْكَ, ولا يؤمن في ذكر العدد أن يدخل فيهم من ليس منهم

إن ذكر عدد أكثر من عددهم

(أو يخرج منهم من هو فيهم)

"But it is better not to limit their number in naming them, because Allaah Ta`aalaa said: *{"Of some of them We have narrated unto you their stories, and of others We have not."}* If a person mentions a specific number, he is not safe from adding among them those who are not from them."

Meaning, if he mentions a number larger than what their actual number was.

"Or excluding from them those who are from them."

إن ذكر عدد أقل من عددهم, يعني أن خبر الواحد على تقدير اشتماله على جميع الشرائط المذكورة في أصول الفقه, لا يفيد إلا الظن, ولا عبرة بالظن في باب الإعتقادات, خصوصاً إذا اشتمل على اختلاف رواية, وكان القول بموجبه مما يفضي إلى مخالفة ظاهر الكتاب, وهو أن بعض الأنبياء لم يُذكر للنبي عليه السلام, ويحتمل مخالفة الواقع, وهو عد النبي عليه السلام من غير الأنبياء, بناء على أن اسم العدد خاص في مدلوله, لا يحتمل الزيادة ولا النقصان

If he mentions a number lower than what their number had been. What this means is that a *Khabr-e-Waahid*, supposing that it includes all of the stipulations mentioned in *Usool-ul-Fiqh*, then even so it does not give a meaning other than speculation, and there is no consideration given to speculation when it comes to the matter of *I`tiqaadaat* (Beliefs), especially when there are differing narrations. The statement (mentioning a specific number) arrives at a conclusion that differs from the apparent of the Kitaab (i.e. the Qur'aan), which is that some Ambiyaa were mentioned to Nabi صلى الله عليه وسلم and some were not. Thus, it carries the possibility of differing from the actual fact, in counting a Nabi as being not from the Ambiyaa or a non-Nabi as being from the Ambiyaa, based on the fact that the number is *khaas* in what it indicates and does nto carry the possibility of increase or decrease.

(وكلهم كانوا مخبرين مبغلين عن الله تعالى)

"All of them informed and delivered (their message) from Allaah Ta`aalaa." \

لأن هذا معنى النبوة والرسالة

Because that is the meaning of *Nubuwwah* and *Risaalah*.

(صادقين ناصحين)

"They were truthful and advisors."

للخلق لئلا تبطل فائدة البعثة والرسالة, وفي هذا إشارة إلى أن الأنبياء عليهم السلام معصومون عن الكذب , خصوصاً فيما يتعلق بأمر الشرائع وتبليغ الأحكام وإرشاد الأمة, أما عمداً فبالإجماع وأما سهواً فعند الأكثرين

For the creation, so that the purpose of being sent and of the Risaalat is not nullified. In this there is an indication that the Ambiyaa عليهم السلام are protected from lying, especially in that which is connected to the *Sharaa'i`* and the delivery of the *Ahkaam* and the guiding of the Ummah. As for purposefully, then there is *ijmaa`* on it, and as for doing so forgetfully, then according to the majority (they do not).

عصمة الأنبياء

The Sinlessness of the Ambiyaa:

وفي عصمتهم عن سائر الذنوب تفصيل: وهو أنهم معصومون عن الكفر قبل الوحي وبعده بالإجماع, وكذا عن تعمد الكبائر عند الجمهور خلافاً للحشوية, وإنما الخلاف في أن امتناعه بدليل السمع أو العقل؟ وأما سهواً فجوزه الأكثرون, وأما الصغائر فتجوز عمداً عند الجمهور خلافاً للجبائي وأتباعه, وتجوز سهواً بالإتفاق, إلا ما يدل على الخسة, كسرقة لقمة والتطفيف بحبة, لكن المحققين اشترطوا أن ينبهوا عليه, فينتبهوا عنه, هذا كله بعد الوحي

Regarding their being protected from all sins there is some detail, and that is: They are protected from *Kufr* prior to *Wahi* and after it, according to *ijmaa`*. Similarly, they are protected from intentionally commiting major sins, according to the majority, contrary to the opinion of the Hashwiyyah. The difference arises in whether the possibility is affirmed through the evidence that is *sam`iyy* or based on logic? As for forgetfully, then the majority regarded it as possible. As for the minor sins, then according to the majority it is possible intentionally, unlike al-Jubbaa'i and his followers. It is possible forgetfully according to *ittifaaq* (unanimous agreement), except for those (minor sins) that point out to lowliness, such as stealing a morsel, and giving a grain less for short measure. However, the Muhaqqiqeen stipulated that after Wahi, they are made away of these things (i.e. minor sins) and thus refrain from them.

وأما قبل الوحي, فلا دليل على امتناع صدور الكبيرة, وذهبت المعتزلة إلى امتناعها, لأنها تجب النفرة المانعة عن اتباعهم, فتفوت مصلحة البعثة, والحق منع ما يوجب النفرة كعهر الأمهات,

والفجور, والصغائر الدالة على الخسة, ومنع الشيعة صدور الصغيرة والكبيرة قبل الوحي وبعده, لكنهم جوزوا إظهار الكفر تقية

As for prior to *Wahi*, then there is no evidence for the impossibility of a major sin coming from them. The Mu`tazilah adopted the view that it is impossible because it would necessitate *nafrat* (dislike) which would act as an impediment from following them, and thus the benefit of their being sent would have been lost. The truth is that those (acts) which necessitate nafrat, like adultery with the mothers, and *fujoor* (vices), and minor sins which indicate lowliness. The Shias denied the possibility of a major or minor sin coming (from the Ambiyaa) before *Wahi* or after it. However, they regarded it as possible that (they) would manifest *Kufr* out of *taqiyyah*.

إذا تقرر هذا, فما نقل عن الأنبياء مما يشعر بكذب أو معصية, فما كان منقولاً بطريق الآحاد فمردود, وما كان بطريق التواتر فمصروف عن ظاهره إن أمكن, وإلا فمحمول على ترك الأولى, أو كونه قبل البعثة, وتفصيل ذلك في الكتب المبسوطة

Once this is established, then that which is narrated regarding the Abmiyaa from the matters which give the perception of a lie or disobedience, then that which is narrated by way of *Aahaad* (solitary reports) is mardood (rejected), and that which is narrated by way of *tawaatur* is averted from the literal meaning if possible. If not, then it is interpreted as leaving off that which is better, or having been prior to being granted *Nubuwwah*. The details concerning this can be found in the lengthier books.

(وأفضل الأنبياء عليهم السلام محمد صلى الله عليه وسلم)

لقوله تعالى:

كُنْتُمْ خَيْرَ أُمَّةٍ

الآية

"The most virtuous of the Ambiyaa عليهم السلام is Muhammad صلى الله عليه وسلم."

Because Allaah Ta`aalaa said:

{"*You are the best Ummah.*"}

ولا شك أن خيرية الأمة بحسب كمالهم في الدين, وذلك تابع لكمال نبيهم الذي يتبعونه, والإستدلال بقوله عليه السلام: أَنَا سَيِّدُ وَلَدِ آدَمَ وَلَا فَخْرَ, ضعيف لأنه لا يدل على كونه أفضل من آدم, بل من أولاده

There is no doubt that the goodness of the Ummah or their best "best" is proportionate to their perfection in Deen, and that follows the perfection of their Nabi whom they follow. As for using as evidence the *Hadeeth*: "I am the leader of the sons of Aadam and that is not a boast." It is *dha`eef*, because it does not point out to Rasoolullaah صلى الله عليه وسلم being better than Nabi Aadam عليه السلام, but rather, better than his offspring.

الملائكة

The Malaa'ikah:

(والملائكة عباد الله تعالى العاملون بأمره)

على ما دل عليه قوله تعالى:

"The Malaa'ikah are the slaves of Allaah Ta`aalaa, carrying out His Orders."

As is mentioned in the *Aayah*:

لَا يَسْبِقُونَهُ بِالْقَوْلِ وَهُم بِأَمْرِهِ يَعْمَلُونَ

{"They do not precede Him in speech, and they act on His Command."}

And the *Aayah*:

لَا يَسْتَكْبِرُونَ عَنْ عِبَادَتِهِ وَلَا يَسْتَحْسِرُونَ

{"They are not arrogant to (carry out) His `Ibaadah and nor are they wearied."}

(ولا يوصفون بذكورة ولا أنوثة)

"They are not described as being male or female."

إذ لم يرد بذلك نقل ولا دل عليه عقل, وما زعم عبدة الأصنام أنهم بنات الله تعالى محال باطل, وإفراط في شأنهم كما أن قول اليهود أن الواحد منهم قد يرتكب الكفر ويعاقبه الله بالمسخ تفريط وتقصير في حالهم

Because nothing of the sort has come from the *naql* (narrations) nor does the intellect point out to it. As for what is claimed by the idol-worshippers, that the Malaa'ikah are the "daughters of Allaah Ta`aalaa", then this is an impossible, *baatil* lie of theirs, and going to excess with regards to the status of the Malaa'ikah, just as the Yahood (Jews) who claimed that the Malaa'ikah even commit Kufr and get punished with disfiguration on account of it, is a disregard and laxity regarding their status.

فإن قيل: أليس قد كفر إبليس, وكان من الملائكة, بدليل صحة استثنائه منهم؟

If it is said: "Did not Iblees commit Kufr, and yet he was from the Malaa'ikah, with the evidence of the validity of his exclusion from them?"

قلنا: لا, بل كان من الجن ففسق عن أمر ربه, لكنه لما كان في صفة الملائكة في باب العبادة ورفع الدرجة وكان جنياً واحداً مغموراً بالعبادة فيما بينهم, صح استثناؤه منهم تغليباً

We say: No. Rather, he was from the Jinn, and he disobeyed the Command of his Rabb. However, because he was included among the Malaa'ikah on account of possessing an attribute like theirs in terms of *`Ibaadah* and having a high rank, but he was a solitary Jinn engrossed in *`Ibaadah* along with them, and thus he was included among them by way of *taghleeb* (i.e. they were the majority, so they were regarded as all).

وأما هاروت وماروت فالأصح أنهما ملكان لم يصدر عنهما كفر ولا كبيرة, وتعذيبهما إنما هو على وجه المعاتبة كما يعاتب الأنبياء على الزلة والسهو, وكانا يعظان الناس, ويعلمان السحر, ويقولان: إنما نحن فتنة فلا تكفر, ولا كفر في تعليم السحر, بل في اعتقاده والعمل به

As for Haaroot and Maaroot, then what is authentic is that they were two Malaa'ikah who had not committed an act of *Kufr* nor a major sin. Their punishment was by way of rebuke, like how the Ambiyaa can be rebuked for a slip up and forgetfulness. They used to admonish the people, and would teach them *sihr*, and would say to them: "We are a test, so do not commit kufr." The *Kufr* is not in the teaching of *sihr*, but rather, in believing in it and acting upon it.

تفضيل بعض القرآن على بعض

The Virtue of Some Parts of the Qur'aan over Other Parts:

(ولله تعالى كتب أنزلها على انبيائه, وبين فيها أمره ونهيه ووعده ووعيده)

"Allaah Ta`aalaa has *Kutub* which He revealed upon His Ambiyaa, and in them He explained His Commands and His Prohibitions, His Promises and His Threats."

وكلها كلام الله تعالى, وهو واحد, وإنما التعدد والتفاوت في النظم المقروء والمسموع, وبهذا الإعتبار كان الأفضل هو القرآن, ثم التوراة ثم الإنجيل ثم الزبور, كما أن القرآن كلام واحد ولا يتصور فيه تفضيل, ثم باعتبار الكتابة والقراءة يجوز أن يكون بعض السور أفضل كما ورد في الحديث, وحقيقة التفضيل أن قراءته أفضل لما أنه أنفع أو ذكر الله تعالى فيه أكثر, ثم الكتب قد نسخت بالقرآن تلاوتها وكتابتها وبعض أحكحامها

All of these *Kutub* are the *Kalaam* of Allaah Ta`aalaa, which is One. The multiplicity and differentiation of them is only with regards to the context that is recited and heard. Taking this into consideration, the most virtuous is the Qur'aan, then the Tawraah, then the Injeel, then the Zaboor.

The Qur'aan is one *Kalaam* and thus it is inconceiveable that there is superiority of some parts of it above others. However, from the aspect of writing and recitation, it is permissible that some *Soorahs* be more virtuous than others as has been mentioned in the *Ahaadeeth*. The *haqeeqat* of this superiority is that the recitation of some parts are more virtuous due to being more beneficial, or the *Dhikr* of Allaah Ta`aalaa in those *Soorahs* (or those *Aayaat*) are more.

The previous *Kutub* were abrogated by the Qur'aan: their recitation, their writing and some of their rulings.

المعراج

The *Mi`raaj* (Ascension):

والمعراج لرسول الله عليه الصلاة والسلام في اليقظة بشخصه إلى السماء ثم إلى ما شاء الله) (تعالى من العلى حق

"The Mi`raaj is *Haqq*, and it is that Rasoolullaah صلى الله عليه وسلم was physically taken (i.e. with his physical body) in a state of wakefulness to the heavens, and thereafter to wherever Allaah Ta`aalaa willed from the exalted places."

أي ثابت بالخبر المشهور, حتى أن منكره يكون مبتدعاً وإنكاره وادعاء استحالته إنما يبتنى على أصول الفلاسفة, وإلا فالخرق والإلتئام على السموات جائز, والأجسام كلها متماثلة, يصح على كل ما يصح على الآخر, والله تعالى قادر على الممكنات كلها, فقوله في اليقظة: إشارة إلى الرد على من زعم أن المعراج كان في المنام, على ما روي عن معاوية أنه سئل عن المعراج فقال: كانت رؤيا صالحة, وروي عن عائشة رضي الله عنها أنها قالت: ما فقد جسد محمد عليه السلام ليلة المعراج

Meaning that it has been affirmed by the report that is *Mash-hoor*, so much so that the one who denies it is regarded as a *Mubtadi`*. The denial of it and the claim that it is impossible is based on the principles of the Philosophers; otherwise, it is possible of heavenly things that there be an infringement of what is customary and a compliance with it. All bodies are similar to each other, so it is valid to say of one what is valid to say of another.

Allaah Ta`aalaa has power of all *mumkinaat* (possible things).

The statement of the author: "In wakefulness," is a reference to a rebuttal of those who claim that the *Mi`raaj* took place as a dream. It is narrated about Hadhrat Mu`aawiyah رضي الله عنه that he was asked about the *Mi`raaj*, so he said: "It was a truthful vision." It is narrated from Hadhrat `Aa'ishah رضي الله عنها that she said: "The body of Muhammad صلى الله عليه وسلم was not absent on the night of Mi`raaj."

وقد قال الله تعالى:

$$\text{وَمَا جَعَلْنَا الرُّؤْيَا الَّتِي أَرَيْنَاكَ إِلَّا فِتْنَةً لِلنَّاسِ}$$

Allaah Ta`aalaa said:

{"*And We did not make the vision which We showed you except a test for mankind...*"}

وأجيب: بأن المراد الرؤيا بالعين, والمعنى ما فقد جسده عن الروح, بل كان مع روحه, وكان المعراج للروح والجسد جميعاً, وقوله بشخصه: إشارة إلى الرد على من زعم أنه كان للروح فقط, ولا يخفى أن المعراج في المنام أو بالروح ليس مما ينكر كل الإنكار, والكفرة أنكروا أمر المعراج غاية الإنكار, بل وكثير من المسلمين قد ارتدوا بسبب ذلك

We respond by saying that the meaning of *Ru'yaa* (vision) in this *Aayah* is the seeing with the physical eye, and the meaning of what was said by Hadhrat `Aa'ishah رضي الله عنها is that his body was not absent from his *Rooh*, i.e. the *Mi`raaj* was with his *Rooh* and his body.

The meaning of the author's statement: "By his person," is a reference to a refutation of those who claim that it was only by his *Rooh*. It is not hidden that *Mi`raaj* in a dream or with the *Rooh* is not from that which was denied with a complete denial, whereas the Kuffaar had denial the *Mi`raaj* with a complete denial. In fact, many Muslims became Murtadd as a result thereof.

وقوله إلى السماء: إشارة إلى الرد على من زعم أن المعراج في اليقظة لم يكن إلا إلى بيت المقدس على ما نطق به الكتاب, وقوله ثم إلى ما شاء الله تعالى: إشارة إلى اختلاف أقوال السلف, فقيل: إلى الجنة, وقيل: إلى العرش, وقيل: إلى قوف العرش, وقيل: إلى طرف العالم, فالإسراء وهو من المسجد الحرام إلى بيت المقدس قطعي, ثبت بالكتاب, والمعراج من الأرض إلى السماء مشهور, ومن السماء إلى الجنة, أو العرش, أو غير ذلك آحاداً, ثم الصحيح أنه عليه السلام إنما رأى ربه بفؤاده لا بعينه

The author's statement, "To the heavens," is a reference to a refutation of those who claim that *Mi`raaj* in a state of wakefulness was only until Bayt al-Maqdis which was mentioned in the Qur'aan.

The meaning of his statement: "And thereafter to wherever Allaah Ta`aalaa willed," is a reference to the different opinions of the Salaf. Some said he went to Jannah, and some said he went until the `Arsh, and some said he went above the `Arsh, and some said he went to the edge of the world.

Thus, *Israa* (the night journey) was from Masjid al-Haraam until Bayt al-Maqdis, and that is absolute. It is affirmed by the Kitaab (Qur'aan). *Mi`raaj* is from the earth to the heavens and is *Mash-hoor* (well-known), and then from the heavens to Jannah, or the `Arsh, or other than that, and that is mentioned in *Khabr-e-Aahad Ahaadeeth*. Then, the *saheeh* (authentic) view is that Rasoolullaah ﷺ saw Allaah Ta`aalaa with his heart, not with his physical eyes.

كرامات الأولياء

The *Karaamaat* (Miracles) of the *Awliyaa*:

(وكرامات الأولياء حق)

"The *Karaamaat* (miracles) of the *Awliyaa* are true."

والولي: هو العارف بالله تعالى وصفاته بحسب ما يمكن, المواظب على الطاعات, المجتنب عن المعاصي, المعرض عن الإنهماك في اللذات والشهوات, وكرامته: ظهور أمر خارق للعادة من قلبه غير مقارن لدعوى النبوة, فما لا يكون مقروناً بالإيمان والعمل الصالح يكون إستدراجاً, وما يكون مقروناً بدعوى النبوة يكون معجزة

A *Wali* is one who is an `*Aarif* (one who has *Ma`rifat*) of Allaah Ta`aalaa and of His *Sifaat* in so far as is possible, and who is continuous upon the obedience of Allaah Ta`aalaa and avoiding disobedience unto Him, the one who avoids becoming engrossed in pleasures and desires (of this Dunyaa). His *Karaamat* is that a matter occurs at his hand which is completely at odds with the natural order of things, and he is not one who claims *Nubuwwah*. If he does not have Imaan and is not a person with *a`maal-e-saalihah*, then such an event occuring at his hands is only deception (*istidraaj*). If he is one who claims *Nubuwwah* (provided it was before the time of Rasoolullaah ﷺ), it would be a *Mu`jizah*.

والدليل على حقية الكرامة ما تواتر عن كثير من الصحابة ومن بعدهم بحيث لا يمكن إنكاره

خصوصاً الأمر المشترك, وإن كانت التفاصيل آحاداً, وأيضاً الكتاب ناطق بظهورها من مريم, ومن صاحب سليمان عليه السلام, وبعد ثبوت الوقوع لا حاجة إلى إثبات الجواز

A proof for the reality of *Karaamaat* is that it is reported with *tawaatur* that *Karaamaat* took place at the hands of Sahaabah and thsoe after them, and thus it is not possible to reject it. Especially when the matter is something common, even if the details of it are reported in solitary reports. Also, the Qur'aan speaks about the occurence of *Karaamaat* for Hadhrat Maryam عليها السلام, as well as by the companion of Nabi Sulaymaan عليه السلام. Since the very occurence of it has already been proved, there is no need to prove the possibility.

ثم أورد كلاماً يشير إلى تفسير الكرامة, وإلى تفصيل بعض جزئياتها المستبعدة, فقال:

(فتظهر الكرامة على طريق نقض العادة للولي, من قطع المسافة البعيدة في المدة القليلة)

Thereafter, the author presents a discussion which hints towards an explanation of what a *Karaamat* is, and an indepth explanation of some of its particulars. He says:

"A *Karaamat* manifests by way of a break in the natural habit of things, for a Wali, such as the travelling of far distances in a short span of time."

كإتيان صاحب سليمان عليه السلام وهو آصف بن برخيا على الأشهر, بعرش بلقيس قبل ارتداد الطرف, مع بعد المسافة

(وظهور الطعام والشراب واللباس عند الحاجة إليها)

كما في حق مريم, فإنه قال تعالى:

Like how the companion of Sulaymaan عليه السلام - and he was Aasif ibn Barkhiyaa, according to the most well-known report - brought the throne of Bilqees in the blink of an eye despite the lengthy distance.

"And the appearance of food, drink and clothing at the time it is needed."

Like how it was in the case of Hadhrat Maryam عليها السلام. Allaah Ta`aalaa said:

كُلَّمَا دَخَلَ عَلَيْهَا زَكَرِيَّا الْمِحْرَابَ وَجَدَ عِنْدَهَا رِزْقاً قَالَ يَا مَرْيَمُ أَنَّى لَكِ هَذَا قَالَتْ هُوَ مِنْ عِنْدِ اللهِ

{"Whenever Zakariyyaa entered the mihraab, he found with her rizq. He said, "O Maryam, how did you get this?" She said, "It is from Allaah."}

(والمشي على الماء)

كما نقل عن كثير من الأولياء

"And walking on water."

As was reported from many of the *Awliyaa*.

(وفي الهواء)

كما نقل عن جعفر بن أبي طالب ولقمان السرخسي وغيرهما

"And in the air."

As was reported from Hadhrat Ja`far ibn Abi Taalib رضي الله عنه and Luqmaan as-Sarakhsi, as well as others.

(وكلام الجماد والعجماء)

واندفاع المتوجه من البلاء, كفاية المهم من الأعداء

"And the speaking of inanimate, solid objects, and of animals."

And the warding off of an approaching calamity, and the protection of enemies from the one who is anxious.

أما كلام الجماد: فكما روي أنه كان بين يدي سلمان وأبي الدرداء رضي الله عنهما قصعة, فسبحت وسمعا تسبيحها

وأما كلام العجماء: فتكليم الكلب لأصحاب الكهف, وكما روي أن النبي صلى الله عليه وسلم قال: بَيْنَا رَجُلٌ يَسُوقُ بَقَرَةً قَدْ حَمَلَ عَلَيْهَا إِذِ الْتَفَتَ الْبَقَرَةُ إِلَيْهِ وَقَالَتْ: إِنِّي لَمْ أُخْلَقْ لِهَذَا إِنَّمَا خُلِقْتُ لِلْحَرْثِ

فَقَالَ النَّاسُ: سُبْحَانَ اللهِ بَقَرَةٌ تَكَلَّمُ, فَقَالَ عَلَيْهِ السَّلَامُ: آمَنْتُ بِهَذَا

As for the speaking of inanimate, solid objects, then it was narrated that once, in front of Hadhrat Salmaan al-Faarisi رضي الله عنه and Hadhrat Abu-d Dardaa رضي الله عنه there was a bowl, and both of them heard the sound of tasbeeh coming from it.

As for the speaking of animals, then an example of this is the dog of the Ashaab-e-Kahf speaking to them, and also what was narrated that Nabi صلى الله عليه وسلم said: "There was a man leading a cow upon which he was using for bearing burdens. The cow turned to him and said, "I was not created to this. I was created for plowing."

The people said, "*Sub-haanallaah*, a cow that speaks?" Rasoolullaah صلى الله عليه وسلم said, "I have brought Imaan in it."

(وغير ذلك من الأشياء)

"And other such (miracles)."

مثل رؤية عمر رضي الله عنه وهو على المنبر بالمدينة جيشه بنهاوند حتى أنه قال لأمير جيشه: يا سارية, الجبل, الجبل, تحذيراً له من وراء الجبل لمكر العدو هناك, وسماع سارية كلامه مع بعد المسافة, وكشرب خالد رضي الله عنه السم من غير تضرر به, وكجريان النيل بكتاب عمر رضي الله عنه, وأمثال هذا أكثر من أن تحصى

ولما استدل المعتزلة المنكرون لكرامة الأولياء بأنه لو جاز ظهور خوارق العادات من الأولياء لاشتبه بالمعجزة, فلم يتميز النبي من غير النبي, أشار إلى الجواب بقوله:

Such as Hadhrat `Umar رضي الله عنه being upon a *mimbar* in the Masjid in Madeenah and yet seeing the Muslim army at Nihaawand, and saying to the Ameer of the army: "O Saariyah, the mountain! The mountain!" Warning him of a plot of the enemy behind the mountain. Hadhrat Saariyah رضي الله عنه heard the words of Hadhrat `Umar رضي الله عنه despite being so far away. Another example is Hadhrat Khaalid رضي الله عنه drinking poison without it harming him. Another example is the river Nile flowing after the letter of Hadhrat `Umar رضي الله عنه was thrown into it. There are innumerable examples such as this.

The Mu`tazilah denied the existence of *Karaamaat*, saying that had they been possible, then it would resemble the *Mu`jizaat* of the Ambiyaa and thus a Nabi would not be distinguishable from a *Wali*.

Imaam an-Nasafi refutes them by saying:

(ويكون ذلك)

أي ظهور خوارق العادات من الأولياء أو الولي الذي هو من آحاد الأمة

(معجزة للرسول الذي ظهرت هذه الكرامة لواحد من أمته, لأنه يظهر بها)

"And that happens - "

Meaning, the manifestation of *khawaariq al-`aadaat* (matters that contradict the norm) at the hands of the *Awliyaa*, which are from the individual members of the Ummah."

"As a *Mu`jizah* for the Rasool in whose Ummah one of the individual members had it occur by his hands, because by (the *Karaamat*) it becomes clear- "

أي بتلك الكرامة

Meaning, by that particular *Karaamat*.

(أنه ولي ولن يكون ولياً إلا وأن يكون محقاً في ديانته, وديانته الإقرار)

باللسان والتصديق بالقلب

"That he is a Wali, and it is not possible for him to be a Wali unless he is upon the Haqq in the matter of his Deen, and his Deen is the admission."

By his tongue and the assent by his heart.

(رسالة رسوله)

"Of the Risaalah of his Rasool."

مع الطاعة في أوامره ونواهيه, حتى لو ادعى هذا الولي الإستقلال بنفسه وعدم المتابعة لم يكن ولياً, ولم يظهر ذلك على يده

والحاصل أن الأمر الخارق للعادة فهو بالنسبة إلى النبي عليه السلام معجزة سواء ظهر ذلك من قبله أو من قبل آحاد من أمته, وبالنسبة إلى الولي كرامة, لخلوه عن دعوى نبوة من ظهر ذلك من قلبه, فالنبي لا بد من علمه بكونه نبياً, ومن قصده إظهار خوارق العادات, ومن حكمه قطعاً بموجب المعجزات, بخلاف الولي

Along with obedience to him in his commands and his prohibitions, so much so that if this *Wali* claims to be independent and that he does not follow that Rasool, then he would not be a *Wali* and this would not take place by his hands.

The summary is that a matter that is a break in the customary way of things, when it is connected to a Nabi, it is a *Mu`jizah*, whether that takes place by his hands or by the hands of someone from his Ummah. When it is connected to a *Wali*, it is a *Karaamat* because he does not lay claim to *Nubuwwah*. The Nabi necessarily knows that he is a Nabi, and he intends the manifestation of *khawaariq al-`aadaat* (matters that contradict the norm), and he must give absolute judgement as to the necessity of the *Mu`jizaat*, and all of this is contrary to the *Wali*.

(وأفضل البشر بعد نبينا)

"The best of mankind after our Nabi - "

والأحسن أن يقال بعد الأنبياء, لكنه أراد البعدية الزمانية, وليس بعد نبينا نبي ومع ذلك لا بد من تخصيص عيسى عليه السلام, إذ لو أريد كل بشر يوجد بعد نبينا إنتقض بعيسى عليه السلام,

ولو أريد كل بشر يولد بعده لم يفد التفضيل على الصحابة, ولو أريد كل بشر هو موجود على وجه الأرض لم يفد التفضيل على التابعين ومن بعدهم, ولو أريد كل بشر يوجد على وجه الأرض في الجملة, إنتقض بعيسى عليه السلام

(أبو بكر الصديق)

It would have been better for him to have said, "The best of mankind after the Ambiyaa". However, what he meant is "after" in terms of time, because there is no Nabi after our Nabi. However, despite that, it is necessary to exclude Nabi `Eesa عليه السلام (from that statement), because if he (the author) intended (by his statement) every person to come into existence after our Nabi صلى الله عليه وسلم, it would contradict Nabi `Eesa عليه السلام. If he intended every person to be born after our Nabi صلى الله عليه وسلم, it would exclude the Sahaabah who were born in his time and before him. If he intended every person to exist on the face of the earth at that time, it would exclude the Taabi`een and those after them. If he intended every person to come into existence on the face of the earth altogether, then again it would exclude Nabi `Eesa عليه السلام.

"Is (Hadhrat) Abu Bakr as-Siddeeq رضي الله عنه."

الذي صدق النبي صلى الله عليه وسلم في النبوة من غير تلعثم وفي المعراج بلا تردد

(ثم عمر الفاروق)

The one who testified to the truthfulness of Nabi صلى الله عليه وسلم in the matter of *Nubuwwah* without any doubting and who testified to his truthfulness in the matter of *Mi`raaj* without any hesitation.

"Then (Hadhrat) `Umar al-Faarooq رضي الله عنه."

الذي فرق بين الحق والباطل في القضايا والخصومات

The one who separated between Haqq and Baatil in matters of judgements and disputes.

(ثم عثمان ذو النورين)

لأن النبي عليه السلام زوجه رقية, ولما ماتت رقية زوجه أم كلثوم, ولما ماتت قال: لَوْ كَانَ عِنْدِيْ ثَالِثَةً لَزَوَّجْتُكَهَا

"Then (Hadhrat) 'Uthmaan Dhun-Noorain رضي الله عنه."

Because Nabi صلى الله عليه وسلم married him to his daughter, Hadhrat Ruqayyah رضي الله عنها, and then to Hadhrat Umm Kulthoom رضي الله عنها after she passed away, and then after she passed away as well he said to him, "If I had a third daughter, I would have given her to you in marriage as well."

(ثم علي المرتضى)

من عباد الله تعالى وخلص أصحاب رسول الله تعالى, على هذا وجدنا السلف, والظاهر أنه لو لم يكن لهم دليل على ذلك لما حكموا بذلك, وأما نحن فقد وجدنا دلائل الجانبين متعارضة, ولم نجد هذه المسألة مما يتعلق به شيء من الأعمال, أو يكون التوقف فيه مخلاً بشيء من الواجبات فيهما, وكأن السلف كانوا متفقين في تفضيل عثمان على علي رضي الله عنهما, حيث جعلوا من علامات السنة والجماعة تفضيل الشيخين ومحبة الختنين, والإنصاف أنه أن أريد بالأفضلية كثرة الثواب فلتتقف جهة, وإن أريد كثرة ما يعده ذوو العقول من الفضائل فلا

"Then (Hadhrat) 'Ali al-Murtadhaa رضي الله عنه."

Al-Murtadhaa meaning "the approved", i.e. by the bondsmen of Allaah Ta'aalaa and the sincere Sahaabah of Rasoolullaah صلى الله عليه وسلم.

Upon this we found the Salaf. The apparent is that had there been no proof for that, they would have ruled in that way. However, we found the evidences of the two sides to be contradictory, and we found that this issue did not have connected to it anything pertaining to *a`maal*, nor does hesitation in this matter cause any confusion with regards to the *waajibaat*. It seems as though the Salaf had *ittifaaq* regarding the superiority of Hadhrat 'Uthmaan رضي الله عنه over Hadhrat 'Ali رضي الله عنه, because they regarded believing in the superiority of Shaykhayn (i.e. Hadhrat Abu Bakr رضي الله عنه and Hadhrat 'Umar رضي الله عنه) and loving the two sons-in-law (i.e. Hadhrat

'Uthmaan رضي الله عنه and Hadhrat 'Ali رضي الله عنه) as being one of the signs of being from Ahlus Sunnah wal-Jamaa'ah. The impartial position is that if what he means by superiority (of Hadhrat 'Uthmaan رضي الله عنه) is having greater reward, then *tawaqquf* (hesitance) would have a point of view. However, if what he means is that Hadhrat 'Uthmaan رضي الله عنه possessed more of those matters which people with sound intellects regard as *fadhaa'il* (virtues), then there is no place for hesitance (i.e. it becomes quite clear why Hadhrat 'Uthmaan رضي الله عنه has been regarded as having a virtue over Hadhrat 'Ali رضي الله عنه).

ترتيب الخلافة

The Order of the *Khilaafah*:

(وخلافتهم)

أي نيابتهم عن الرسول في إقامة الدين بحيث يجب على كافة الأمم الإتباع

"And their *Khilaafat*."

Meaning, their leadership of the Ummah after Rasoolullaah صلى الله عليه وسلم, in establishing the Deen in such a manner that it was *waajib* upon the rest of the Ummah to follow them.

(على هذا الترتيب)

"Is in this order."

أيضاً يعني أن الخلافة بعد رسول الله صلى الله عليه وسلم لأبي بكر, ثم لعمر, ثم لعثمان, ثم لعلي, رضي الله عنهم, وذلك لأن الصحابة قد اجتمعوا يوم توفي رسول الله صلى الله عليه وسلم في سقيفة بني ساعدة واستقر رأيهم بعد المشاورة والمنازعة على خلافة أبي بكر رضي الله عنه, وأجمعوا على ذلك, وتابعه علي رضي الله عنه على رؤوس الأشهاد, بعد توقف كان منه, ولو لم تكن الخلافة حقاً له لما اتفق عليه الصحابة, ولنازعه علي رضي الله عنه, كما نازع معاوية, ولاحتج عليهم, لو كان في حقه نص, كما زعمت الشيعة, وكيف يتصور في حق أصحاب رسول الله صلى الله عليه وسلم الإتفاق على الباطل, وترك العلم بالنص الوارد؟ ثم إن أبا بكر رضي الله

عنه لما أيس من حياته دعا عثمان رضي الله عنه, وأملى عليه كتاب عهده لعمر رضي الله عنه, فلما كتب عثمان ختم الصحيفة وأخرجها إلى الناس, وأمرهم أن يبايعوا لمن في الصحيفة فبايعوا, حتى مرت بعلي فقال: بايعنا لمن كان فيها, وإن كان عمر رضي الله عنه

Meaning, after Rasoolullaah صلى الله عليه وسلم the Khilaafah was for Hadhrat Abu Bakr رضي الله عنه, then Hadhrat `Umar رضي الله عنه, then Hadhrat `Uthmaan رضي الله عنه, then Hadhrat `Ali رضي الله عنه. That is because on the day Rasoolullaah صلى الله عليه وسلم passed away, the Sahaabah gathered in Saqeefah Bani Saa`idah and unanimously decided, after consultation, to appoint Hadhrat Abu Bakr رضي الله عنه as the Khaleefah. They had *ijmaa`* upon that, and Hadhrat `Ali رضي الله عنه gave *bay`ah* to him in the presence of witnesses as well, after some *tawaqquf* on his part.

If the Khilaafah had not been a right of Hadhrat Abu Bakr رضي الله عنه, the Sahaabah would not have had *ittifaaq* on it, and Hadhrat `Ali رضي الله عنه would have disputed with him regarding it like how Hadhrat Mu`aawiyah رضي الله عنه had disputed with Hadhrat `Ali رضي الله عنه regarding the *Khilaafah*, and he would have used evidence against had there been any *nass* on his having the right (to have it first), like what is claimed by the Shias. How can it ever be conceived that the Sahaabah of Rasoolullaah صلى الله عليه وسلم would have had *ittifaaq* upon *baatil*? And that they would abandon *nass* which had come (regarding Hadhrat `Ali رضي الله عنه, as the Shias claim)? Thereafter, when Hadhrat Abu Bakr رضي الله عنه was at the end of his life, he called Hadhrat `Uthmaan رضي الله عنه and dictated to him a letter wherein he gives the Khilaafah over to Hadhrat `Umar رضي الله عنه. After Hadhrat `Uthmaan رضي الله عنه completed writing the letter, he stamped it and took it out to the people, and he commanded them to give *bay`ah* to the one who is named in it, so they gave *bay`ah*. When he passed by Hadhrat `Ali رضي الله عنه, he said, "We give *bay`ah* to whomsoever is mentioned therein, even if it be `Umar رضي الله عنه."

وبالجملة: وقع الإتفاق على خلافته, ثم استشهد عمر رضي الله عنه وترك الخلافة شورى بين ستة: عثمان, وعلي, وعبد الرحمن بن عوف, وطلحة, والزبير, وسعد بن أبي وقاص رضي الله عنهم, ثم فوض الأمر خمستهم إلى عبد الرحمن بن عوف ورضوا بحكمه, فاختار عثمان, وبايعه

بمحضر من الصحابة, فبايعوه وانقادوا لأوامره ونواهيه, وصلوا معه الجمع والأعياد, فكان إجماعاً, ثم استشهد وترك الأمر مهملاً, فاجتمع كبار المهاجرين والأنصار على علي رضي الله عنه, والتمسوا منه قبول الخلافة, وبايعوه لما كان أفضل أهل عصره, وأولاهم بالخلافة

In summary: There was *ittifaaq* upon the *Khilaafah* of Hadhrat 'Umar رضي الله عنه. Thereafter he became Shaheed and left the decision of appointing the next Khaleefah upto the *Shoora* of six Sahaabah: Hadhrat 'Uthmaan رضي الله عنه, Hadhrat 'Ali رضي الله عنه, Hadhrat 'Abdur Rahmaan ibn 'Awf رضي الله عنه, Hadhrat Talhah رضي الله عنه, Hadhrat Zubair رضي الله عنه and Hadhrat Sa'd ibn Abi Waqqaas رضي الله عنه. Thereafter, five of the six left the matter upto Hadhrat 'Abdur Rahmaan ibn 'Awf رضي الله عنه and were pleased with whatever decision he gives, so he chose Hadhrat 'Uthmaan رضي الله عنه and gave *bay'ah* to him in the presence of the Sahaabah, and thereafter they all gave *bay'ah* to him and submitted to his commands and prohibitions, and performed with him Salaat al-Jumu'ah and the Salaats of the two 'Eids, and thus his *Khilaafah* was by *ijmaa'* of the Sahaabah. Thereafter he became Shaheed and left the matter open, and the seniormost of the Muhaajireen and Ansaar chose Hadhrat 'Ali رضي الله عنه and sought from him that he accept the *Khilaafah*, and they gave *bay'ah* to him because he was the most virtuous person alive at that time (i.e. after the demise of the previous three Khulafaa رضي الله عنهم) and was the most deserving of *Khilaafah* from those who remained.

وما وقع من المخالفات والمحاربات لم يكن عن نزاع في خلافته, بل عن خطأ في الإجتهاد, وما وقع من الإختلاف بين الشيعة وأهل السنة في هذه المسألة وادعاء كل من الفريقين النص في باب الإمامة, وإيراد الأسئلة والأجوبة من الجانبين, فمذكور في المطولات

As for what occured of differences and wars, then it was not because of a dispute regarding his *Khilaafah*, but rather, due to an error in *ijtihaad*. As for the dissension between Ahlus Sunnah wal-Jamaa'ah and the Shias in this issue, and the claiming of each side *nass* regarding the issue of *Imaamat*, and the questions and answers on both sides, then this can be found in the most extensive books.

مدة الخلافة

The Duration of the Khilaafah:

(والخلافة ثلاثون سنة ثم بعدها ملك وإمارة)

"The *Khilaafah* was for 30 years, and thereafter there was *mulk* (kingship) and *imaarah* (rulership)."

لقوله عليه السلام: الْخِلَافَةُ بَعْدِيْ ثَلَاثُوْنَ سَنَةً ثُمَّ تَصِيْرُ مُلْكاً عَضُوْضاً, وقد استشهد علي رضي الله عنه على رأس ثلاثين سنة من وفاة رسول الله صلى الله عليه وسلم, فمعاوية ومن بعده لا يكونون خلفاء, بل كانوا ملوكاً وأمراء, وهذا مشكل, لأن أهل الحل والعقد من الأمة قد كانوا متفقين على خلافة الخلفاء العباسية, وبعض المروانية, كعمر بن عبد العزيز مثلاً

ولعل المراد أن الخلافة الكاملة التي لا يشوبها شيء من المخالفة وميل عن المتابعة تكون ثلاثين سنة, وبعدها قد يكون وقد لا يكون

Because of the *Hadeeth*: "The *Khilaafah* after me will be for 30 years, and thereafter there will be biting kingship."

Hadhrat `Ali رضي الله عنه passed away on the 30th year after the demise of Rasoolullaah صلى الله عليه وسلم; thus, Hadhrat Mu`aawiyah رضي الله عنه and those who came after him would (according to this narration) not have been Khulafaa, but rather, kings and rulers, but this is a difficult problem, because the Ahl-ul-Halli wal-`Aqd (the People of Power and Authority) from the Ummah had *ittifaaq* upon the *Khilaafah* of the Abbasid Khulafaa and some of the Marwaani (i.e. Umayyad) Khulafaa like Hadhrat `Umar ibn `Abdil `Azeez, for example. Thus, perhaps the meaning of the Hadeeth is that the "complete *Khilaafah*" in which there is differences of opinion and inclination away from following (the Khaleefah) will last for 30 years, and thereafter such a *Khilaafah* may exist and may not exist (i.e. may exist for some Khulafaa but not for others.)

ثم الإجماع على أن نصب الإمام واجب, وإنما الخلاف في أنه هل يجب على الله تعالى و على الخلق بدليل سمعي أو عقلي؟

والمذهب أنه يجب على الخلق سمعاً لقوله عليه السلام:

مَنْ مَاتَ وَلَمْ يَعْرِفْ إِمَامَ زَمَانِهِ مَاتَ مِيْتَةً جَاهِلِيَّةً

Thereafter, there is *ijmaa`* that to choose a Khaleefah is *waajib*. The difference arises regarding whether the appointment (of the Khaleefah) must be done by Allaah Ta`aalaa or by the creation, and whether the basis (for appointment) is (dalaa'il that are) *sam`iyy* or *`aqliyy* (based on logic).

The correct view is that it is *waajib* upon the creation and the *wujoob* is based on *dalaa'il* that are *sam`iyy*, because of the *Hadeeth*:

"Whosoever passes away not recognising the Imaam (i.e. Khaleefah) of his time (i.e. has not given *bay`ah* to a Khaleefah) then his death is a death of *jaahiliyyah*."

ولأن الأمة قد جعلوا أهم المهمات بعد وفاة النبي صلى الله عليه وسلم نصب الإمام, حتى قدموه على الدفن, وكذا بعد موت كل إمام, ولأن كثيراً من الواجبات الشرعية يتوقف عليه, كما أشار إليه بقوله:

Also, because the Ummah after the passing away of Rasoolullaah صلى الله عليه وسلم regarded the most important thing to be the appointment of a Khaleefah, so much so that the burial of Nabi صلى الله عليه وسلم was postponed until a Khaleefah was appointed. The same is the case after the demise of every Khaleefah. Also, many of the *waajibaat* of the Sharee`ah require a Khaleefah. This is hinted to by the author when he says:

والمسلمون لا بد لهم من إمام يقوم بتنفيذ أحكامهم, وإقامة حدودهم, وسد ثغورهم, وتجهيز) جيوشهم, وأخذ صدقاتهم, وقهر المتغلبة والمتلصصة وقطاع الطريق, وإقامة الجمع والأعياد, وقطع المنازعات الواقعة بين العباد, وقبول الشهادات القائمة على الحقوق, وتزويج الصغار (والصغائر الذين لا أولياء لهم, وقسمة الغنائم

ونحو ذلك من الأمور التي لا يتولاها آحاد الأمة

"The Muslims need to have an Imaam (i.e. Khaleefah) who enforces the *Ahkaam* (of Sharee`ah), and carries out the *hudood*, and protects the frontiers (of the Muslim lands), and prepares the armies, and collects the Zakaat, and subjugates those who try to get the upper hand (over the Muslims) as well as the robbers and highway men, and establishes the Jumu'ah and the `Eids, and cuts off the disputes which occur between the Muslims, and accepts the receiving of testimonies based on rights, and arranges the marriage of young men and young women that have no *wali* (guardian), and distributes the spoils of war."

And other than that from the matters which cannot be run by the individual members of the Ummah.

فإن قيل: لِمَ لا يجوز الإكتفاء بذي شوكة في كل ناحية؟ ومن أين يجب نصب من له الرياسة العامة؟

قلنا: لأنه يؤدي إلى منازعات ومخاصمات مفضية إلى اختلال أمر الدين والدنيا, كما يشاهد في زماننا هذا

فإن قيل: فليكتف بذي شوكة له الرياسة العامة إماماً كان أو غير إمام, فإن انتظام الأمر يحصل بذلك كما في عهد الأتراك

If it is said: "Why not suffice with men of power in each field (of these fields, i.e. rather than having just one Khaleefah)? And from where do you find that it is *waajib* to appoint one who has general leadership?"

We say: "That (i.e. men of power in each field) would lead to disputes and quarrels which would end up in disorder in matters of Deen and matters of Dunyaa, as is witnessed in our time.

If it is said: "Then suffice with having a man of authority having general leadership whether he is an Imaam (i.e. Khaleefah) or not, because the system of rule would be achieved by that, like in the era of the Turks."

قلنا: نعم, يحصل بعض النظام من أمر الدنيا, ولكن يختل أمر الدين, وهو المقصود الأهم, والعمدة العظمى

فإن قيل: فعلى ما ذكر من أن مدة الخلافة ثلاثون سنة يكون الزمان بعد الخلفاء الراشدين خالياً عن الإمام فتعصي الأمة كلهم, وتكون ميتتهم ميتة جاهلية

قلنا: قد سبق أن المراد الخلافة الكاملة, ولو سلم فلعل بعدما دور الخلافة ينقضي دون دور الإمامة, بناء على أن الإمام أعم, وانتفاء الأخص لا يوجب انتفاء الأعم, لكن هذا الإصطلاح مما لم نجده للقوم, بل من الشيعة من يزعم أن الخليفة أعم, ولهذا يقولون بخلافة الأئمة الثلاثة دون إمامتهم, وأما بعد الخلفاء العباسية فالأمر مشكل

We say: "Yes, some of the Dunyaa matters would have been achieved through that; however, the matters of Deen would be in disorder despite them being the most imporant and the greatest reliance (being upon them)."

If it is said: "According to what has been mentioned, the period of Khilaafah lasts for 30 years, and thus after that time there is no Imaam Khaleefah), and that means the entire Ummah is disobedient and their deaths are like the death of *jaahiliyyah*."

We say: "It has already been mentioned that the intended meaning of the Hadeeth is "Complete Khilaafah". Even if it were to be submitted, then perhaps after it the era of the Khilaafah ends without the era of the *Imaamat* ending, because the term Imaam is more general, and the denial of what is specific does not entail the denial of what is more general. However, we have not seen this technicality used by any people other than the Shias, those who claimed that Khaleefah is more general, and for this reason they speak of the Khilaafah of the "three Imaams", not their "*Imaamat*". As for after the Abbasid Khulafaa, then the matter is difficult.

(ثم ينبغي أن يكون الإمام ظاهراً)

"Thereafter, it is necessary that the Imaam (Khaleefah) be one who is seen, apparent."

ليرجع إليه, فيقوم بالمصالح ليحصل ما هو الغرض من نصب الإمام

So that people may go to him, and that he may take care of the needs of people, thus fulfilling the purpose of the appointment of an Imaam.

(لا مختفياً)

"Not hidden away."

من أعين الناس, خوفاً من الأعداء, وما للظلمة من الإستيلاء

(ولا منتظراً)

From the eyes of people, out of fear of the enemy and of being conquered by the oppressors.

"Nor awaited."

خروجه عند صلاح الزمان, وانقطاع موارد الشر والفساد, وانحلال نظام أهل الظلم والعناد, لا كما زعمت الشيعة خصوصاً الإمامية منهم, أن الإمام الحق بعد رسول الله صلى الله عليه وسلم علي رضي الله عنه, ثم ابنه الحسن, ثم أخوه الحسين, ثم ابنه علي زين العابدين, ثم ابنه محمد الباقر, ثم ابنه جعفر الصادق, ثم ابنه موسى الكاظم, ثم ابنه علي الرضا, ثم ابنه محمد النقي, ثم ابنه علي التقي, ثم ابنه الحسن العسكري, ثم ابنه محمد القائم المنتظر المهدي, وقد اختفى خوفاً من أعدائه, وسيظهر فيملأ الدنيا قسطاً وعدلاً كما ملئت جوراً وظلماً, ولا امتناع في طول عمره وامتداد أيامه كعيسى والخضر عليهما السلام, وغيرهما

His coming out will be at the appropriate time, at the cutting off of the sources of evil and corruption, and at the loosing of the system of the people of oppresion and rebellion. (The correct position) is not like what is claimed by the Shias, especially the Imaamiyyah Shias among them, that the "true Imaam" after Rasoolullaah صلى الله عليه وسلم was Hadhrat `Ali رضي الله عنه, then his son, Hadhrat Hasan رضي الله عنه, then his brother, Hadhrat Husain رضي الله عنه, then his son, Imaam Zayn-ul-`Aabideen, then his son, Muhammad al-Baaqir, then his son, Ja`far as-Saadiq, then his son, Moosaa al-Kaazhim, then his son, `Ali ar-Ridhaa, then his son, Muhammad an-Naqi, then his son, `Ali at-Taqi, then his son, Hasan al-`Askari, then his son, Muhammad al-Qaa'im an-Muntazhar al-Mahdi, who has hidden away out of fear of his enemies. They claim that when he emerges, he will fill the *Dunyaa* with equity and justice just as it had been filled with injustice and oppression.

It is not impossible (they say) for his life to be that long and his days to be that extended, because the same is the case with Nabi `Eesa عليه السلام, Hadhrat Khidhr عليه السلام and others.

وأنت خبير بأن اختفاء الإمام وعدمه سواء في عدم حصول الأغراض المطلوبة من وجود الإمام وأن خوفه من الأعداء لا يوجب الإختفاء بحيث لا يوجد منه إلا الإسم, بل غاية الأمر أن يوجب

اختفاء دعوى الإمامة كما في حق آبائه الذين كانوا ظاهرين على الناس ولا يدعون الإمامة, وأيضاً
فساد الزمان واختلاف الأراء واستيلاء الظلمة, أحتياج الناس إلى الإمام أشد وانقيادهم له أسهل

You (the reader) are well-aware that for an Imaam to be hidden away or for him to be non-existent is the same, because either way the objectives of Khilaafat are not attained. His fear of his enemies should not require his hiding, since nothing but the name "Khaleefah" now exists; rather, the end of the matter is that fear does require him to hide his claim to the *Imamaat*, just as in the case of his fathers who appeared among men but did not claim the *Imaamat*. Also, when the times are corrupt and differences are many and the tyrants and oppressors have seized power, the people's need for an Imaam is greater, and their submission (to such an Imaam) becomes easier.

الأئمة من قريش

The Khaleefahs Must Be From the Quraish:

(ويكون من قريش, ولا يجوز من غيرهم, ولا يختص ببني هاشم)

وأولاد علي رضي الله عنه, يعني يشترط أن يكون الإمام قرشياً لقوله عليه السلام: الأَئِمَّةُ مِنْ قُرَيْشٍ

وهذا إن كان خبر واحد, لكن لما رواه أبو بكر رضي الله عنه محتجاً به على الأنصار ولم ينكره أحد, فصار مجمعاً عليه, لم يخالف فيه إلا الخوارج وبعض المعتزلة

"The (Khaleefah) must be from the Quraish, and it is not permissible for him to be from other than them, but he does not have to be from Banu Haashim."

Nor from the sons of Hadhrat `Ali رضي الله عنه. Meaning, it is stipulated that the Imaam be a Qurashi, because of the Hadeeth: "The A'immah are from the Quraish."

Even though this is a *Khabr-e-Waahid*, however, because Hadhrat Abu Bakr رضي الله عنه had narrated it in the presence of the Sahaabah, using it as proof against the Ansaar, and not a single Sahaabi denied it, it became something that is *mujma` `alayhi* (agreed upon by *ijmaa`*), and no one had a difference regarding it except the Khawaarij and some of the Mu`tazilah.

ولا يشترط أن يكون هاشمياً أو علوياً, لما ثبت بالدليل من خلافة أبي بكر وعمر وعثمان رضي الله عنهم مع أنهم مع أنهم لم يكونوا من بني هاشم, وإن كانوا من قريش, فإن قريشاً إسم لأولاد النضر بن كنانة, وهاشم هو أبو عبد المطلب جد رسول الله صلى الله عليه وسلم, فإنه محمد بن عبد الله بن عبد المطلب بن هاشم بن عبد مناف بن قصي بن كلاب بن مرة بن كعب بن لؤي بن غالب بن فهر بن مالك بن النضر بن كنانة بن خزيمة بن مدركه بن إلياس بن مضر بن نزار بن معد بن عدنان.

فالعلوية والعباسية من بني هاشم, لأن العباس وأبا طالب إبنا عبد المطلب, وأبو بكر قرشي لأنه إبن أبي قحافة عثمان بن عامر بن عمرو بن كعب بن لؤي, وكذا عمر, لأنه ابن الخطاب بن نفيل بن عبد العزى بن رباح بن عبد الله بن قرط بن رزاح بن عدي بن كعب, وكذا عثمان لأنه ابن عفان بن أبي العاص بن أمية بن عبد شمس بن عبد مناف

It is not stipulated that the Imaam be an Haashimi or an `Alawi, because it is affirmed with evidence the *Khilaafat* of Hadhrat Abu Bakr, Hadhrat `Umar and Hadhrat `Uthmaan رضي الله عنهم, despite the fact that they were not from Bani Haashim, but they were from the Quraish. That is because Quraish is a name for the children of an-Nadhr ibn Kinaanah, and Haashim was the father of `Abdul Muttalib, the grandfather of Rasoolullaah صلى الله عليه وسلم, because he is Muhammad ibn `Abdillaah ibn `Abdil Muttalib ibn Haashim ibn `Abdi Manaaf ibn Qusayy ibn Kilaab ibn Murrah ibn Ka`b ibn Lu'ayy ibn Ghaalib ibn Fihr ibn Maalik ibn an-Nadhr ibn Kinaanah ibn Khuzaimah ibn Mudrikah ibn Ilyaas ibn Mudhar ibn Nizaar ibn Ma`add ibn `Adnaan.

The `Alawis and the `Abbaasiyyah (Abbasids) are from Bani Haashim, because Hadhrat `Abbaas رضي الله عنه and Abu Taalib were the sons of `Abdul Muttalib. Hadhrat Abu Bakr رضي الله عنه was a Qurashi, because he was ibn Abi Quhaafah, `Uthmaan ibn `Aamir ibn Ka`b ibn Lu'ayy. Similarly, Hadhrat `Umar رضي الله عنه was ibn al-Khattaab ibn Nufail ibn `Abdil `Uzzaa ibn Rabaah ibn `Abdillaah ibn `Qurat ibn Razaah ibn `Adi ibn Ka`b. Similarly, Hadhrat `Uthmaan رضي الله عنه was ibn `Affaan ibn Abi-l `Aas ibn Umayyah ibn `Abdi Shams ibn `Abdi Manaaf.

عصمة الإمام

The Sinlessness of the Khaleefah:

(ولا يشترط)

في الإمام

(أن يكون معصوما)

"It is not stipulated - "

For the Imaam.

"That he be *ma`soom* (sinless)."

لما مر من الدليل على إمامة أبي بكر مع عدم القطع بعصمته, وأيضاً الإشتراط هو المحتاج إلى الدليل, وأما في عدم الإشتراط فيكفي عدم دليل الإشتراط

إحتج المخالف بقوله تعالى:

لَا يَنَالُ عَهْدِيْ الظَّالِمِيْنَ

Because of what has preceded of evidence for the *Imaamat* of Hadhrat Abu Bakr رضي الله عنه, along with the non-existence of *qat`iyy* evidence of him being *ma`soom*. Also, it is the duty of the one who makes this claim to bring the evidence for it. As for the absence of this stipulation, then sufficient as evidence is the fact that there is no evidence for its stipulation.

Those who disagree cite as proof the *Aayah*:

{"*My Covenant is does not include the Zhaalimeen (wrong-doers; oppressors; tyrants).*"}

وغير المعصوم ظالم فلا ينال عهد الإمامة

They say, anyone who is not *ma`soom* is a *zhaalim* (wrong-doer) and does he will not receive the Covenant (mentioned in the *Aayah*), which is that of *Imaamat*.

والجواب: المنع, فإن الظالم من ارتكب معصية مسقطة للعدالة مع عدم التوبة والإصلاح, فغير المعصوم لا يلزم أن يكون ظالماً, وحقيقة العصمة: أن لا يخلق الله تعالى في العبد الذنب مع بقاء قدرته واختياره, وهذا معنى قولهم هي لطف من الله تعالى يحمله على فعل الخير, ويزجره عن الشر, مع بقاء الإختيار تحقيقاً للإبتلاء, ولهذا قال الشيخ أبو منصور رحمه الله تعالى: العصمة لا تزيل المحنة وبهذا يظهر فساد قول من قال إنها خاصية في نفس الشخص أو في بدنه, يمتنع بسببها صدور الذنب عنه, كيف ولو كان الذنب ممتنعاً لما صح تكليفه بترك الذنب, ولما كان مثاباً عليه؟

The answer is to preclude this, because the *zhaalim* is the one who perpetrates an act of disobedience which brings about the downfall of `adaalat (justice), without making *tawbah* and *islaah* (reforming himself). Thus, the one who is not *ma`soom* is not necessarily a *zhaalim*. The *haqeeqat* of `ismat (being protected from sin) is that Allaah Ta`aalaa does not create within the bondsman the sin, despite the fact that the bondsman retains the ability and free-choice (to perpetrate the sin if he wanted to). This is the meaning of their statement: "It is a Kindness from Allaah Ta`aalaa which leads the person on to do good and restrains him from doing evil, despite him retaining *ikhtiyaar* (choice) as a verification of the (reality of) the test." For this reason, Imaam Abu Mansoor al-Maatureedi رحمة الله عليه said: "`*Ismat* does not remove the trial." By this, the corruption of the statement of the one who says that this *`ismat* is a special characteristic of the soul of the person or of his body, on account of which characteristic no sin comes from him, becomes clear. How can this be the case, when if it was impossible for him to commit a sin in the first place, then what is the meaning of him being made *mukallaf* (held responsible by the Sharee`ah) to not commit the sin, and why would he be rewarded for not doing it (if he cannot do it anyway)?

(ولا أن يكون أفضل أهل زمانه)

"Nor that he be the most virtuous person of his era."

لأن المساوي في الفضيلة, بل المفضول الأقل علماً وعملاً, ربما كان أعرف بمصالح الإمامة ومفاسدها, وأقدر على القيام بموجبها, خصوصاً إذا كان نصب المفضول أدفع للشر, وأبعد عن

إثارة الفتنة, ولهذا جعل عمر رضي الله عنه الإمامة شورى بين ستة, مع القطع بأن بعضهم أفضل من البعض

فإن قيل: كيف صح جعل الإمامة شورى بين الستة مع أنه لا يجوز نصب إمامين في زمان واحد؟

قلنا: غير الجائز: هو نصب إمامين مستقلين يجب طاعة كل منهما على الإنفراد, لما يلزم من ذلك من إمتثال أحكام متضادة, وأما في الشورى فالكل بمنزلة إمام واحد

Because the one who is equal to him in virtue, or rather, the one who is less than him in virtue, less than him in `*ilm* and in `*amal*, can sometimes have more knowledge concerning the needs and duties of *Imaamat* (than the person with the most virtue) as well as the corruptions, and more capable of taking care of its duties, especially if the appointment of this one who is less in virtue would better repel evil and be further from the outbreak of fitnah. For this reason, Hadhrat `Umar رضي الله عنه left the choice of the next Khaleefah up to the *Shoora* of six Sahaabah, despite knowing with certainty that some of them are superior to others.

If it is said: How could it be valid to leave the *Imaamat* up to the Shoora of six (Sahaabah) despite the fact that it is not permissible to have two Imaams in one time?

We say: What is impermissible is to appoint two independent Imaams each of whom it is waajib to obey, by themselves, because of what that entails of having to follow orders that are contradictory. As for in the case of *Shoora*, then each of them takes the place of one Imaam.

شروط الولاية

The Conditions for Assuming the *Khilaafah*:

(ويشترط أن يكون من أهل الولاية المطلقة الكاملة)

أي مسلماً, حراً, ذكراً, عاقلاً, بالغاً, إذ ما جعل الله للكافرين على المؤمنين سبيلاً, والعبد مشغول بخدمة المولى مستحقر في أعين الناس, والنساء ناقصات عقل ودين, والصبي والمجنون قاصران عن تدبير الأمور, والتصرف في مصالح الجمهور

(سادساً)

"It is stipulated that he be from the people who have complete, unrestricted authority."

Meaning, he must be a Muslim, free, male, sane and an adult. Because, Allaah Ta`aalaa has not made a way for the Kaafirs over the Mu'mineen, and the slave is busy with serving his master and seen as low in the eyes of people, and the women are deficient in intellect and Deen, and the child and the madman are deficient in terms of managing affairs and managing the welfare of the people.

"An administrator."

أي مالكاً للتصرف في أمور المسلمين بقوة رأيه ورويته ومعونة بأسه وشوكته

(قادراً)

بعلمه وعدله وكفايته وشجاعته

Meaning, a person who possesses management over the affairs of the Muslims with the strength of his thinking and his deliberation, and the help of his strength and might.

"Capable."

Meaning, by his knowledge, his justice, his competence and his courage.

(على تنفيذ الأحكام وحفظ حدود دار الإسلام, وإنصاف المظلوم من الظالم)

إذ الإخلال بهذه الأمور مخل بالغرض من نصب الإمام

(ولا ينعزل الإمام بالفسق)

أي بالخروج عن طاعة الله تعالى

"Of carrying out the *Ahkaam* and protecting the borders of Daar-ul-Islaam, and giving the oppressed justice against the oppressor."

Because a deficiency in these matters equals an absence of the fulfillment of the objective of appointing an Imaam in the first place.

"The Imaam is not removed (from power) on account of *fisq*."

Meaning, on account of him leaving the obedience of Allaah Ta`aalaa.

(والجور)

أي الظلم على عباد الله تعالى, لأنه قد ظهر الفسق وانتشر الجور من الأئمة والأمراء بعد الخلفاء الراشدين, والسلف قد كانوا ينقادون لهم, ويقيمون الجمع والأعياد بإذنهم, ولا يرون الخروج عليهم, ولأن العصمة ليست بشرط للإمامة إبتداء فبقاء أولى

وعن الشافعي رحمه الله تعالى أن الإمام ينعزل بالفسق والجور, وكذا كل قاض وأمير, وأصل المسألة: أن الفاسق ليس من أهل الولاية عند الشافعي رحمه الله, لأنه لا ينظر لنفسه فكيف بنظر لغيره, وعند أبي حنيفة رحمه الله هو من أهل الولاية حتى يصح للأب الفاسق تزويج ابنته الصغيرة, والمسطور في كتب الشافعية أن القاضي ينعزل بالفسق بخلاف الإمام, والفرق أن في انعزاله ووجوب نصب غيره إثارة الفتنة, لما له من الشوكة, بخلاف القاضي

"Or on account of tyranny."

Meaning, oppressing the bondsmen of Allaah Ta`aalaa. This is because *fisq* and oppression had come from Imaams and leaders after the Khulafaa-e-Raashideen, and despite that the Salaf submitted to their authority, and established the Jumu`ah and `Eids with their permission, and did not believe in rebelling against them. Also, because `*ismat* is not a condition for the validity of *Imaamat* in the first place (i.e. in becoming a Khaleefah), so (for him to remain in power) is even more so.

According to Imaam ash-Shaafi`ee رحمة الله عليه, the Imaam is removed from power on account of *fisq* and oppression, and the same goes for any such Qaadhi or Ameer. The basis for this issue is that according to Imaam ash-Shaafi`ee رحمة الله عليه, a *faasiq* is not a person of *wilaayat* (authority), because such a person does not look after himself so how can he look after others? According to Imaam Abu Haneefah رحمة الله عليه, such a person remains from the people of *wilaayat*, so much so that the father who is a *faasiq* can arrange the marriage of his young daughter. It is written in the books of the

Shaafi'iyyah that the Qaadhi is to be removed on account of *fisq*, contrary to the Imaam. The difference between the two is that in the case of removing the Imaam (i.e. Khaleefah) and necessitating the appointment of another, it can lead to fitnah, due to the power he has, and this is not the case with the Qaadhi.

وفي رواية النوادر عن العلماء الثلاثة أنه لا يجوز قضاء الفاسق

According to the *riwaayat* of *an-Nawaadir*, from the three `Ulamaa (i.e. Imaam Abu Haneefah, Imaam Abu Yusuf and Imaam Muhammad), the judging (as a Qaadhi) by a *faasiq* is not permissible.

وقال بعض المشايخ: إذا قلد الفاسق إبتداء يصح ولو قلد وهو عدل ينعزل بالفسق, لأن المقلد إعتمد عدالته فلم يرض بقضائه بدونها, وفي فتاوى قاضي خان: أجمعوا على أنه إذا ارتشى لا ينفذ قضاؤه فيما ارتشى, وأنه إذا أخذ القاضي القضاء بالرشوة لا يصير قاضياً ولو قضى لا ينفذ قضاؤه

Some of the Mashaayikh said: "If a person was a *faasiq* initially, and he is put in power as the Imaam, then it is valid. However, if he was put in power whilst he was just, and thereafter he becomes a *faasiq*, then he is to be removed, because the one who put him in power did so relying on his `adaalat* (justice) and is thus not pleased with his judging in the absence of that condition.

In *Fataawaa Qaadhi Khaan* it is mentioned: "They had *ijmaa`* that if a judge passes a particular judgement on account of a bribe he had taken, then his judgement is not enforced (in that matter in which he had taken a bribe), and if a Qaadhi takes the position of Qaadhi through a bribe, he does not become a Qaadhi, and if he passes a judgement, it is not carried out."

(وتجوز الصلاة خلف كل بر وفاجر)

"Salaah is valid behind every pious person and sinner."

لقوله عليه السلام:

صَلُّوا خَلْفَ كُلِّ بِرٍّ وَفَاجِرٍ

Because of the *Hadeeth*:

"Perform Salaah behind every *birr* (pious person) and *faajir* (sinner)."

لأن علماء الأمة كانوا يصلون خلف الفسقة وأهل الأهواء والمبتدع من غير نكير, وما نقل عن بعض السلف من المنع عن الصلاة خلف الفاسق والمبتدع فمحمول على الكراهة, إذ لا كلام في كراهية الصلاة خلف الفاسق والمبتدع, وهذا إذا لم يؤد الفسق أو البدعة إلى حد الكفر, وأما إذا أدى فلا كلام في عدم جواز الصلاة

Because the `Ulamaa used to perform Salaah behind people who were *faasiqs*, Ahl-ul-Ahwaa (people of desires) and innovators (*mubtadi`*) without any rejection. As for what has been narrated from some of the Salaf, that they forbid performing Salaah behind a *faasiq* and a *mubtadi`* (innovator), then it is interpreted as being a reference to *karaahat* (i.e. being *makrooh*), and there is no debate regarding Salaah behind a *faasiq* and *mubtadi`* as being *makrooh*. However, this is in the case where his *fisq* or *bid`ah* does not reach the level of *Kufr*. If it does so, then there is no disagreement regarding the invalidity of Salaah behind him.

ثم المعتزلة وإن جعلوا الفاسق غير مؤمن لكنهم يجوزون الصلاة خلفه لما أن شرط الإمامة عندهم عدم الكفر, لا وجود الإيمان بمعنى التصديق والإقرار والأعمال جميعاً

The Mu`tazilah, even though they regard the *faasiq* as not being a Mu'min, they permit Salaah behind him, because according to them, the condition for *Imaamat* is the absence of *Kufr*, nor necessarily the presence of Imaan which is *tasdeeq*, *iqraar* and *a`maal* altogether.

(ويصلى على كل بر وفاجر)

"*Janaazah Salaah* is performed for every Muslim, be he a pious person or be he a *faajir* (sinful transgressor)."

إذا مات على الإيمان للإجماع, ولقوله عليه السلام:

If he dies upon *Imaan*, and there is *ijmaa`* on this, because of the *Hadeeth*:

لَا تَدْعُوا الصَّلَاةَ عَلَى مَنْ مَاتَ مِنْ أَهْلِ الْقِبْلَةِ

"Do not leave off (*Janaazah*) *Salaat* for the one who dies from the Ahl-e-Qiblah."

فإن قيل: أمثال هذه المسائل إنما هي من فروع الفقه, فلا وجه لإيرادها في أصول الكلام, وإن أراد أن اعتقاد حقية ذلك واجب وهذا من الأصول فجميع مسائل الفقه كذلك

If it is said: These *masaa'il* are from the sub-branches of *Fiqh* and thus have no place being mentioned in the *Usool* of *'Ilm-ul-Kalaam*, and if he (the author) intends by it that it is *waajib* to believe in these things being Haqq, and this is from the *Usool*, then all of the *masaa'il* of *Fiqh* are like this.

قلنا: إنه لما فرغ من مقاصد علم الكلام من مباحث الذات والصفات والأفعال والمعاد والنبوة والإمامة على قانون أهل الإسلام وطريق أهل السنة والجماعة, حاول التنبيه على نبذ من المسائل التي يتميز بها أهل السنة من غيرهم مما خالف فيه المعتزلة أو الشيعة أو الفلاسفة أو الملاحدة, أو غيرهم من أهل البدع والأهوا, سواء كانت تلك المسائل من فروع الفقه أو غيرها من الجزئيات المتعلقة بالعقائد

We say: After he (Imaam an-Nasafi) completed the discussion regarding the objectives of *'Ilm-ul-Kalaam*, from the discussions pertainin to the *Dhaat*, the *Sifaat*, the Actions, the *Ma`aad* (world to come), the Nubuwwah, the *Imaamah*, according to the laws of the People of Islaam and the path of Ahlus Sunnah wal-Jamaa`ah, he tried to draw attention to some *masaa'il* wherein Ahlus Sunnah wal-Jamaa`ah are distinguished from those who differ with them such as the Mu`tazilah, the Shias, the Philosophers, the atheists, or other than them from the people of *bid`ah* and *ahwaa* (desires), regardless of whether those *masaa'il* pertain to the sub-branches of *Fiqh* or other than it from the particulars that are connected to *`Aqaa'id* (beliefs).

(ويكف عن ذكر الصحابة إلا بخير)

"The Sahaabah are not to be mentioned except with goodness."

لما روي في الأحاديث الصحيحة من مناقبهم ووجوب الكف عن الطعن فيهم, لقوله عليه السلام:

Because of what has been narrated in the *Saheeh Ahaadeeth* regarding their virtues and the obligation of refraining from insulting any of them. It is mentioned in the *Hadeeth*:

لَا تَسُبُّوا أَصْحَابِي فَلَوْ أَحَدُكُمْ أَنْفَقَ مِثْلَ أُحُدٍ ذَهَباً مَا بَلَغَ مُدَّ أَحَدِهِمْ وَلَا نَصِيْفَهُ

"Do not insult my Sahaabah, for if one of you were to give in *sadaqah* gold equal to the mountain of Uhud, it would not equal a *mudd* or even half a *mudd* (given by) one of them."

ولقوله عليه السلام:

أَكْرِمُوْا أَصْحَابِيْ فَإِنَّهُمْ خِيَارُكُمْ

الحديث

ولقوله عليه السلام: اللهَ اللهَ فِيْ أَصْحَابِيْ لَا تَتَّخِذُوْهُمْ غَرَضاً مِّنْ بَعْدِيْ, فَمَنْ أَحَبَّهُمْ فَبِحُبِّيْ أَحَبَّهُمْ وَمَنْ أَبْغَضَهُمْ فَبِبُغْضِيْ أَبْغَضَهُمْ

ومن آذاهم فقد آذاني ومن آذاني فقد آذى الله ومن آذى الله فيوشك أن يأخذه, ثم في مناقب كل من أبي بكر الصديق وعمر وعثمان وعلي والحسن والحسين وغيرهم من أكابر الصحابة أحاديث صحيحة, وما وقع بينهم من المنازعات والمحاربات فله محامل وتأويلات, فسبهم والطعن فيهم إن كان مما يخالف الأدلة القطعية فكفر, كقذف عائشة رضي الله عنها, وإلا فبدعة وفسق

And the *Hadeeth*:

"Honour my Sahaabah for they are the best of you."

And the *Hadeeth*:

"Fear Allaah, fear Allaah regarding my As-haab. Do not take them as a target after me. Whosoever loves them, loves them because he loves me, and whosoever hates them, hates them because he hates me. Whosoever harms them has harmed me, and whoever harms me has (tried to) harm Allaah, and whoever (tries to) harm Allaah, he will soon be seized (by `*Adhaab*)."

Thereafter, regarding the virtues of each of these Sahaabah, namely, Hadhrat Abu Bakr رضي الله عنه, Hadhrat `Umar رضي الله عنه, Hadhrat `Uthmaan رضي الله عنه, Hadhrat `Ali رضي الله عنه, Hadhrat Hasan رضي الله عنه, Hadhrat Husain رضي الله عنه, and other than them from the seniors (*Akaabir*) of the Sahaabah, there are many *Saheeh Ahaadeeth*. As for what occured between some of them of disputes and wars, then there are reasons and interpretations for these. Thus, insulting them, if it is from that which opposes the decisive proofs, it is *Kufr*, like the one who accuses Hadhrat `Aa'ishah رضي الله عنها; else, it is *bid`ah* and *fisq*.

وبالجملة: لم ينقل عن السلف المجتهدين والعلماء الصالحين جواز اللعن على معاوية وأعوانه, لأن غاية أمرهم البغي والخروج عن طاعة الإمام الحق, وهو لا يوجب اللعن, وإنما اختلفوا في يزيد بن معاوية, حتى ذكر في الخلاصة وغيرها أنه لا ينبغي اللعن عليه ولا على الحجاج لأن النبي عليه السلام نعى عن لعن المصلين ومن كان من أهل القبلة, وما نقل من لعن النبي عليه السلام لبعض من أهل القبلة فلما أنه يعلم من أحوال الناس ما لا يعلمه غيره, وبعضهم أطلق اللعن عليه, لما أنه كفر حين أمر بقتل الحسين رضي الله عنه, واتفقوا على جواز اللعن على من قتله أو أمر به أو أجازه أو رضي به, والحق أن رضا يزيد بقتل الحسين واستبشاره بذلك وإهانة أهل بيت النبي عليه السلام مما تواتر معناه وإن كان تفاصيلها آحاداً, فنحن لا نتوقف في شأنه بل في إيمانه لعنة الله عليه وأنصاره وأعوانه

In summary: it is not reported from any of the Salaf who were Mujtahideen, or from the pious `Ulamaa, the permissibility of cursing Hadhrat Mu`aawiyah رضي الله عنه or those who were with him, because the limit of their matter was to rebel and to go out of the obedience of the Imaam (Khaleefah of the time) who was rightful, and that does not require cursing. Rather, they (the Mujtahideen) had differences of opinion regarding Yazeed ibn Mu`aawiyah, so much so that it is mentioned in *al-Khulaasah* and other books that it is not appropriate to curse him (Yazeed) or Hajjaaj, because Rasoolullaah صلى الله عليه وسلم forbade cursing those who perform Salaah and those who are from the Ahl-ul-Qiblah.

As for what has been reported concerning Rasoolullaah صلى الله عليه وسلم cursing some people from Ahl-ul-Qiblah, then that is because he knew from the conditions of people that which others do not know.

Some (of the Mujtahideen) unrestrictedly applied curse upon (Yazeed), because (according to them) he committed *Kufr* by ordering the killing of Hadhrat Husain رضي الله عنه. They (Mujtahideen) had *ittifaaq* regarding the permissibility of cursing whoever killed Hadhrat Husain رضي الله عنه, or ordered it, or permitted it, or was pleased with it. The truth is that Yazeed being pleased with the killing of Hadhrat Husain رضي الله عنه and rejoicing on account of it and his lowering the family members of Rasoolullaah صلى الله عليه وسلم is from those things the meaning of which has been reported with tawaatur, even if the details are transmitted through solitary reports. However, we do not do *tawaqquf* regarding his status; we only do *tawaqquf* regarding his Imaan (i.e. whether he was a Mu'min or not). The curse of Allaah Ta`aalaa be upon him and his helpers.[1]

(ونشهد بالجنة للعشرة المبشرة الذين بشرهم النبي عليه الصلاة والسلام)

"We testify (entry to) Jannah for the `*Asharah Mubash-sharah* (The Ten Promised Jannah) who were given the glad-tiding (of Jannah) by Nabi صلى الله عليه وسلم."

بالجنة حيث قال النبي عليه السلام: أَبُوْ بَكْرٍ فِيْ الْجَنَّةِ, وَعُمَرُ فِيْ الْجَنَّةِ, وَعُثْمَانُ فِيْ الْجَنَّةِ, وَعَلِيٌّ فِيْ الْجَنَّةِ, وَطَلْحَةُ فِيْ الْجَنَّةِ, وَالزُّبَيْرُ فِيْ الْجَنَّةِ, وَعَبْدُ الرَّحْمَنُ بْنُ عَوْفٍ فِيْ الْجَنَّةِ, وَسَعْدُ بْنُ أَبِيْ وَقَّاصٍ فِيْ الْجَنَّةِ, وَسَعِيْدُ بْنُ زَيْدٍ فِيْ الْجَنَّةِ, وَأَبُوْ عُبَيْدَةَ بْنِ الْجَرَّاحِ فِيْ الْجَنَّةِ

وكذا يشهد بالجنة لفاطمة والحسن والحسين, لما وري في الحديث الصحيح أن فاطمة سيدة نساء أهل الجنة وأن الحسن والحسين سيدا شباب أهل الجنة

Rasoolullaah صلى الله عليه وسلم said: "Abu Bakr is in Jannah; `Umar is in Jannah; `Uthmaan is in Jannah; `Ali is in Jannah; Talhah is in Jannah; Zubair is in Jannah; `Abdur Rahmaan ibn `Awf is in Jannah; Sa`d ibn Abi Waqqaas is in Jannah; Sa`eed ibn Zaid is in Jannah and Abu `Ubaydah ibn al-Jarraah is in Jannah."

Also, we bear witness of (entry into) Jannah for Hadhrat Faatimah رضي الله عنها, Hadhrat Hasan رضي الله عنه and Hadhrat Husain رضي الله عنه, due to what has been narrated in the Saheeh Hadeeth that Hadhrat Faatimah رضي الله عنها is the leader of the women of Jannah, and that Hadhrat Hasan and Hadhrat Husain رضي الله عنهما are the leaders of the youth of Jannah.

وسائر الصحابة لا يذكرون إلا بخير, ويرجى لهم أكثر مما يرجى لغيرهم من المؤمنين, ولا نشهد بالجنة أو النار لأحد بعينه بل نشهد بأن المؤمنين من أهل الجنة والكافرين من أهل النار

---

[1] However, the official stance of the Akaabireen of Deoband is to refrain from cursing Yazeed.

(ونرى المسح على الخفين في السفر والحضر)

The Sahaabah as a whole are not to be mentioned except with goodness, and what is hoped for them is greater than what is hoped for other than them from the Mu'mineen.

We do not bear witness for (entry into) Jannah or Jahannam for anyone specifically; rather, we bearness that the Mu'mineen are the people of Jannah and the Kaafireen are the people of Jahannam.

"And we view (as permissible) *masah 'alal khuffain*, on a journey and during residence."

لأنه وإن كان زيادة على الكتاب لكنه ثابت بالخبر المشهور, وسئل علي بن أبي طالب رضي الله عنه عن المسح على الخفين فقال: جعل رسول الله صلى الله عليه وسلم ثلاثة أيام ولياليهن للمسافر, ويوماً وليلة للمقيم

وروى أبو بكر عن رسول الله صلى الله عليه وسلم أنه رخص للمسافر ثلاثة أيام ولياليهن وللمقيم يوماً وليلة, إذا تطهر فلبس خفيه, أن يمسح عليهما

Because it, even though it is additional upon the Qur'aan, but it is affirmed with *Ahaadeeth* that are *Mash-hoor*. Hadhrat `Ali ibn Abi Taalib رضي الله عنه was asked regarding *masah `alal khuffain*, so he said: "Rasoolullaah صلى الله عليه وسلم made it three days and three nights for the *musaafir*, and one day and one night for the *muqeem* (resident)."

Hadhrat Abu Bakr رضي الله عنه narrates from Rasoolullaah صلى الله عليه وسلم that he gave concession for the *musaafir* (to make *masah*) for three days and three nights, and for the *muqeem* (to make *masah*) for one day and one night, if he wore the *khuffain* after being in a state of *wudhoo*.

وقال الحسن البصري رحمه الله: أدركت سبعين نفراً من الصحابة رضي الله عنهم يرون المسح على الخفين

ولهذا قال أبو حنيفة رحمه الله: ما قلت بالمسح حتى جاءني فيه دليل مثل ضوء النهار

وقال الكرخي: إني أخاف الكفر على من لا يرى المسح على الخفين, لأن الآثار التي جاءت فيه في حيز التواتر

Imaam Hasan al-Basri رحمة الله عليه said: "I met seventy groups of the Sahaabah رضي الله عنهم and all of them regarded *masah `alal khuffain* (as being permissible)."

For this reason, Imaam Abu Haneefah رحمة الله عليه said: "I did not give (the *Fatwaa* of permissibility) of masah until the evidence came to me like the light of day."

Imaam al-Karkhi said: "I fear *Kufr* for the one who denies *masah `alal khuffain*, because the *Aathaar* concerning it are *mutawaatir*."

وبالجملة: من لا يرى المسح على الخفين فهو من أهل البدعة, حتى سئل أنس بن مالك رضي الله عنه عن أهل السنة والجماعة فقال: أن تحب الشيخين, ولا تطعن في الختنين, وتمسح على الخفين

(ولا نحرم نبيذ التمر)

وهو أن ينبذ تمر أو زبيب في الماء فيجعل في إناء من الخزف فيحدث فيه لذع كما للفقاع لكأنه نهي عن ذلك في بدء الإسلام لما كانت الجرار أواني الخمور, ثم نسخ فعدم تحريمه من قواعد أهل السنة والجماعة, خلافاً للروافض, وهذا بخلاف ما إذا اشتد فصار مسكراً, فإن القول بحرمة قليله وكثيره مما ذهب إليه كثير من أهل السنة والجماعة

In summary: the one who does not regard as valid *masah `alal khuffain*, then he is from the Ahl-e-Bid`ah. Hadhrat Anas ibn Maalik رضي الله عنه was asked regarding Ahlus Sunnah wal-Jamaa`ah, so he said: "It is that you love Shaykhain, that you do not revile the two *Khatans* (sons-in-law, i.e. Hadhrat `Uthmaan رضي الله عنه and Hadhrat `Ali رضي الله عنه), and that you perform *masah `alal khuffain*."

"We do not prohibit *nabeedh* made from dates."

This means that the dates or raisins are brewed in water and then put in an earthern container, until it acquires a burning taste like there is in *fuqqaa`* (a kind of drink. It seems as though it was prohibited in the beginning of Islaam when jars were the containers for alcohol, but then (the prohibition) was abrogated. Thus, the absence of its prohibition is from the foundations of Ahlus Sunnah wal-Jamaa`ah, contrary to the Rawaafidh. However, this permission is in the case where it does not become severe and thus turn into an intoxicant, because the verdict regarding the prohibition of alcohol, be it a little or a little, is from that which was held by the majority of Ahlus Sunnah wal-Jamaa`ah.

الولي

The *Wali* (Saint)

(ولا يبلغ الولي درجة الأنبياء)

لأن الأنبياء معصومون مأمونون عن خوف الخاتمة, مكرمون بالوحي ومشاهدة الملك, مأمورون بتبليغ الأحكام وإرشاد الأنام بعد الإتصاف بكمالات الأولياء, فما نقل عن بعض الكرامية من جواز كون الولي أفضل من النبي كفر وضلال, نعم, قد يقع تردد في أن مرتبة النبوة أفضل أم مرتبة الولاية, بعد القطع بأن النبي متصف بالمرتبتين, وأنه أفضل من الولي الذي ليس بنبي

(ولا يصل العبد)

"The *wali* does not reach the rank of the Ambiyaa."

Because the Ambiyaa are *ma`soom*, protected from fear of a bad ending (*soo'-ul-khaatimah*), honoured with *Wahi* and by seeing the *Malak* (i.e. Jibreel عليه السلام). They are commanded with *tableegh* of the *Ahkaam* and guiding the people, after having been attributed with the perfections of the *Awliyaa*. What has been narrated from some of the Karraamiyyah that it is possible for a *Wali* to be superior to a Nabi, is *Kufr* and deviation. Yes, some confusion has occurred regarding which is better: the rank of *Nubuwwah* or the rank of *Wilaayah*? However, there is certitude that a Nabi is attributed with most ranks, and that he is superior to a *wali* who is not a Nabi.

"And the bondsman (of Allaah Ta`aalaa) does not reach - "

ما دام عاقلاً بالغاً

(إلى حيث يسقط عنه الأمر والنهي)

As long as he is sane, and an adult.

"A stage where the Commands and Prohibitions (of the Sharee'ah) fall away."

لعموم الخطابات الواردة في التكاليف, وإجماع المجتهدين على ذلك, وذهب بعض المباحيين إلى أن العبد إذا بلغ غاية المحبة وصفا قلبه واختار الإيمان على الكفر من غير نفاق سقط عنه الأمر والنهي, ولا يدخله الله تعالى إلى النار بارتكاب الكبائر, وبعضهم إلى أنه يسقط عنه العبادات الظاهرة من الصلاة والصوم والزكاة والحج وغير ذلك

وتكون عبادته التفكر, وهذا كفر وضلال, فإن أكمل الناس في المحبة والإيمان هم الأنبياء خصوصاً حبيب الله تعالى, مع أن التكاليف في حقهم أتم وأكمل, وأما قوله عليه السلام: إِذَا أَحَبَّ اللهُ عَبْداً لَمْ يَضُرُّهُ ذَنْبٌ

فمعناه أنه عصمه من الذنوب فلم يلحقه ضررها

Due to the generality of the addresses that have come regarding *takleef*, and the *ijmaa`* of the Mujtahids upon that. Some of the *Mubaahiyyeen* (Halaalizers) held the view that when the person reaches a certain level of Love for Allaah Ta`aalaa and his heart beomces pure, and he chooses *Imaan* over *Kufr* without any *Nifaaq*, that the Commands and Prohibitions of the Sharee'ah fall away from it and that Allaah Ta`aalaa will not enter such a person into Jahannam even if he perpetrates major sins. Some of them claimed that the "*zhaahiri*" (external) `*Ibaadaat* fall away from such a person, such as Salaah, fasting, Zakaat, Hajj, etc. His `*Ibaadah* then becomes nothing more than "*tafakkur*" (contemplation).

This is a belief of *Kufr* and deviation. The most perfect of mankind in Love for Allaah Ta`aalaa and *Imaan* were the Ambiyaa, especially the Beloved of Allaah Ta`aalaa, but despite that, the *takleef* (responsibilities imposed by the Sharee'ah) remained upon them; in fact, even more perfect and more complete in their case.

As for the *Hadeeth*: "When Allaah loves a slave, a sin will not harm him."

What it means is that Allaah Ta`aalaa will protect him from the sins and thus their harm does not reach him.

(والنصوص)

من الكتاب والسنة تحمل

(على ظواهرها)

"And the *nusoos*."

From the Qur'aan and Sunnah.

"Are carried upon their literal meanings."

ما لم يصرف عنها دليل قطعي كما في الآيات التي يشعر ظواهرها بالجهة والجسمية ونحو ذلك

لا يقال: ليست هذه من النص, بل من المتشابه

لأنا نقول: المراد بالنص هاهنا ليس ما يقابل الظاهر والمفسر والمحكم, بل ما يعلم أقسام النظم على ما هو المتعارف

As long as there is no *qati`yy daleel* to take it away from the literal meaning, like in the case of the *Aayaat* which give the impression (to one who does not know) of a direction for Allaah Ta`aalaa, or having a body, etc.

It is not to be said: "Those are not *nusoos*. Rather, those are from the category of *al-Mutashaabih*."

Because we say: "The meaning of *nass*, here, is not that which is opposite to *zhaahir*, and *mufassar*, and *muhkam*. Rather, it is that which encompasses all the conventional divisions of the context."

(فالعدول عنها)

أي عن الظواهر

(إلى معان يدعيها أهل الباطن)

"Thus, to turn away from them."

Meaning, the literal meanings.

"To meanings that are claimed by the Ahl-e-Baatin (People of the Inner Meaning)."

وهم الملاحدون, وسموا الباطنية لادعائهم أن النصوص ليست على ظواهرها بل لها معان باطنة لا يعرفها إلا المعلم, وقصدهم بذلك نفي الشريعة بالكلية

(إلحاد)

أي ميل وعدول عن الإسلام, واتصال واتصاف بكفر, لكونه تكذيباً للنبي عليه السلام فيما علم مجيئه به بالضرورة

They are Heretics. They were called al-Baatiniyyah because of their claim that the nusoos of Qur'aan and Sunnah are not to be taken upon the literal meanings, but rather, upon "hidden meanings" which none knows except the Teacher. What they intended by that is to completely remove the Sharee`ah.

"Is heresy (to do so)."

Meaning, to do so is to turn away from Islaam and to become connected and attributed with *Kufr*, because doing so is denial of Rasoolullaah صلى الله عليه وسلم in that which is known by necessity to have been brought by him.

وأما ما يذهب إليه بعض المحققين من أن النصوص محمولة على ظواهرها ومع ذلك ففيها إشارات خفية إلى دقائق تنكشف على أرباب السلوك, يمكن التطبيق بينهما وبين الظواهر المرادة, فهو من كمال الإيمان ومحض العرفان

(ورد النصوص)

بأن ينكر الأحكام التي دلت عليها النصوص القطعية من الكتاب والسنة, كحشر الأجساد مثلاً

As for what was adopted by some of the *Muhaqqiqeen*, that the *nusoos* are to be interpreted upon their literals and along with that there are hints towards hidden meanings and finer details that are unveiled to the Masters of *Sulook*, and it is possible to join between those meanings and the *zhaahiri* meanings whic are intended, then that is the perfection of *Imaan* and pure `*Irfaan* (Recognition).

"And rejection of the *nusoos*."

By rejecting the *Ahkaam* which the nusoos point out to, the *nusoos* that are decisive from the Qur'aan and the Sunnah, like the resurrection of the bodies, for example.

(كفر)

لكونه تكذيباً صريحاً لله تعالى ورسوله عليه السلام, فمن قذف عائشة بالزنا كفر

(واستحلال المعصية)

صغيرة كانت أو كبيرة

"Is *Kufr*."

Because to do is to clearly deny Allaah Ta`aalaa and His Rasool صلى الله عليه وسلم. For example, like the one who accuses Hadhrat `Aa'ishah رضي الله عنها.

"And "Halaalizing" disobedience."

Be it major or minor.

(كفر)

إذا ثبت كونها معصية بدليل قطعي, وقد علم ذلك فيما سبق

(والإستهانة بها كفر , والإستهزاء على الشريعة كفر)

"Is *Kufr*."

It its being disobedience is proved with *daleel* that is *qat`iyy*, and that is known from what has preceded.

"To regard it as insignificant is *Kufr*, and to mock any aspect of the Sharee`ah is *Kufr*."

لأن ذلك من أمارات التكذيب

وعلى هذه الأصول يتفرغ ما ذكر في الفتاوى من أنه إذا اعتقد الحرام حلالاً فإن كان حرمته لعينه وقد ثبت بدليل قطعي يكفر, وإلا فلا, بأن تكون حرمته لغيره أو ثبت بدليل ظني, وبعضهم لم يفرق بين الحرام لعينه ولغيره, فقال: من استحل حراماً قد علم في حين النبي عليه السلام تحريمه, كنكاح ذوي المحارم, أو شرب الخمر, أو أكل ميتة, أو دم, أو لحم خنزير, من غير ضرورة, فكافر, وفعل هذه الأشياء بدون الإستحلال فسق, ومن استحل شرب النبيذ إلى أن يسكر كفر

Because that is from the signs of denial.

Based on these *Usool*, that which has been explained in the *Fataawaa* becomes clear: if a person beloves something haraam to be *halaal*, then, if its *hurmat is li-`aynihi* (due to itself) and is affirmed with *qati`yy daleel*, then he becomes a Kaafir. If it is not, such as if its *hurmat is li-ghayrihi* (due to something else) or affirmed with *zhanni daleel*, then he does not become a Kaafir. Some of them did not differentiate between *haraam li-`aynihi* and *haraam li-ghayrihi*, so they said: Whosoever "Halaalizes" something that is *haraam* and was known to be *haraam* during the time of Rasoolullaah صلى الله عليه وسلم, like *nikaah* with *mahrams*, or drinking *khamr*, or eating carrion, or blood, or swine meat without necessity, then he becomes a Kaafir. To do these things without regarding them as *halaal* is *fisq*. Whosoever believes that *nabeedh* that is left until it becomes intoxicating is permissible to drink, becomes a Kaafir.

أما لو قال لحرام: هذا حلال, لترويج السلعة أو بحكم الجهل لا يكفر

ولو تمنى أن لا يكون الخمر حراماً أو لا يكون صوم رمضان فرضاً لما يشق عليه لا يكفر, بخلاف ما إذا تمنى أن لا يحرم الزنا وقتل النفس بغير حق, فإنه كفر, لأن حرمة هذه الأشياء ثابتة في جميع الأديان موافقة للحكمة

ومن أراد الخروج عن الحكمة فقد أراد أن يحكم الله بما ليس بحكمة, وهذا جهل منه بربه

If a person says regarding something that is *haraam*: "This is *halaal*," then if it was for the purpose of selling his merchandise or due to ignorance, then he does not become a Kaafir.

If a person wishes that *khamr* was not *haraam*, or that fasting in Ramadhaan was not *fardh*, due to it being difficult upon him, then he is not a Kaafir. However, if he wishes that *zinaa* was not *haraam* or that killing someone unjustly was not *haraam*, then he becomes a Kaafir, because the hurmat of these things is affirmed in all religions and is in conformity with wisdom.

Whosoever desires to exit from wisdom, he had intended that Allaah Ta`aalaa shoud rule with that which is not *Hikmah* (Wisdom), and this is ignorance on his part regarding his Rabb.

وذكر الإمام السرخسي في كتاب الحيض أنه لو استحل وطء امرأته الحائض يكفر, وفي النوادر عن محمد رحمه الله أنه لا يكفر, وهو الصحيح, وفي استحالة اللواطة بامرأته لا يكفر على الأصح

ومن وصف الله بما لا يليق أو سخر باسم من أسمائه أو بأمر من أوامره أو أنكر وعده ووعيده يكفر, وكذا لو تمنى أن لا يكون نبي من الأنبياء على قصد استخفاف أو عداوة, وكذا لو ضحك على وجه الرضا لمن تكلم بالكفر, وكذا لو جلس على مكان مرتفع وحوله جماعة يسألونه مسائل ويضحكونه ويضربونه بالوسائد يكفرون جميعاً, وكذا لو أمر رجلاً أن يكفر بالله, أو عزم على أن يأمره بكفر, وكذا لو أفتى لامرأة بالكفر لتبين من زوجها, وكذا لو قال عند شرب الخمر أو الزنا: بسم الله, وكذا إذا صلى لغير القبلة أو طهارة متعمداً, يكفر, وإن وافق ذلك القبلة, وكذا لو أطلق كلمة الكفر إستخفافاً لا اعتقاداً إلى غير ذلك من الفروع

Imaam as-Sarakhsi mentions in *Kitaab al-Haidh* that if a man "Halaalizes" intercourse with his wife during haidh, he becomes a Kaafir. However, it is mentioned in *an-Nawaadir* from Imaam Muhammad رحمة الله عليه that he does not become a Kaafir, and that is the correct view. WIth regards to halaalizing sodomy with ones's wife, the person who does so does not become a Kaafir, according to the most correct opinion.

Whosoever attributes Allaah Ta`aalaa with that which is not befitting, or mocks any Name from His Names, or any Command from His Commands, or rejects His Promise or His Threat, such a person becomes a Kaafir. Similarly, if a person wishes that a certain Nabi had not been a Nabi, out of considering him insignificant or out of enmity, this person becomes a

Kaafir. Similarly, if a person utters words of Kufr and another person laughs out of pleasure at what this Kaafir had said, then he becomes a Kaafir as well (both the one who uttered it and the one who was pleased with it are Kaafirs).

Similarly, if he were to sit on a high place, surrounded by people asking him *masaa'il*, and making him laugh, and hitting him with pillows, all of them become Kaafirs (because this is making a mockery of an aspect of Deen, which is that of *ta`leem*, or answering *masaa'il*, or issuing *Fataawaa*. Whosoever mocks any aspect of Deen becomes a Kaafir, and whosoever is pleased with any aspect of Deen being mocked becomes a Kaafir.)

Similarly, if a person commands another person to become a Kaafir, he himself becomes a Kaafir. Even if he just makes the resolve to tell this person to become a Kaafir, he becomes a Kaafir.

If a person gives a woman a *Fatwaa* saying that she can get divorced from her husband by uttering words of Kufr, he (the one who gave the *Fatwaa*) becomes a Kaafir.

If a person, at the time of drinking wine or committing *zinaa*, says: "*Bismillaah*," he becomes a Kaafir.

If a person intentionally performs Salaah without wudhoo, or intentionally performs Salaah whilst not facing the Qiblah, he becomes a Kaafir (because to do so is to treat Salaah as a thing of mockery and a game). Even if it turns out that the person actually was facing the Qiblah, even though he had intended facing a different direction, he still becomes a Kaafir (because what matters is his niyyat to face in a direction other than the Qiblah).

If a person utters words of *Kufr*, he becomes a Kaafir even if he does not believe those words, but he just uttered those words out of treating the Deen insignificantly, or treating the matter of *Kufr* and *Irtidaad* insignificantly (i.e. so he mockingly utters those words).

There are many other examples like this.

(والياس من الله تعالى كفر)

"To despair of Allaah (i.e. of the *Rahmah* of Allaah Ta`aalaa) is *Kufr*."

لأنه لا ييأس من روح الله إلا القوم الكافرون

Because no one despairs of relief from Allaah except the people that are Kaafiroon.

(والأمن من الله تعالى كفر)

إذ لا يأمن مكر الله إلا القوم الخاسرون

"And feeling safe from (the Punishment) of Allaah is *Kufr*."

Because no one regards himself as secure from the Plan of Allaah except those who are losers.

فإن قيل: الجزم بأن العاصي يكون في النار يأس من الله تعالى وبأن المطيع يكون في الجنة أمن من الله, فيلزم أن يكون المعتزلي كافراً, مطيعاً كان أو عاصياً, لأنه إما آمن أو آيس, ومن قواعد أهل السنة أن لا يكفر أحد من أهل القبلة

قلنا: هذا ليس بيأس ولا أمن, لأنه على تقدير العصيان لا ييأس أن يوفقه الله تعالى للتوبة والعمل الصالح, وعلى تقدير الطاعة لا يأمن أن يخذله الله فيكتسب المعاصي, وبهذا يظهر الجواب عما قيل إن المعتزلي إذا ارتكب كبيرة لزم أن يصير كافراً ليأسه من رحمة الله تعالى, ولاعتقاده أنه ليس بمؤمن, وذلك لأنا لا نسلم أن اعتقاد استحقاقه النار يستلزم اليأس, وأن اعتقاد عدم إيمانه المفسر بمجموع التصديق والإقرار والأعمال بناء على أن انتفاء الأعمال يوجب الكفر, هذا والجمع بين قولهم لا يكفر أحد من أهل القبلة وقولهم يكفر من قال بخلق القرآن واستحالة الرؤية أو سب الشيخين أو لعنهما, وأمثال ذلك مشكل

If it is said: The certitude that a disobedient one will be in Jahannam is despairing from Allaah Ta`aalaa, and certitude that the obedient one will be in Jannah is feeling safe from the `*Adhaab* of) Allaah Ta`aalaa, and that necessitates that the Mu`tazilah are Kaafirs, whether they are obedient or disobedien, because either they are feeling secure (from the `*Adhaab* of Allaah Ta`aalaa) or they are despairing. From the foundations of Ahlus Sunnah is that they do not make *takfeer* of anyone who is from the Ahl-ul-Qiblah.

We say: This is not despairing or feeling secure, because supposing that he is disobedient, he does not despair that Allaah Ta`aalaa might grant him the *tawfeeq* to make *tawbah* and do good deeds, and supposing that he is obedient, he does not feel secure that Allaah Ta`aalaa might forsake him and thus he will acquire sins. From this the answer becomes clear to that which was said, i.e. that if a Mu`tazili commits a major sin he becomes a Kaafir because of his despairing from the *Rahmah* of Allaah Ta`aalaa and because of his belief that he is not a Mu'min. That is because we do not submit that his believing that he is deserving of Jahannam necessitates despairing, and that the belief of the absence of Imaan that is explained (as being together) with tasdeeq, and iqraar, and *a`maal-e-saalihah*, based on the fact taht the absence of *a`maal* necessitates *Kufr* (according to them).

There is difficulty in joining between the statement, "*Takfeer* is not made of anyone from the Ahl-ul-Qiblah," and the statements, "Whosoever claims that the Qur'aan is created becomes a Kaafir," and: "Whosoever says that the Vision is impossible becomes a Kaafir," and: "Whosoever insults Shaykhain becomes a Kaafir," and others like that.

(وتصديق الكاهن بما يخبره عن الغيب كفر)

لقوله عليه السلام:

مَنْ أَتَى كَاهِناً فَصَدَّقَهُ بِمَا يَقُوْلُ فَقَدْ كَفَرَ بِمَا أُنْزِلَ عَلَى مُحَمَّدٍ عليه السلام, والكاهن هو الذي يخبر عن الكوائن في مستقبل الزمان ويدعي معرفة الأسرار ومطالعة علم الغيب, وكان في العرب كهنة يدعون معرفة الأمور, فمنهم من كان يزعم أن له رئيا من الجن وتابعة تلقى إليه الأخبار, ومنهم من كان يدعي أنه يستدرك الأمور بفهم أعطيه, والمنجم إذا ادعى العلم بالحوادث الآتية فهو مثل الكاهن

"To assent to what a *kaahin* (diviner) informs one of the Unseen (*Ghayb*) is *Kufr*."

Because of the *Hadeeth*:

"Whosoever goes to a *kaahin* (diviner) and regards as truthful that which he says, then he has disbelieved in that which was revealed upon Muhammad." صلى الله عليه وسلم. The *kaahin* is the one who informs regarding what will happen in the future, and he claims to possess knowledge of the secrets and knowlwedge of the Unseen. Among the Arabs there had been *kaahins* who claimed knowledge of matters. Among them were those who claimed that he has visions from the Jinn and information is granted to him from them. Among them were those who claims that comprehends matters with an understanding that was given to him. The *munajjim* (astrologer), when he claims knowledge of events that are to occur, then he is like the *kaahin* (diviner)."

وبالجملة: العلم بالغيب أمر تفرد به الله تعالى, لا سبيل إليه للعباد إلا بإعلام منه تعالى, وإلهام بطريق المعجزة أو الكرامة, أو إشراد إلى الإستدلال بالأمارات فيما يمكن ذلك فيه, ولهذا ذكر في الفتاوى أن قول القائل عند رؤية هالة القمر: يكون المطر, مدعياً علم الغيب لا بعلامة كفر, والله أعلم

(والمعدوم ليس بشيء)

In summary: *`Ilm-ul-Ghayb* (Knowledge of the Unseen) is exclusive to Allaah Ta`aalaa. There is no way for people to attain it except through being informed by Allaah Ta`aalaa, such as *ilhaam* by way of a *mu`jizah* or *karaamat*, or being guided towards deducing from signs in those matters wherein it is possible. For this reason, it is mentioned in the *Fataawaa* that if a person says, when seeing a ring around the moon, that: "There will be rain," claiming thereby knowledge of the *Ghayb*, and not saying it as a sign (i.e. saying that there is a possibility of rain deducing from this sign), then he becomes a Kaafir.

And Allaah Ta`aalaa knows best.

"That which is *ma`doom* (non-existent) is not a thing."

إن أريد بالشيء الثابت المتحقق, على ما ذهب إليه المحققون من أن الشيئية ترادف الوجود والثبوت, والعدم يرادف النفي, وهذا حكم ضروري لم ينازع فيه إلا المعتزلة القائلين بأن المعدوم الممكن ثابت في الخارج, وإن أريد أن المعدوم لا يسمى شيئاً فهو بحث لغوي مبني على تفسير الشيء أنه الموجود أو المعدوم, أو ما يصح أن يعلم أو يخبر عنه, فالمرجع إلى النقل وتتبع موارد الإستعمال

(وفي دعاء الأحياء للأموات وتصدقهم)

If what is meant by "a thing" is that which is affirmed and verified as having a reality, according to what was adopted by the Muhaqqiqoon (verifiers), that *ash-Shay'iyyah* (being a thing) is synonymous with existent and affirmation, and non-existence is synonymous with negation. This is a necessary judgement which no one disputes regarding except the Mu`tazilah, those who say that the non-existent thing is which possible is affirmed in the outside world. If what is intended is that the non-existent thing is not named a thing, then that is a linguistic subject of discussion based on the explanation of a thing "*shay*" that it is existent or non-exisent, or that which is valid to be known or informed about. Thus, the source to return to is *naql* and to follow-up on the sources of usage (of the words).

"And in the living making *Du'aa* for the dead, and giving *sadaqah* (charity) on their behalf."

أي تصدق الأحياء

Meaning, the living giving *sadaqah* on behalf of the dead.

(عنهم)

"On their behalf."

أي عن الأموات

Meaning, on behalf of the dead.

(نفع لهم)

"There is benefit for them."

أي للأموات, خلافاً للمعتزلة تمسكاً بأن القضاء لا يتبدل, وكل نفس مرهونة بما كسبت, والمرء مجزى بعمله لا بعمل غيره

ولنا ما ورد في الأحاديث الصحاح من الدعاء للأموات خصوصاً في صلاة الجنازة, وقد تواتره السلف فلو لم يكن للأموات نفع فيه لما كان له معنى

قال صلى الله عليه وسلم: مَا مِنْ مَيِّتٍ يُصَلِّيْ عَلَيْهِ أُمَّةٌ مِّنَ الْمُسْلِمِيْنَ يَبْلُغُوْنَ أَنْ يَكُوْنُوْا مِائَةً كُلُّهُمْ يَشْفَعُوْنَ لَهُ إِلَّا شُفِعُوْا فِيْهِ

Meaning, for the dead. This is contrary to the opinion of the Mu`tazilah who claimed that *Qadhaa* (Pre-Destination) does not change, and every sould has a pledge of that which is acuiqred, and a person is recompensed for his own actions, not the actions of others.

We have as evidence that which is narrated in the authentic *Ahaadeeth*, with regards to making *Du`aa* for the dead, especially in *Janaazah Salaat*. It is reported from the Salaf by way of tawaatur; thus, if there had been no benefit to the dead (in doing so), then it would have been meaningless.

Rasoolullaah صلى الله عليه وسلم said:

"There is no *mayyit* (deceased) upon whom a group of the Muslims performs (*Janaazah*) *Salaat*, and their number amounts of 100, all of them interceding for him except that their intercession will be accepted regarding him."

وعن سعد بن عبادة أنه قال: يا رسول الله, إن أم سعد ماتت, فأي الصدقة أفضل؟ قال: سَقْيُ الْمَاءِ, فحفر بئراً وقال: هذه لأم سعد

وقال عليه السلام: الدُّعَاءُ يَرُدُّ الْبَلَاءَ, وَالصَّدَقَةُ تُطْفِئُ غَضَبَ الرَّبِّ

وقال عليه السلام: إِنَّ الْعَالِمَ وَالْمُتَعَلِّمَ إِذَا مَرَّا عَلَى قَرْيَةٍ فَإِنَّ اللهَ يَرْفَعُ الْعَذَابَ عَنْ مَقْبَرَةِ تِلْكَ الْقَرْيَةِ أَرْبَعِينَ يَوْماً

والأحاديث والآثار في هذا الباب أكثر من أن تحصى

Hadhrat Sa`d ibn `Ubaadah رضي الله عنه narrates that: "I said, Yaa Rasoolallaah, Umm Sa`d passed away, so what *sadaqah* is best (i.e. to give on her behalf)?" He said: "A drink of water (i.e. constructing a well)." So he dug a well and said, "This is for Umm Sa`d."

Rasoolullaah صلى الله عليه وسلم said: "Du`aa averts calamity, and sadaqah extinguishes the Anger of Ar-Rabb (Allaah Ta`aalaa)."

Rasoolullaah صلى الله عليه وسلم said: "The teacher and the student, when they pass by a village, then indeed Allaah raises the `*Adhaab* from the graveyard of that village (i.e. the Muslims therein) for 40 days."

The *Ahaadeeth* and *Aathaar* concerning this issue are innumerable.

(والله تعالى يجيب الدعوات ويقضي الحاجات)

لقوله تعالى:

أُدْعُوْنِيْ أَسْتَجِبْ لَكُمْ

"And Allaah Ta`aalaa answers the *Du`aas* and fulfills the needs."

Allaah Ta`aalaa said:

{*"Call upon Me, I will answer you."*}

ولقوله عليه السلام: لَا يَزَالُ يُسْتَجَابُ لِلْعَبْدِ مَا لَمْ يَدْعُ بِإِثْمٍ أَوْ قَطِيْعَةِ رَحِمٍ, مَا لَمْ يَسْتَعْجِلْ

ولقوله عليه السلام: إِنَّ رَبَّكُمْ حَيٌّ كَرِيْمٌ, يَسْتَحْيِيْ مِنْ عَبْدِهِ أَنْ يَّرْفَعَ إِلَيْهِ يَدَيْهِ فَيَرُدَّهُمَا صَفَراً

واعلم أن العمدة في ذلك صدق النية, وخلوص الطوية, وحضور القلب, لقوله عليه السلام:

أُدْعُوا اللهَ وَأَنْتُمْ مُوْقِنُوْنَ بِالْإِجَابَةِ, وَاعْلَمُوْا أَنَّ اللهَ لَا يَسْتَجِيْبُ الدُّعَاءَ مِنْ قَلْبٍ غَافِلٍ لَاهٍ

Rasoolullaah صلى الله عليه وسلم said: "The *Du`aas* of the bondsman (of Allaah Ta`aalaa) continues to be answered so long as he does not make *Du`aa* for something sinful or the severance of family ties, (and) as long as he does not hurry (i.e. become impatient)."

Rasoolullaah صلى الله عليه وسلم said: "Your Rabb is Living, Generous. He does not like to turn back the hands of his bondsmen empty after they had been raised to Him."

Know that the reliance in this is upon the truthfulness of the *niyyat*, and the sincerity of aim, and the presence of the heart, because Rasoolullaah صلى الله عليه وسلم said:

"Make *Du`aa* to Allaah while being certain of *ijaabah* (your *Du`aas* being answered), and know that Allaah does not answer the *Du`aa* of a heedless, thoughtless heart."

واختلف المشايخ في أنه هل يجوز أن يقال: يستجاب دعاء الكافر؟ فمنعه الجمهور لقوله تعالى:

وَمَا دُعَاءُ الْكَافِرِيْنَ إِلَّا فِيْ ضَلَالٍ

ولأنه لا يدعو الله, لأنه لا يعرفه, ولأنه وإن أقر به فلما وصفه بما لا يليق به فقد نقض إقراره, وما روي في الحديث من أن دعوة المظلوم وإن كان كافراً تستجاب, فمحمول على كفران النعمة, وجوزه بعضهم لقوله تعالى حكاية عن إبليس:

The Mashaayikh had differences of opinion regarding whether or not it is permissible to say: "Allaah accepts the *Du`aa* of a Kaafir." The majority prohibited it, becaues of the *Aayah*:

{"*The Du`aa of the Kaafireen is only in error.*"}

And because a Kaafir does not make *Du`aa* to Allaah, because he does not recognise Allaah. And also because, even if he were to admit (the Existence of Allaah Ta`aalaa), he attributes to Allaah that which is not befitting of Him, and thus he contradicts his *iqraar* (admission). As for what has been narrated in the *Hadeeth*, that the *Du`aa* of a *mazhloom* (oppressed one), even if he is a Kaafir, is answered, then it is interpreted as referring to *Kufr* in terms of ingratitude (i.e. not an actual Kaafir, but a Muslim who is ungrateful unto Allaah Ta`aalaa).

Some of the Mashaayikh regarded it as permissible, because of the *Aayah* narrating the story of Iblees:

أَنْظِرْنِيْ إِلَى يَوْمِ يُبْعَثُوْنَ

فقال الله تعالى:

إِنَّكَ مِنَ الْمُنْظَرِيْنَ

وهذه إجابة, وإليه ذهب أبو القاسم الحكيم السمرقندي وأبو النصر الدبوسي

{"*Grant me respite until the Day of Resurrection.*"}

So Allaah Ta`aalaa said:

{*"You are from those granted respite."*}

This is answering his *Du`aa*. This position was held by Abu-l Qaasim al-Hakeem as-Samarqandi and Abu-n Nasr ad-Daboosi.

وقال الصدر الشهيد: وبه يفتى

(وما أخبر النبي عليه الصلاة والسلام من أشراط الساعة)

أي علاماتها

As-Sadr Ash-Shaheed said: "The *Fatwaa* is upon that."

"And that which Nabi صلى الله عليه وسلم informed of from the conditions of the Hour."

Meaning, its signs.

(من خروج الدجال ودابة الأرض ويأجوج ومأجوج, ونزول عيسى عليه السلام من السماء, وطلوع الشمس من مغربها فهو حق)

لأنها أمور ممكنة أخبر بها الصادق

قال حذيفة بن أسيد الغفاري: اطلع رسول الله علينا ونحن نتذاكر فقال: مَا تَذَاكَرُونَ؟ قلنا: نَذْكُرُ السَّاعَةَ, قال: إِنَّهَا لَنْ تَقُومَ حَتَّى تَرَوْا قَبْلَهَا عَشَرَ آيَاتٍ, فذكر الدخان والدجال والدابة وطلوع الشمس من مغربها, ونزول عيسى بن مريم ويأجوج ومأجوج وثلاثة خسوف: خسف بالمشرق, وخسف بالمغرب, وخسف بجزيرة العرب, وآخر ذلك نار تخرج من اليمن تطرد الناس إلى محشرهم

"Such as the emergence of Dajjaal, and the Daabbatul Ardh, and Ya'jooj and Ma'jooj, and the descension of Nabi `Eesa عليه السلام from the heaven, and the rising of the sun in the west: all of it is Haqq."

Because they are matters that are possible, and which the Truthful One has informed us about.

Hadhrat Huzaifah ibn Usaid al-Ghifaari رضي الله عنه said: "Rasoolullaah صلى الله عليه وسلم once visited us whilst we were discussing among ourselves, so he said: "What are you discussing?" We said: "We are discussing the Hour." He said: "It will not come until you see before it 10 signs." He then mentioned the smoke, Dajjaal, the Daabbatul Ardh, the rising of the sun from the west, the descending of Nabi `Eesa ibn Maryam عليه السلام, Ya'jooj and Ma'jooj, and three earthquakes: an earthquake in the east, an earthquake in the west, and an earthquake in the Jazeeratul `Arab (Arabian Peninsula). The last of them is a fire which will come out from Yemen and which will push people towards the *mahshar* (plains of resurrection)."

والأحاديث الصحاح في هذه الأشراط كثيرة جداً, فقد روى أحاديث وآثار في تفاصيلها وكيفياتها, فلتطلب من كتب التفسير والسير والتواريخ

(والمجتهد)

في العقليات والشرعيات الأصلية والفرعية

(قد يخطئ ويصيب)

The Authentic *Ahaadeeth* regarding these signs are many. *Ahaadeeth* and *Aathaar* have been narrated concerning their details and how they will be, so those who wish to do so may check them up in the *Kutub* of *Tafseer*, and *Siyar* and *Taareekh* (history).

"And the Mujtahid."

In matters pertaining to logic as well as Sharee`ah, whether fundamental or branch matters.

"May be incorrect or may be correct."

وذهب بعض الأشاعرة والمعتزلة إلى أن كل مجتهد في المسائل الشرعية الفرعية التي لا قاطع فيها مصيب, وهذا الإختلاف مبني على اختلافهم في أن لله تعالى في كل حادثة حكماً معيناً, أم حكمه في المسائل الإجتهادية, ما أدى إليه رأي المجتهد؟

وتحقيق هذا المقام أن المسألة الإجتهادية إما أن لا يكون لله تعالى فيها حكم معين قبل اجتهاد المجتهد أو يكون وحينئذ إما أن لا يكون من الله عليه دليل أو يكون, وذلك الدليل إما قطعي أو ظني, فذهب إلى كل احتمال جماعة

Some of the Ash`aris and the Mu`tazilis adopted the view that the Mujtahid, in masaa'il of Sharee`ah, be they fundamental or branch matters which are not absolute, is always correct. This difference of opinion is based on their difference of opinion regarding whether or not Allaah Ta`aalaa has a specific Judgement in every occurence, or whether His Judgement in matters of ijtihaad is that at which the opinion of the Mujtahid has arrived.

The verification of this position is that *masaa'il ijtihaadiyyah* are such that either Allaah Ta`aalaa does not have, concerning them, a specific Ruling prior to the *ijtihaad* of the Mujahid, or He has. And if He has, then either there is no proof from Allaah concerning it or there is. And if there is, then that daleel is either *qat`iyy* or *zhanni*.

Each *Jamaa`ah* adopted a different possibility (regarding these issues).

والمختار أن الحكم معين وعليه دليل ظني, إن وجده المجتهد أصاب, وإن فقده أخطأ, والمجتهد غير مكلف بإصابته لغموضه وخفائه, فلذلك كان المخطئ معذوراً, بل مأجوراً, فلا خلاف على هذا المذهب في أن المخطئ ليس بآثم, وإنما الخلاف في أنه مخطئ إبتداء وانتهاء, أي بالنظر إلى الدليل والحكم جميعاً, وإليه ذهب بعضهم المشايخ, وهو مختار الشيخ أبي منصور, أو انتهاء فقط, أي بالنظر إلى الحكم حيث أخطأ فيه, وإن أصاب في الدليل حيث أقامه على وجهه مستجمعاً لشرائطه وأركانه, فأفتى بما كلف به من الإعتبارات, وليس عليه في الإجتهاديات إقامة الحجة القطعية التي مدلولها حق البتة

والدليل على أن المجتهد قد يخطئ وجوه:

The chosen view is that the Ruling (of Allaah Ta`aalaa) is specific and there is *daleel* for it that is *zhanni*. If the Mujtahid finds it, he is correct, and if he does not find it, he is incorrect. The Mujtahid is not made *mukallaf* with getting it right due to its obscurity and being hidden. For this reason, the Mujtahid who errs is excused; in fact, he is even rewarded. There is no difference of opinion regarding the view that the Mujtahid who errs is not sinful. The difference of opinion is only whether he errs at both the beginning and at the end (of his *ijtihaad*), i.e. by looking at both the *daleel* and the ruling. Some of the Mashaayikh adopted that view, and that is also the chosen view of Shaykh Abu Mansoor (i.e. Imaam al-Maatureedi). Or whether it is at the ending only, i.e. by looking at the ruling because it is in the ruling that he erred. And if he is correct in the *daleel* by having put it in its proper place, having gathered its stipulations and pillars, and issues a *Fatwaa* with that which he has been made *mukallaf* of in terms of texts. In matters of *ijtihaad* he is not responsible for establishing an absolute evidence in which the thing to be proved is an absolute truth.

The evidence that a Mujtahid can err is from different points:

الأول: قوله تعالى:

فَفَهَّمْنَاهَا سُلَيْمَانَ

والضمير للحكومة أو الفتيا, ولو كان كل من الإجتهادين صواباً لما كان لتخصيص سليمان بالذكر جهة, لأن كلاً منهما قد أصاب الحكم حينئذ وفهمه

الثاني: الأحاديث والآثار الدالة على ترديد الإجتهاد بين الصواب والخطأ بحيث صارت متواترة المعنى, قال عليه السلام: إِنْ أَصَبْتَ فَلَكَ عَشَرَ حَسَنَاتٍ, وَإِنْ أَخْطَأْتَ فَلَكَ حَسَنَةٌ

The first is the *Aayah*:

{"So we gave Sulaymaan the understanding of it."}

The pronoun refers to legal authority or to the Fatwaa. If each of the ijtihaads had been correct, then there would have been no meaning in specifying Nabi Sulaymaan عليه السلام with mention, because in that case both Nabi Daawood عليه السلام and Nabi Sulaymaan عليه السلام would have been correct and arrived at the correct conclusion and understood it.

The second point is: the *Ahaadeeth* and *Aathaar* which point out to *ijtihaad* wavering between being correct or being incorrect, so that the idea (that one can err) is *mutawaatir* in terms of meaning. Rasoolullaah صلى الله عليه وسلم said: "If you are correct (i.e. in *ijtihaad*), you will get 10 rewards, and if you err, you will get one reward."

وفي حديث آخر جعل للمصيب أجرين وللمخطئ أجراً واحداً

وعن ابن مسعود: إن أصبتُ فمن الله وإلا فمني ومن الشيطان

وقد اشتهر تخطئة الصحابة بعضهم بعضاً في الإجتهادات

الثالث: أن القياس مظهر لا مثبت, فالثابت بالقياس ثابت بالنص معنى, وقد أجمعوا على أن الحق فيما ثبت بالنص, واحد لا غير

In another *Hadeeth* it has been mentioned that the one who gets it right will get two rewards and the one who errs gets one reward.

Hadhrat `Abdullaah ibn Mas`ood رضي الله عنه said: "If I am correct, then it is from Allaah, and if I am incorrect, then it is from me and from Shaytaan."

It is well-known that Sahaabah-e-Kiraam would say one another is wrong with regards to certain *ijtihaad* (*masaa'il*).

The third point is: *qiyaas* (analogical deduction) makes something apparent but does not affirm. That which is affirmed by *qiyaas* is affirmed by *nass* in terms of meaning. They had *ijmaa`* that the Haqq which is affirmed by nass is only one, not more.

الرابع: أنه لا تفرقة في العمومات الواردة في شريعة نبينا عليه السلام بين الأشخاص, فلو كان كل مجتهد مصيباً لزم اتصاف الفعل الواحد بالمتنافيين من الحظر والإباحة, أو الصحة والفساد, أو الوجوب وعدمه

وتمام تحقيق هذه الأدلة, والجواب عن تمسكات المخالفين يطلب من كتابنا التلويح في شرح التنقيح

(ورسل البشر أفضل من رسل الملائكة, ورسل الملائكة أفضل من عامة البشر, وعامة البشر أفضل من عامة الملائكة)

The fourth point is: there is no distinction made in terms of generalities that occur in the Sharee`ah of our Nabi صلى الله عليه وسلم between individuals. If every Mujtahid was correct, it would necessitate the description of a single action with mutually negating opinions such as being both impermissible and permissible (at the same time), or valid and invalid, or *waajib* and not *waajib*.

The completion of the verification of these evidences, and the response to that which is held onto by the opponents, is found in our *Kitaab: at-Talweeh fee Sharh at-Tanqeeh*.

"The Rusul of mankind are better than the Rusul of the Malaa'ikah, but the Rusul of the Malaa'ikah are better than the majority of mankind. However, the majority of mankind (i.e. Muslims) are better than the majority of the Malaa'ikah."

أما تفضيل رسل الملائكة على عامة البشر فبالإجماع, بل بالضرورة, وأما تفضيل رسل البشر على رسل الملائكة, وعامة البشر على عامة الملائكة فلوجوه:

الأول: أن الله تعالى أمر الملائكة بالسجود لآدم عليه السلام على وجه التعظيم والتكريم, بدليل قوله تعالى حكاية:

أَرَأَيْتَكَ هَذَا الَّذِيْ كَرَّمْتَ عَلَيَّ

أَنَا خَيْرٌ مِّنْهُ خَلَقْتَنِيْ مِنْ نَارٍ وَّخَلَقْتَهُ مِنْ طِيْنٍ

As for the superiority of the Rusul of the Malaa'ikah over the majority of mankind, then that is established by *ijmaa`*; in fact, by necessity. As for the superiority of the Rusul of mankind over the Rusul of the Malaa'ikah, and the superiority of the majority of mankind (i.e. Muslims) over the majority of Malaa'ikah, then that is due to certain points:

The first is that Allaah Ta`aalaa commanded the Malaa'ikah to perform sujood to Nabi Aadam عليه السلام by way of respect and honouring, as is evidenced by the *Aayah*:

{"Do You see this one whom You have honoured above me?"}

And the *Aayah*:

{"I am better than him. You created me from fire and You created him from sand."}

ومقتضى الحكمة: الأمر للأدنى بالسجود للأعلى, دون العكس

Wisdom necessitates that the one who is lower in status be commanded to perform *sujood* to the one who is higher in status - not the other way around.

الثاني: أن كل واحد من أهل اللسان يفهم من قوله تعالى:

وَعَلَّمَ آدَمَ الْأَسْمَاءَ كُلَّهَا

الآية

The second is that everyone of the people of the language understands from the *Aayah*:

{"*And Allaah taught Aadam the names of everything.*"}

أن القصد منه إلى تفضيل آدم على الملائكة, وبيان زيادة علمه, واستحقاقه التعظيم والتكريم

That the purpose behind this was for the superiority of Nabi Aadam عليه السلام over the Malaa'ikah, and to show the additional knowledge he has (above theirs), and his deserving of honour and respect.

الثالث: قوله تعالى:

إِنَّ اللَّهَ اصْطَفَى آدَمَ وَنُوحًا وَّآلَ إِبْرَاهِيمَ وَآلَ عِمْرَانَ عَلَى الْعَالَمِينَ

The third is the *Aayah*:

{"*Indeed, Allaah has chosen Aadam, and Nooh, and the family of Ibraaheem and the family of `Imraan above the `aalameen (worlds).*"}

والملائكة من جملة العالم وقد خص من ذلك بالإجماع عدم تفضيل عامة البشر على رسل الملائكة, فبقي معمولاً به فيما عدا ذلك, ولا خفاء في أن هذه المسألة ظنية يكتفي فيها بالأدلة الظنية

الرابع: أن الإنسان يحصل الفضائل والكمالات العلمية والعملية مع وجود العوائق والموانع, من الشهوة والغضب وسنوح الحاجات الضرورية الشاغلة عن اكتساب الكمالات, ولا شك أن العبادة وكسب الكمالات مع الشواغل والصوارف أشق وأدخل في الإخلاص, فيكون أفضل

The Malaa'ikah are a part of the `*Aalam*. It has been specified from that, by *ijmaa`*, that the majority of mankind (i.e. Muslims) are not superior to the Rusul of the Malaa'ikah, but the rule remains in operation in that which is besides that. It is not hidden that this *mas'alah* is *zhanni* and suffices with evidences that are *zhanni*.

The fourth point is that *insaan* (mankind) achieves virtues and perfections in knowledge and action despite of impediments and hindrances such as lust, anger, and the recurrence of necessities which preoccupy him from the acquisition of perfections. And, there is no doubt that to perform `*Ibaadah* and acquire perfections along with the presence of preoccupying factors and distractions is much more difficult and thus much more deeply engrossed in *ikhlaas* (sincerity), and for this reason it is better.

وذهبت المعتزلة والفلاسفة وبعض الأشاعرة إلى تفضيل الملائكة, وتمسكوا بوجوه:

The Mu`tazilah, the Philosophers and some of the Ash`aris adopted the view that the Malaa'ikah are superior, and they used as proof the following points:

الأول: أن الملائكة أوراح مجردة كاملة بالفعل, مبرات عن مبادئ الشرور والآفات, كالشهوة والغضب, وعن ظلمات الهيولي والصورة, قوية على الأفعال العجيبة, عالمة بالكوائن ماضيها وآتيها من غير غلط

The Malaa'ikah are pure souls, perfect in actions, free from the origins of evil and (*Roohani*) maladies such as lust, anger, and the darknesses of *hayooli*, and form, and they have power over amazing actions, and they have knowledge of the past and future of things without error.

والجواب: أن مبنى ذلك على أصول الفلاسفة دون الإسلامية

The response is that those things are based on the principles of the Philosophers rather than the principles of Islaam.

الثاني: أن الأنبياء مع كونهم أفضل البشر, يتعلمون ويستفيدون منهم, بدليل قوله تعالى:

The second point is that the Ambiyaa, despite being the greatest of mankind, they learn and benefit (from the Malaa'ikah), and the proof for this is the *Aayah*:

$$\text{عَلَّمَهُ شَدِيدُ الْقُوَى}$$

{"He was taught by one severe in power (i.e. Jibreel عليه السلام)."}

وقوله تعالى:

$$\text{نَزَلَ بِهِ الرُّوحُ الْأَمِينُ}$$

And the *Aayah*:

{"Ar-Rooh Al-Ameen (The Trustworthy Rooh) descended with it."}

ولا شك أن المعلم أفضل من المتعلم

And there is no doubt that the teacher is better than the one who is taught.

والجواب: أن التعلم من الله, والملائكة إنما هم المبلغون

The response is that the teaching comes from Allaah Ta`aalaa, and the Malaa'ikah simply convey it.

الثالث: أنه قد اضطرد في الكتاب والسنة تقديم ذكرهم على ذكر الأنبياء, وما ذلك إلا لتقدمهم في الشرف والرتبة

والجواب: أن ذلك لتقدمهم في الوجود, أو لأن وجودهم أخفى, فالإيمان بهم أقوى, وبالتقديم أولى

The third point is that there are many cases in the Qur'aan and Sunnah where the Malaa'ikah are mentioned before the mention of the Ambiyaa, and that is not for any reason except due to their superiority in terms of honour and status.

The response to this point is: that is because they existed (before mankind), or because their existence is more hidden, and thus *Imaan* in them is stronger, and mentioning them first is better.

الرابع: قوله تعالى:

$$\text{لَنْ يَسْتَنْكِفَ الْمَسِيْحُ أَنْ يَكُوْنَ عَبْداً لِلهِ وَلَا الْمَلَائِكَةُ الْمُقَرَّبُوْنَ}$$

The fourth point is the *Aayah*:

{*"The Maseeh (i.e. Nabi `Eesa* عليه السلام*) would never disdain being a bondsman of Allaah, nor would the Malaa'ikah who are near (to Him)."*}

$$\text{فإن أهل اللسان يفهمون من ذلك أفضلية الملائكة من عيسى عليه السلام, إذ القياس في مثله الترقي من الأدنى إلى الأعلى}$$

The people of the language understand from that the superiority of the Malaa'ikah over Nabi `Eesa عليه السلام, because the *qiyaas* in a case like that is to *taraqqi* (ascend) from that which is lower to that which is higher.

$$\text{يقال: لا يستنكف من هذا الأمر الوزير ولا السلطان, ولا يقال: السلطان ولا الوزير, ثم لا قائل بالفضل بين عيسى عليه السلام وغيره من الأنبياء}$$

It is said: "The wazeer would not disdain this matter, nor would the sultaan." It is not said: "The sultaan would not disdain this matter, nor would the wazeer." Thereafter, there is no one who said who is superior between Nabi `Eesa عليه السلام and the rest of the Ambiyaa.

$$\text{والجواب: أن النصارى إستعظموا المسيح, بحيث يرتفع مع أن يكون عبداً من عباد الله, بل ينبغي أن يكون إبناً له, لأنه مجرد لا أب له, وقال تعالى:}$$

The response is that the Christians revered Nabi `Eesa عليه السلام in such a manner that they considered him too high despite the fact that he was a bondsman from the bondsmen of Allaah.; They even claimed that he is the son (of Allaah) simply because he has no father.

Allaah Ta`aalaa said:

$$\text{وَأُبْرِئُ الْأَكْمَهَ وَالْأَبْرَصَ وَأُحْيِيْ الْمَوْتَى}$$

{*"I heal the blind and the leper, and I bring the dead back to life (by the Permission of Allaah)."*}

بخلاف سائر عباد الله من بني آدم, فرد عليهم بأنه لا يستنكف من ذلك المسيح ولا من هو أعلى منه في هذا المعنى, وهم الملائكة الذين لا أب لهم ولا أم, ويقدرون بإذن الله تعالى على أفعال أقوى وأعجب من إبراء الأكمه والأبرص وإحياء الموتى, فالترقي والعلو إنما هو أمر التجرد وإظهار الآثار القوية, لا في مطلق الشرف والكمال, فلا دلالة على أفضلية الملائكة

Unlike the rest of the bondsmen of Allaah Ta`aalaa from Bani Aadam. Allaah Ta`aalaa refuted them by saying that the Maseeh will not disdain from that, nor those who are higher than him in this meaning, which are the Malaa'ikah, for the Malaa'ikah have no fathers or mothers, and they are able to do - by the Permission of Allaah - such actions which are more powerful and more amazing than even the healing of the blind and the lepers and bringing the dead back to life. Their exaltion and eminense is only in being (i.e. coming into existence without the medium of parents) and manifesting powerful signs, not in terms of absolute honour and perfection. Thus, there is no proof for the superiority of the Malaa'ikah (above the Ambiyaa).

والله أعلم بالصواب وإليه المرجع والمآب

Allaah Ta`aalaa knows best what is correct, and to Him is the return.

تَمَّتْ بِإِذْنِ اللهِ تَبَارَكَ وَتَعَالَى وَاللهُ وَلِيُّ التَّوْفِيْقِ

وَالْحَمْدُ لِلهِ رَبِّ الْعَالَمِيْنَ

Translation completed on: 23rd of Jumaadal Ukhraa, 1439 - 11th of March, 2018.

OUR PUBLICATIONS

Available on Amazon

Logic for Beginners
Translation of تيسير المنطق

The Creed of Imam Tahawi
Arabic with *English* & *Farsi* translation

Sharh Al-Aqeedah An-Nasafiyyah
English Translation

Solving Tarkeeb
Translation of حلّ تُرْكِيْب

Arabic Tutor: Arbi Ka Mu'allim
(Volumes 1, 2, 3, 4)

From the Treasures of Arabic Morphology - من كنوز الصرف

Simplified Principles of Fiqh
Translation of آسان اصول فقه

Miftah ul Qur'an
(Volumes 1, 2, 3, 4)

Masail Al Qudoori Made Easy
Question Answer Format (English)

Al-Hizbul A'zam (Pocket Size)

Tajweed for Beginners

Muhammad (SAW) - A Mercy unto mankind

Etiquettes for Teachers
آداب المعلمین

Etiquettes for Students
آداب المتعلمین

Hadhrat Mufti Mahmood Hasan Gangohi رحمة الله علیه

Hadhrat Moulana Maseehullah Khan Saahib Sherwaani رحمة الله علیه

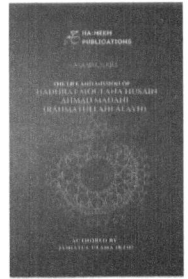
The Life and Mission of Hadhrat Moulana Husain Ahmad Madani رحمة الله علیه

Hadhrat Moulana Muhammad Qaasim Nanotwi رحمة الله علیه

www.ingramcontent.com/pod-product-compliance
Lightning Source LLC
Chambersburg PA
CBHW021054080526
44587CB00010B/251